Praise for

THE BIG PICTURE

"Epstein peels away the Hollywood façade and gives a nuts-and-bolts view of how the six entertainment empires—Viacom, Fox, NBC/Universal, Time Warner, Sony, and Disney—create and distribute intellectual property. . . . A fascinating look at the unbelievable efforts that must be coordinated to produce a film." —*Booklist*

"Illuminating." —*The New York Times*

"Engrossing. . . . This is the new indispensable text for anyone interested in how Hollywood works." —*Publishers Weekly (starred review)*

"Edward Jay Epstein is here to tell us that when it comes to Hollywood these days, we've got it all wrong.

"Epstein argues, and most persuasively, that we persist in thinking about Hollywood in terms that no longer exist: the 'dream factories' that were the old studios—MGM, RKO, Paramount, Columbia, Fox, Universal and Warner Bros—where movies were the only products, stars and lesser actors were bound to studios by rigid contracts, and theaters were owned by the studios that supplied them. . . . [Epstein] is a bulldog researcher, he's brought a great deal of interesting material together and he has interesting things to say." —*The Washington Post Book World*

ALSO BY EDWARD JAY EPSTEIN

Inquest: The Warren Commission and the Establishment of Truth

Counterplot: Garrison vs. the United States

News from Nowhere: Television and the News

Between Fact and Fiction: The Problem of Journalism

Agency of Fear: Opiates and Political Power in America

Cartel: A Novel

Legend: The Secret World of Lee Harvey Oswald

The Rise and Fall of Diamonds: The Shattering of a Brilliant Illusion

Who Owns the Corporation?: Management vs. Shareholders

Deception: The Invisible War Between the KGB and the CIA

The Assassination Chronicles: Inquest, Counterplot, and Legend

Dossier: The Secret History of Armand Hammer

THE BIG PICTURE

THE BIG PICTURE

☆ Money and Power in Hollywood ☆

Edward Jay Epstein

RANDOM HOUSE TRADE PAPERBACKS ☆ NEW YORK

2006 Random House Trade Paperback Edition

Copyright © 2005 by E. J. E. Publications, Ltd., Inc.

Published in the United States by Random House, an imprint of The Random House Publishing Group, a division of Random House, Inc., New York.

RANDOM HOUSE TRADE PAPERBACKS and colophon are trademarks of Random House, Inc.

Originally published in hardcover in the United States by Random House, an imprint of The Random House Publishing Group, a division of Random House, Inc., in 2005.

LIBRARY OF CONGRESS CATALOGING-IN-PUBLICATION DATA
Epstein, Edward Jay.
The big picture: money and power in Hollywood / by Edward Jay Epstein.
p.   cm.
Includes index.
ISBN 0-8129-7382-8
1. Motion picture industry—California—Los Angeles—Finance.   2. Motion picture industry—United States—Finance.   3. Motion picture industry—Economic aspects—California—Los Angeles.   4. Motion picture industry—Economic aspects—United States.   I. Title.
PN1993.5.U65E67 2005
384'.83'0979494—dc22   2004050874

Printed in the United States of America

www.atrandom.com

468975

Book design by Casey Hampton

For Clay Felker

Contents

THE BIG PICTURE

I

The Two Hollywoods

The Twilight of the Gods

On March 20, 1948, the elite of Hollywood, braving freezing temperatures and gale-force winds, filed past the newsreel cameras into the Shrine Auditorium in Los Angeles for the twentieth annual presentation of the Academy Awards. Once inside, they discovered a stage that had been transformed into a towering birthday cake, with twenty giant Oscar statuettes in place of candles.

The studios had much to celebrate that night. Their movies, the most democratic of all art forms, had become the principal mode of paid entertainment for the vast majority of Americans. In an average week in 1947, 90 million Americans, out of a total population of only 151 million, went to a movie, paying on the average forty cents for a ticket. Nor was this massive outpouring, about two thirds of the ambulatory population, the product of expensive national marketing campaigns. It was simply the result of regular moviegoers going to see whatever was playing at their neighborhood theaters.

Most of these moviegoers didn't go to the theater to see a particular film. They went to see a program that included a newsreel; a short comedy film, such as the Three Stooges; a serial, such as Flash Gordon; animated cartoons, such as Bugs Bunny; a B feature, such as a western; and finally, the main attraction. In 1947 in America, movie houses were more ubiquitous than banks. There were more than eighteen thousand neighborhood theaters. Each had only one auditorium, one screen, one speaker (located behind the screen), one projection booth, and one marquee. Every week, usually on Thursday, a UPS truck picked up the previous week's reels and delivered the new ones. The new film's title on the marquee and the listings for it in the local newspapers constituted all the advertising most movies got.

Virtually all of these movies and shorts came from regional exchanges owned and operated by seven distribution companies that were, in turn, owned by seven Hollywood studios: Paramount, Universal, MGM, Twentieth Century–Fox, Warner Bros., Columbia, and RKO. In little over a generation, these studios had perfected a nearly omnipotent mechanism for controlling what the American public saw and heard. It was known, collectively, as the studio system.

These studios had their common origins in the arcades, nickelodeons, and exhibition halls of the silent-film era. Their founders, self-made and self-educated Jews, had been part of the late-nineteenth- and early-twentieth-century wave of immigration from Eastern Europe. They had worked at menial jobs as ragpickers, furriers, errand boys, butchers, junk peddlers, and salesmen and then gone into the business of showing movies. Here they found an enthusiastic audience, especially among those not yet fully literate in English, and a great deal of competition for it. To rise above their competitors, they instinctively sought what later economists would call "economies of scale." Louis B. Mayer, the founder of MGM, borrowed money to expand from a single theater in Haverhill, Massachusetts, to a small group of theaters that he combined into a "circuit"—so called because the reels of a single movie could be sent by bicycle from one theater to the next (with showtimes cut so close that sometimes one theater was showing the first reel of a film while another theater was showing the last), allowing multiple screenings of—and multiple admissions for—the movies he rented from film exchanges. As their circuits expanded, these entrepreneurs began opening their own film exchanges and distributing movies to other theater owners, but they still

made most of their money from tickets bought at their own box office—
so called because the cash went into locked boxes.

When they found that they could not get enough movies on a regular
basis from independent moviemakers, these new distributors took the
next step and started making their own films. Initially, their studios were
in the East, but as their production expanded after the turn of the century, they came under increased pressure from the Edison Trust, the legal
entity formed by Thomas A. Edison to control the basic patents on movie
cameras and projectors in America. The Trust filed a constant stream of
lawsuits against the nascent film companies, who finally decided to relo-
cate their studios a continent's width away from the reach of the Trust's
East Coast lawyers. They chose the newly incorporated village of Hollywood, California—a place they could control—for their new home.

In less than a generation, these entrepreneurs had literally gone from
rags (or furs) to riches. By the 1940s, the studio heads were among the
highest-paid executives in the world. Having come from poverty, they
reveled in this wealth and dubbed themselves moguls—an appellation
that, although perhaps not strictly appropriate since it originally referred
to absolute *Moslem* rulers, became part of their identity. Louis B. Mayer,
who had scavenged rags as a newly arrived immigrant and at nineteen
did not have, as his son-in-law David O. Selznick later put it, "the price of
a sandwich," was in 1947 the highest-paid executive in America, with an
annual salary from MGM of $1.8 million.

The studios produced nearly five hundred films in 1947—features
and B movies. While marketing strategies varied slightly from studio to
studio, the movie business in 1947 was a relatively simple affair. The studios did not license their films to television or other media or license their
characters for toys, games, T-shirts, or other merchandise. Foreign markets provided some revenue, but that income was mostly offset by high
taxes—Britain had a 75 percent import tax, for example—and most European and Asian countries had restrictions on currency repatriation. As a
result, profits from abroad were almost impossible to retrieve.

In short, studios looked to a single source for virtually all their money:
the American box office. In 1947 the six major studios earned over 95 percent of their revenue from their share of ticket sales (called "rentals,"
since it was technically the "rent" theaters paid for films) at North American movie houses. This came to $1.1 billion, which made movies, after

grocery stores and automotive sales, America's third-largest retail business.

The studios were able to harvest this windfall extremely efficiently because they controlled almost all the movie theaters. MGM, Warner Bros., Paramount, Twentieth Century–Fox, and RKO had their own theater chains, which produced about half of their total revenue, while Columbia and Universal controlled chains of theaters less directly through their distribution arms. Among the theaters under studio control were most of the first-run houses in major cities in the United States and Canada, where films had their premieres. During these first runs, films got their reviews, garnered publicity, and generated the word of mouth that served as the principal form of advertising. Thanks to their direct ownership of the theaters, studios were able to determine where, when, and for how long their films played in their first run. Such engagements could extend for many months while studios prepared the subsequent release to neighborhood theaters. For example, in 1947, Samuel Goldwyn's *The Best Years of Our Lives* was still playing at New York's Astor Theater, owned by MGM through its Loews subsidiary, six months after its premiere.

In addition, the studios indirectly controlled almost all independently owned theaters, which included most of the neighborhood and second-run movie houses, through ironclad contracts that forced the theater owners to commit to show a given number of films (usually ten) in a so-called block. If they did not accept a block, they got no studio films at all—which meant they did not have the star names to attract an audience. Only a few dozen art theaters that showed foreign films could afford to turn down this "blind-bidding" arrangement.

Not only were the studios able to control the bookings of their films, but they enjoyed a monopoly on the resulting revenue. Stars, directors, writers, and other talent did not share in it. Neither did producers. In rare cases these participants might receive a share of the eventual profits, but never of the studio's rentals.

The studios were further aided by low distribution and marketing costs. Because films opened in only a handful of theaters in major cities before moving on to other regions, the same prints and posters could be used first in the Northeast and later on in the South and West. Distribution costs therefore were low, averaging only about $60,000 a film in

1947. Further, there were no national advertising campaigns, and since theaters paid a good part of local advertising and stars freely supplied the publicity on radio and in newsreels, the advertising budgets averaged less than $30,000 a picture.

What remained after these distribution and advertising costs were deducted from the rental revenue were the studios' net receipts. In 1947 these totaled approximately $950 million.

To ensure a profit, studios obviously had to produce their films for less money than their net receipts totaled. To maximize their economies of scale, each studio had organized what amounted to a film factory, with staff and equipment that could operate around the clock. On their soundstages, shadowless light was cast by vast arrays of arc lamps, artificial weather was whipped up by wind, rain, and snow machines, and seas were created in indoor pools. On their back lots, exotic locales could be replicated and filled with extras dressed from the stocks of costumes and other props stored in their warehouses. For example, in 1947, MGM shot the adventure movie *The Three Musketeers*, which was set in seventeenth-century France, entirely on its soundstages and back lots.

The studios' technological apparatus included synchronous back ground projection, which allowed them to seamlessly integrate actors in current films with stock footage from their extensive film libraries and with film shot elsewhere by second units. They also had animation cameras to convert miniaturized models, puppets, and other replicas into the illusion of full-scale phenomena. To do all this, a veritable army of electricians, camera operators, seamstresses, makeup artists, set dressers, sound engineers, and other technicians were paid weekly wages. The MGM studio in Culver City, which in 1947 was the largest of the studios, could churn out on its soundstages six different films at the same time. With the aid of these assembly-line facilities, feature films could be shot in less than a month, and some B films were shot in a week.

Under this factory system, studios were also able to keep a tight rein over their product. Frank Capra wrote in a letter to *The New York Times* in 1939 that "about six producers today pass on about 90 percent of the scripts and edit about 90 percent of the pictures." These producers reported to the studio chief, who was directly responsible to the studio's owners.

The studios also had locked up all the stars who attracted audiences to movie theaters in a contractual arrangement called the star system. In 1947, 487 actors and actresses—including such marquee names as Bing Crosby, Bob Hope, Betty Grable, Gary Cooper, Ingrid Bergman, Humphrey Bogart, Clark Gable, John Wayne, Alan Ladd, and Gregory Peck—were under such contracts. Since these contracts usually ran seven years, precluded the actors from working elsewhere, and had renewal options, the stars were, for that period at least, essentially the studios' chattel. They had to play every part and perform every bit of publicity assigned to them. If they balked, they could be suspended without pay, as Lana Turner was in 1947 by MGM when she initially refused a part in *The Three Musketeers*. With no further recourse and facing the prospect of not being allowed to work at the height of her stardom, she finally acceded to MGM's casting and played the part.

In addition, studios could rent stars out to other studios for more than their salaries and pocket the difference. Joan Crawford, under contract to MGM, was loaned to Columbia for *They All Kissed the Bride* in 1942; and Bette Davis, under contract to Warner Bros., was loaned to RKO for *The Little Foxes* in 1941.

The contracts also usually gave the studios control of the stars' public image to further their publicity campaigns for their movies. This meant, in practice, that studios could script stars' interviews and dictate their public utterances, photographic poses, and gossip-column items. They could order them to alter their facial appearance, hair color, biographical details, and, as was commonly done, their name. Issur Danielovitch, for example, had his name changed to Kirk Douglas, Marion Morrison to John Wayne, and Emanuel Goldenberg to Edward G. Robinson.

In return, the studios provided their contract actors with an annual salary, roles in major films, and publicity in the media that they owned or controlled, which included newsreels and fan magazines. Whatever publicity benefits stars enjoyed by being contractually linked to a studio, however, their salaries were relatively low compared with the additional revenue they produced at the box office. In 1947 even highly successful stars, such as Clark Gable, made on average less than $100,000 a film. Until their contracts ran their course, stars could not increase their fees as they became more popular with audiences and more prominent in the entertainment media. The star system, in effect, allowed the studios to brand their products via the personas they had created—for example, a

James Cagney gangster film, a Roy Rogers western, a Clark Gable romance—and take the full profits from them.

By locking in actors' salaries, Hollywood studios were able to control the cost of manufacturing their products. Indeed, virtually all their films made money. Since the average cost of producing a film in 1947, including all studio overhead, was only $732,000, and the average net receipts for a studio feature amounted to $1.6 million, filmmaking was a lucrative enterprise for studios. Less successful films might eke out a profit of only a few thousand dollars, but the hits that appealed to a broad adult audience, like *The Best Years of Our Lives,* made profits in excess of $5 million.

But the studio moguls wanted more from their invention than mere profits. Not entirely secure with their rapid ascent to wealth, they also wanted the kind of respect, admiration, and status that would reinforce their position. This social part of the equation had been formally recognized some twenty years earlier, in 1927, at a dinner at the Ambassador Hotel, when Louis Mayer had proposed to thirty-five other top studio executives that they institute a way to honor Hollywood's (i.e., their own) achievements. The result was the establishment of the Academy of Motion Pictures Arts and Sciences and its annual ritual of bestowing honors in the form of Academy Awards.

The Oscar for the Best Motion Picture of 1947 went to Twentieth Century–Fox's *Gentleman's Agreement.* Adapted from the book of the same title by Laura Z. Hobson, the black-and-white film included the studio contract players Gregory Peck, Celeste Holm, John Garfield, and Dorothy McGuire. The Moss Hart script, like those of most of Hollywood's feature films, had all the elements of a classic narrative: a beginning, a middle, and an end; rising and falling action; conflict, confrontation, and resolution. It also had a character with whom the audience could readily identify in Philip Green (Gregory Peck), a gentile magazine writer who pretended to be Jewish so he could report firsthand on anti-Semitism. The conflict was almost entirely an intellectual one, resolved without mayhem or bloodshed. Nor was there any sex, nudity, profanity, or even suggestive language, all of which was proscribed by the studios' own censorship system.

Director Elia Kazan also won an Oscar for *Gentleman's Agreement.* The thirty-eight-year-old stage director had been retained by Twentieth

Century–Fox after the studio had bought the book, commissioned and approved Moss Hart's script, and assigned all the major roles to its contract stars. Like almost all other directors under the studio system, Kazan arrived at the beginning of principal photography and departed when it ended. The director's job was to exact the best performance from the actors and technicians within a shooting schedule prepared by the studio.

Twentieth Century–Fox executives, including studio head Darryl F. Zanuck, reviewed Kazan's daily progress during the twelve weeks of production. Zanuck then supervised the film's editing and musical score. Absolute authority over the creative process had been invested in the studio head ever since Irving Thalberg at MGM had perfected the system in the late 1920s. Zanuck had produced 170 of Fox's films, and *Gentleman's Agreement*, which he had supervised from start to finish, was no exception.

When Kazan accepted the Oscar for *Gentleman's Agreement* that night, the film was still, four months after opening at the Mayfair Theater in New York, in its first run. Even at this point, without having yet moved to neighborhood theaters, it had already earned back the $2 million it had cost to make. Although it was a cerebral film intended mainly for adults, it could reasonably be expected to draw a much larger audience once it was released more widely because, like all studio features, it would be part of a theater program that included a B film for teenage audiences and cartoons for children.

On that cold night in March 1948, all the signs seemed to indicate that the system was still operating almost flawlessly, and many of the old faces were there to attest to it. For the Academy Awards' twentieth anniversary, all the original moguls were present except Carl Laemmle, the founder of Universal, who had died, and William Fox, the founder of Twentieth Century–Fox, who, after nearly succeeding in taking over MGM in 1929, had gone bankrupt and then to prison for attempting to bribe a judge in his bankruptcy case. But if there is one lesson Hollywood teaches, it is that looks can be deceiving, and in 1948 the world of American moviemaking was on the verge of radical and irreversible change.

Although it was not evident in their demeanor that night, the power elites gathered at the awards ceremony knew that ominous storm clouds were amassing on the horizon. Hollywood was becoming the principal target of the House Un-American Activities Committee's efforts to uncover Communist subversion. In 1947 a large number of writers, actors, and directors had been called before the committee and asked to name subversives in the film industry. Many of those who refused to cooperate were then cited for contempt of Congress, and ten of them, the so-called Hollywood Ten, had to choose between prison and flight from the country. Caught in this bind, many leading writers—including Joseph Losey, Ben Barzman, and Donald Ogden Stewart—had moved abroad to avoid being subpoenaed.

The studios, rather than defying the congressional inquisition, had declared that anyone who invoked his or her constitutional right against self-incrimination or refused to cooperate by naming names would be fired and blacklisted. The Screen Actors Guild, headed by Ronald Reagan, in turn supported the studios, which had hired ex–FBI agents to help them weed out employees who had a politically suspect past. The smiles and jokes during the awards ceremony notwithstanding, the ugly issue of what constituted loyalty was threatening to tear apart the social fabric of the film community.

Another cloud was even darker and more threatening. For nearly ten years, in *U.S.* v. *Paramount et al.*, the Justice Department had been pressing an antitrust suit against the studios, alleging that the studios' control over the means by which movies were distributed and exhibited constituted an illegal restraint of trade under the Sherman Anti-Trust Act. The lower courts had decided in favor of the Justice Department, and the studios were running out of appeals. To settle the case, the government had demanded that the studios end their block booking and divest themselves of either their distribution arms or their theaters. In either case, they would lose control over what was shown—and that control, as every studio owner realized, was the jugular of the studio system. RKO—the weakest of the studios—was on the verge of breaking ranks and signing a consent decree. If it did, the other studios would come under tremendous, if not irresistible, pressure to follow suit. And once they did, the studio system would be dead.

The darkest cloud on the horizon, however, was the advent of an alternative entertainment medium: television. To be sure, at that point the new technology offered only a few hours of primitive programming a day in black and white, but it offered that at no cost to the consumer. Advertisers, not the audience, paid the broadcasters. The Hollywood studios had attempted to hobble this infant medium, if not kill it, by refusing to let the networks show films from their libraries or use their facilities to produce programs. Nevertheless, the television broadcasters were finding alternatives: live sports, news, game shows, and independent movies. And, although there were only 1 million sets in American homes in 1947, television manufacturers were expecting that number to quadruple by 1949. If these projections were realized, it would only be a matter of time before a good part of the 90 million people who paid to see movies at theaters would choose instead to watch free television. Since the studios were almost entirely dependent on this audience for their revenues, any substantial decrease would be an economic disaster.

Disturbing as these developments might have seemed to the studio owners, there was at least one man in the audience that night who had a more optimistic appreciation of the future: Walt Disney. Tellingly, perhaps, he won no Academy Award that night. Instead, the Oscar for best animation was awarded to the Warner Bros. cartoon *Tweetie Pie*.

Considered something of an oddball by the hardheaded moguls, the boyish-looking Disney had chosen to remain outside the studio system. Although his animation studio by now employed more than one thousand artists and technicians, he was not even a member of the Movie Producers Association or the distributor of his own movies. Instead, he relied on RKO to get his films into theaters.

Disney had a different strategy from the other studio heads. Unlike them, he did not have any stars under contract or own any theaters. While their studios made their money from ticket sales, he made most of his from licensing Mickey Mouse and other characters for toys, books, filmstrips, and newspapers.

To the other studio heads' mystification, he was enjoying success with his seemingly crazy ideas. In 1934 Disney had begun work on a feature-length cartoon that the chiefs of the conventional Hollywood studios derided as "Disney's Folly": *Snow White and the Seven Dwarfs*. At the time, the major studios believed that adults, not children, were the principal audience for movies, and that cartoons, which usually ran no more than five minutes, were merely adjuncts used to entertain children during weekend matinees. So Disney's announcement that he would make an eighty-three-minute cartoon out of a Grimms fairy tale seemed like madness. Apparently confirming his perceived lack of touch with reality, Disney planned to spend three times the average Hollywood budget making the film. With the continuing Depression threatening their viability, the studio heads could not fathom how he could ever earn back this sum at the theaters.

But Disney was working from a different concept: he believed that children, with adults in tow, could be the driving force of the entertainment industry. His surprising success with *Snow White and the Seven Dwarfs*—which would become the first film in history to gross $100 million—demonstrated that the potential of the child audience had been severely underestimated by Hollywood: in the case of *Snow White and the Seven Dwarfs,* children were going to see it over and over again, just as they did with other cartoons. (Children's tickets on the average cost only twenty-five cents; approximately 400 million of them had been sold for *Snow White* between 1937 and 1948).

Snow White and the Seven Dwarfs was more than just a successful box-office event, however. It was also the first film to have a soundtrack—including such hit songs as "Someday My Prince Will Come"—that became an enormously successful record, as well as the first film to have a merchandising tie-in. And, most important as far as the Disney model was concerned, it had multiple licensable characters—Snow White, seven dwarfs, and a wicked witch—who took on long lives of their own, first as toys and later as theme-park exhibits.

With *Snow White and the Seven Dwarfs*, Disney had done more than define a new audience for movies; he had suggested the future course of the entertainment business overall. In it, the real profits would come not from squeezing down the costs of producing films but from creating out of them intellectual properties that could be licensed in other media over long periods.

But even as the studio system tottered under the tripartite threat of television, HUAC, and an antitrust lawsuit in 1948, this was not a future Hollywood saw or, if it did—as when Louis Mayer was advised by his top executive that MGM was pursuing "business that no longer exists"—wanted to embrace. Disney was regarded by the moguls who still ruled the industry as a whimsical eccentric. Little did they suspect that his Pied

Piper strategy would prevail and that they themselves would soon enough be dancing to his tune.

The New System

February 29, 2004. A very different elite made their way along the red carpet into the newly built Kodak Theater for the seventy-sixth presentation of the Oscars. Many of the stars were now paid representatives for fashion and cosmetic companies, walking product placements for a worldwide broadcast that Hollywood publicists claimed, with their usual hyperbole, would reach 1 billion viewers. (In fact, according to the Nielsen rating, the event was seen that night in 43.5 million homes.) The lobby through which they passed contained a gauntlet of five-foot-high sepia-tinted photographs of stars—including Grace Kelly, Jack Nicholson, Marlon Brando, Halle Berry, Tom Hanks, and Julia Roberts—mounted on Plexiglas panels that hung in front of beaded white walls designed to suggest an old-time movie screen. These outsized images, like almost everything else in the meticulously planned ceremony, memorialized the past glory of Hollywood. Not that the glory of the present was being ignored—the auditorium itself had been specially outfitted to accommodate thirty-six strategically placed television cameras.

Although outwardly much of the 2004 awards ceremony seemed to resemble its predecessors from the days of the studio system—the statuettes, the celebrity presenters opening sealed envelopes, the acceptance speeches, the special awards, the self-deprecating jokes by the master of ceremonies—Hollywood was now a very different place, operating according to a very different logic. The physical plants of the great Hollywood studios, with their soundstages and back lots, still existed in somewhat diminished form, and most of the studios still bore the same names and logos, such as Paramount's mountain peak, Universal's globe, and Fox's searchlights. But beneath their outward appearance, they were radically different enterprises. They were now international corporate empires, with their shares traded on stock exchanges in New York, Tokyo, and Sydney and their debt managed by global banking syndicates. Movies now were just one of their many businesses.

Columbia Pictures was now owned by the Sony Corporation, a Japanese electronics conglomerate that manufactured everything from computers to PlayStations and owned music, television-broadcasting, and insurance companies. Sony also owned TriStar Productions, CBS Records, and the studio in Culver City once owned by MGM. (In 2004, it would gain control of MGM itself—and its film library.)

The Warner Bros. studio was now owned by Time Warner, a giant conglomerate that contained the Internet assets of America Online; the media assets of Time, Inc., which included HBO; the cable and entertainment assets of Turner Entertainment, which included New Line Cinema; and the movie, television, and music assets of Warner Communications.

The Fox studio was now owned by News Corporation, an Australia-based media company whose properties included newspapers, magazines, a television network, cable networks, and satellite broadcasting in Europe, North America, South America, and Asia.

The Universal studio was now owned by General Electric, America's largest industrial company, in partnership with Vivendi Entertainment, a huge French conglomerate. Its properties included the NBC television network, the USA cable networks, USA Films, and the Universal theme parks.

The Paramount and RKO studios were now both owned by Viacom International, a media company that owned the CBS and UPN television networks; MTV, Nickelodeon and other cable networks; Blockbuster video stores; the Infinity radio networks; and Viacom Outdoor Advertising billboards.

And the Walt Disney animation studio had grown into the Walt Disney Company. It now owned—with its $19 billion acquisition in 1996 of CapitalCities/ABC Corporation—a television network, a radio network, cable networks, theme parks, cruise ships, and other assets, all of which made it, as its then-chairman Michael Eisner once put it, "a true full-service entertainment enterprise . . . in the vast entertainment firmament."

Despite the differences among them, the six entertainment giants still had three fundamental things in common.

First, whereas in the days of the studio system making movies for theaters had been the one and only business of studios, the movie business itself was now a relatively unimportant part of each conglomerate's financial picture. Even when all the earnings from movies' theatrical releases, video and DVD sales, and television licensing—both domestic and international—were included in their movie businesses, they accounted for only a small part of each company's total earnings. In 2003 Viacom earned 7 percent of its total income from its movie business; Sony, 19 percent; Disney, 21 percent; News Corporation, 19 percent; Time Warner, 18 percent; and General Electric, if it had counted Universal Pictures as part of its conglomerate that year, less than 2 percent. So while the film business may have held great social, political, or strategic significance to each company, it was no longer the principal way any of them made their money.

Second, unlike their predecessors, who made their profits at the box office, all six companies now routinely lost money on theatrical release (or, as it is now called, "current production"). Consider, for example, the Disney film *Gone in 60 Seconds*. Although a not-otherwise-memorable car-theft movie starring Nicolas Cage, it had been singled out for its commercial success by Disney chairman Michael Eisner in the company's 2000 annual report, where it was described as one the company's biggest "hits." As far as the public—and shareholders—knew, the movie's impressive-sounding worldwide box-office gross of $242 million amounted to an immense profit. But the company's confidential financial statements, issued semiannually to the movie's profit participants over the next four years, tell a different story.

Disney paid $103.3 million to physically produce the movie—the so-called negative cost. Then, just to get the film physically into theaters in America and abroad, it had to pay another $23.2 million—$13 million for prints and $10.2 million for the insurance, local taxes, customs clearances, reediting for censors, and shipping fees. Next Disney spent $67.4 million on advertising worldwide. Finally, it had to pay $12.6 million in "residual fees" in accordance with agreements it had with various guilds and unions. Altogether, then, it cost the studio $206.5 million to get this film—and its audiences—into the theaters.

The so-called gross—a figure authoritatively reported in the media as if it was the amount a movie earned for its studio—also proved elusive. Most of the $242 million collected at the box offices never made it to Disney's coffers. Theaters kept $139.8 million. Disney's distribution arms—Buena Vista and Buena Vista International—collected only $102.2 million for a film on which it had spent $206.5 million. And this calculation does not include Disney's cost in paying its own employees in its production, distribution, and marketing arms or the interest on the millions it had laid out. When this overhead ($17.2 million) and interest ($41.8 million) were included, the loss on the theatrical release of this "hit" was over $160 million by 2003.

Nor was *Gone in 60 Seconds* an aberration. In 2003, a relatively good year, the six studios lost money on the worldwide theatrical release of most of their titles, or their current production. These losses stemmed not from malfeasance, mismanagement, or flawed decisions about the content of the films but from the economic realities of the new era.

The massive moviegoing audience that had nurtured the studio system simply no longer exists. In contrast to the 4.7 billion movie tickets sold in America in 1947, there were only 1.57 billion tickets sold in 2003. So, even though the population had almost doubled, movie theaters sold 3.1 billion fewer tickets than they had in 1947. Television, as well as other diversions, had so reduced the audience that less than 12 percent of the population bought a ticket in an average week. And the six studios could not count on getting even this small fraction of its former audience. To settle the federal antitrust suits in 1949, they had sold their own theaters and discontinued their block-booking contracts with the independent theaters. As a consequence, they had lost control over what was shown in theaters. The theater owners, not the studio heads, now decide which films to show and for how long. And the theater owners no longer restrict their bookings to only major studio releases. So the six studios now have to compete with studioless studios (such as MGM, DreamWorks, and Artisan Entertainment), as well as other independent filmmakers, for the desirable times and screens at the multiplexes. Indeed, the six major studios, including their subsidiaries, accounted for less than half of the 473 films released in the United States in 2003. As a result, their take from the American box office totaled only about $3.23 billion.

Just as in the old days, studios still have to pay the distribution expenses on their films. But now they also have to create a new audience for each and every movie. This requires creating and paying for intensive television advertising as well as making enough prints for simultaneous openings in thousands of theaters to take advantage of that advertising. In 2003, just the prints required for the opening of a studio film cost, on average, $4.2 million. The advertising averaged another $34.8 million a title. But while the studios spent an average of $39 million per film just to get audiences and prints into American theaters, they recovered from the box office only $20.6 million on average per film. So in 2003 they wound up paying more to alert potential moviegoers and supply theaters with prints for an opening than they were getting back from those who bought tickets. (The story was similar with overseas theaters, for which, in addition to prints and advertising, the studios had to pay the cost of dubbing and additional editing to tailor the films to foreign audiences.) These new marketing costs had grown so large by 2003 that even if the studios had somehow managed to obtain all their movies for free, they would still have lost money on their American releases.

But studios, of course, did *not* make these movies for free. And, to make matters far worse, the costs of producing a film have also risen astronomically. At the end of the studio-system era, in 1947, the cost of producing an average studio film, or negative cost, was $732,000. In 2003 it was $63.8 million. To be sure, the dollar had decreased in value sevenfold between 1947 and 2003, but even after correcting for inflation, the cost of producing films had increased more than sixteen times since the collapse of the studio system.

Part of the studios' cost problem is the result of stars being freed from their control. Instead of being tethered to studios by seven-year contracts, stars are now auctioned off—with the help of savvy agents—to the highest bidder for each film. Since there are fewer desirable stars than film projects, they can command eight-digit fees. By 2003, the top stars were getting not only between $20 and $30 million a film in fixed compensation and perks but a percentage of the film's total revenue after repaying cash outlays.

For example, Arnold Schwarzenegger received, according to his contract, a $29.25 million fixed fee for his role in the 2003 film *Terminator 3: Rise of the Machines,* as well as a $1.5 million perk package that included private jets, a fully equipped gym trailer, three-bedroom deluxe suites on locations, round-the-clock limousines, and personal bodyguards. In addition, once the film reached its cash break-even point, his contract guaranteed him 20 percent of the gross receipts from all sources worldwide (including video, DVD, theatrical box office, television, and licensing). Under any scenario—whether the film failed, broke even, or made a profit—the star was assured of making more money than the studio itself. In this new era, stars, not studios, reap the profit their brand names bring to a film.

In 2003 the six studios—Paramount, Fox, Sony, Warner Bros., Disney, and Universal—spent $11.3 billion to produce, publicize, and distribute to theaters around the world 80 films under their own imprints. They spent another $6.7 billion on 105 films produced by their so-called independent subsidiaries, such as Miramax, New Line, Fox Searchlight, and Sony Classic. Of this $18 billion in expenditures (which did not include the cost of abandoned projects), the studios recovered only $6.4 billion from their share of the world box office, leaving them with a deficit of more than $11 billion after their movies had played in all the theaters in the world.

In the days of the studio system, numbers like this would have meant bankruptcy. But the studios in the new system no longer expect to earn their profits from showing their products in movie theaters. As Frank Biondi, who served as studio chief at both Paramount and Universal, put it, "Studios nowadays almost always lose money on current production."

This brings us to the third, and probably most significant, feature that the six studios now have in common. They all make the bulk of their profits from licensing their filmed entertainment for home viewing. Even as late as 1980, most of the studios' worldwide revenues still came from movie theaters. At that point, no matter how large the success of hits such as *Love Story*, *Jaws*, or *Star Wars* proved to be, all the studios were losing money on their overall movie business. The deus ex machina that transformed the movie business, as shown in Table 1, was not the selection of better movies—as studio chiefs would later claim—but the prodigious expansion in home viewing that came as a result of the video player, cable networks, pay TV, and the DVD. By 2003 the studios were taking in almost five times as much revenue from home entertainment as from theaters.

As the studios' profit center shifted from movie theaters to retail stores, they all made a further adjustment in their business strategies. Since the six major studios now produced relatively few films, they needed to increase their "throw weight," as one Paramount executive termed it, to persuade merchandisers like Wal-Mart to cede them the strategic shelf space for their videos. So, beginning in the 1990s, they either bought existing independent distributors—such as Miramax, Di-

TABLE 1. MAJOR STUDIO WORLDWIDE REVENUES, 1948–2003
INFLATION ADJUSTED IN 2003 DOLLARS (BILLIONS)

Year	Theater	Video/DVD	Pay TV	TV, Free	Total	Theater Share (%)
1948	6.9	0	0	0	6.9	100
1980	4.4	0.2	0.38	3.26	8.2	53
1985	2.96	2.34	1.041	5.59	11.9	25
1990	4.9	5.87	1.62	7.41	19.8	25
1995	5.57	10.6	2.34	7.92	26.43	21
2000	5.87	11.67	3.12	10.75	31.4	19
2003	7.48	18.9	3.36	11.4	41.1	18

mension New Line Cinema, October Films, Gramercy Pictures, Focus Features, and USA Films—or created their own "independent" subsidiaries—such as Sony Pictures Classics, Paramount Classics, and Warner Independent Pictures—to acquire the rights to foreign movies and low-budget movies made outside of Hollywood's purview. As a result of their search for "throw weight," the studios came to dominate much, if not all, of the independent film business as well.

By 2003, the home-entertainment share had, thanks in large part to the sales of more than a billion DVDs, reached $33 billion. Since the advertising and other marketing costs associated with them are minimal, these sales provided a veritable ocean of bottom-line profits, which the studios now count on to offset the massive losses from their films' theatrical releases. Theatrical releases now serve essentially as launching platforms for licensing rights, much like the runways at haute couture fashion shows.

Part of what makes the shift to the home-entertainment market so significant is the shift in audiences that goes along with it. By far the most important segment of the studios' home-entertainment audience in 2003 was children and teens, who use television sets for hours on end, either to watch programs on cable channels and networks or to play movie videos, music videos, and games. These younger consumers, prized by advertisers since they heavily influence their parents' purchases, also buy many of the toys and much of the clothing and other paraphernalia licensed by the studios.

The six entertainment companies' sway over—and interest in—this young audience goes beyond the home-television market. They publish most of the books read by children, they record most of the music listened to by children—Disney alone accounting for 60 percent—they own most of the theme parks visited by children on their vacations, and they license most of the characters whose images appear in the toys, clothes, and games consumed by children. To capture this valuable audience, studios no longer focus on making films that appeal mainly to grown-ups, as their predecessors from the studio-system days did. By 2003, all six Hollywood studios had adopted the strategy first foreshadowed by Walt Disney sixty-six years earlier, when *Snow White and the Seven Dwarfs* appeared—making films specifically aimed at youth.

While Disney's animation process cleared the first path to this young audience, the digital revolution of the new millennium has widened that path to a thoroughfare. The new elite of computer-graphic establishments includes Industrial Light & Magic (the postproduction house owned by George Lucas, director-producer of the *Star Wars* movies), Lightstorm Entertainment (the company owned by James Cameron, director of *Titanic*), and Pixar Animation Studios (led by Steve Jobs, founder of Apple Computer). With its proprietary computer programs and loose networks of computer wonks, this new generation of technology consumes an increasingly large share of the studios' budgets. Beyond the financial implications, the new division of labor between the camera and the computer is also changing, for better or worse, the aesthetics of movies themselves.

Consider the movie that won eleven Oscars that night in 2004, including the one for the Best Motion Picture of 2003: *The Lord of the Rings: The Return of the King.* The celebration that the studios had invented for their own validation was now dominated by a children's fantasy movie. Time Warner's wholly owned subsidiary, New Line Cinema, had produced it not as a single entity but as part of a franchise, a trilogy with *The Lord of the Rings: The Two Towers* and *The Lord of the Rings: The Fellowship of the Ring*, all of which had been shot simultaneously in New Zealand in late 1999 and early 2000 and then released separately in 2001, 2002, and 2003. The triple production cost $281 million. Unlike *Gentleman's Agreement*, which, like almost all other films in the studio system, was created by camera operators photographing actors, *The Lord of the Rings: The Return of the King* was created mainly by computer animators. More than one thousand separate shots in the film—over 70 percent of the total number of shots—were not filmed by a camera at all. These parts of the movie were created by digital technicians working for autonomous computer-graphics houses in far-flung parts of the world. Some shots were created from scratch, while others combined live acting with digitally created layers. Unlike the single crew—thirty-nine technicians in all—who filmed the actors in *Gentleman's Agreement* in close enough proximity to see and hear them on the set, most of the digital compositors, inferno artists, rotoscope artists, digital modelers, digital wranglers, software developers, and motion-capture coordinators working on *The Lord of the Rings: The Return of the King* were separated in both time and space from the action on the set and had virtually no personal contact with the actors, director, production staff, or even one another. While the process in this case yielded stunning results—attested to by those eleven Oscars—it also augured a future for Hollywood that would be much more dependent on the manipulations of the computer than on those of the camera.

This shift has not gone unnoticed by outside critics, who berate the studios for wasting money on lavish productions and extravagant advertising campaigns, suggesting that Hollywood's studios fail to appreciate the "logic" of their own industry. But the studios may understand more than their critics give them credit for. Even though they lost more than $11 billion in 2003 on movies shown in theaters, they more than made up that deficit from licensing products from those movies to the global home-entertainment market. They have now all come to realize—as Disney did a half century earlier—that the value they create lies not in the tickets they sell at the box office but in the licensable products they create for future generations of consumers.

F. Scott Fitzgerald noted, in his final, unfinished novel, *The Last Tycoon*, that most people in Hollywood had at best only a fragmentary understanding of the movie business; "not a half dozen men," he wrote, "have been able to keep the whole equation of pictures in their heads."

By the dawning of the third millennium, the "whole equation" of what had replaced the studio system had become even more complex. At the heart of it is a sexopoly: six global entertainment companies—Time Warner, Viacom, Fox, Sony, NBC Universal, and Disney—that collude and cooperate at different levels to dominate filmed entertainment. It is these six companies that choose the images that constitute a large part of the world's popular culture, and it is these six companies that will continue to shape the imagination of a universe of youth for generations to come. Nostalgia for the old studios notwithstanding, their Hollywood is the new Hollywood.

Not surprisingly, the decisions of these six companies about the movies they make—the logic of the new Hollywood—is largely driven by money. But economic considerations are not the whole story. Social and political logics—involving status, honor, solidarity with stars, and other, less tangible, considerations—also form a critical part of the equation. If the big picture continues to remain elusive to the outside world, shrouded in self-generated myths and misplaced nostalgia, that is not accidental. The major studios, for example, go to considerable lengths to conceal the revenues from their moviemaking enterprise from investors, financial analysts, and journalists—even though they make this data available to one another through their trade organization, the MPA (on condition that the MPA keep it secret from the public). They manage this concealment, even in their own financial reporting, by combining their movie earnings with those of unrelated businesses, such as licensing television programs (or even, in the case of Paramount, theme parks). The rationale given by one savvy top studio executive for this "blurring" is "to avoid showing Wall Street how volatile the movie business is and how tricky are its profit margins." Studios are willing to camouflage short-term losses on their movies because movies, not television sales or theme park operations, are their principal source of prestige and satisfaction in Hollywood. In more ways than one, today's movie business works to keep its audience—and, to some extent, its own players—in the dark.

☆ Part One ☆

THE NEW SYSTEM

2

The Creators

The original studio system was devised by a handful of turn-of-the-century entrepreneurs in the business of showing movies. They were all self-made men, and in building their studios, they followed a common path typified by Paramount founder Adolph Zukor.

Zukor left Hungary in 1889 at the age of sixteen, arriving in New York with $40 sewn inside his vest. He worked as a furrier, stitching pieces of hides into stoles; by the time he was twenty-seven, he had established his own successful fur business. The profits from this business he in turn invested in a string of amusement arcades that featured a new invention by Thomas Edison: a hand-cranked machine that, for the cost of a few pennies dropped in the slot, created the illusion of motion by rapidly repeating still pictures. By 1903, these "motion pictures," as Edison called them, had proved so immensely popular, especially among the largely illiterate immigrant population in New York, that they took in more than a million pennies annually. Since there were many competitors in the arcade business, Zukor soon moved on to small movie theaters—called nickelodeons because they charged five cents—in which a projectionist rather than the patron generated the illusion. To keep the theater seats filled, the movies were changed every week.

Rather than depend on other producers to supply new movies, Zukor eventually began producing them himself in New York. There was, however, an obstacle to expanding this production in the East: Thomas Edison's Motion Picture Patents Company. Edison, it will be recalled, held patents on both the camera and the projector, and (along with a company called American Mutoscope, which had patented similar devices) had formed what came to be called the Trust. Not only did the Trust have patents on the hardware necessary for filmmaking, but it had contractually bound the Eastman Kodak Company, the principal manufacturer of raw stock, not to sell film to any producer that it did not license. When independent producers in New York, Boston, and other major filmmaking centers tried to buy raw film stock and cameras elsewhere, the Trust aggressively threatened litigation, reinforced by cooperative police involvement, to harass if not outright prohibit them. To evade the Trust's lawyers, these nascent studios had to resort to constant deception. For example, some producers had their cameramen hide the real cameras in the back of trucks while displaying out front dummy cameras that were not covered by the Trust's patents.

However, as Neal Gabler astutely points out in his history of the early film moguls, *An Empire of Their Own*, the conflict between the Trust and the independent producers went beyond patent rights and the profits that flowed from them. The battle also concerned "cultural, philosophical [and] religious" issues. The men who ran the Trust were mainly Anglo-Saxon, Protestant Americans, with positions in the traditional business establishment; the independent producers, of which Zukor was one of the largest, were Jewish immigrant outsiders. In the face of this cultural divide and the Trust's strong-arm tactics, Zukor decided to move his production to the other side of the continent, where the Trust would find less sympathetic courts, politicians, and police. Hollywood, it turned out, was just the escape he was looking for.

Hollywood had been little more than barley fields and orange groves until 1903, when a real-estate syndicate headed by Harry Chandler, the future newspaper tycoon, and General Moses Sherman, a railroad millionaire, bought the rural acreage and, connecting it to Los Angeles by a one-track trolley line, managed to incorporate it as a municipality. Then they built the Hollywood Hotel on Hollywood Boulevard and began pitching lots to prospective buyers in the East. Zukor, on the lookout for cheap real estate, was happy to buy. By 1916 he had consolidated the theater, distribution exchanges, and production facilities he controlled into a single studio, and Paramount Pictures was born.

The stories of the other studio founders are remarkably similar. Carl Laemmle, who began in America as an errand boy, founded Universal Pictures in 1912. William Fox, who began as a street peddler, founded Fox in 1915. Warner Bros. was founded eight years later by Jack and Harry Warner, who began as butchers. Louis B. Mayer, a onetime ragpicker, organized Metro-Goldwyn-Mayer in 1924. That same year, Harry Cohn, who got his start as a sheet-music salesman, founded Columbia Pictures.

Not all the founders remained in power until the end of the studio system (Carl Laemmle, the oldest among them, died in 1939 at the age of seventy-two, and William Fox went bankrupt in the Great Depression and saw his studio taken over by Darryl Zanuck, who had the distinction of being the only non-Jew among the studio-era moguls), but the studios remained basically personal fiefdoms, and they continued to fulfill the purpose for which the moguls had created them: providing theaters and exchanges in America with movies. When the moguls were finally replaced, it was by a very different group of men. Not only did they come from more varied backgrounds, but their focus was not limited to making a single product. They were empire builders.

Walt Disney: The Genius of the New System (1901–1966)

Walter Elias Disney, even if he would not have cast himself in the role, was the principal architect of the new studio system. Born on December 5, 1901, to Protestant middle-class parents in Chicago, Disney was four years old when his family moved to a farm near Marceline, Missouri, where his fascination with barnyard animals began. When he was nine, the family moved to Kansas City, where Walt delivered newspapers, attended elementary school, and, on Saturdays, took drawing classes at the Kansas City Art Institute.

Shortly after America went to war with Germany in 1917, the sixteen-year-old Disney used his artistic skills to forge an earlier date on his birth certificate so he could enlist. He spent one year in France as a Red

Cross ambulance driver. After returning to Kansas City in 1919, he worked briefly as an artist for an advertising agency, where he met Ub Iwerks, an extraordinary animator of Dutch origin. The two men decided to go into business together producing humorous trailers—called "Laugh-O-Grams"—for local movie theaters. Since neither man had much interest in the business side of things, however, the venture quickly ran out of money.

In 1923 Disney left Kansas to join his brother Roy in California. He had no job, references, or savings, but he had an idea: he wanted to animate cartoons for the movies. Although Roy had very little money himself, he managed to loan his twenty-one-year-old brother the $50 he needed to go into the animated-movie business.

With that stake, Walt Disney opened a small workshop on Hollywood's Kingswell Avenue in October 1923. The rent was $10 a month. He bought a used camera, built an animation table out of discarded lumber, and officially opened for business, making shorts that combined live action and animation. It was a one-man operation. He wrote the scripts. He drew the pictures. He photographed them, one by one, and edited the results.

After working around the clock for two months, Disney managed to complete his first film, *Alice's Day at Sea*. It was eleven minutes long and told the story of a young girl, Alice, dreaming of fish in the sea. Alice was played by a child; the fish were animated. In December he sold the film to a small distributor, Winkler Films, for $1,500. He was on his way.

By the spring of 1924, after he had produced four more Alice films, Disney persuaded his mentor, Ub Iwerks, to come to Hollywood and become the chief animator of Walt Disney Films. In 1928, based on an idea suggested by Disney, Iwerks drew the anthropomorphic rodent who would make history. Disney soon hit on the name Mickey Mouse, which almost immediately caught the public's imagination.

To establish his new hero, Disney took full advantage of the new technology of sound. At that point animation was easier to synchronize to sound than live action was, with less artificial results, so the new cartoons were especially impressive and theaters were eager to rent them to demonstrate the new technology. Within a year, Mickey Mouse "talkies" were playing in thousands of theaters across the nation and proved an immense success.

As money poured in for the Mickey Mouse cartoons, Disney could have chosen to take the path of the major studios. He was already using actors and camera crews in some semianimated shorts, such as the Alice films. With his growing resources, he could have signed actors to long-term contracts and created a stable of stars, purchased showcase theaters, and formed a distribution arm. He could have competed at the box office for the broad audience, and he could have established a full-fledged studio. But he chose not to become part of the studio system or even to join the Motion Picture Association.

Disney preferred to remain an outsider. As a Protestant from the Midwest, he had no connection with, or affinity for, the Jewish immigrant culture that ran the major studios, or the moguls themselves, whom he referred to as "those Jews." Further, he had no association with the stars, producers, directors, agents, and writers who constituted the Hollywood colony by that time. And unlike men such as Adolph Zukor, Louis Mayer, Jack Warner, or the other studio moguls of the time, he lacked the hawkeyed business temperament to churn out films on an assembly line. Equally significant, Disney, even more than the studio moguls, sought a level of personal control that could not be exerted over live stars, no matter how ironclad their contracts. Animation, on the other hand, gave him nearly total control, and he exercised it, insisting that his artists continue to draw—and redraw—characters until they met with his approval.

Ironically, in bypassing the Hollywood system, Disney chose a route that, though he could not have foreseen it at the time, would not only ultimately create greater wealth than that amassed by all the moguls combined but would replace their studio system altogether.

With Mickey Mouse, Disney had discovered the source for a vast universe of profits that extended well beyond the American box office: children at home and play around the world. He began exploiting this vast market by extracting the characters created by his movies and licensing them to other industries. As early as 1932, he licensed Mickey Mouse to watch manufacturers—the character's gloved hands pointing to the time—and then to book publishers, clothing companies, and toy manufacturers.

Nor was the boon of character licensing limited to America; since anthropomorphic animals required little, if any, verbal exposition, they easily crossed language and cultural barriers. In Japan, Mickey Mouse became Miki Kuchi and the second-most popular figure in Japan (behind only the emperor). In France he became Michel Souris, in Spain Miguel Ratoncito, and so on. Eventually, local fan clubs were established for Mickey Mouse products in more than thirty countries.

By the mid-1930s, Disney, unlike the moguls at the major studios, was well on his way to creating universal properties—not restricted by timeliness, cultural barriers, or nationality—that could be licensed to every enterprise that appealed to children. By 1935, at the height of the Great Depression, Disney's royalties from his characters were providing considerably more profits than the movies in which they starred. (A single Disney-created character, Mickey Mouse, would eventually earn more from licensing fees and theme-park admissions than the total profits of all the studios combined during that decade.)

To expand his array of extractable characters, Disney began producing feature-length animated films, beginning with *Snow White and the Seven Dwarfs* in the mid-1930s. Since drawing each and every frame of a full-length movie would be prohibitively expensive, he used, as he had in previous cartoons, transparent sheets called "cels"—short for *celluloids*— which contained the various moving parts of characters. By overlaying different cels on top of one another, Disney's animators could achieve different permutations of motions without redrawing each frame. Like the computer programs that would come a half century later, these cels enabled artwork to be done mechanically by technicians.

With the phenomenal success of the *Snow White and the Seven Dwarfs* soundtrack—the first soundtrack to become a record—Disney realized the Pied Piper power of music to attract young audiences to his products. In 1940, he produced *Fantasia*, which combined classical music with his animated characters. For its opening, he devised a sound system called Fantasound, which not only introduced stereophonic sound in films but, with its ninety speakers and sonic legerdemain, created the illusion for the audience of being surrounded by the movie. (Such surround sound was merely an adumbrating of the three-dimensional entertainment illusion that would become the hallmark of Disney's later theme parks.)

As his empire expanded, Walt Disney found that he could no longer depend on RKO, which had been taken over by the multimillionaire Howard Hughes, to satisfactorily distribute his films. He was especially disappointed at its handling of his feature-length nature documentaries, such as *The Living Desert*, and in the early 1950s he ended the long-term relationship and established his own distribution arm, Buena Vista International. In doing so, Disney finally became a full-service studio.

Because his company's main profits came from the children who bought the products he licensed, the new medium of television did not pose the sort of threat to Disney that it did to the major studio heads. In fact, where the moguls saw only crises, Disney saw a golden opportunity: television could bring his licensees' products directly into the homes of families. While the major studios were boycotting the new technology, Disney began selling the networks his *Mickey Mouse Club* and other programs. Not only did the networks pay him for these programs, but almost every minute of them functioned as free advertising for his licensed characters.

In 1954, Disney also managed to get ABC, the newest of the three television networks, to help him finance an even more permanent platform for his characters: Disneyland, in Anaheim, California. Here was a mass-entertainment form that went beyond the two-dimensional limits of movies, television, and comic strips and allowed children to interact with three-dimensional simulacrums of Mickey Mouse, Donald Duck, Dumbo, and other Disney characters (all played by costumed park employees called "cast members"). The park would occupy 160 acres and would feature only Disney-approved products. In exchange for a one-third interest in the park and Disney's commitment to produce a weekly television series, ABC guaranteed a $4.5 million loan for the theme park and contributed $500,000 in cash. The television series, *Disneyland* (later *Walt Disney Presents* and then *Walt Disney's Wonderful World of Color*), essentially served as a weekly advertisement—in prime time on Sunday night—for Disney's products, including the theme park itself.

Disney's choice of a television network as his initial partner in Disneyland proved a brilliant success: in its first year 3 million visitors passed through the theme park's gates. (In 1962 ABC sold back to Disney its share in the park.) Since Disney insisted on maintaining a private apartment over the firehouse on Main Street in Disneyland—a street designed after the main street in Marceline, Missouri, where he had lived as a boy—some observers saw the theme park as Disney's personal indulgence or, as one observer put it, "the world's biggest toy for the world's biggest boy." But Disneyland was far more than a personal indulgence; it was the logical extension of the strategy that Disney had devised for bypassing the Hollywood studios and building an empire of the mind—or, at least, of children's minds. Every structure in the enclosed park—including rides, restaurants, parking lots, and even rest rooms—was designed to reinforce the imagery of Disney characters in the minds of children. At its opening on July 18, 1955, Disney vowed that "Disneyland will never be completed, as long as there is imagination left in the world."

In keeping with this effort to stir children's fertile imaginations with Disney-branded rides, exhibits, and characters, Disney recruited a permanent design team called Imagineers, which continued under his successors. In this quest, Disney also acquired the licensing rights in 1961 to the popular children's book *Winnie the Pooh*, whose characters alone would generate nearly $6 billion a year in retail sales by 2003.

While the major studios were waging a losing battle to hold on to the remnants of the movie-theater audience by whatever means they could—producing epic three-hour films such as *Ben-Hur* and elongating theater screens with technologies such as CinemaScope—Disney was thriving by embracing the new medium of television—and in the process expanding the presence of his characters in the places where children lived, played, and vacationed.

Walt Disney died of lung cancer in 1966, but his vision survived. His brother Roy, who succeeded him, continued the "Disney way" of using the theme parks, television programs, children's books, and movies to establish and enhance the value of the Disney characters. "*Integration* is the key word around here," he explained. "We don't do anything in one line without giving a thought to its likely profitability in our other lines."

Even though Michael Eisner, who became Disney's chairman in 1984, greatly expanded the company by buying the ABC network, the ESPN network, and other assets, he insisted that the company's "key objective" remain the same as Walt Disney's: developing "powerful brand and character franchises." He reassured shareholders in 2000, "Once you're inside Disneyland's gates, the outside world disappears." By now, Hollywood— as well as Wall Street—understood that marketing licensable characters to audiences of children was a serious business.

COURTESY OF CORBIS

Lew Wasserman: The Insider (1913–2002)

Louis Wasserman was born on the ides of March, 1913 in Cleveland, the son of Orthodox Jews from Russia. After graduating from Glenville High School in 1930 and changing his first name to Lew, he began his career in show business, working as a publicist for vaudeville acts.

At the age of twenty-three, Wasserman took a job in the mail room of the Music Corporation of America's office in Chicago. It was menial work, but MCA, as it was called, was a company that fit his ambitions. MCA had been founded in 1924 by Jules Stein, then still a medical student. By 1935, it had become one of the leading bookers of bands, singers, and musical acts. Through its connections with radio stations, musicians' unions, and nightclubs, it was at the heart of the entertainment business, which is where Wasserman wanted to be.

Alert, shrewd, and enthusiastic, Wasserman quickly moved from the mail room to Stein's outer office. By the time he was twenty-five, he had become not only a go-getting agent but Stein's protégé. In 1938 Stein sent Wasserman to Los Angeles to expand MCA's client list in Hollywood. For Wasserman, who had immersed himself in Hollywood movies since he was a child, it was a dream assignment. With the imprimatur of Stein, who was on a first-name basis with the studio moguls, he had no trouble blending into the Hollywood colony. Unlike Disney, who was a born outsider, the articulate, politically artful, and socially adept Wasserman gravitated toward the inner sanctums of power.

By 1946, although Dr. Stein remained chairman, Wasserman had become president of MCA. While not a visionary like Disney, Wasserman had great business acumen and focused it on an issue of great interest to the directors, producers, actors, and lawyers in his community: compensation. He saw that the then-current star system, in which the stars contractually agreed to a fixed salary for seven years, was the mechanism by which the studios captured for themselves the earnings that stars' public recognition added to their films. Stars, including the ones he represented, understandably wanted a larger share of these earnings, but Wasserman—and other agents—had virtually no leverage in negotiations as long as the studios maintained their effective monopoly over the theaters. If stars did not renew their studio contracts, or broke them, they had nowhere else to turn. But Wasserman foresaw that if the Department of Justice succeeded in its suit to break that monopoly, the stars' position would be greatly strengthened, as would the talent agencies that got 10 percent of their fees.

So, as president, Wasserman aggressively expanded MCA's movie business, both by signing stars and by acquiring other talent agencies. By 1948, MCA represented almost half of the stars under contract to studios, and Wasserman himself represented such top stars as Bette Davis, Errol Flynn, James Stewart, and director Alfred Hitchcock.

Later that year, when the Justice Department finally prevailed in *U.S. v. Paramount* and one studio after another signed consent decrees that ended their domination of theater bookings, the door opened to independent producers, who could finally begin to compete with the studios for mass audiences—and the stars who attracted them. This development left Wasserman in a powerful position to renegotiate the contracts of the leading stars that MCA represented. In 1950 he arranged a percentage deal for the actor James Stewart. Instead of the $50,000 Stewart had received just two years earlier from Fox for his starring role in *Call Northside 777*, Stewart would get half of the profits of his next movie, *Winchester 73*, from Universal.

Wasserman devised the percentage deal not as part of any grand vision but as a practical way to get more money for MCA's clients and, through its 10 percent agent's cut, for MCA itself. But the percentage deal forever changed the relationship between the studios and the stars, producers, and directors. Wasserman did not single-handedly cause this seismic change—with the disintegration of the studio system, it was inevitable that stars would recapture a large part, if not all, of the value that they had been deprived of under the star system—but he took full advantage of it by supplying the studios with stars, directors, producers, and writers (all of whom were MCA clients) who were tied together in what were called "packages." In an ironic twist, this arrangement bore a similarity to the now banned studio practice of block booking: if a studio wanted the star, it also had to accept the other clients in the package. For example, when Columbia wanted the actor Dean Martin, whom MCA represented, for the film *Who Was That Lady?* Wasserman "packaged" him with the rights to the play it was based on and the actors Tony Curtis and Janet Leigh, whom MCA also represented. MCA then took a 10 percent commission on the entire package, which included the star's pay.

The new arrangement that Wasserman pioneered helped to redefine the function of studios. Instead of being factories that employed their own capital and contractual labor to turn raw materials into movies, they became service organizations that arranged for others with capital, both financial and artistic, to participate in movies and share in the profits. Under this new system, talent agencies like MCA often packaged the talent, including script, director, and actors. Then independent production companies, such as Sam Spiegel's Horizon Films, produced the movies. And studios provided the physical facilities, distribution, marketing, and part or all of the financing. The proceeds from the box office, and whatever other rights could be sold around the world, belonged no longer solely to the studio but to the various participants in the alliance, including stars, directors, and producers.

Like Disney, Wasserman also saw the enormous opportunities presented by the new medium of television. For Disney, television was a means of extending his imagery, and licensable brand, to children. For Wasserman, it was an opportunity to make money for MCA and consolidate its position in Hollywood. He saw that the initial unwillingness of the studios to license their film libraries and rent their production facilities to a competing medium had resulted in an enormous need for television programming. So with the aid of MCA's subsidiary, Revue Productions, which had originally been established to film live bands, he helped to satisfy this demand by producing low-budget game shows, such as *Truth or Consequences*, and other "telefilm" programs, such as *General Electric Theater* (which MCA client Ronald Reagan hosted).

Before Wasserman could use MCA's pool of talent for these telefilms, he had to persuade the Screen Actors Guild (SAG) to waive its prohibition against talent agencies acting as producers. The issue was the conflict of interest posed by a talent agency having to choose between the maximum compensation for the talent it represented and the minimum expenses for the film it was producing. In 1952, with the help of Ronald Reagan and Walter Pidgeon, president and vice president, respectively, of SAG, Wasserman negotiated a secret ten-year waiver. Under it, MCA was able to use its own roster of celebrity talent in telefilm series.

To appreciate the tremendous impact of Wasserman's decision to involve MCA in television, consider his packaging of the series *Alfred Hitchcock Presents*. Even though Hitchcock himself was fully occupied directing feature movies at Paramount and considered television an inferior medium, Wasserman proposed that the well-known director lend his name to the series that would be aired by the CBS network and paid for in advance by a single sponsor, Bristol-Myers. Revue would do all the actual work, including writing, casting, and directing the half-hour episodes. All Hitchcock would have to do was appear in a one-minute teaser that would begin and end each episode. In return for this minimal involvement, he would own part of the rerun rights (which he then signed over to MCA in exchange for stock in the company). Eventually, the deal was completed and MCA went on to produce 268 episodes of the hit series, which were sold over and over again to local television stations in syndication. (As a result of MCA buying back the rights for shares, Hitchcock became MCA's third-largest shareholder, behind Dr. Stein and Wasserman himself.)

By 1959, MCA, which had already become the principal provider of talent for all the movie studios, had also become the dominant force in providing television with programming, which included everything from *The Ed Sullivan Show,* Ted Mack's *Original Amateur Hour,* and *The Jackie Gleason Show* to *The Millionaire, The Liberace Show,* and *KTLA Wrestling.* With the stunning acquisition of Paramount's entire film library, it could now also license old movies to television stations.

Even with this library—and Revue—MCA could not fully satisfy the prodigious appetite of the television industry for filmed entertainment—especially after color television was introduced in 1957. For that, Wasserman needed a full-fledged studio. So in 1959 he set his sights on what had become the long-standing sick man of Hollywood: Universal.

The fortunes of Universal, Hollywood's first film factory, had begun to decline in the mid-1930s, along with the health of its founder, Carl Laemmle. Laemmle's appointment of his son, Junior—as a gift on his twenty-first birthday—to head the studio brought it to the verge of collapse. In 1936 he had no choice but to cede control to a Wall Street group that had been lending Universal money; they in turn sold control of the studio to British movie tycoon J. Arthur Rank.

Like his American counterparts, Rank had put together a vertically integrated studio in Britain that, with the help of British import and censorship regulations, controlled most of the country's movie business. Rank bought Universal not because he needed its production facilities but because he needed a foothold in America. Since Universal—along with the other Hollywood studios—used block booking to get its films into theaters, he assumed that it could include his British films, along with Hollywood films, in the blocks it offered theaters in the United States. Since by this time Universal was making mainly B movies, he first merged it with a production company called International Pictures, which was producing A features, creating Universal International Pictures.

As it turned out, Rank had won a battle but not the war. His plan to join Universal with his British company foundered when the Department of Justice made it clear that it would no longer allow the block booking that had been the rationale for the entire acquisition in the first place. So in 1952 Rank and the other investors sold Universal International to Decca Records, a music company headed by Milton Rackmil.

In 1959 Wasserman, who had developed a previous relationship with Rackmil through supplying talent that MCA represented to Decca's music business, offered to buy just the soundstages and back lots of Universal Studios for its television production. Rackmil, desperately short of capital, accepted the deal.

After modernizing the new studio and using MCA's contract clients, Wasserman began mass-producing telefilm programs with the same efficiency that the defunct studio system had once mass-produced films.

The licensing of the television shows MCA owned to local stations—the process known as syndication—also produced a burgeoning stream of cash, since the networks had already paid most, if not all, the production costs. Wasserman used this huge influx of money to buy the rest of Universal—and its corporate parent, Decca Records—for $160 million in 1962. With its newly acquired assets—including a film-distribution arm, a music-publishing company, and a library of thousands of feature and short films—MCA was now a full-fledged studio as well as a talent agency.

MCA could not remain in both businesses, however. For one thing, its SAG waiver was due to expire at the end of 1962. But far more important, the Justice Department, concerned about MCA's growing power over the entertainment industry, was threatening a potentially disastrous antitrust suit. Under this pressure, Wasserman decided that MCA's future lay in producing programs and films, not representing stars. Stein concurred, and MCA abruptly closed down the talent agency. All of MCA's clients received a terse letter releasing them from their contracts.

Even though he was no longer their agent, Wasserman remained an informal advisor, if not a godfather, to many of Hollywood's stars, directors, writers, and producers. He also maintained working relationships with the many lawyers, politicians, and studio executives he had dealt with behind the scenes for decades, not only in negotiating deals for Hollywood talent but in finding mutually acceptable ways to resolve sensitive issues in the film industry, ranging from congressional investigations into Communist influence to Hollywood disputes with unions. With the connections he had assiduously cultivated throughout the community, he had become Hollywood's consummate insider.

After Dr. Stein retired as chairman of MCA in 1973, Wasserman assumed full control and went on to turn MCA into an immensely successful studio. Finally, in 1990, fifty-five years after his first day on the job as a mail clerk, he decided to sell the company. At that point, the Matsushita Electric Industrial Company of Japan—the world's largest manufacturer of video recorders under the Panasonic brand—was, like Sony, preparing for the digital DVD player that would eventually replace the VCR, and it offered $6.59 billion for the studio and its library. In accepting this offer, Wasserman launched Universal on an international odyssey.

COURTESY OF GLOBE AGENCY

Steve Ross: The Magician (1927–1992)

Steven J. Ross was born in Brooklyn in 1927. When he was three, his father, Max, changed the family name from Rechnitz to Ross in the hope that the more easily pronounced name would help to build his contracting business. It didn't. Max Ross went bankrupt during the Depression and lost whatever money he had earned.

Steve Ross understood very early that he would have to make his own way in the world. At the age of thirteen, already six feet tall, he began hanging around illusion shops on Montague Street in Brooklyn, fascinated by the magic tricks they offered. While these tricks dazzled and confused other patrons, he intuitively grasped the principles of deception behind each trick. One of these principles was the so-called "card force," which operated by giving the "mark," who in those days was usually a relative or friend, the illusion of free choice when, in reality, he had no choice. It could be done by asking a mark to pick from a deck that, unbeknownst to him, had all the same cards, or by maneuvering a selected card into the mark's hand. When skillfully applied, the principle of card force, or false choice, had many uses beyond the world of magic. Years later, sitting in his private Gulfstream jet, Ross recalled jokingly, "It always worked with cards, it sometimes worked with women, and it usually worked in business."

By playing cards—especially gin rummy and poker—for money, Ross earned enough to put himself through Paul Smith Junior College. Belying the old adage "Lucky at cards, unlucky at love," with women he also did well, courting and winning eighteen-year-old Carol Rosenthal. She was not only vivacious and beautiful, but her father, Edward Rosenthal, owned Riverside Chapel, a lucrative funeral home. After they were married in 1954, Ross went to work as a funeral director for his father-in-law.

Before long, Ross was applying his powers of persuasion to convince his father-in-law to diversify. At his urging, the Rosenthal business merged with Kinney Services, a small conglomerate that owned parking lots, rental cars, office-cleaning services, and real estate. In 1962 Ross became Kinney's head.

In the mid-1960s, Ross, still fascinated by illusion, used shares of Kinney stock to acquire more than a dozen entertainment companies, among them National Periodicals, the publisher of *Mad* magazine; Licensing Corporation of America, which licensed characters to toy companies; and Ashley Famous, the second-largest talent agency in America after the William Morris Agency. While his new publishing, licensing, and talent businesses were not particularly profitable, they were the means to an end: creating an entertainment conglomerate. For this, Ross knew he would need a studio. He set his sights on Warner Bros.

Warner Bros., like the other major studios, had been unable to make money from its movies after most of its audience abandoned theaters for television. Its record company, Reprise (a joint venture with Frank Sinatra), was making some money but was still not profitable enough to keep the studio, with its high fixed costs, afloat. Jack Warner, the last surviving founding brother of the studio, had sold his shares in the mid-sixties to Seven Arts Productions, a Canadian television distributor, which itself was on shaky financial ground. The new company, Warner Bros.–Seven Arts, still unable to finance its capital needs, finally put itself up for sale to the highest bidder. Ross bought it in 1969 for $400 million in Kinney stock.

Ross was not concerned with Warner Bros.' short-term operating losses. Like Disney, he conceived of a studio as a reservoir of licensable material, or "intellectual property" as it is called in the legal world, and the Warner Bros. library had more than three thousand titles.

With his studio in place, Ross now split his company into two separate entities: Kinney National, which his father-in-law would run (and which would include the funeral homes, parking lots, and other nonentertainment businesses), and Warner Communications International, which Ross himself would lead.

Unlike Disney, who had shunned the Hollywood culture as if it was some alien life form, Ross reveled in it. He may have been less well connected to the community leaders than Wasserman was, but he made every effort to accommodate them. He flew stars in his corporate jet to gatherings at Las Brisas in Acapulco, the San Pietro Hotel in Positano, and his summer home on Georgica Pond in East Hampton. He could be extremely generous with his guests. In 1976, for example, he flew a dozen of them from New York to Las Vegas in his corporate jet, provided luxurious rooms for them adjacent to the Frank Sinatra suite at the Caesars Palace hotel, and, after offering to use his skills at magic to win money for them on the condition that they remain in the suite for one hour, returned with $70,000 in Caesars Palace chips. These chips he then divided among his guests as "their share of his winnings."

It was not merely that he enjoyed the company of such luminaries as Steven Spielberg, Barbra Streisand, and Clint Eastwood; this purposeful socializing was part of his strategy for transforming the corporate image of a New York–based holding company into one befitting a worldwide entertainment conglomerate.

Ross used his skills, charm, and magic to persuade other entertainment companies to merge with Warner Communications, eventually acquiring three major record labels—Atlantic, Asylum, and Elektra Records—and making Warner Communications one of the world's five largest music companies. He also acquired DC Comics, the comic-book giant (thereby providing the studio with access to characters like Batman and Superman), and Atari, an electronic-game maker, for its arcade and home-entertainment interests.

Like Disney and Wasserman, Ross made moviemaking part of a broader entertainment strategy, but unlike them, he was not satisfied owning just content—in the form of films, music rights, television programs, and books—and the means to produce it. He also wanted to own the means to deliver entertainment to people's homes. Cable offered such a capability.

Originally, in the 1950s, cables had been strung up from jerry-built antennas by local entrepreneurs, often without any municipal regulations, to enable rural audiences to get better reception of over-the-air television in their homes. By the late 1970s, aided by federal regulations requiring stations to provide their programs free to cable users, cable had penetrated over half of American homes.

Most of the smaller cable operators by this point had been taken over by larger telecommunications companies. Such companies, even though they had large numbers of subscribers, typically lost money, at least on their balance sheets, because of an accounting practice that required them to deduct from their earnings a fixed percentage of the cost of their cables and other fixed assets for their "depreciation," since, in theory, they would have to be periodically replaced (even if, in fact, cables lasted generations). Ross sought to relieve the telecommunications companies of this book-keeping embarrassment. He bought the cable businesses of Continental Telephone Corporation, Television Communications Corporation, and Cypress Communications Corporation. Together they had about 400,000 subscribers. Although it was a business that required a large investment to connect cables to homes, Ross deemed the risk a worthwhile one and borrowed the money to add to their existing cable systems.

To Ross, cable was much more than an alternative to broadcast television. For one thing, since there was room on cables for hundreds of different channels, it offered the potential of creating cable networks that segregated audiences by their particular interests for advertisers. In Atlanta, Robert Edward "Ted" Turner III, a flamboyant entrepreneur, had already demonstrated that a small UHF television station with an audience of fewer than 100,000 viewers could be transformed into a cable network by leasing interconnections from telephone companies and licensing old movies. Taking advantage of a loophole in its movie-licensing agreement with the studios, Turner's "superstation" supplied these movies to cable systems throughout America. If Turner could create a cable network "out of thin air," Ross proposed that executives at Warner Communications, with all its resources, could do the same.

To this end, Warner Bros. formed a partnership with American Express—Warner Amex Satellite Entertainment Company—which, in the 1980s, launched such cable networks as Nickelodeon (mainly for children over nine) and MTV (for teenagers).

Another major application of cable, in Ross's view, was as a means of delivering Warner Bros.' movies into homes. When he had first been briefed by Warner Bros. executives about the plan to sell his company's films to independent video stores, which would then rent them to customers for $2 a night, he shook his head in disbelief, according to an executive at the briefing. He asked: "Can we really expect millions of busy people to get in their car, drive to a store, pick out a movie, stand in line, fill out a rental agreement, pay a deposit, drive home, play it on their VCR, and then, the next day, repeat the procedure in reverse to return it?" Even if all that happened, Warner Bros. would have to yield control of its films to, and split the revenues with, video stores. At best, he saw video rentals as a stopgap measure.

Ross saw the cable system he was assembling piece by piece as a far more efficient way of delivering films into homes on demand. But what most excited him was a project that Warners had begun in 1977 in Columbus, Ohio, called Qube Television. It was the first commercial experiment in what would come to be known as interactive television. Unlike over-the-air (including satellite) broadcasting, cable wiring could be used to send as well as receive signals. It could allow viewers, while watching programs on one channel, to signal back on another channel by clicking on their remote control. With cable, "people could vote for the ending they wanted," Ross explained.

Indeed, voting for a preferred ending was only one of the myriad possibilities promised by the new technology. Viewers could also vote in a poll, respond to an advertising offer, or order a movie that would be shown over their television. While the customer base in Columbus was too small for it to be economically feasible, Ross remained convinced that such an interactive cable service represented a future in which there would be no videotapes, no video stores, no returns, no inventory, and, most important, no intermediaries. The studios would directly provide consumers with the films, concerts, and sports they wanted to see and charge them on their monthly cable bill. Ross assigned Dr. Peter Goldmark, the former head of CBS's research laboratory, the task of developing such an interactive system. Always an optimist, Ross assumed that the technology would emerge and borrowed heavily to accelerate Warners' acquisition of cable companies.

Next he set his sights on Time, Inc., the publishing empire founded in 1923 by Henry Luce. Aside from owning dozens of magazines, including its flagship, *Time*, the company owned the second-largest cable system in America (after John Malone's cable giant TCI). In addition, Time, Inc., owned Home Box Office (HBO), the principal pay-television channel in America. In engineering a merger of the two companies in 1989, Ross also fused two disparate corporate cultures: "a WASPy blue-chip institution" and a "swinging pop-entertainment conglomerate," in the words of a Time executive. The potential clash notwithstanding, the "beauty of the deal" for Ross was expressed in a single word: cable.

Although the resulting company, Time Warner, became a media company without peer in America, Ross was determined to provide it with a powerful base in Japan—the second-largest economy in the world. In 1991 he met in Los Angeles with Joichi Aoi, chairman of Toshiba and, having been briefed on progress that the Japanese electronics giant was making on a digital disc for video, proposed that their companies join together in a strategic alliance. According to Toshiba executives, he suggested that "a simple disc available for, say, $26, the equivalent of a theater ticket, plus parking and a tub of popcorn," could prove immensely successful with American audiences.

The following year Toshiba became a minority partner in Time Warner Entertainment, a newly organized entity that contained all of Time Warner's movie, television, and cable interests. One of the first orders of business was to create a cartel-like partnership to develop the DVD.

Although Ross did not live to see it (he died of prostate cancer in 1992), his instincts about the future were right: cable connections and that "simple disc"—the DVD—have proven to be key elements in the entertainment economy.

Akio Morita: The Engineer (1921–1999)

Akio Morita, the eldest son of Kyuzaemon Morita, was born wealthy. For fourteen generations, a Kyuzaemon Morita had ruled the House of Morita and its sake brewery in Osaka, Japan, and Akio was expected, on his father's death, to take the name Kyuzaemon and assume his rightful place. From the time he was six, he had sat by his father's side at family gatherings, the heir apparent. At the age of ten he joined the board of directors and was taught to taste and sample the sake.

But Morita, who had studied physics at Osaka University, aspired to more than continuing a three-hundred-year-old sake empire. By the time he graduated in 1944, an American firebombing campaign had decimated much of the imperial Japan of his ancestors. He received a draft notice and went to work during the final year of the war for the Naval Office of Aviation Technology at Yokosuda on Tokyo Bay.

When the war ended in 1945, Morita decided to break with his family's long-standing tradition and not to go into the sake business. Instead, he asked his father's permission to go to Tokyo, which was in ruins, to build an engineering company with Masaru Ibuka, an extraordinary inventor whom Morita had met at the naval lab. His father not only gave him permission but agreed to finance the new company. Tokyo Telecommunications Engineering Corporation, the company that would eventually become Sony Electronics, began in a bombed-out basement, and the partnership of the two men who started it was to continue for the rest of their lives.

Morita's first undertaking was to manufacture rice cookers for a malnourished Japanese population. He was, as he described himself, a passionate tweaker of gadgets. He had grown up in Nagoya surrounded by foreign-made appliances and enjoyed dismantling them to see how they worked and whether he could reassemble them. Now he wanted to improve the rudimentary appliances available to the Japanese survivors of the war. In addition to rice cookers, the new company made portable lights, heating pads, and other much-needed devices in his ravaged country.

The American occupation authorities had granted Japanese companies a special export quota for the American market to encourage the rebuilding of Japanese industry. To take advantage of that, Morita sought electronic products that could be manufactured with cheap Japanese labor and exported to America. The most promising of these was a sound recorder. The then-current design for these machines used thin strands of wire to record sound on, but wire was difficult to obtain in postwar Japan, so Morita began looking into machines that could record on a tape made of paper.

His research efforts paid off when he discovered that in the 1930s a German company, AEG, had devised a technology called AC biasing for using AC current to record sound on tape. After the defeat of Germany, an American army unit had commandeered a prototype machine that used this technology, and one of the soldiers in the unit, John Mullin, had become interested enough in the process to patent it in America. In 1949 Morita bought the Japanese license for AC biasing from Mullin for $2,500 and began manufacturing tape recorders.

Morita made his first trip to America in 1953. He was relatively small by American standards, and ghostly thin, with delicate features and jet black hair. But what most impressed those he met on his trip was an intense focus, expressed with unblinking eyes; he had a look that projected unmistakable confidence and strength.

In New York he befriended Adolph Gross, a Jewish businessman, and through this and other relationships fostered what was to become a lifelong affinity for the Jewish culture. He was struck by the similarity between the Jews and the Japanese. According to Irving Sagor, the first of a long line of Jewish executives hired to run Sony's American operations, Morita "felt Jews were smart, imaginative, and very compatible with the Japanese in temperament and ways of looking at the world." John Nathan, in his biography of Sony, suggests that Morita's Judeaphilea proceeded from seeing Jews sharing with the Japanese "the sense of being foreign" to the American business culture. In any case, on his return to Japan, he told his executives to recruit Jews whenever possible—and they did. (In the decades that followed, the top executives of Sony included Edward Rosinay, Ernest Schwartzenbach, Harvey Schein, Ron Sommer, Walter Yetnikoff, and Michael Schulhof, all of whom were Jewish.)

By the mid-1950s, Morita's company was the world's largest exporter of tape recorders to the United States. As the world's appetite for Japanese electronics expanded, so did the fortunes of the company now called Sony, a name Morita derived from the transliteration in Japanese of the Latin word for sound, *sonus*. (Morita believed *Sony* had an international ring to it, and he wanted to build an international company.) Because Sony had the license in Japan for the AC-biasing process, its profits extended even beyond its prodigious output: all other Japanese manufacturers who subsequently made tape recorders were required to pay Sony a royalty.

With the phenomenal success of its tape recorders, Sony firmly established its niche: global home entertainment. Morita meanwhile began searching for other electronics to sell under the Sony brand. In many cases, especially where existing products were too complex to be operated by average consumers, he had his engineers redesign them, making whatever compromises were necessary, so that the public could learn to work them. By the late 1950s, Sony was the world's leading exporter of color televisions, radios, and other home-entertainment devices.

Then, in the early 1980s, Morita's company enjoyed another breakthrough. With its European partner, Philips Electronics, Sony had developed and patented a radically new system for encoding sound—one that converted sound from the analog form in which it occurred, and was heard, into a digital stream of just two characters: zeroes and ones. The advantage this revolutionary system offered was reusable storage, and its development had been prompted, in part, by a personal whim. Morita, an aficionado of Western classical music, had wanted to be able to hear a seventy-minute symphony—Beethoven's Ninth—without interruption. With the new technology, the entire symphony could be fitted onto a six-inch plastic disc.

This system, introduced in 1982, begat the now ubiquitous compact disc, or CD (on the sale of every one of which Sony and Philips continue to receive a royalty). It also provided the basis for the digital sound now used in movies, satellite television, and computers.

Morita had already revolutionized global entertainment with the Walkman, another invention with a casual beginning. Morita's founding partner, Ibuka, now nearing eighty, mentioned one day that he greatly missed being able to listen to classical music in stereo on long international flights. In a matter of days, Morita had Sony's engineers modify a small, monaural tape recorder (called a Pressman because it had been developed for traveling journalists) into an even smaller stereo player connected to a pair of headphones. Morita then took the "portable stereo" to his golf club on the weekend and demonstrated it to his friends. A month later the Walkman was rushed into production. Morita was convinced, even if his marketing executives had reservations, that the Walkman, with its extreme portability, would appeal to teenagers who wanted to listen to music while they bicycled, skateboarded, and played games. Like Walt Disney, Morita never underestimated the power of youth at play.

Even before Morita changed the way the public heard music, he and his engineering staff realized the possibility of changing the way people watched television by developing a home video recorder. Up until the mid-1970s, viewers had to watch programs when they were aired, in what is called real time. A videotape recorder would change all that by enabling people to view programs when it was convenient for them to do so. Morita called it "time shifting." A video recorder for commercial applications, such as studio recording, had already been developed by Ampex, a California engineering company. But that machine weighed a half ton, cost $800,000, recorded only twenty minutes of programming on expensive two-inch-wide tape, and needed a two-man crew to operate it. Morita bought the rights to it, as he had done previously with the audio recorder, and set out to redesign it for home use. He ordered his engineers to make it small enough to fit on top of a television set and to redesign it so it could record an hour-long program on relatively inexpensive quarter-inch-wide tape, could be sold for less than a $1,000, and could be operated by any consumer (especially children, who adapt easily to new things).

As daunting as the task sounded, Sony's engineers managed, bit by bit, to accomplish it. They reduced the thickness of the tape by 25 percent. They reduced the width of each track from eighty-five to sixty microns by using a different magnetic powder on the tape. By using a different recording angle and recording only half the signal, they extended the running time by 75 percent. The resulting product, the Betamax (which means "brushstroke painting" in Japanese), went on sale in New York in February 1976 for $1,295.

Not surprisingly, this device enormously increased the potential for home entertainment. Not only did viewers no longer have to be at home at the time programs were broadcast to watch them but they could buy or rent programs, including movies, self-improvement tapes, and pornography, to view on their own television. With this device they could now, as Morita called it, time-shift programs that had been broadcast when they were at work, school, or watching another program. He reasoned it would vastly increase television viewing. As one Betamax ad proclaimed in 1976, "NOW YOU DON'T HAVE TO MISS KOJAK BECAUSE YOU ARE WATCHING COLUMBO (OR VICE VERSA)."

Meanwhile, at MCA/Universal, Lew Wasserman was watching these developments and taking a decidedly less sanguine view. He saw the Betamax as a direct challenge to what was then the studios' single most valuable asset—their libraries of movies and television programs. If the public could freely make copies of *Kojak* and *Columbo,* they could make copies of anything that appeared on television for themselves and their friends. The result would be that the studios would make less money from the thousands of titles in their libraries, since there would be less demand from television stations to rebroadcast them. Wasserman was not opposed to the concept of selling films to the public (MCA itself had under development a device called Discovision, which would allow consumers to buy prerecorded movies from the studios), but he did not want consumers to be able to freely record them. So he made an appointment to see Morita at Sony's New York headquarters on the pretext of discussing a possible business relation between Sony and MCA/Universal.

After much banter, he suddenly announced that he planned to sue Sony unless Morita withdrew the Betamax from the market, explaining that all the studios would back him and that Sony would surely be defeated.

Morita was taken aback, not so much by the ultimatum but by the breach of traditional business etiquette. According to James Lardner's authoritative book on the video issue, Morita told Wasserman that in Japan it is not traditional to call a meeting to discuss business and then threaten a lawsuit. He reportedly said, "When we shake hands, we will not hit you with the other hand." Moreover, even though Morita was told by his American advisors that Wasserman would carry out his threat, he was not about to give up the machine that his engineers had so ingeniously perfected. While the breach may have added insult to injury, the video recorder had the potential to create a vast new home audience for Sony products.

The ensuing court battle over the legality of the video recorder, *Universal* v. *Sony*, lasted almost eight years before it was finally decided in 1984 in Sony's favor. Paradoxically, even though Wasserman had to abandon Discovision, the court defeat would turn out to be a great, if unforeseen, victory for the Hollywood studios, especially for Disney (which had joined Wasserman in the litigation in 1977). Just months after the case was lost, Roy E. Disney, Jr., Walt's nephew, brought in a new management team headed by Michael D. Eisner, a tall, articulate New Yorker who had previously helped revitalize both movie and television production at Paramount. Although many executives at Disney still opposed releasing the studio's library of animated movies on video on the grounds that it would diminish, if not kill, their value as rereleases in movie houses, Eisner overrode this objection, pointing out that the success of Walt Disney, dating back to his use of "synchronous sound" in cartoons, had always been based on embracing the possibilities of new technology. The Disney classics consequently were issued as videos and, within a decade, accounted for seven of the ten top-selling videos of all time, providing a new El Dorado of profits.

A further unexpected twist to Sony's victory in court was that even while it made possible an enormously profitable video market for the Hollywood studios, it turned out to be a bittersweet one for Morita. His willingness to litigate American-style had established the legality of the home video recorder, but in doing so, he had paved the way for Sony's rival, Matsushita, to establish its own format, called VHS. After having fought the Hollywood studios in court, Morita was unable to persuade them to put out a sufficient number of titles in the Betamax format to compete with VHS. In addition, although the VHS had far inferior quality to the Betamax, it provided almost twice the running time, which allowed users to record an entire movie without changing the cassette. By the time Sony engineers were able to increase the running time of the Betamax, it had already lost the format war. (The only silver lining was that Matsushita had to pay Sony a small royalty on every video it sold for the use of the digital sound.)

This defeat made it clear to Morita that technologically superior hardware and patents were not by themselves enough to dominate the home-entertainment business; he also needed control over the software—in this case, the films and television programs—to ensure a format's success with consumers and against its competitors. The principal architect that Morita depended on to realize this strategy was Norio Ohga. Morita had recruited Ohga as his protégé while Ohga was still pursuing an extraordinary career as an opera singer and symphony conductor. When he joined Sony in 1959 at the age of twenty-nine, Morita promised him he would succeed him—a promise he kept. After entering into a joint venture with CBS—CBS/Sony Records—Ohga convinced Morita to buy the record division of CBS for $2 billion in 1986 by persuading Morita that "software and hardware are like the two front wheels of a car," and that without both wheels, a car cannot be steered. The acquisition not only made Sony the third-largest music company in the world overnight but helped assure the success of the CD launch. "If I owned a movie studio, Betamax would not have come out second-best," Morita concluded. In accepting Ohga's "automobile wheel" analogy, Morita not only steered a new course for Sony but helped alter the direction of Hollywood.

The technology that would radically transform movies as a home entertainment was the digital disc. By the late 1980s, it had become clear to Sony—as well as its principal rivals in Japan—that the same digital technology that had resulted in the CD could also be applied to movies. Indeed, there was no conceptual difference between the ones and zeroes that represented the information in a Beethoven symphony and those that represented the picture element, or "pixels," in a Hollywood movie. For movies, the digital disc would not only provide a much higher quality viewing experience than was then possible from videotape but would also permit instant navigation to any part of the movie. The practical difficulty came in fitting the digits for both sound and picture on a six-inch disc, which required using computer circuitry to compress the information. By early 1988, Sony's competitor Toshiba already had on its drawing boards a prototype of what would become the digital versatile disc or DVD, and its other traditional rival, Matsushita, was not far behind. If Morita's analysis of Sony's Betamax failure applied prospectively, victory in the crucial race to develop the digital format would go not to the fleetest or even the most technically competent electronics manufacturer, but to the one that controlled a Hollywood studio with a vast library of movies. In 1988, after Ohga assessed the prospects in Hollywood, Morita set his sights on the studio Columbia Tristar Pictures.

Columbia had never recovered from the collapse of the studio system. Plagued by financial scandals, such as the one involving embezzled funds and fake checks in 1977, it had hovered on the verge of bankruptcy until it was temporarily rescued by the New York merchant bank Allen & Company. Then, in 1982, Allen & Company sold a controlling interest to Coca-Cola for $700 million. Coca-Cola then attempted to broaden its base by buying all of TriStar Productions (a combined venture of CBS, Time Inc.'s Home Box Office, and Columbia). Columbia TriStar, as the company was now called, vastly expanded its television capabilities by acquiring Screen Gems, Embassy, and Merv Griffin Productions. These companies not only produced new television shows and series, but their past episodes constituted a library of thousands of programs that could be rented to local television stations in syndication. By the mid-1980s, virtually all of the studio's profit was coming from its library of twenty-two thousand television programs. Its movie production, which Coca-Cola had counted on to elevate its standing as an entertainment company, was consistently losing money.

Consequently, Coca-Cola, a premier marketing company in its own right, saw little future in remaining involved in the Hollywood venture. In 1989 Morita offered the starting price of $3.4 billion, a relatively high price, and Coca-Cola accepted his offer.

Morita was willing to pay Coca-Cola a premium price for Columbia because his vision had now gone beyond the conventional business of producing movies. The future he saw for Sony was in home entertainment, not theaters, and he reasoned that ownership of a Hollywood studio and its library would provide the software "wheel" that would be necessary to launch the digital format that would come to dominate home entertainment. Sony thus became the first Japanese company to acquire a Hollywood studio, a move not lost on its principal rivals in the race to control the hardware for the digital revolution. Matsushita and Toshiba followed suit, Matsushita buying MCA-Universal in 1991 for $6.1 billion, and Toshiba ponying up $1 billion to become a minority partner in Time Warner Entertainment in 1992.

As Sony moved into Hollywood, Morita came to the realization that controlling a single studio, even one with a library of titles as extensive Columbia Tristar's, would not provide the critical mass needed to assure the success of establishing the digital revolution. Morita therefore set out to find a powerful corporate ally in Hollywood.

In Japan, the tradition of *zaibatsu* encourages corporations to work together to achieve their goals, but in the United States, antitrust laws often discourage such collaborations. So Morita had to find a way of arranging an alliance that did not conflict with the American antitrust laws. Ironically, a pending lawsuit that was being brought against Sony by Warner Bros. for hiring away two Warner Bros. executives, Peter Guber and Jon Peters, provided Morita with the opening he was looking for.

To end the dispute, Steve Ross was demanding that Warner Bros. be compensated in three ways. First, he wanted Sony to swap Columbia's studio in Burbank, which was adjacent to the Warner Bros. studio, for a larger studio in Culver City that had once belonged to MGM, which Ross had acquired when he bought the Lorimar television-production company. Ross did not need two studios in different parts of Los Angeles. Second, Ross wanted Sony to allow Warner Bros. to act as a sales agent for selling Columbia's huge library of television programs to cable channels, charging it a 15 percent sales commission. He suggested that this arrangement would greatly enhance the leverage the Warners sales force had over cable stations and, in doing so, benefit Sony because the Warners sales force was, according to the analysis he presented, getting more than twice what the Sony sales force was getting for similar material. Moreover, each sale would be contingent on Sony's approval, and if Sony could get a better price for any program, it could sell it itself. So, as Ross put it, Sony had "nothing to lose."

Third, Ross wanted a half interest in Columbia House, the music and video mail-order business that Sony had acquired from CBS. Warner Music had been one of Columbia House's vendors, selling them records at wholesale prices, which Columbia House used to attract new subscribers to its mail-order club. But Warner Music was threatening to withdraw as a vendor—a move that, since it was supplying over one third of Columbia House's music, would greatly weaken the club's appeal. Ross, using his well-honed card-force technique, made the case that instead of withdrawing, Warner Music should become a full-fledged partner (and therefore not charge Columbia House for the records it was supplying). He reasoned that by combining the music labels of Warner with those of Sony, Columbia House would greatly increase its sales—and value (even though Sony would only own half of it).

To Ross's surprise, Morita agreed to all his terms. Ross was now able to consolidate Warner Bros. into a single studio, gain great leverage over cable stations by marketing both the Columbia and Warner Bros. television libraries, and become a 50/50 partner in Sony's mail-order music and video business. The settlement was reported in the press as a great victory for the American companies over their Japanese rivals, with an article in *Vanity Fair* going so far as to suggest that it was considered in Hollywood to be "Pearl Harbor Revenged."

But Morita had his own reasons for agreeing to Ross's deal, and being intimidated by the threat of Warner Bros. suing Sony was not one of them. Morita, raised as a prince in an Osaka dynasty, was anything but timid. After all, when Sony's Betamax technology had been at stake in 1976, he had tenaciously stood his ground against Lew Wasserman, and all the other Hollywood studio heads, for eight years in American courts, and prevailed. But Sony's technology was not at stake this time—at least not directly.

From Morita's perspective, the only cost to Sony was money. The proposed deal would give Warner Bros. a more geographically convenient studio, and Sony would get one that required modernizing—a project that, though expensive, fit in well with Morita's plan to build a facility capable of state-of-the-art digital work. As for the joint-marketing television deal, it simply involved, as in all *zaibatsu* arrangements, the junior partner in an area deferring to the senior partner. In cable television,

Warner Bros. was clearly the senior partner, and as such, it had good reason to coordinate the sales, especially since its much more powerful marketing arm could get better prices from cable stations. So, even with the 15 percent sales commission, Sony might make more money by deferring to Warner Bros. If not, it could return to selling its own films.

But as Morita saw it, the real benefit for Sony, in the best *zaibatsu* tradition, was to be found in the Columbia House alliance, because he needed an ally, though for different reasons. Giving Ross the half interest in Columbia House was, to be sure, a costly concession, but he saw it as a necessary one. Columbia House was already planning to expand its mail-order business beyond CDs to videos and DVDs. With Warner Bros.' library of 6,500 movie titles of its own and 2,500 pre-1986 MGM titles, along with Columbia TriStar's almost equally formidable library, Sony would definitely have the critical mass needed to make the DVD launch successful.

Morita also needed to reach agreement on a common format for the DVD with Toshiba, another Japanese electronics giant, which by then was a strategic partner (and part owner) of Warner Bros., as well as with Philips, which had been a long-term strategic partner of Sony's on the CD. Warner Bros. had meanwhile had the other studios, except for Fox, meet together to work out "disc specifications that would satisfy them as major producers of movies," according to the then-head of Warner Bros. home entertainment. "These were not requirements—just a perfectly legal 'wish list.' " After some wrangling, Sony accepted these proposed standards. Once that accommodation was reached in the late 1990s, the DVD, backed by the joint resources of Warner Bros. and Sony, would quickly establish itself in world markets.

Morita, who died in 1999, rarely set foot in Hollywood. Unlike Ross and Wasserman, he had almost no contact with stars, directors, and producers and was not familiar with many of their Hollywood movies. Indeed, like Disney, he found its celebrity culture alien. Yet, by engineering the digital platform for the DVD, digital television, and the game console, he helped usher in the new Hollywood.

In the tradition of a prince, he organized his succession well, beginning with Norio Ohga, the extraordinary renaissance man he had lured out of classical music. When Ohga retired in 1995 to return to his career as a symphony conductor, Nobuyuki Idei, who had fittingly led the home video division, took his place. Both men followed Morita's lead in transforming Sony from a conventional manufacturer of hardware to a company that delivers to consumers a wide range of digitalized entertainment. In the 2000 annual report, Idei noted that despite the company's proven success in adapting inventions—such as color television sets, CDs, video recorders, Walkmen, camcorders, and PlayStations—Sony now seeks to "revolutionize itself." The goal is, as the company's leaders described it, to embed "our intellectual assets into products." They look forward to a time when Sony will earn the bulk of its money not from manufacturing products but from the playing, and replaying, of proprietary digital versions of the entertainment itself. It is a transformation very much in the spirit of Morita himself.

Rupert Murdoch: The Revolutionary (1931–   )

Keith Rupert Murdoch was born in Melbourne, Australia, at the height of the Great Depression in 1931. Like Akio Morita, he came from a wealthy family, and like Morita, he came to the movie business relatively late in life. His first pursuit was newspapers.

Murdoch's father, Sir Keith, the son of a clergyman, had built a chain of newspapers, opened Australia's first radio station, and owned a vast forest in Tasmania before dying a multimillionaire in 1952. At that time Rupert was in his final year at Worcester College, Oxford.

When his father died, most of his assets went to his wife. Rupert Murdoch's inheritance was limited to a single small Australian newspaper, the *Adelaide News*. That, as well as a dose of extraordinary self-confidence, was all Murdoch needed to form News Corporation. Until that time, Australian newspapers had always been local operations based on local advertising, but Murdoch broke that pattern in 1964 by creating Australia's first national newspaper, *The Australian*. In addition, he began acquiring other newspapers, television stations, and, most lucrative of all, the Australian syndication rights for several American television programs. Lack of ready capital did not deter his insatiable appetite for expansion; he fearlessly mortgaged the newspapers and television stations he already owned to buy new ones. Nor did opposition from established owners discourage him; he enjoyed overcoming opposition and winning. As William Shawcross wrote, describing Murdoch's life from a later vantage point, "His life had been an unending assault upon the world. One battle had followed another. More newspapers, more television, more power."

By the late 1960s, Murdoch had become the most powerful media owner in Australia, and by then, Australia was no longer enough. In 1969 he began expanding his realm to Britain by buying newspapers there. First he bought the *News of the World*, a raunchy, cheaply run tabloid with a Sunday circulation of 6 million readers, followed by *The Sun*, another tabloid with a circulation just under a million. He subsequently bought two papers at the heart of the establishment: the *Sunday Times*, which had a circulation of 3 million, and the daily *Times*, which was the oldest and most respected newspaper in the British commonwealth.

Although these holdings represented enormous power, Murdoch, like all the other press lords in Britain, still had to acquiesce to two powerful unions, the National Graphical Association (NGA) and the Society of Graphical and Allied Trades (SOGAT), which for over a century had had what appeared to be an unbreakable stranglehold over printing and delivering newspapers. They, not the press lords, determined the staffing levels and the employment rules that stipulated, in large measure, who did what at the newspapers. If a press lord, no matter how powerful, attempted to oppose their dictates, his newspapers would either not get printed or—if they were printed elsewhere—not get delivered.

In the mid-1980s, Murdoch decided to do what no other press lord had ever tried: break both unions. It required stealth, deception, new technology, and incredible nerve.

He needed stealth to keep the unions from learning of his plan to move all four of his newspapers to Wapping in London's Docklands. If they found out, they would surely shut down all the papers, killing his cash cows before he had prepared an alternative. The loss could bankrupt his empire. Deception was required to mislead the unions as to why he was constructing a new facility in Wapping. His cover story was that it was to publish a new newspaper called the *London Post.* In fact, the *London Post* would never actually be published. Like Patton's nonexistent First Army in the Allies' deception plan to conceal D day in World War II, the *London Post* was a decoy.

Murdoch needed new technology to bypass the job of hard typing on hot metal Mergenthaler linotypes—or, in the case of headlines, handsetting the type—a process that required more than two thousand NGA union members. To this end, he contracted with Kodak in America to secretly build him a state-of-the-art computerized printing system called Atex, from which journalists on their consoles could do the work of the unionized typesetters. He also bought a fleet of eight hundred delivery trucks in Australia and had two thousand drivers secretly trained to deliver his newspapers throughout the United Kingdom.

Finally, to carry out his audacious plan, he needed steel nerves as well as miles of razor wire and hundreds of armed guards to prevent the unions from attacking the plant at Wapping once it was up and running. If they broke through his perimeter, he might never be able to put his plan into effect.

On January 24, 1986, without any prior warning, Murdoch's four newspapers moved in the middle of the night from historic Fleet Street—London's newspaper center for more than one hundred years—to Wapping. The unions, still not realizing that Murdoch had the technology to publish all four papers without union typesetters and delivery men, called a strike. The strike, which violated their contract, allowed Murdoch to fire all the union members without giving them any severance pay.

Within a month, Murdoch had defeated the unions. By doing so, he revolutionized British newspaper publishing, to say nothing of British politics. Not incidentally, the value of his four newspapers more than tripled as a result.

The man who once told an interviewer that his life consisted of "a series of interlocking wars" was now ready to launch his next offensive—this time on a global scale.

Murdoch had already bought a number of American publications—so many of them, in fact, that by 1977 *Time* ran a cover of him standing astride the towers of the World Trade Center, looking like King Kong, above the caption "Aussie Press Lord Terrifies Gotham." At that point he owned the *San Antonio Express News, New York Post, National Star, New York* magazine, and *The Village Voice.* In the 1980s he bought *TV Guide,* as well as book publishers on both sides of the Atlantic—Harper & Row in New York and Collins in London—which he merged into a single entity, HarperCollins. But these investments in conventional publishing, as substantial as they were, were just his means of gathering the credentials, political influence, and financial resources for his more far-reaching global goal: to build a home-entertainment empire that would literally span the world. Like his Wapping operation, it would be based on new technology that bypassed established institutions, even the restrictions of local governments. Its means of delivery would not even be limited to the terrestrial confines of earth; it would be in outer space.

Murdoch had in his sights the Clarke Ring, named after the science fiction writer Arthur C. Clarke. Clarke had predicted that in this ring, located precisely 22,300 miles above the earth, manmade satellites could move around the earth in a geosynchronous orbit that would enable them to remain over any chosen city or area. In such an orbit, they could serve as a network of broadcasting platforms.

Unlike cable systems, satellites could not be used for two-way communications such as the interactive television that had captured Steve Ross's imagination. But Murdoch was not disturbed by this. He firmly believed in one-way communications: that those who own the media should control, and take responsibility for, all its content. He assumed such control when he published his newspapers, and he would later favor for the Internet a system called "push technology," whereby content, rather than being sought after, was "pushed" into selected computers. Satellites, in any case, had an overriding advantage for Murdoch: unlike cable, which was essentially local, they were truly global. Not only could they cover every important market in the world, but their orbits in the Clarke Ring were free of the constraints of national law. In one technological leap, Murdoch would be able to bypass the need for television stations and licenses and be able to beam programming to the entire world.

In pursuit of this bold vision, in 1983 Murdoch bought a controlling interest in Britain's Sky Television, a company that through the European Space Agency already had access to a satellite in the Clarke Ring. With it, he began broadcasting to Europe. Unlike conventional networks, which allowed free reception of their programs (and charged advertisers for access to the audience), Sky Television required viewers to pay to subscribe to its service.

Murdoch realized that without paying customers, the entire extraterrestrial concept would fail. So he created a think tank of researchers to find out how to persuade people around the world to pay to receive television, a medium they were accustomed to getting for free. The answer Murdoch found was movies. He decided that he needed to buy a Hollywood studio. Like Morita, Murdoch envisioned a studio not as an end in itself but as a convenient means to an end.

Later that same year Murdoch tried to buy Warner Bros. But in Steve Ross he had met his match. Ross blocked his bid by arranging in a complicated exchange to buy the television stations owned by the Chris-Craft Corporation. Since Murdoch was not yet an American citizen, he was not allowed to own television stations in the United States. Stymied by Ross's legerdemain, he next turned his attention to Twentieth Century–Fox.

The Fox studio had fallen on hard times. After the studio system fell apart, Twentieth Century–Fox had sold a large portion of its real estate to the developers who created Century City and had invested in new projection technologies, such as its CinemaScope, in an attempt to attract an audience for epic-sized films, such as *Cleopatra*. Despite three decades of such heroic effort, it now found itself unable to compete with home entertainment and had put itself up for sale.

In 1981 Marvin Davis, a billionaire oil and gas driller, and Marc Rich, an immensely successful oil trader, joined forces to buy Fox for $703 million. They hired Barry Diller, then head of Paramount, to run it. Soon afterward, however, Rich, a target of a federal investigation into his oil-trading activities with Iran, fled the country.

Rich's sudden departure gave Murdoch the opening he was seeking. He first bought Rich's half share in 1985. Two years later he bought the remainder from Davis at a premium price. As the sole owner of Fox, Murdoch now had a dependable source for films.

Murdoch then bought the holding company Metromedia for some $2 billion. Metromedia owned a group of ten television stations in New York, Los Angeles, and other large markets. To accommodate the prohibition against foreigners owning American television stations, Murdoch now gave up his Australian citizenship and became an American. He also bought a residence befitting an entertainment mogul: the Beverly Hills mansion of Jules Stein, the founder of MCA.

Murdoch next turned his attention to creating a grander structure for his newly acquired television stations. Seven of his ten stations, although they were located in some of the largest markets, did not have network affiliations and could not get them because other stations in those markets had long-standing affiliations with CBS, NBC, and ABC. Since these three were the only national networks, Murdoch's unaffiliated stations were less desirable outlets for national advertisers and, consequently, less profitable.

Murdoch solved this problem—as he had done when he had broken the British trade unions and when he moved broadcasting into the Clarke Ring—by bypassing the established order. He created a fourth network, called the Fox Television Network, which became the first new television network since CBS, NBC, and ABC had been created in the 1930s.

Murdoch reasoned that a network required nothing more than programming and outlets in major markets. With the Fox studio he could create the programming, and with the former Metromedia stations he had outlets in seven of the largest markets, reaching 22 percent of American homes. To these he would add stations either as affiliates or outright acquisitions. No major capital investment in technology was necessary, since the Fox programming could be sent over rented lines and satellites. It would broadcast fewer hours a week than ABC, CBS, and NBC, but it would be a full-fledged network that could attract national advertisers.

In addition to the Fox network, Murdoch assembled, through a string of other acquisitions, four cable networks—the Fox Children's Network, the Fox Sports Network, the Fox Family Network, and the Fox News Network. Meanwhile, he continued to globalize his satellite pay-television systems. In Asia he bought Star Television, whose satellites reached China, Japan, Australia, and India. In Latin America he created coventures to provide satellite service that covered most of its major cities. He also created strategic alliances with existing cable pay-television channels in Italy, Germany, Spain, and the United States.

This worldwide expansion was not without risks. By making these daring acquisitions, Murdoch had gravely strained the financial resources of News Corporation. Even the increased cash flow from his four automated newspapers at Wapping was not sufficient to pay the enormous start-up cost of global satellites. By December 1990, News Corporation had amassed a staggering $7.6 billion of debt, much of it in short-term bank loans, that had to be renewed—or "rolled over"—every month by borrowing new money to repay the expiring debt (and accumulated interest). This enormous debt had been parceled out to more than one hundred different banks around the world. On December 6, while meeting with one bank in Zurich, Murdoch learned that another bank in Pittsburgh had refused to roll over its share of the debt and was demanding repayment. Murdoch knew that if he repaid one bank, many others would follow with the same demand. The ensuing panic would almost certainly bankrupt his company and force him to liquidate the empire that he had spent twenty-five years building.

Murdoch, who had prided himself on controlling his own destiny, now had to put his fate in the hands of a banking consortium led by Citibank. He had a trump card, however. The banks could not *afford* to liquidate his empire. Many of his assets—such as the complex mosaic of satellite-systems pieces, the Fox network, *TV Guide*, and the Fox studio— were dependent for their value on his own vision of a global delivery system for entertainment and news. If the banks took them over they would probably suffer enormously, selling them piecemeal to parties lacking the totality of his vision. This was some consolation, but he also needed a backup plan. On December 20, 1990, he flew in his private Gulfstream jet from Aspen, where one of his top executives had just been badly injured in a skiing accident, to Cuixmala, Mexico, to the estate of the financier

Sir James Goldsmith. He meticulously explained his critical situation to Goldsmith in an effort to raise temporary financing in the event that the Citibank consortium failed. Goldsmith, despite his admiration of Murdoch, was not in a position to help.

As it turned out, Citibank did succeed in arranging the refinancing, and Murdoch, having avoided bankruptcy, decided to merge his Sky Television satellite company with its only real rival in Britain, BSB. Murdoch called it an "opportunistic" decision. By doing so, he eliminated the competition in Britain.

In 2003 Murdoch managed to get control of the final piece of his extraterrestrial design: the Hughes Electronic Company, whose DirecTV unit's satellites beamed television programs to American consumers. Founded in 1932 by the industrialist (and movie mogul) Howard Hughes to produce airplanes, bombs, and electronics, the company was acquired in 1985 by General Motors and transformed into a state-of-the-art communications company that pioneered satellite television in the United States and to which over half of the viewers with satellite receivers subscribed. When General Motors first put it up for sale in 2001, EchoStar, the only other satellite broadcaster in the United States, outbid Murdoch with an offer of $27 billion. But working behind the scenes in Washington, Murdoch's lobbyist argued successfully that a merger of DirecTV and EchoStar would create a monopoly in restraint of trade, and after the EchoStar bid was rejected, Murdoch bought control in a complicated deal for only $6.6 billion—a tribute to his political acumen, if not his connections.

With his acquisition of DirecTV, Rupert Murdoch was rapidly approaching the realization of a vision that had a decade earlier seemed quixotic, if not from the realm of science fiction: satellites orbiting in the Clarke Ring, seamlessly beaming movies, television, and sports events to a paying global audience. To be sure, it had taken tens of billions of dollars in precarious loans to rocket these satellites into space, build ground stations, supply consumers with antennas, and outmaneuver competitors; and because of the enormous debts incurred in the process, the company was still losing money. But Murdoch now had direct, unfettered access to audiences everywhere. He told financial analysts gathered at the annual Morgan Stanley Media and Communications Conference in 2003 that if "content is king," as fellow entertainment mogul Sumner Redstone liked to say, distribution is queen. And his means of distribution included satellites orbiting the earth as well as terrestrial television networks and cable channels. In 2003 his satellite companies—now headed by his thirty-year-old son, James Murdoch—dominated pay television in Britain, Europe, Australia, Asia, and Latin America. In addition, his broadcast network, twenty-three television stations, and three cable networks in America gave him access to general audiences there. As for content, his Fox studio assured him of product for these networks. If Morita's efforts had created a digital form for entertainment, Murdoch's vision had created a means of delivering it to consumers on a global scale.

Sumner Redstone: The Lawyer (1923–)

Sumner M. Rothstein was born in the low-income West End of Boston in 1923. Like Ross, he grew up in the shadow of the Depression. "We didn't have a bathroom in our apartment, but I never felt deprived," he later recalled. As poor as his family was, he went to the movies every Saturday for the matinee and dreamed of someday owning a movie studio. His father, Mickey Rothstein, did what he needed to do to support his family during these lean years—selling linoleum floors, driving a truck, hauling garbage, and running restaurants. When Sumner was still in school, his father anglicized the family name to Redstone to avoid any accidental confusion with the gangster Arnold Rothstein.

Redstone attended a public school, Boston Latin, that was one of the best schools in America. He proved to be an exceptional student and was accepted to Harvard at the age of sixteen. Earning credit for his wartime work with the elite group that broke the Japanese ciphers, he graduated in a near-record two and a half years. His father by this time had gone into the movie-theater business, buying theaters and opening one of the first drive-ins in America in Valley Stream, New York.

Sumner meanwhile went on to Harvard Law School. After graduating in 1947, he moved to Washington, D.C. There he worked as a special assistant at the Department of Justice, which was then pressing the antitrust case, *U.S.* v. *Paramount et al.,* that would end the studio system. Even though Redstone did not work on the case, he had an interest in its outcome. Not only had his family's chain of theaters grown, but he was still nursing his own dream of someday owning a Hollywood studio.

When he returned to Boston in 1954, Redstone took over the stewardship of the family company, the Northeast Theater Corporation. He was determined to expand the family holding company, which he renamed National Amusements Corporation, and he began driving around America looking for sites. He took with him, he later recalled, stacks of "blank contracts" so he could buy any promising property immediately. "Whatever cash flow National Amusements had we used for expansion," he notes in his autobiography.

Even with its armada of some fifty drive-in theaters by 1958, National Amusements could not compare in size with the major chains of indoor theaters, like Loews, which had hundreds of screens. Since the studios favored these larger chains by giving them their premier movies, National Amusements' drive-ins were often unable to get the first-run movies they needed to attract large audiences. So Redstone, whose tenure at the Justice Department had taught him how to wave the antitrust flag, decided to demand that the studios give his drive-ins their films at the same time that they played elsewhere. When they refused his request, he filed suit against them all— Paramount, Warner Bros., Columbia Pictures, Twentieth Century–Fox, and Universal. He knew that he was taking a grave risk, since these studios were his main suppliers, but he was confident that the law was on his side.

The studios, after all, had agreed not to discriminate against theaters in the consent decree they had signed in the late 1940s. The problem was that a consent decree cannot be enforced in court by a private party; it can only be enforced by the government. Redstone, however, found a way around this limitation: conspiracy law. He alleged that the studios were acting in a broad conspiracy to circumvent the decree. Redstone brought the case to trial in Virginia, where one of his drive-ins had been denied a first-run film. He saw himself, as he would in later encounters, as David battling Goliaths. But he had, as he would later entitle his autobiography, "a passion to win," and he prevailed. He also so impressed the independent theater owners with his grit that they elected him president of the National Association of Theater Owners.

The fact that Redstone had identified the Hollywood studios as conspirators did not preclude him from later attempting to buy one. Coming to the conclusion in the late 1970s that there was little future in the theater business, he invested in two studios: Twentieth Century–Fox (buying roughly 5 percent of its shares) and Columbia Pictures (buying 10 percent). He had the idea of possibly making an offer for a controlling interest of one of them once he had the capital, but in the meantime Fox was taken over by the oilman Marvin Davis and Columbia was taken over by Coca-Cola. Although this delayed his dream of owning a studio, he made a profit of more than $26 million in the two sales.

Redstone was still buying theaters and biding his time when, in 1979, he had an experience that forever changed his life. He was at the Copley Plaza hotel in Boston when suddenly the room was engulfed in flames. The entire hotel was ablaze. Redstone suffered burns on more than half his body, and doctors predicted he would not survive.

But he did survive, and when he recovered he realized, as he later told an interviewer, that "success isn't built on success; it's built on failure, frustration, and sometimes catastrophe." Surviving when he was not expected to made him more determined than ever to realize his dream.

In 1987, at the age of sixty-three, Redstone finally found his route to Hollywood in the form of Viacom International, a company that had been created by CBS as a corporate structure for its library of syndicated programs and its cable systems. In 1970, in a move engineered by Lew Wasserman and other studio owners, the FCC had passed the Financial Interest and Syndication Rule, known as fin-syn, which effectively took the television networks out of the business of producing their own television series. So, in 1973, CBS spun off the stock in Viacom to its shareholders, cutting its ties with the now independent company.

Viacom then had an extraordinary piece of good fortune. At Warner Communications Steve Ross, who was buying cable systems, decided to buy American Express's cable-television business, but because his company was already heavily in debt, he had to raise a large part of the capital for the transaction by selling some of its assets. So he decided to sell three of his company's fledgling cable networks—MTV, Nickelodeon, and Showtime—since that divestment meant avoiding the legal problems that might arise from his company owning both cable systems and cable networks. Since Ross did not want to sell these networks to a competing studio, he offered them to Viacom, which was then still a tiny company, for $510 million.

To raise the money for the purchase, Viacom issued bonds, which caused its share price to fall precipitously, since the cable assets it was acquiring were not yet profitable. Seeing that its market price had fallen well below the value of its assets, Viacom's management offered to take the company "private" by buying it themselves from the stockholders for $1.8 billion.

Redstone, assessing that Viacom's management's bid was far too low, saw his opportunity. He bought about 20 percent of the stock and then offered $2.1 billion for the remaining 80 percent. A bidding war between him and management ensued, and he won—at a cost of $3.4 billion. By borrowing against the assets of National Amusements, of which he now owned two thirds, and the assets he would get from Viacom, he financed the deal.

On June 3, 1987, Redstone took control of Viacom and promptly sold off its local cable systems and some other assets to pay down the debt. What remained was the MTV, Nickelodeon, Showtime, and Movie Channel cable networks and the library of television programs. MTV and Nickelodeon not only collected fees both from advertisers and cable systems throughout America but were themselves brand names that, in the tradition established by Walt Disney, could be exploited to sell products throughout the world. The library contained thousands of television series that could be licensed in syndication, some for as much as $4 million an episode.

Showtime and The Movie Channel (TMC) were another matter, however. They both were pay-television channels that had not been able to acquire enough subscribers to cover their operating costs. Redstone quickly discovered that the problem lay not in Showtime and TMC's management but in the business strategy of their rival, Time, Inc.

Time, which was then in the process of merging with Warner Communications, owned both HBO, which had two thirds of the pay-TV subscribers in America, and many cable systems in major cities, including Manhattan Cable in New York, through which subscribers could receive pay-TV channels. Each of Time's cable systems constituted a natural monopoly in its area, allowing it to exclude pay-TV channels that otherwise would compete with HBO. Not surprisingly, both Showtime and TMC had been excluded from the areas in which Time was gatekeeper. "We were competing against HBO for movies and had to pay the same amount in licensing fees to the studios," Redstone writes, "but we were denied millions of potential viewers by Time's refusal to give us access to its cable systems." Time was already the second-largest owner of cable systems, and its impending merger with Warner Communications would mean that the resulting company, Time Warner, would have monopolistic sway over even more cable systems.

As he had done before in his David versus Goliath suit against the studios, Redstone sought redress in the courts. "He was a born litigator, and looked at every issue from the bottom up," a Viacom executive recalled. Redstone sued Time for $2.4 billion under the Sherman Anti-Trust Act, charging it with a conspiracy to monopolize the pay-television business in the United States. His timing proved brilliant. Time, concerned that the documents it would have to reveal in the discovery process could impede the merger with Warner Communications, came to terms with Redstone out of court. The settlement gave Viacom, aside from a significant cash payment, access to the viewers on the Time Warner cable systems for Showtime and TMC. In the process, in addition to turning pay TV into a profitable enterprise for Viacom, Redstone himself received a valuable education on the tacit ways in which giant conglomerates can use their power to stifle competition. "I learned that size matters," he reflected.

With the cash settlement in hand, Redstone could now move on to acquiring the studio he had dreamed of owning since he was a child. Ever since taking over Viacom, he notes in his autobiography, "I had my eye on Paramount Pictures."

Like the other original studios, Paramount had lost its independence. Gulf + Western Industries, an international conglomerate run by Charles Bluhdorn, had bought it in 1966 to take advantage of its tax losses in the movie business. After Bluhdorn died, his conglomerate got into financial trouble, and in 1993 Paramount, as well as the company's other assets, was put up for sale.

Redstone initially offered $8.2 billion for Paramount, 10 percent in cash and the balance in nonvoting Viacom stock. (Since Redstone would have two thirds of the voting stock in Viacom, he would still retain undisputed control.) But before Redstone could close the deal, Barry Diller, a former Paramount and Fox executive who now headed the QVC Home Shopping Network, made a superior offer of $9.9 billion. To secure the deal, Redstone realized he would have to make an immense cash offer that Diller could not meet. He knew this involved a risk, but as the fire in Boston had taught him, "to succeed, you have to live dangerously." He offered $10 billion in cash.

Since Viacom did not have that sum, it would have to borrow it, and even with its improved balance sheet, it did not have sufficient earnings to get a $10 billion loan. So Redstone needed a partner with enough cash flow to persuade the banks to make the huge loan. He found that partner in Blockbuster Entertainment. Blockbuster, which had once been a shabby string of video stores, had been acquired by H. Wayne Huizenga after he made a fortune in the waste-disposal business, and under his watch the company had grown to become a national chain of video stores that dominated the video-rental business. Concerned about competing video-distribution systems, such as pay-per-view, Huizenga had also acquired Spelling Entertainment, with its huge library of television programs, and Republic Pictures' library, which owned NBC's pre-1972 television shows.

By acquiring Blockbuster with Viacom stock, Redstone now had enough earnings to secure the bank loans he needed to buy Paramount, but at a cost that greatly diluted his ownership of Viacom. His holding company, National Amusements, which had previously owned 80 percent of Viacom's shares, now owned only 20 percent (although it still controlled the company through a separate class of voting shares). As a result, the value of Redstone's investment in Viacom fell sharply. Before the merger in July 1993, Viacom shares (including preferred) were worth $5.99 billion on the New York Stock Exchange, and Redstone's share of that was valued at $4.8 billion. After the merger in March 1994, Viacom's shares were worth only $6.2 billion, and Redstone's share of that was worth $1.8 billion. Redstone accepted this $3 billion loss on paper philosophically as "the price for gaining a studio." He explained, "Not everything is about the bottom line." The Paramount studio represented a dream he had been pursuing for over half a century—a dream of power, status, and a sense of achievement.

Once the merger went through, Redstone's most immediate problem was the tenuous financial situation at Blockbuster. He found that each of its ten thousand stores was paying the studios $65 a copy for videos and at that price could not afford to buy more than twenty copies of even the most popular titles. Twenty copies of a single title per store cost $13 million and was still so far from satisfying customer demand that Redstone determined that about 30 percent of Blockbuster's potential customers were leaving the stores empty-handed on any given opening weekend. Worse, after the opening week, the demand for these copies greatly slackened, and Blockbuster could not return the copies. Redstone called the results "managed dissatisfaction," meaning that the price paid for not overordering copies was that a large number of customers were routinely disappointed each week. "What other business treats its customers like that?" he asked.

Redstone decided to use the power of his enlarged conglomerate to fundamentally change the relationship between the studios and the video stores, and in 1997 he came up with a radical scheme of "revenue sharing." The plan called on studios effectively to loan Blockbuster a hundred or more copies of new releases per store. These so-called "licensed copies" would satisfy the opening demand and allow Blockbuster to guarantee that titles would be in stock. Instead of paying $65 for these copies, Blockbuster would advance the studios only about $4 for the manufacturing costs of the video, and then pay them 40 percent of the rental money it collected from its customers. After the opening, copies they did not need for rentals would either be returned to the studios or sold to customers as "previously viewed" (which would cover the amount advanced for the manufacturing costs). Redstone further offered to hook up the computers in every Blockbuster store to those of the studios, or an intermediary, so that the studios could monitor all the transactions. In effect, instead of Blockbuster being the studios' customer, it would become their partner.

In addition to offering the studios the carrot of a 40 percent share of rental revenues, Redstone showed them a stick. If they refused to go along with his plan, he told them that the alternative was that Blockbuster might go out of business. And if they lost Blockbuster, they would lose a large share of the entire video-rental market. "We are not going to pay [$65 a tape]," he warned a Warner Bros. executive. "If we continue that way, we are going to destroy our business—and you will go down with us. The studios can't live without a video-rental business—we are your profit—and this business is going into the toilet."

Each studio had to weigh the possibility that if it rejected Redstone's ultimatum, other studios, including Paramount, might wind up with hundreds of copies of their movies in Blockbuster, while it alone would be shut out. All the major studios eventually acquiesced. They then offered the revenue-sharing plan to other video chains. But most of these chains lacked the sophisticated computer systems or otherwise did not qualify and thus lost many of their customers to Blockbuster (which increased its share of video rentals from under 40 percent in 1997 to over 50 percent in 2002).

With revenue sharing, the studios, for their part, got a far greater measure of control over their video releases. They could choose the titles they considered most profitable to sell and flood the stores with them. Also, as a side payment for accepting the change, Redstone agreed to give the studios so-called "output deals," in which Blockbuster agreed to buy outright a specified number of B titles not included in the revenue-sharing plan.

Not only had Redstone increased Blockbuster's profitability with his imaginative plan, but he had converted the rental business into a predominantly new-release business, with each store carrying hundreds of copies of a video during its opening week.

On the heels of this victory, Redstone, the onetime David who had now proven himself to be a Goliath able to dictate terms to the studios, began looking for further conquests. "The paradigm was Disney's acquisition of ABC," Redstone explained. It demonstrated that the government would permit the consolidation of a studio and a network. Redstone reasoned that since the various divisions of Viacom—including Paramount, MTV, and Spelling Entertainment—produced twenty-eight hours of television programming a week, which was roughly ten times its total feature-film production, owning a network would provide a very profitable "fit," as he put it. In 1998 he found an immense one: the television giant CBS. He paid $34 billion in Viacom stock for the acquisition, which gave him two separate networks—CBS and United Paramount Network (UPN)—a dozen television stations in major markets, the largest group of radio stations in America, the largest billboard company in the world, and five cable networks.

Redstone estimated that with the acquisition of CBS, Viacom would control over a third of the audience through which national advertisers reach their customers and earn $10 billion a year in advertising revenue. To maintain these audiences, Viacom needed a continuing stream of new movies, TV programs, and other material. "We use our content to build these audiences," he explained. Selling these audiences to advertisers was now, as he put it, Viacom's "core business."

Redstone, like Ross and Murdoch, was an empire builder, with, if anything, an even more insatiable appetite for large acquisitions— witness Viacom, Paramount, Blockbuster, and CBS, followed then by the Nashville Network, Country Music Network, Black Entertainment Television, and Infinity Broadcasting. Through them, he had assembled an entertainment conglomerate that controlled many of the principal routes—including radio, television, cable, and billboards—that were of interest to national advertisers in America.

For Redstone, viewers were the means, and advertisers were the end. Movies, instead of merely attracting ambulatory audiences to movie theaters, as they had in the era of the studio system, now served to deliver home audiences to advertisers. He thus made studios integral parts of the vast advertising-entertainment complexes that manufacturers and merchants depended on to sell their products.

David Sarnoff: The Delivery Boy (1891–1971)

David Sarnoff, by creating both a movie studio and a television network, pioneered the link between movies and home entertainment that would become the backbone of the new system. Born in the Jewish ghetto of Uzlian, Russia, in 1891, Sarnoff emigrated to America with his family in 1900. His first job was as a newsboy. While hawking Yiddish newspapers on the streets of New York's Lower East Side, he taught himself English and, with the help of a telegraph key, the new international language of

COURTESY OF CORBIS

Morse code. Fascinated by wireless communications, a technology even newer than movies, he soon became a telegraph operator at the New York office of the Marconi Wireless Telegraph Company. One fateful day—April 14, 1912—he found an opportunity to use the technology in a way no one could have anticipated. He had been given the job of sitting in the show window of Wanamaker's Department Store in New York, demonstrating the telegraph to curious onlookers, when he intercepted the message from a ship at sea: "Titanic ran into iceberg, sinking fast." With a great presence of mind, he managed to telegraph a passing steamer that was picking up some of the HMS *Titanic*'s survivors. When it replied, he—and Marconi—became the prime news source on the disaster.

By 1916, Sarnoff had further impressed his superiors at Marconi with his resourcefulness in a memorandum describing how small radio receivers, then considered no more than novelty "music boxes," could become "a household utility." "The idea is to bring music into the house by wireless," he writes. The music could then be followed by news and other programming. With this memo, he was laying the conceptual foundation for what would become, some fifty years later, one of the largest consumer-based industries in America: home entertainment.

Marconi, seeing the potential in Sarnoff's idea, put him in charge of the project. Then, in 1919, as a result of World War I and other international pressures, the company sold its American assets to the General Electric Company, the manufacturing giant—originally known as the Edison General Electric Company—that had grown out of Thomas Edison's patents. Though only twenty-eight, Sarnoff was put in charge of reorganizing the Marconi assets for General Electric into the Radio Corporation of America (RCA).

At RCA Sarnoff wasted no time in designing the means to send music over the air to the home radios he had envisioned. With the approval of General Electric, he secretly negotiated to buy the broadcasting technology of AT&T, then the telephone monopoly, and with it created NBC, with two radio networks, the Red and the Blue. The Red network went on the air in November 1926, with a four-hour demonstration that included performances by the New York Symphony Orchestra, opera soprano Mary Garden, comedian Will Rogers, and six dance bands.

Since he knew it would be years, if not decades, before NBC would be profitable, Sarnoff's next move was to turn to technology that could be immediately—and lucratively—exploited: talking movies. In 1927 there were more than twenty-one thousand silent-movie houses in America. But as *The Jazz Singer* had demonstrated that year, the "talkie" was the future of movies, and Sarnoff foresaw that soon all the silent-movie houses, as well as the Hollywood studios, would have to buy new sound equipment.

In hopes that RCA could capitalize on this coming trend, he licensed from GE, RCA's corporate parent, a process called Pallophotophone, which recorded sound on movie film.

To give his company a further edge, he also created a new movie studio—by combining RCA's recording equipment division with the Keith-Albee-Orpheum Circuit, then the largest independent theater and vaudeville chain, and the Film Booking Office, an independent studio and distributor owned by financier Joseph P. Kennedy. This merger resulted in the formation of the last major studio, Radio-Keith-Orpheum Pictures, or RKO, in 1928. Sarnoff insisted that the logo of the new studio be a radio tower radiating out signals—a harbinger of the broadcast technology still to come.

With RKO, and its theaters, as a wedge, RCA within a few years was dominating the sound-equipment business. By this time, General Electric, concerned that its control of RCA might put it at risk of being targeted in an antitrust suit, decided to spin off its growing communication empire to its shareholders. So in 1932 RCA—which now included the two NBC radio networks and a controlling interest in the RKO studio—became an independent company.

Sarnoff, now in full control of RCA, then decided to sell the company's interest in the RKO movie studio. As far as he was concerned, the movie studio had always been no more than a convenient means to an end—the establishment of RCA's sound technology. Since the conversion to talking movies was now complete, he was ready to move on to another promising technology: television.

While Sarnoff had been busy organizing the NBC radio networks, two scientists, J. L. Baird in England and C. F. Jenkins in the United States, had successfully demonstrated in the mid-1920s that both pictures and sound could be transmitted between distant points through electrical signals. This feat had opened Sarnoff's eyes to the potential of an enormously powerful new medium of mass communications that would operate with the simplicity of radio but provide visual as well as aural pictures of the world. Before television could become a reality, however, the technology would have to be developed for broadcasters to send the signals on a continuous basis and for the public to receive them. By the early 1930s, Sarnoff was convinced that his company had the wherewithal to develop these technologies in a way that was economically feasible. RCA would engineer and then manufacture the sets; NBC would develop the means to broadcast the programs.

Meanwhile, the political issue of just who would own and license the airwaves over which television would be transmitted was being raised in Washington. In the Communications Act of 1934, Congress declared the airwaves to be public property and established the Federal Communications Commission (FCC), a government agency whose members would be appointed by the president but responsible to Congress, to regulate access to them. In the mid-1930s, the FCC began by licensing television stations to local entities throughout the country for a six-year period on the condition that the stations serve the public interest—a mandate that included the requirement that stations provide news and other public-service programs to viewers free of charge.

Since television stations, unlike movie theaters, could not directly charge the audience for the programs they saw, they had to find another means of support. The answer was advertising: stations would charge sponsors for access to their audience.

Television finally became a reality at the 1939 World's Fair in New York, when Franklin Delano Roosevelt became the first president to appear on a television broadcast. Immediately afterward Sarnoff made his grand announcement: RCA was introducing the first commercial TV set, which had a twelve-inch screen and cost $650 (then about half the price of an automobile). Sarnoff then had NBC launch the first commercial television station in New York City, WNBT, and arranged for General Electric and other advertisers to sponsor programs on it. Despite all his careful and farsighted plans, Sarnoff encountered an obstacle he could not control. In 1941, before television had a chance to take hold, World War II intervened.

Sarnoff, though he was fifty by this time, volunteered his services in 1942, and General Dwight D. Eisenhower, impressed with his grasp of technological issues, promoted him to the rank of brigadier general and made him his wartime communications advisor.

Despite General Sarnoff's patriotic contribution to the war effort, the FCC remained steadfast in its objection to his company's control of two of the three networks—NBC's Red Network and Blue Network—that were to become the backbone of television after the war. (The third network, the Columbia Broadcasting System [CBS], was owned by William Paley.) Sarnoff accommodated the FCC in 1943 by selling the smaller Blue Network, which became the American Broadcasting Company (ABC).

As the postwar television industry developed, NBC, CBS, and ABC each came to own outright five stations—the maximum allowed by the FCC—in major cities. To reach the rest of the country, each network made arrangements for its programs to be carried by stations it did not own, called affiliates, during the four hours in the evening that became known as "prime time." The affiliated stations, in turn, got the right to sell a limited amount of local advertising on the nationally sponsored programs. When, during the 1950s, networks could no longer find single sponsors for a given program—such as Philco for *The Philco Television Playhouse*, R. J. Reynolds Tobacco for the *Camel Caravan*, and General Electric for the *General Electric Theater*—they began producing their own programs and selling commercial time on them to multiple advertisers.

General Sarnoff remained the chairman of RCA until 1970. Asked once about the function of the broadcast networks he had been instrumental in establishing, he answered, "Basically, we're the delivery boys." Despite his modest formulation, it was the nationwide delivery system of broadcast television that Sarnoff pioneered that enabled those who followed him to build the enormous entertainment empires of today.

After Sarnoff died in 1971, the nonbroadcasting assets of RCA were sold off piece by piece, and in 1985, after the Justice Department relaxed its antitrust criteria, General Electric bought the final piece, NBC—the network it had been forced to divest fifty-three years earlier. Although NBC proved a profitable acquisition, General Electric's management became increasingly convinced, as all the other networks merged with movie studios in the 1990s, that NBC would find itself at a competitive disadvantage in acquiring movies and other programming. "The numbers made the case," an NBC executive explained. The enormous increase in network outlays for studio movies and programs during that decade are evident in Table 2.

Once merged together with studios, networks tended to buy a huge share, if not all, of their movies, cartoons, and programs from their corporate sibling. ABC, for example, bought more than 70 percent of its programs from its Disney units. While these in-house deals might not fit the theories of classical free-market economics, they gave studio-network combinations a larger share than they might otherwise have of the $5.07 billion network purchases in 2003. In addition, as network purchases established series for future sales, it gave the studios with networks an advantage in syndication and foreign markets, which amounted to another $5.48 billion in 2003. NBC, the only network without an in-house studio to supply it, decided to remedy the disparity by buying a movie studio. At that point, the best bet was Universal, which had undergone a wrenching sojourn of corporate upheavals after Wasserman had sold it to Matsushita in 1990.

In 1995, with the Japanese economy in a deep recession, Matsushita had decided it could not afford the financial burden of a Hollywood studio and sold a controlling interest in Universal to Seagram, a Canadian beverage company, for $5.7 billion.

Edgar Bronfman, Jr., whose family had founded and controlled Seagram, and who had dropped out of college to be a songwriter and music

TABLE 2. NETWORK CONTRACT PURCHASES FROM U.S. STUDIOS
(MILLIONS)

Year	Movies and Cartoons	TV Programs	Total
1993	$259	$1,124	$1,383
1997	$978	$2,259	$3,237
2002	$1,329	$2,501	$3,830
2003	$1,759	$3,310	$5,069

producer, personally took charge of the movie studio. In 1998 Bronfman bought PolyGram NV for $10.4 billion and combined PolyGram and Universal's record labels, creating the world's largest music company.

The record business, which had been incidental to Wasserman's vision, became central to Bronfman's. Instead of an enterprise based on manufacturing, distributing, and selling products, as his family had done in their liquor business and Wasserman had done in the movie business, Bronfman envisioned one based heavily on licensing music, movies, and other properties. The Internet would play a critical role in distributing such licensed intellectual properties to consumers around the world.

While Wasserman had viewed television production as the heart of the studio's profitability, Bronfman decided to get out of the television-production business by selling most of Universal's domestic television and cable assets, including its library of programs. He did this in a roundabout way. Universal under Wasserman had jointly created the USA cable network with Paramount, and now Universal and Paramount's parent, Viacom, each owned half of it. Bronfman's perspective was different. On the theory that the cable interests owned by Viacom, including MTV and Nickelodeon, might influence the USA Networks programming, he had Universal sue in federal court to force Redstone to sell Viacom's half interest in USA to Universal. Redstone, a former antitrust lawyer, saw no gain in such litigation, and sold his company's share for $1.7 billion. Bronfman then merged the USA Networks, and, in addition, all of Universal's other domestic cable and television interests, into Barry Diller's company, Home Shopping Network, which owned home-shopping networks, radio stations, and electronic ticket-reservation services. For these assets, Universal got 46 percent of the stock of Home Shopping Network, which it agreed to vote in support of Diller's management. As a result of this complicated transaction, Universal effectively turned over its cable and television business, which for other studios provided a main engine of profit, to Diller's company, now renamed USA Networks.

Then, in 2000, the young Bronfman, under family pressure to make a profit, sold the entire company to the French corporate giant Vivendi, under the leadership of its forty-three-year-old chairman, Jean-Marie Messier. Less than three years later, forced to the brink of bankruptcy by its chairman's huge acquisitions, Vivendi fired Messier, then put Universal up for sale.

Enter General Electric, which offered to merge Universal and NBC into a new entertainment conglomerate of which it would own 80 percent and Vivendi 20 percent. In October 2003, when Vivendi accepted the offer, NBC Universal was created. The new vertically integrated giant would supply programs and movies from its studio and library to an immense audience through NBC, a television network that reached virtually the entire population in America; fourteen local television stations in New York, Los Angeles, Chicago, and other metropolitan areas; six cable networks (USA, Trio, Bravo, the Sci Fi Channel, CNBC, and, in partnership with Microsoft, MSNBC); and the leading Spanish-language network, Telemundo (which, with fifteen stations and thirty-two affiliates, reached over 90 percent of Hispanic homes in America). It would also own the Universal theme parks in Florida and California, which drew an audience second only to Disney's theme parks, and overseas, through its partnership with Viacom, major theater chains in Europe and Japan, as well as United International Pictures, the largest foreign distributor of movies and home-entertainment products. Meanwhile, Vivendi, the junior partner in the new conglomerate, would continue to control Canal Plus, with its global cable and pay-TV interests, and Vivendi Universal Music, the world's largest record company.

The merger of NBC and Universal also provided some measure of closure to the century-long shaping of Hollywood. The gap between moviemakers and industrial America that first emerged at the outset of the twentieth century—when Universal Pictures fled to Hollywood to distance itself from the Edison interests, which later evolved into General Electric—had now closed. The television networks, once so feared by the moguls, had, with this final merger, become fully unified with the studios.

NBC Universal was not the only postmillennium consolidation. After the death of Steve Ross, Time Warner had also expanded its domain. First, it acquired Turner Entertainment—the $8 billion media empire created by the cable pioneer Ted Turner that included CNN, the all-news network; the Turner cable networks; Turner Network Television; the Cartoon Network; Turner Classic Movies; and New Line Cinema. Then, in 2000, it merged with the Internet behemoth AOL, which gave it a powerful presence on the Internet.

The six entertainment giants—Viacom, Time Warner, NBC Universal, Sony, Fox, and Disney—today rule the universe of entertainment. Between them, they own all six broadcast networks in America. These networks—NBC, CBS, ABC, Fox, UPN, and the Warner Bros. Network—establish the hit series that are eventually syndicated. They also own sixty-four cable networks whose reach accounts for most of the remainder of the prime-time television audience. Indeed, between over-the-air and cable networks, the big six control over 96 percent of the programs that carry commercial advertising during prime time. They also own the broadcast rights to all the sporting events prized by advertisers—including the Olympics, the Super Bowl, the Indianapolis 500, *Monday Night Football*, and the World Series—as well as the major commercial radio networks, making corporations that want to sell their products or establish their brands on a national scale heavily dependent on them for access.

These six companies further control the television networks depended on by advertisers to reach children under twelve—including the Disney Channel, Nickelodeon, Nick at Nite, the Cartoon Network, the ABC Family Network, and Fox Kids—and those designed for younger teens, including MTV, Fox Sports, ESPN, and the Warner Bros. Network.

The six companies also dominate the worldwide distribution of movies, a studio business Steve Ross once described, with considerable justification, as a "money machine." The studios' distribution arms, along with their subsidiaries, make the arrangements necessary for theaters

TABLE 3. THE SEXOPOLY: THE COMBINED MARKET SHARE HELD BY VIACOM, FOX, NBC UNIVERSAL, TIME WARNER, SONY, AND DISNEY

Category	Properties of All 6 Companies	Market Share
U.S. Film Distribution		96% of Total U.S. Rentals
Major Studio	Disney, Paramount Fox, Universal, Warner Bros., Sony	71%
Specialty Distributors	New Line, USA, Miramax, Fox Searchlight, Fine Line, HBO, Dimension, Sony Classic, Paramount Classic	25%
Prime Time Television		98% of U.S. Ad Revenues
Broadcast	NBC, ABC, CBS, FOX, WB, UPN	(70%)
Cable	USA, Comedy Channel, ESPN, CNN, TNT, BET, MTV, VH1, Nickelodeon, Disney, Fox Kids, ABC, Nick at Nite, Family Network, Sci Fi, Bravo, Fox Sports, Cartoon Network, TBS	(28%)
Non-Prime Time Television		75% of Local Ad Revenues
• Local Stations	63 Stations	(41%)
• Cable	More Than 100 Cable Networks	(34%)
Pay TV	HBO, Showtime, Cinemax	Share of Subscribers 80%
Radio	Infinity, NBC, ABC, Disney, CBS, Fox	Share of Advertising 65%

throughout the world to show both movies produced by their own studios and those licensed from independent American and foreign filmmakers, and, in return, levy a distribution fee that generally amounts to one third of all the revenue received from theaters.

In addition, they control a large part of the entertainment media, including magazines (such as *People, InStyle,* and *Entertainment Weekly*), TV and radio interview shows (such as *Today, The Tonight Show with Jay Leno,* and the *Late Show with David Letterman*), and cable channels that publicize movies (such as E!, VH1, and MTV).

The creators of this new system—Disney, Wasserman, Ross, Morita, Murdoch, Redstone, and Sarnoff—and their associates and successors had redefined Hollywood into a vast entertainment economy dominated by six corporate giants. These six companies now focused not on the moviegoers who had once driven the movie business but on the far more lucrative and ubiquitous home audience. And, like the modern Pied Pipers they are, they now reaped their greatest rewards from the children and teenagers in that audience.

But before the six companies could realize their full potential, they had one more challenge to overcome. They had to achieve true global reach by overcoming any barrier that might prevent their product from appealing to any audience in the world.

3

Americanizing the World

When Hollywood created itself at the beginning of the twentieth century, it had a universal product in silent movies. Their highly visual action—brawls, chases, flirtations, and slapstick humor—could be broadly understood. Whatever further explanations were necessary were furnished in caption boards that could be inserted into the films in multiple languages. As it turned out, however, the political barriers to international success proved more formidable than the linguistic ones. In the early 1900s, driven by concerns about the economic, political, and cultural consequences of Hollywood's products, foreign governments, especially those in Europe, placed import restrictions on American films.

The studios fought back successfully by persuading the U.S. government that since American movies were a potent means of advancing America's image abroad, it should actively assist Hollywood in its efforts to market films overseas. To this end, in 1917 President Woodrow Wilson, after declaring Hollywood an "essential industry," created the Foreign Film Service. He explained, "The film has come to rank as the very highest medium for the dissemination of public intelligence and as it speaks a universal language it lends itself importantly to the presentation of

America's plans and purposes." With America preparing to enter the First World War, the studios' cause was further aided by the fact that Britain and its other European allies were in no position to resist, and their quotas on American films were thus abolished.

After the war, Hollywood studios not only expanded their distribution centers throughout Europe but also bought interests in leading European filmmakers, including UFA, then Germany's largest studio. By 1926, American films accounted for nearly three quarters of the box office of Europe, and European ticket sales provided Hollywood with at least one third of its revenue.

Paradoxically, the advance of sound technology temporarily set back Hollywood's domination of foreign markets. The talkies allowed American directors to use subtler humor, quick repartee, local slang, and more convoluted stories. As a result, movies became less accessible to foreign audiences. Language now did become a barrier, and that barrier gave European studios the opportunity to compete.

In the 1930s, backed by their governments, studios in France, Italy, Germany, and other European countries began making films in their own languages. The Hollywood studios' first response to this was to begin producing foreign versions of their own films. Paramount, for example, built in France a studio in which as many as twelve different sets of actors, speaking as many different languages, reused the sets, costumes, and shooting scripts of the original Hollywood film. These faithful copies could not succeed, however, lacking the Hollywood stars that attracted audiences. The Hollywood studios then tried dubbing their films instead. Although this was a much cheaper solution than reshooting, it initially suffered from a severe technical limitation: the dubbed voices could not be convincingly synchronized with the actors' lip movements. This disparity between lips and words effectively broke the illusion of the movie. The studios finally tried subtitles but found that many foreign moviegoers couldn't understand them, either because they were illiterate or because they lacked the corrective glasses to see them. As a result, by the mid-1930s, Hollywood still found itself in Europe at a comparative disadvantage to the foreign studios.

This technical disadvantage was greatly compounded by the war clouds once again gathering over Europe. Foreign governments, concerned over the power of propaganda inherent in this powerful medium, began to apply rigorous censorship limitations on American films. After war finally broke out, Hollywood studios were so hamstrung by the difficulties of marketing their films overseas that they began to restrict their efforts exclusively to producing movies designed specifically for American audiences.

When the war ended in 1945, the studios again had access to foreign markets. The American occupation of Germany, Italy, Austria, South Korea, and Japan not only made the world safer for democracy but made it—or at least the non-Communist part of it—safer for Hollywood's movies. But now a new obstacle was put in place: to conserve their currency reserves, many foreign governments—including those of Britain, France, and Italy—had imposed restrictions on repatriating money. This meant that the studios could not recoup the expenses involved in overseas distribution because they were prohibited from converting their earnings in foreign currencies to American dollars. Consequently, up until the late 1940s, overseas film sales remained, as one executive put it, "a marginal activity."

Then, in the early 1950s, the dam finally broke—for good this time. With the disintegration of the studio system and the loss of much of the moviegoing audience to television, producers needed to find both new sources of financing for their projects and new audiences. Many of them began making coproduction deals with European studios. In return for providing money and facilities to make the films, European distributors were given the rights to foreign markets in so called presales.

The Hollywood studios, meanwhile, which had reorganized their operations after consenting to the antitrust decree of 1948, quickly moved to reclaim these foreign markets from independent producers by greatly expanding their distribution arms in Europe and Asia. By now, they had also further perfected the technique of synchronously dubbing films in foreign languages, making them more competitive with local films. Furthermore, since the antitrust decree did not limit the block booking of theaters outside the United States, the studios could use raw marketing muscle, backed by strategic visits from American film stars at foreign openings and film festivals, to get the best times and theaters for their movies. They found that European audiences, as well as those in Japan and Latin America, could be fed the same diet of action, fantasy, and event films that appealed to American audiences. "Decisions on what films to make were motivated largely by American sensibilities," Peter Guber recalled when he was an executive at Columbia Pictures in 1968.

As a result, even without catering to foreign tastes—or foreign casting (except when necessary to obtain foreign subsidies and tax breaks)—by the end of the century, the six major studios—Paramount, Universal, Disney, Warner Bros., Sony, and Fox—had succeeded in replacing largely local films in European and Asian markets with their own. Their share of the box office in Europe and Japan grew from 30 percent in 1950 to over 80 percent by 1990. Disney also gave a concrete embodiment to this Americanization concept with its foreign theme parks, such as Tokyo Disneyland in Japan and Euro Disneyland in France.

Even relatively successful foreign films were now being remade as American films rather than enjoying wider distribution in their original versions. The French comedy *Trois Hommes et un Couffin* (Three Men and a Cradle), for example, became *Three Men and a Baby* (1987), starring Tom Selleck, Ted Danson, and Steve Guttenberg. Similarly, the French thriller *La Femme Nikita* became 1993's *Point of No Return*, with Bridget Fonda, Gabriel Byrne, and Anne Bancroft; the Spanish drama *Abre Los Ojos* (Open Your Eyes) became *Vanilla Sky*, with Tom Cruise, Kurt Russell, and Cameron Diaz; and the Japanese horror movie *Ringu* (Ring) became *The Ring*, with Naomi Watts, Brian Cox, and Jane Alexander. Such "Americanization," as one Disney executive described it, involved not just adding American stars and locales but changing the plots, and often the endings, to convert the films into "transnational products." In the 1988 Franco-Dutch hit *The Vanishing*, for example, not only were Jeff Bridges, Sandra Bullock, and Kiefer Sutherland substituted for the French and Dutch actors Bernard-Pierre Donnadieu, Gwen Eckhaus, and Gene Bervoets, but the film was given a different ending: instead of the hero slowly suffocating to death, he is saved by the heroine after an action-packed fight.

The message of such Americanized remakes, amply reinforced by meager results of the non-American movies in international distribution, was that local stars, even though they could still attract local audiences, were no longer suitable for a global product. By the end of the twentieth century, it had become clear abroad that access to world markets required American-style movies with, if possible, American stars.

While it may have been driven in large part by Hollywood studios, the Americanization of much of the world's movie and television industry has not wanted for foreign cooperation and participation. Rupert Murdoch demonstrated through his acquisition of Twentieth Century–Fox the value, if not the necessity, of controlling a rich feedstock of American movies in building his company, News Corporation, into a truly global media empire. Although he still held that News Corporation's "roots, heart and culture are unmistakably Australian" when he moved the company's base to America in 2004, he also recognized, as he put it in a conference call to investors, "the reality that we are a U.S.–based global company."

Meanwhile, in Germany, Leo Kirch, the entrepreneurial son of a small winemaker, had recognized early on the value of acquiring an American film library. In 1959, when West German television stations, which were then all owned by the government, wanted to show only one or two American films a week, Kirch persuaded Warner Bros. to license him the German-language television rights to their entire four-hundred-movie library for $2.7 million. Borrowing the entire sum from state-controlled banks in Germany on his bet that German stations would eventually become dependent on American movies—a gamble that proved successful—he then bought all the other American studios' film libraries, making his KirchMedia the dominant (and in many cases exclusive) supplier of popular American movies to the German television audience.

As his fortune from American movies increased, Kirch used his new wealth to cultivate important politicians and cultural icons in Germany, establishing, for example, a highbrow classical-music channel with the legendary conductor Herbert von Karajan. He also moved more deeply into television. In the late 1980s Kirch and his partners created Sat.1, one of Germany's first private broadcasters, and in 1996 they spent some $2.8 billion to found Premiere, Germany's digital pay-TV service. To attract viewers, Kirch relied heavily on American movies, signing contracts for over $1 billion with the six major studios for licensing rights to their products in Germany. To fill out his programming, he also bought exclusive rights to sports events. He funded this impressive expansion into pay TV by again borrowing heavily from banks in Germany. By 2002 his companies' debt had grown to nearly $9 billion, and their inability to meet his financial commitments had brought the company to the verge of bankruptcy.

Enter Rupert Murdoch, a man whose own expansion into pay TV had brought him perilously close to bankruptcy a decade earlier. After acquiring 22 percent of KirchMedia, Murdoch saw an opportunity to further extend his dominance over his now successful global pay-TV empire. Kirch fought back. Warning that "Murdoch is a shark" who will "eat us," Kirch was able to enlist the support of German politicians to pressure the state banks to block Murdoch from acquiring the company. He could not, however, keep his company. When Murdoch stepped aside, Haim Saban, Murdoch's former equal partner in Fox Family Worldwide, reached a deal with the banks to buy KirchMedia's television assets and film library for $2.2 billion. Since Saban had made his fortune by licensing, editing, dubbing, and changing Japanese cartoon series, notably the *Mighty Morphin Power Rangers,* for world television markets, he had the necessary experience to continue the Americanization of television fare in Germany.

Meanwhile, in France, Jean-Marie Messier, a rising star of the corporate establishment in the late 1990s, was embarking on an even grander mission: to create a Murdoch-style global empire based on American movies and music. As a member of a best-and-brightest French administrative elite known as Enarchs—a moniker for graduates of the prestigious ENA, the Ecole National d'Administration—Messier moved easily between the interlocked banks and corporations of France. In 1990, at the age of thirty-two, Messier had become the youngest partner of the investment bank of Lazard Frères in Paris, and only seven years later he was named chairman of the Compagnie Generale des Eaux, a company that had been created by imperial decree in 1853, and that was, even before Messier's intervention, in two businesses related only by French politics: water supply and media. As the water supplier for half the cities in France, the company enjoyed great influence with local French politicians, many of whom had come to depend on its contributions; and, as a result of its political standing, the government had allowed it to acquire a controlling interest in two French media institutions: Canal Plus, the powerful French pay-TV channel, and Havas, one of France's largest publishing groups.

In 1996 Messier moved to transform the company into a full-fledged entertainment and communications enterprise. He made multibillion-dollar investments in Internet assets, including buying AOL France and launching Vizzavi (a portal for Europe's population of web surfers, cellular-telephone users, and satellite-television users) as well as acquiring pay-TV channels in Belgium, the Netherlands, Poland, and Italy for Canal Plus. He also changed the company's name to Vivendi (derived from the Latin "to live"), which he believed had a more international-sounding ring, and adopted a new mission: "to provide audiences throughout the world with entertainment and information across all distribution platforms." His goal, as he told one of his American investment bankers, was to create a company that would "out-Murdoch" Murdoch. Meanwhile, he planned to spin off the company's industrial water assets into a separate entity.

Even though Vivendi already controlled a film studio in Paris—StudioCanal, through Canal Plus, French films could not attract the audiences Messier sought for his global "distribution platforms." If it was to emulate Murdoch's empire, Vivendi needed to buy an American studio with an extensive library. So when Edgar Bronfman, Jr., offered to sell Vivendi all of Seagram, including the Universal studio and Universal Music, in 2000, Messier bought it for $31 billion and then combined it with Canal Plus and Vivendi's other media assets into Vivendi Universal.

With this acquisition, however, Messier had to confront the French government's policy of protecting the French film industry from the encroachment, and competition, of American movies. Through the 1990s, the French government had excluded this subsidy from both the General Agreement on Trade and Tariffs (GATT) and the World Trade Organization treaty on the grounds of a "cultural exception," with the minister of education, Jacques Lang, asserting that French movies, even if not commercially successful, were a crucial part of the cultural heritage of the nation—a claim he traced back to the invention of the *Cinématographe* by Louis and Auguste Lumière in 1894. Now, with the acquisition of Universal, Messier proclaimed—in English, at a press conference in New York City, no less—"The French cultural exception is dead."

With his French company now part of the global system, Messier proceeded to extend his American assets, paying $11.6 billion to reacquire the Universal television properties that Bronfman had sold to Barry

Diller's company, $1.5 billion to acquire a stake in the EchoStar satellite network (which was then in competition with Murdoch to buy DirecTV), and $2.2 billion to buy the publisher Houghton Mifflin. In a now familiar development, the spree left Messier's company submerged in debt, and in 2002, after suffering a catastrophic $17 billion loss—the largest corporate loss in French history—Messier was fired. In the subsequent merger with General Electric, Vivendi was then relegated to junior-partner status (owning only 20 percent).

Although Messier failed in his ambition to create a French-owned global media empire, he did succeed in forcing France to confront the new logic of the global entertainment economy, and in doing so, he helped breach one of the last bastions of resistance to Americanization in Europe.

By 2004, American movies had by and large conquered the globe—not vice versa. Although the studios subsumed immense international investments, they produced an essentially American product that dominated not only movie theaters but also video stores, television, and pay-TV outlets in the commercially important markets throughout the world. This left the six entertainment empires—Viacom, Sony, Time Warner, NBC Universal, Fox, and Disney—like their predecessors in the bygone studio system, with a final problem to solve: how to manage destructive competition among them without tripping the alarm of antitrust laws.

4

The Sexopoly

People of the same trade seldom meet together, even for merriment and diversion, but the conversation ends in a conspiracy against the public, or in some contrivance to raise prices.

—Adam Smith, *The Wealth of Nations*

The six entertainment giants may be paradigms of capitalism, but capitalism has two faces. One is that of a continuing competition that drives down prices for consumers, the other of an equally pervasive cooperation that prevents interlopers from competing in established markets. The six entertainment empires—Viacom, Fox, NBC Universal, Time Warner, Sony, and Disney—are capable of showing both faces simultaneously, like the famous "rabbit or duck" illusion, one face concealed inside the other.

The contemporary collaboration parallels earlier arrangements in the older studio system. In 1922, concerned by the threat of government censorship, the silent-film studios created, at Louis B. Mayer's behest, the Motion Picture Association of America (MPAA). Because it was classified as a trade organization, it was exempt from antitrust law. With this exemption, the studio owners used the MPAA both to negotiate labor agree-

ments with unions and to lobby politicians to enact legislation that favored them.

The Motion Picture Producers and Distributors of America, or Hays Office, though better known for its censoring activities, also served as a highly effective tool of collaboration for the studios. This in-house censorship tool allowed the major studios to act in concert to standardize the controversial content of movies—including depictions of drug addition, divorce, family planning, and interracial marriage. It went so far as to require that even married couples sleep in twin beds onscreen. By promulgating a set of rules, the Motion Picture Production Code ("the Code"), that applied to all films played in theaters, the studios not only prevented competition among themselves on salacious or controversial subjects—a "race to the bottom," in the words of one Paramount executive—but they also headed off the possibility of foreign or independent competitors distributing such fare to American theaters, since the release of such movies likewise would be precluded by this censorship instrument.

The moguls also used their trade organization to lobby the government to sanction the contrivances they employed to maintain their control over the entire industry. To this end, for example, the MPAA drew up the Code of Fair Competition for the Motion Picture Industry—a set of regulations permitted under the Depression-era National Industrial Recovery Act of 1933. The practices it legitimized under the rubric of "fair competition" in fact eliminated any possibility of competition. These included the previously discussed block booking, which allowed studios to force-feed independently owned theaters their movies, as well as "zoning" and "clearances"—practices that effectively gave the studios the power to decide exactly where and for how long theaters could show first-run, second-run, and third-run movies. With the aid of "full-line forcing," studios could dictate what program accompanied their movies in theaters, including advertising; and they could set "minimum admission prices," further preventing independently owned theaters from competing by lowering their admission price. Any theater that refused to abide by the studios' "fair-competition" practices could be found in violation of the code, which was, in turn, backed by law. Although the National Industrial Recovery Act was found unconstitutional in 1935, the studios continued for over a decade to apply these "trade practices" to maintain their near-monopoly on the distribution of films.

On a more tacit level, the studio moguls also cooperated with one another to perpetuate the star system. Initially, they entered into "nonproselytizing agreements," in which studio heads agreed not to attempt to lure away other studios' stars. Stars who refused to abide by their contract would not find employment at another studio. When this practice finally came under scrutiny, studios found an equally effective means for achieving the same objective: the so-called "loan-out." Instead of denying rival studios the use of their stars (and, by doing so, increasing the risk that the stars might not renew their contracts when the time came), the studios began loaning one another the stars they needed. The usual arrangement, which applied even to actors of the stature of Gary Cooper, Clark Gable, Vivien Leigh, and Jimmy Stewart, was that the borrowing studio paid the loaning studio the star's contractual wages plus a garnish of 10 percent.

In theory, these loan-outs were also available to independent producers, but a Department of Justice analysis of loan-outs found that over 90 percent of them were to other major studios (and almost all the remainder were to producers associated with major studios). By making it exceedingly difficult, if not impossible, for independent and foreign producers to obtain stars, the moguls reinforced their grip on the production, distribution, and exhibition of movies in America.

Abroad, in 1945, the studios created what amounted to their private cartel. Called the Motion Picture Export Association (MPEA), it had as part of its stated mission "to respond to the barriers aimed at restricting the importation of American films" and to "re-establish American films in the world market" after the conclusion of World War II. It accomplished this mission by acting as a single distributor of American studio films in West Germany, France, Britain, Italy, Spain, Japan, and other overseas markets. As it had all of the studios' films to choose from, it could stagger their play dates so as to minimize the possibility that they competed with one another for the same audience. It also used block booking and other such practices, even after they had been declared in violation of antitrust laws in the United States, to force foreign theaters to take their American product, even if this meant excluding locally produced films. If theaters dared to turn down the offer, they got no American films at all.

Like other classic cartels, the MPEA allocated profits to its members, the studios, by a formula. Each studio's share of the total profits was determined by its share of box-office receipts in the United States. If, for example, Paramount's share of the American box office was 27 percent, it would get 27 percent of the foreign profits, even if none of its films had been profitable overseas. By agreeing to this division of the foreign market, the studios eliminated any competition among themselves that might allow foreign theater owners to negotiate with any one of them for better terms.

By 1957, however, everything had changed. The studio system had disintegrated, and the studios, now faced with competition from independent and foreign-based producers, ended the MPEA arrangement and began organizing their own distribution arms to sell their films abroad. The MPEA also changed, becoming a liaison with foreign governments or, as it now described itself, a "State Department" for Hollywood.

The New Collaboration

By the 1970s, television had become the dominant entertainment medium, and the studios could no longer count on habitual moviegoers. Instead, they had to recruit their audience for each movie from television watchers by buying commercial time on network (and later cable) television. The problem was that the cost of these advertising campaigns could easily exceed the return from ticket sales if the ads did not succeed in attracting a large proportion of their target audience. If another studio simultaneously attempted to recruit the same demographic audience— for example, white teenage girls—for the same opening weekend, often by placing their ads on the same TV show, the potential audience would be confused and divided. Even if one studio vastly outspent the other, it could not be sure that part of the audience it had attracted might not defect to the rival film if both were playing at the same multiplexes. The competition would likely result in failure for both studios. On the other hand, if this collision could be averted, and one of the studios was to reschedule its picture for a period when there would be no competition, both studios would likely benefit. But they could not simply coordinate their openings to eliminate competition, as the MPEA had done abroad, since that form of coordination would risk violating the antitrust laws. In 1978, with network advertising costs spiraling upward and multiplex runs for films getting ever shorter, the studios needed what Steve Ross called "a legal way to avoid competing head-to-head."

The ingenious solution the studios found was in a small private research firm called the National Research Group (NRG). NRG would determine the relative demographic appeal of all studio films through telephone polls, calling people who had not (yet) seen the movies and asking if they had heard of them. The firm would then analyze the data and circulate the results to its subscribers (i.e., all the studios). As a result, each studio would learn from the NRG reports when its film was on a collision course with a competitor's film, and either it or its competitor—usually, whichever studio had the lower numbers in the NRG report—would then reschedule to avoid the "head-to-head" opening. This cooperation, though it involved no direct communications that could set off antitrust alarms, nevertheless greatly reduced disadvantageous competition.

The transformation of the studios into entertainment conglomerates only increased their need for cooperation. The fact that they now earned most, if not all, their profits from licensing video, television, pay-TV, and other nontheatrical rights made it crucial that each of them have unimpeded access to the global entertainment market. And since the gateways to it in the form of rental chains, cable networks, television stations, and satellites were often controlled by subsidiaries of the other giants, some degree of cooperation among them was necessary. The opportunities to substitute tacit cooperation for out-and-out competition presented themselves under the mantra of "strategic alliances."

Since the Justice Department still scrutinized possible collusion in the distribution of theatrical movies, most of these new arrangements involved areas not covered by the 1948 antitrust decree, such as video, DVD, pay TV, television licensing, and other ancillary markets. The level of such collaboration in the guise of strategic alliances can be gauged by the following axes formed within the sexopoly by 2003.

The Sony–Time Warner Axis

Although Akio Morita's deep fascination with the Jewish business culture extended to Hollywood, and he once said of himself, "I am a kind of Japanese Jew," he also realized that Sony was at a disadvantage in competing against the American-owned companies in Hollywood. As a foreign-owned company, Sony was legally prohibited from owning television stations or broadcast networks in the United States, which meant it had to rely on American-owned companies for this crucial gateway to home entertainment. So Morita needed an American ally. As previously described, the legal settlement with Steve Ross over the recruitment by Sony of Warner Bros. executives Peter Guber and Jon Peters, as expensive as it was, laid the groundwork for just the alliance Sony needed. Together the two companies controlled the licensing rights to nearly 40 percent of the films and television programs held by all the studios.

Sony also decided to license its films exclusively to Time Warner subsidiary HBO. This arrangement gave HBO access to films it needed to maintain its dominant position in pay TV in the United States, while giving Sony, which had no pay-TV outlet of its own in America, a means of reaching the millions of pay-television subscribers. Further extending the axis, Sony became an equity partner with Time Warner in overseas pay television by investing in HBO Asia in Japan and HBO Ole in Europe.

The 50/50 partnership with Time Warner in Columbia House— which through its mail-order business was the leader in the direct marketing of CDs in the United States—was further reinforced by a joint venture for distributing music in Britain. By 2001, with their combined music labels, the coventures between Time Warner and Sony provided over half of all mail-order CD sales in the world. Even more significant, this mail-order business, which eventually included video clubs, provided Sony and Time Warner with the means to advance the DVD format.

To assure the success of this format, Sony and Time Warner also had to find a way to prevent DVDs that were first released in the United States from being sold in countries in which the DVD, or even the movie, had not yet been released. Otherwise, DVDs could undermine the release of the major studios' films in foreign markets. The solution was to divide the world into "regions" (not unlike the "zones" used by the older studio system before it ran afoul of antitrust laws) and compel manufacturers of DVD players to implant a circuit that would prevent playing movies from one region in another region. For example, a DVD released in the United States (region 1) would not play on equipment sold in Japan (region 2). To avoid any antitrust issues, Sony and Toshiba, which was then a partner in Time Warner, negotiated a joint patent agreement that contained a so-called content scrambling system (CSS) as part of the patent. The announced purpose of this system was to stop consumers from copying DVDs in violation of copyright laws, but folded into it was the circuit that blocked consumers from watching DVDs in a different region, even though it was legal for them to do so. As a result of this scheme, all licensed manufacturers of DVD players had to enforce the studios' division of markets by using the prescribed circuitry. Then, to make sure consumers didn't themselves rewire or bypass this circuit, Sony, Time Warner, and their partners in the DVD launch successfully lobbied Congress to insert a provision into the Digital Millennium Act of 2000 to make it a felony for anyone, even the owner of a DVD player, to tamper with the CSS.

Meanwhile, the only potential rival format, DVX, which had been briefly supported by Paramount, Fox, and Disney, failed to get off the ground. The Sony–Time Warner collaboration had triumphed. In doing so, it had provided the studios with a single digital platform: the zone-restricted DVD.

But the DVD was merely the first stage of their digital plan. In 2001, in a move that was in line with both Ross's earlier vision of bypassing video stores and Morita's concept of freeing digital products from the storage disc, container, and packaging, Time Warner joined Sony in an arrangement to deliver films directly into homes. Under this new system, digitalized movies would be sent over the Internet to television sets, computers, PlayStations, and digital storage devices (which could play them back at a future time). This came close to "the holy grail," as one Warner Bros. executive explained, because it provided a means for Sony and Time Warner to continuously rent out their vast libraries without having to deal with any physical product. Even Internet companies like Amazon.com, which were essentially mail-order houses, had to buy, package, and ship via postal service the items that were ordered. And if customers were dissatisfied, there was the cost of retrieving the products. But in the Sony–Time Warner concept, there would be no actual product, just an access code that would be both provided and billed over the Internet.

In addition, Sony and Time Warner planned to jointly distribute computer games over the Internet. In 2001 the two giants signed a memorandum of understanding outlining a plan for Sony to integrate into its PlayStations access to some services of Time Warner's AOL division, such as its instant messaging. With access to these services, PlayStation owners, by subscribing to AOL, could play games with one another over the Internet. Since computer games were already producing more revenue (and profits) than movies in the theater, Sony and Time Warner clearly recognized the benefits of embracing this new world of computer entertainment.

This new world that Sony and Time Warner sought to create through their alliance required one further element: control over their digitalized content even after they had sold and delivered it. If consumers could replay movies, programs, and games whenever they liked, and make them available to others, then Sony, Time Warner, and other studios would lose control over much of the future value of their libraries. So they, as well as the other entertainment empires, have joined together in a lobbying effort to get the government to require all manufacturers of digital television sets and projectors to embed an encryption chip in their products that would prevent them from playing any digital entertainment— including digital television, movies on DVD, and computer games— without an authorizing signal. The signal might be included in the television transmission or DVD for a given number of viewings; for additional usage, consumers would pay for a signal to be sent over the Internet, cable, or telephone lines. With such an innovation in place, studios finally would be able "to retain control over their content even after they sold it," as one studio video executive explained.

To this end, and through the MPAA (which between 1966 and 2004 was headed by Jack Valenti, former aide to President Lyndon Johnson), the concerned studios have threatened to withhold all their movies and cartoons from digital television until control over digital television sets, in the form of built-in encryption devices, is ceded to them. The lobbying of Congress to make encryption chips mandatory (and the disabling of them a punishable offense) has given Sony and Time Warner, together with the other studios, one more reason to cooperate.

The Sony–NBC Universal Axis

Sony also made an alliance with Universal to further its music business. Both companies faced a common challenge: although their subsidiaries, Sony Music and Universal Music Group, sold about half of the world's recorded music on CDs and tape cassettes, websites—most notably Napster—were freely distributing music, including their own labels, in a digital format called MP3. In keeping with Morita's *zaibatsu* philosophy, the two corporate giants decided to join forces. After successful litigation to force these Internet interlopers out of business, they themselves entered into an alliance to dominate Internet music. Their joint venture, called Pressplay, began as a online subscription service in which they would sell their music in the MP3 format on the two largest Internet portals, Yahoo! and Microsoft's MSN. The buyers would receive their requested music in digital form over the Internet, and they could then download it either onto their computers or directly onto an MP3 portable player. In 2003, after Napster was driven out of business by litigation, Sony and Universal disposed of their interest in Pressplay.

The two companies then expanded their alliance into conventional music stores with the so-called MAP (minimum advertised price) program. Through it, they made the advertising funds that they provided to retail stores conditional on the stores not featuring a lower CD price in their ads or in-store promotions. Any retailer who reduced the manufacturer's suggested price in any ad or in-store promotion, no matter who paid for the ad, was subject to financial penalties. Sony and NBC Universal were soon joined by two other large music companies, BMG Music (which in 2003 merged its operation with Sony) and EMI. Together, these four corporations accounted for approximately two thirds of recorded music. Since the music companies did not fix actual prices, just advertised ones, the MAP scheme was found not to violate U.S. antitrust laws.

The NBC Universal–Viacom Axis

The NBC Universal and Viacom axis traces back to the powerful bond that Lew Wasserman cultivated with Charles Bluhdorn, the financier who bought Paramount in 1966. The "special relationship" that developed between Universal and Paramount was "unique" in Hollywood, according to Sid Sheinberg, Wasserman's deputy and successor. "Bluhdorn loved Wasserman and respected him—worshipped him, literally," Sheinberg said to a reporter.

After MCA took over Universal in 1962, Wasserman found that its overseas distribution unit was losing massive amounts of money because the cost of maintaining offices and operating showcase theaters in dozens of countries greatly exceeded the proceeds it collected from foreign theaters showing Universal films. Since Paramount was having the same problem, Wasserman proposed a solution: combining the two studios' overseas distribution. Since by doing so they would not only cut their overhead in half but would greatly increase the marketing muscle they could bring to bear on foreign chains, Bluhdorn readily agreed to the creation of Cinema International Corporation in 1970.

Then, with the help of Sidney Korshak, an influential Hollywood lawyer, the two men approached the financier Kirk Kerkorian, who had bought and merged two studioless studios—MGM and United Artists— into MGM-UA. The resulting consortium—one third owned by Universal, one third owned by Paramount, one third owned by Kerkorian—changed its name to United International Pictures, or UIP. (In 1999 Kerkorian pulled MGM-UA out of the consortium, selling his shares back to Paramount and Universal.)

The partners also owned, either individually or jointly through UIP, a large number of theaters in foreign cities (which was permissible under the 1948 antitrust settlement), including Famous Players, the second-largest chain of theaters in Canada; United Cinemas International, the largest chain in Britain and France; and UCI cinemas, which had nine hundred screens in Japan, Germany, Spain, Italy, Brazil, Portugal, and Taiwan, including many of the showcase theaters.

The Universal-Paramount partnership, with its overseas distribution consortium and ownership of foreign theaters, has in place abroad many of the elements of the former studio system. In 2003, UIP was the single-largest distributor of films in the international markets, handling not only all the movies of Universal and Paramount but most of those of the "studioless studios," including USA Films, DreamWorks, Focus, and Artisan. Since its overseas operations are not restricted by American antitrust laws, UIP can use practices such as block booking, clearances, and blind bidding, all of which are now proscribed in the United States. In most cases it offers only output deals, in which it, not the theater owner, selects the films to be shown over specified periods. If theater owners want any of the major films UIP offers, such as *Jurassic Park*, they also have to show other films that they would not necessarily have selected. (The partnership extends to the international distribution of videos and DVDs as well.)

These profits overseas depend in large measure on the marketing success of major Universal and Paramount films in the United States. If a film has an enormously successful opening at the American box office, it tends to become more valuable to foreign chains, and UIP can use it as a "locomotive" in its output deals. Universal's *The Mummy*, for example, served to pull ten other films through output deals in Japan, Germany, Italy, and Spain. On the other hand, if few films emerge as locomotives in a given year, UIP may not be able to get as many films into foreign theaters and will therefore make less money. Consequently, both Universal and Paramount have a very powerful incentive to create the maximum number of locomotives for UIP. In practice, this means coordinating their American openings so as not to undermine one another's potential locomotives by releasing films that directly compete with them.

News Corporation–Disney Axis

In 2001 Disney and News Corporation formed a joint venture to deliver films directly to American consumers through a technology called Video-On-Demand (VOD), which, if successful, would replace the weakest link in the distribution chain, the video store. Instead of the consumer renting a video or DVD, he would order it via his remote control, telephone, or home computer, and it would be charged to his credit card and be instantly available on his television. Like a video, the movie could be seen at the customer's convenience, and even paused and replayed during a defined time period. Unlike the more futuristic Sony–Time Warner scheme, this plan relies on the cable box rather than the Internet as the point of entry into homes. Initially, the alliance would sell new releases from Fox, Disney, and their subsidiaries over existing cable-TV channels.

It would then, if successful, be expanded to include all the movies, cartoons, television programs, and entertainment fare in the combined libraries of Disney and Fox.

Like the Sony–Time Warner plan, the Disney–News Corporation partnership is intended to bypass intermediaries—such as video stores, cable channels, and television stations—to assume the sort of direct relationship with customers that has not existed since the halcyon days of the studio system. In doing so, however, it faces a new problem. Whereas there was little danger in the days of the studio system that large and fragile 35-millimeter prints would be pirated and duplicated, home computers have now made it possible for people to copy and replay digitalized movies. To counter this threat, the Disney–News Corporation axis has joined forces with the Sony–Time Warner axis in their previously mentioned effort to pressure the government to implement an encryption requirement that would leave them, and not their customers, in control of the digitalized material they provide.

Disney and News Corporation are also partners in fifty-nine foreign countries in the pay-television business. In sports, the two giants are joint owners of ESPN-Star, which offers eleven channels of sports programming in Asian countries.

This mutually beneficial alliance answered what were previously unmet needs for both companies. Disney had the children's programs familiar to foreign audiences and, through its subsidiary ESPN, major sports events of international interest, but it had no satellite pay-television channels. News Corporation, on the other hand, through its Sky and Star television companies, controlled 90 percent of the pay channels abroad but lacked the children's programming it needed to attract subscribers, especially in Asia.

The alliance emerged again in July 2001, when Murdoch was forced to sell the Fox Family Worldwide to settle a dispute with the network's co-owner, Haim Saban (the international entrepreneur—born in Egypt, raised in Israel, and naturalized as an American citizen—who had sold the rights to the *Mighty Morphin Power Rangers* and other cartoons to News Corporation in return for a half interest in Fox Family Worldwide). Murdoch arranged to sell the entire network, including a library of some three thousand hours of children's programs from Saban, to Disney for $5.3 billion in cash (with Disney also assuming the network's debt). Despite having sold them, because of the ESPN-Star arrangement between Fox and Disney, Murdoch would still have available on his pay-TV networks Saban's *Mighty Morphin Power Rangers* and other children's programs.

The alliance further extended to movies. Disney provided the Star satellites with exclusive rights to all its theatrical movies and had a similar arrangement with Sky satellites in Europe and Latin America. To establish movies that would be a major attraction for viewers in Asia, and eventually for the joint video-on-demand service in the United States, Fox and Disney of course had a mutual interest in coordinating the release of their major films, so as to not undermine each other's marketing campaigns by competing for the same audience at the same time.

The cooperation of the six giants goes well beyond the few alliances described here. For example, Viacom's MTV and News Corporation's British Sky Broadcasting jointly own the Nickelodeon cable channel in Britain, and News Corporation and Sony jointly own Sky Perfect, the main pay-TV channel in Japan.

While the studios themselves may compete with one another for stars, publicity, box-office receipts, and Academy Awards, their corporate parents in fact make most of their money from cooperating with one another in less traditional (and visible) markets, such as cable, video, and pay TV. The issue of how these profits are disbursed—or even defined—in this tangle of relationships hinges on a concept that helps define the new Hollywood: the clearinghouse.

The Clearinghouse Concept

The studios are basically distributors, banks, and owners of intellectual copyrights.

—Richard Fox, Warner Bros.' vice president

In the heyday of the studio system, studios were conceived of as vast factories manufacturing movies as if they were an industrial product. They controlled the entire means of production, from soundstages and back lots to writers and stars. They even had deals with the trade unions that made it prohibitively expensive for any outsider to compete. Most important, they controlled their point of sale—the movie theaters—by stipulating when their films opened and for how long they played. Even as late as 1949, the anthropologist Hortense Powdermaker was on solid ground in describing Hollywood as a "dream factory" engaged in the "mass production of prefabricated daydreams."

But the factory metaphor no longer adequately explains the organizations that replaced the studio system. Although they still call themselves studios and, in most cases, have retained their original names—Fox,

Warner Bros., Universal, Disney, and Paramount—they no longer operate as they once did.

The main task of today's studio is to collect fees for the use of the intellectual properties they control in one form or another and then to allocate those fees among the parties—including themselves—who create, develop, and finance the properties. It is now essentially a service organization, a dream clearinghouse rather than a dream factory. As clearinghouses, they are very different creatures from their predecessors, and this difference is as apparent from looking at their financial reporting as it is from looking at their products.

Consider, for example, the financial profile of one of the largest postindustrial companies in the United States, with a stock-market value of $75 billion in 2001. Its impressive-sounding $25.4 billion in revenues and $800 million in reported income for the previous year were "pro forma." Pro forma, which literally means "in the form of," is an intellectual construct used on balance sheets in which financial results are adjusted to, in management's view, better represent the future prospects of a company. Pro forma results, for example, often exclude expenses that management deems anomalies. Since, according to a comprehensive study by Dow Jones & Company, such pro forma assumptions tend to give a much more optimistic picture of corporate earnings than were actually achieved, they tend to substitute a world seen through management's rose-colored lenses for the existing one.

In the case of the company in question, the pro forma results included profits and losses of newly acquired companies as if these companies had always been under the company's ownership and the results had been a part of its own operations. Additionally, this company managed to remove from its books the massive losses incurred by its Internet operations by spinning them off as separate businesses and issuing a new class of stock for them to its shareholders.

This company also cofinanced many of its capital-intense projects in 2000 with the aid of off-the-books corporations. These corporations, acting as its partner, in turn borrowed much of the money from international banks, incurring debts that did not appear on the company's balance sheet. In addition, billions of dollars of costs for its projects were listed as capital expenses because they had not begun generating revenue.

Since only a small portion of capital expenses are counted against earnings, this accounting maneuver greatly increased its reported profits.

With some of its off-the-book corporations, the company also took advantage of foreign accounting rules to disguise potentially disastrous developments. For example, if it had used American accounting standards in reporting on its subsidiary in France, it would have had to show that subsidiary as being over $2 billion in the red, with $2.5 billion in debt and only $69 million of shareholder equity, but with the aid of much more liberal French accounting standards, the company was able to show that subsidiary in the black with a debt of only $1 billion and shareholder equity of $1.1 billion.

As a corporate empire with operations all over the world, this company also engaged in billions of dollars of transactions with financial institutions, including contracts to buy or sell foreign currencies, treasury bills, and interest-rate options at various future dates. While such "hedging" operations are intended to guard against fluctuations in foreign exchange and interest rates, they can also produce gains or losses when the financial results are different from the expected ones. The company also created a captive insurance company to insure its own businesses. By adjusting the rates and premiums it charged itself regardless of the risk involved, it could further shape the financial picture of itself that it presented to the outside world.

Finally, this company provided its top executives with generous compensation packages, including high salaries, year-end bonuses, and stock options. (The issuance of stock options, tied to the performance of the company's stock, gave executives a very powerful incentive to report on the company's results as optimistically as possible.) For the 1998–2000 period, for example, its CEO received $699.1 million through his salary, bonuses, and the increased value of his stock options. The company also provided generous severance packages to departing executives who might otherwise cast a negative light on the company, paying one president $140 million on his departure after eleven months on the payroll. It also did not count the stock options it granted executives as an expense, on the theory that they were not executive compensation but were rearrangements of the corporate finance structure. The cost of these stock options was in excess of half a billion dollars between 1995 and 2000. If this company had counted these payouts as executive compensation, it would have commensurately reduced its reported earnings.

This company was not Enron, WorldCom, or any other firm whose name has become synonymous with accounting scandals. It was the company whose name has become synonymous with family entertainment: the Walt Disney Company. Clearly, Mickey's handlers had been to business school.

To be sure, Disney's use of such postindustrial accounting methods was not unique among the big six entertainment behemoths. In fact, the company's practices were more conservative than some of its corporate brethren's in Hollywood. If early Hollywood had been "built on phony accounting," as David O. Selznick had famously remarked, then it had adumbrated many elements of postindustrial corporation. The six companies—Disney, Viacom, Fox, Time Warner, NBC Universal, and Sony—all used the pro forma tactic to exclude reporting certain categories of expenses; they all applied certain flexible accounting measures such as EBIDTA (earnings before interest, depreciation, taxes, and amortization), which allowed them to exclude what otherwise would be hefty depreciation charges for their cables, satellites, and other capital investments; and they employed imaginative financial concepts—such as future revenue recognition, reserve reversal, and debt allocations among partly owned subsidiaries—to paint for the public a more optimistic picture of their future. By engaging in these practices, the six companies added billions of dollars to their book value. Of course, at some point there must be a reckoning between accounting constructs and reality. In 2002, for example, AOL Time Warner was forced to recognize a loss of $54 billion for overestimating its past intangible goodwill. (Shortly thereafter, it changed its name back to Time Warner.)

The six entertainment giants had some justification for their accounting methods. They were responding to a changed world in which the external measures of performance had become far more ambiguous. Under the old system, movies were financed, produced, and fully owned by a single studio. Today few, if any, movies are the product of a single entity. Studios now outsource the making and financing of most of their movies and television series to off-the-book corporations (not unlike those used by Enron). The studio's partners in these corporations are often represented by corporate shells designed to protect their owners—including equity financiers, production companies, directors, and stars—from exposure to taxes, legal liability, unfavorable press, and other complications that could arise. Such vehicles technically "lend" the services of their principals to productions, receive the compensation, and disburse it in ways that best serve their tax situation. For example, Arnold Schwarzenegger lent his services to *Terminator 3* through his corporate front, Oak Productions, Inc., which in turn entered into a complex tax-reimbursement agreement aimed at avoiding additional tax liabilities that might occur from filming and distributing the movie abroad.

Complicating matters further, many corporate shells, if not the participants themselves, are domiciled in countries with different tax laws, accounting rules, and qualifications for obtaining government subsidies, which the partners require that the studios take into account.

Nor are these off-the-books entities restricted to production companies for individual films. Paramount's and Universal's jointly owned international-distribution arm, UIP, operates as a highly profitable off-the-books foreign-based corporation.

Another wrinkle of the new system has to do with anticipating future earnings for any given product. Unlike the revenue flow in the older system, in which movies usually returned almost all their money in a year, the income now flows in over the lifetime of licensable rights, which could last for many decades. Determining the value of these distant streams of earnings requires making assumptions about the future entertainment environment.

Consider, for example, the concept of "branding" products—such as toys, dolls, and game characters—for future audiences. Universal's *Jurassic Park* "became a brand that meant dinosaurs," Michael Wolf, a consultant to Universal, notes. "The [dinosaur] theme-park ride is one of the most successful attractions in Universal Studios in Hollywood and Florida. The home videos flew off the shelves, selling $454 million. Merchandise sales, including toys and video games, reached an estimated $1.5 billion. Adding in other revenue streams, Universal built a $5 billion brand empire [by 2000]." The process by which Universal estimates that brand's value for its shareholders, partners, and banks requires projecting children's enthusiasm and parents' buying habits well into the future.

Because they no longer exclusively own these valuable rights, studios are usually obliged to share the proceeds from them with other participants, including equity partners, coproducers, music publishers, stars, directors, and writers. But as the clearinghouses for this income, it is also up to them to decide who gets what share of the proceeds among the participants (including themselves). Even if elusive, these decisions have an enormous impact on the wealth of not only the studios but the Hollywood community.

When revenue flows in, it is the studio that decides (initially at least) who is entitled to what part of it, and when, and under what conditions. If any other participants do not agree with these decisions, their recourse is limited, since the studios usually control the information on which these payments are based. The operation has been likened by one studio executive to the financial equivalent of a "black box," in which "money constantly gets paid in and out."

All six studios manage to conceal the dimensions of these licensing rights by submerging them in broader, catchall categories in their financial reports. Consider, for example, the treatment of video income in the studios' annual reports. NBC Universal lumps it in under "filmed entertainment," along with the income from its movies, television, music publishing, mail-order sales, home-shopping networks, and multiplex chains; Disney records it under "studio entertainment," along with the income from movies, animation, and record labels; Time Warner puts it under "filmed entertainment," along with the income from its movies, character licensing, and licensing of its library to television; Sony and News Corporation file it under "Pictures" and "Film Entertainment" respectively, along with the income from their movies, television-production, and library sales to television; and Viacom records it under the even broader "entertainment," where it is mixed in with the income from theme parks, foreign movie theaters, music publishing, and library sales to television. The enormous income from television production—a single series in syndication such as *Cheers* can bring in more than $150 million in profit—is even harder to find. Viacom, for example, reports the earnings from Paramount Television not as part of the studio's entertainment earnings but under that of its CBS television and KingWorld divisions.

This concealment is no accident. Each studio has thousands of films and television programs on which money is collected and paid out each year. The more opaque the black box and the less information available to outsiders, the easier it is for the studio to control the allocations. Meanwhile, the money that remains in the black box, even temporarily, serves as part of a studio's de facto working capital.

The more money the clearinghouse manages to retain, and the longer it retains it, the greater its de facto profit (even if that sum does not appear in its official financial statements as such).

Inflows into the Clearinghouses

The first concern of the clearinghouse is maximizing the amount of money that flows into the studio's coffers from *all* sources. Even before a film goes into production, money often flows into the clearinghouse from outside investors. In addition to coproducers, financial partners, and foreign tax shelters, these investors include so-called "civilians," who invest primarily to partake in the glamour, glory, or art of the film business.

For the most part, during the era of the studio system civilians played only a bit part as coproducers. In the late 1920s, with two thirds of the population standing in line to buy movie tickets, the studios did not need outside money to finance their film factories. Any temporary gap between their payroll expenses and box-office receipts—often no more than ninety days—was filled by loans from banks that had no qualms about lending the studios money. With the end of the studio system, however, the studios were forced to turn to outside financing, in the form of either direct investments or services.

By the 1980s, the studios had found a wide variety of ways to recruit civilians. Disney, for example, received more than a billion dollars between 1985 and 1990 from investments in partnerships called Silver Screen Partners I and II. For an investment of as little as $50,000, participants were granted the rights to identify themselves with a Hollywood studio and, in some cases, to visit the set while the film was in production. (If the film actually made money, they were also entitled to a share of the profits.) The proceeds from these "partners" financed a large part of Disney's film production.

Paramount found civilian investors abroad who wanted to take advantage of loopholes in the foreign tax laws in the 1990s. In Germany, for example, the tax code then permitted movie investors to deduct from their taxes in a single year the full amount that they committed to a film company. For Germans in a tax bracket that required them to pay 80 percent of their ordinary earnings to the government, this provision meant that by investing in a movie an amount equal to their earnings, which they could borrow, they would not have to pay any tax whatsoever. When, and if, they were repaid in the future, the money constituted a "capital gain," which was taxed in Germany at only 30 percent. Other countries, including France, Ireland, and Australia, had similar loopholes for film productions, provided that some of their actors and locations were used in the film. As a result, billions of dollars that otherwise would have gone to foreign tax collectors went to Hollywood studios.

When Sumner Redstone took over Paramount, he instituted what he termed a "risk-averse" financing strategy, requiring that all the studio's films receive at least 25 percent of their financing from outside investors. Part of this was to come from foreign tax shelters and the rest from "equity partners," who, unlike mere financial partners, have a say in the casting, production, and marketing decisions in movies in which they invest. Some of these equity partners are well-known civilians—multimillionaires like Paul Allen, Ronald Perelman, Michael Steinhardt, Ted Fields III, Philip Anschutz, and Kerry Packer—who made their fortunes in other realms and now want an association with Hollywood. As one of them explained, "It's the ante one pays to get into the game."

Equity partners usually invest through independent production companies—such as New Regency, Spyglass, Village Roadshow, and Phoenix—that maintain ongoing relationships with the studios. To spread their risk, these companies usually arrange deals for multiple pictures to which they commit hundreds of millions of dollars. Their own shareholders put up part of this money, and the rest is borrowed from banks that specialize in financing film ventures. One bank alone, J.P. Morgan Chase, recorded $3.5 billion in outstanding film loans in 2000, and two others—Bank of America and Crédit Lyonnais—reportedly extended more than a billion dollars in similar loans.

The independent production company and its multimillionaire backers often enjoy limited risk, since the bank loans are made on a "nonrecourse" basis, which means that the banks do not have recourse against the equity partners and cannot collect the money from them if the films themselves fail to produce the money to pay them back. As risky as this may sound for banks, banks in turn protect themselves against loss by insisting that the equity partners insure the loans, with the insurer guaranteeing to pay the banks the difference between what they receive from the films and the amount outstanding on the loans. In theory, the banks then are safe and can profit from the relatively high interest on the loans themselves. In practice, however, the insurance companies (which are mainly headquartered in Bermuda, the Channel Islands, and other regulation-free havens) sometimes refuse to pay, preferring to force the banks to sue them. (In 2000 there were at least ten separate lawsuits filed by banks against insurance companies involving $600 million in guaranteed bank loans on films.) Such problems notwithstanding, banks still find it profitable to fund the studios' equity partners.

In some cases, there may also be coproducers who are full partners with a studio—for example, Disney and Universal teamed up with Fox on *Master and Commander*—and fund a large portion of the production cost. In other cases, a coproducer may contribute not cash but substantial services, such as digitalization and animation. For example, Pixar, a state-of-the-art computer-animation enterprise, had an agreement with Disney from 1994 to 2004 to produce seven computer-animated feature films—including such hits as *Toy Story, A Bug's Life, Monsters, Inc.,* and *Finding Nemo*—that Disney would then market and distribute.

There may also be advance payments from toy manufacturers, game makers, and other licensees for rights to use the characters from upcoming films. Entertainment-based characters accounted for over $114 billion in retail sales of licensed products in 2002 and produced an estimated $1.7 billion for the studios. (Not surprisingly, the largest portion of this money went to a single studio: Disney.) A much smaller amount is received on many films from various companies—such as Coca-Cola, Nike, and Coors—for so-called product placement (the insertion of logos or products in movies and television shows). Some money is also taken in from the presale of certain foreign markets.

If necessary, the studio then adds whatever additional funds are needed to make up for any shortfalls prior to the film's release. Here it can either draw from its own capital or borrow from banks.

A few months after a film is released, the clearinghouse receives the "rentals," as the studio's share of the box office is called, from the theaters via the studio's distribution arms. Initially, most of this money comes from the large national chains in North America—such as Cineplex Odeon, Regal, and AMC—who own among them over half the multiplexes in the United States. The division of the box-office receipts varies from movie to movie, but the studios on average wind up with between 45 and 60 percent of the box office. (For their part, theaters get the balance, and keep all the profits from the sale of popcorn, soda, and other items at the concession stands.)

The next major infusion of cash is from the nontheatrical release, which includes airlines' in-flight entertainment, hotels' pay-per-view contracts, and the U.S. military's theaters. With airlines, the license fee for each title is based on the number of flights on which the films are shown, regardless of the number of passengers who actually watch or pay to see it. Hotels also pay a flat fee. With military posts—where there is a potential audience of some 6 million soldiers, sailors, civilian technicians, and their dependents—the studios usually collect 50 percent of paid admissions. Films can garner substantial amounts from these markets. *Gone in 60 Seconds,* for example, earned $3.8 million from these nontheatrical venues.

Studios' distribution arms also handle films produced by independent and foreign filmmakers. For this service, they usually charge one third of all the revenues collected from theaters and video stores (after they recover all of the advertising, print, and other marketing expenses). Usually, these outside films make relatively small contributions to the clearinghouses—merely helping "to keep the lights on," as one studio general manager put it, but occasionally their share can be substantial. For example, Sony's distribution arm, Sony Classic Films, earned $70 million in 2000 for handling the independently made martial-arts film *Crouching Tiger, Hidden Dragon.*

Money flows in more sporadically from the distribution of the film abroad. In most foreign markets, the studios use their own distribution arms (or, in the case of Universal and Paramount, their jointly owned UIP company), but in some markets, they use local distributors. Some films, especially action-oriented ones, earn more abroad than in the United States. *Gone in 60 Seconds,* to continue with its saga, earned for Disney $56.1 million abroad, almost $10 million more than it earned from American theaters.

While money from the major markets—Japan, Germany, Britain, France, Australia, Italy, and Spain—is usually repatriated back within a year of the release, collecting money in smaller markets, or ones with currency restrictions, can take years.

The single-largest flow of money usually comes from video and DVD sales, which begin usually about six months after the film is released, and compared with the small stream from theater rentals, it is a tidal wave. Even before DVD sales became significant, Sumner Redstone estimated that Blockbuster alone wrote checks to the major studios for rental videos alone amounting to $3.9 billion a year. By 2003, the six studios' annual take from videos and DVDs had risen to $17.9 billion.

The next major source of money is television licensing, which extends over decades for many films, beginning with "pay-per-view," and ending with local television stations around the world.

Meanwhile, record companies pay the studios royalties for the soundtracks they release on CDs and cassettes. Some soundtracks sell millions of records—*The Lion King* soundtrack, for example, sold more than 3 million copies—and, over the years, can earn tens of millions of dollars.

In addition, there is the syndication of studio-owned television series that television networks and stations pay to license. After their first-run network broadcasts, the episodes generally become part of the studios' libraries. In 2003 the six studios earned $7.2 billion worldwide from the sale of television programs.

Finally, even after films and television programs are distributed, rebates under various nomenclatures continue to flow in to the studios' coffers. For example, according to one top executive, the rebate from film labs (based on volume) to his studio usually amounted to between $200 and $300 a print—and can amount to $800,000 on a movie. Even if these sums are not always visible in a studio's financial reporting, they can be substantial.

Outflows from the Clearinghouses

Money begins leaving the clearinghouse well before films go into production or, in many cases, are even approved. Each studio has thousands of employees—including executives, lawyers, bookkeepers, publicists, technicians, and salespeople—who are paid each week regardless of whether the studio is making any films. The Sony studio, for example, had seven thousand full-time employees in 2003.

The studios also constantly dole out money to acquire intellectual properties and convert them into scripts that might, in turn, meet with the approval of directors, stars, studio executives, merchandising partners, and equity investors. Not all scripts manage to clear all these initial hurdles, of course. According to the estimate of one high-ranking Paramount executive, only one out of ten writing projects financed by the studios is ever given the green light.

But the torrential outflows come once the film is approved for production. Initial payments must be made to talent agencies and other financial representatives for stars, directors, and other so-called above-the-line talent. Fees must also be paid at this point to the producers who initiated the project.

Money then has to be advanced into the film's production account to hire the army of workers who will prepare the illusion, and, once the production is under way, to pay the weekly cost of equipment rental, caterers, location expenses, film stock, laboratory processing, transportation, insurance, musicians, and all the other myriad expenses.

Often another small fortune must be paid to independent vendors, such as Industrial Light & Magic, for computer graphics, digital effects, puppets, inserts, titles, and trailers. In some cases, like *Godzilla*, these bills can be in the tens of millions of dollars. Then there are the postproduction costs of editing, postsynchronizing sound, mixing the various tracks, color balancing, and negative cutting.

When the film is finally ready for release, money has to be paid to laboratories to make prints for American and foreign distribution. The average cost for a single print is about $1,500 (before rebates). So for a major film like *Spider-Man 2*, which required four thousand prints in 2004, the cost of prints can be $6 million for just the U.S. opening. In 2003, the print bill for the six studios (and their subsidiaries) came to $540 million for U.S. distribution alone.

Before a film opens, studios must create an audience for it—by advertising. This requires another massive outflow. In 2003 studios spent an average of $34.8 million a title for advertising. Although their subsidiaries spent less on their films—an average of $12.8 million per title in 2003—the total for the six studios came to more than $4.1 billion. When films later open abroad, the studios have to spend additional money—more than $3 billion in 2003—to market films in those countries, as well as pay shipping, bonding, custom clearance, insurance, and other expenses.

Studios' home-entertainment divisions, meanwhile, have to prepare videos and DVD versions for different markets. This may entail reediting, remixing, and redoing the color balancing, and, in the case of DVDs, reauthoring, which includes adding features not in the theatrical film and which can cost between $30,000 and $50,000 per title. The videos and DVDs, as well as their containers, also have to be manufactured and shipped to warehouses for both U.S. and foreign distribution. There are also advertising expenses associated with videos and DVDs, including posters, television ads, and in-store displays, as well as sales commissions and the cost of returned videos. A knowledgeable Viacom executive estimated that these expenses amount to between $4 and $5 per copy.

Studios also expend money to produce television series. Unlike movies, these series almost always go into production with guaranteed buyers—the television networks—which advance licensing fees to show them on their networks for their first season. These fees, however, usually cover only between 60 and 80 percent of the cost of making the shows.

Allocations from the Clearinghouse

The most important job of the clearinghouse is to divvy up the money that remains after the outflows between the studio and other participants. For any given movie, numerous people—including the director, producers, actors, writers, musicians, and even technicians—may be due a share of the proceeds from the clearinghouse. Since the terms on which they participate vary, each studio employs a large contingent of lawyers, accountants, and negotiators to ensure that these terms coincide as closely as possible with the studio's own interests. And the studio's interests obviously lie in maximizing its share and keeping the remaining funds in the clearinghouse for as long as possible.

In 2003, the clearinghouses all took in more money in worldwide revenues than they disbursed in expenses and payments. If they had simply shared the entire balance that remained in their coffers with all their partners and other participants in the movies, they would have greatly reduced their own profits. Instead, the clearinghouses manage to exclude a large portion of the cash flow from the allocation by employing complicated royalty formulas. Consider home video, which provided the six studios with more than $17 billion in 2003. To calculate their "gross" for videos and DVDs, including their revenue sharing on rentals, the studios use a royalty system that is used nowhere else in the movie business. It originated in 1976, when videos consisted mainly of exercise and pornography tapes and were sold by independent distributors to small stores. Since the distributors allowed the stores to return unsold copies long after they were issued, it was difficult to calculate retail sales. So, instead, in an arrangement similar to the one then used in the music business, the distributors agreed to pay the producers a flat 20 percent of the wholesale price, regardless of how many videos were returned; this payment, considered a "royalty," became the notional gross for calculating payments to the artists or other participants.

Even as early as 1981, Steve Ross saw the potential windfall for the studios in this royalty arrangement. If the studio also became the video distributor, two different "grosses" could be generated for its clearinghouse accounting: one derived from the studios' total sales of videos and the other derived from the 20 percent royalty fee. In effect, one of the studio's divisions, the home-entertainment unit, would keep 80 percent and would pay another one of its divisions, the movie studio, a 20 percent royalty. The beauty of this plan was not lost on the other studio executives; by the mid-1980s, all the studios had established their own home-entertainment divisions, and the 20 percent royalty had become the "industry standard."

Initially, when only a small number of videos of each title were sold, the cost of transferring movies onto a master tape, recording copies on blank cassettes, packaging them with artwork, warehousing them, selling them, and reimbursing stores for the returned copies could run from $30 to $40 a cassette, absorbing most of the revenue that home-entertainment divisions retained after paying the studio the 20 percent royalty. But as the video business developed into a multibillion-dollar global enterprise and hundreds of thousands of copies of a title were sold, these production costs fell dramatically, to below $4 a copy. As a result, the profit on videos that sold for the wholesale price of $65, even after paying a royalty of 20 percent, or $13, could be as much as $48. Meanwhile, the $13 royalty is booked as the video's "gross rentals" by the clearinghouse—from which distribution expenses and residual payments are deducted.

How this self-dealing worked in practice is illustrated by the treatment of the video sales for *Gone in 60 Seconds*. By 2002, Buena Vista

Home Entertainment International, a wholly owned division of Disney, had earned $198 million from sales and rentals of videos and DVDs of the movie. Of this sum, Buena Vista paid another Disney subsidiary, Walt Disney Pictures, a 20 percent royalty, or $39.6 million, as if Buena Vista International and Walt Disney Pictures were separate companies engaged in an arm's-length transaction. This $39.6 million then became the video's gross rentals, from which $20 million was deducted—$12.6 million for the video-distribution fee and $7 million for expenses—leaving only $18.4 million credited to the film. Meanwhile Disney retained in its home-entertainment account the $159 million that remained after it paid the $39.6 million "royalty." To be sure, it had expenses—about $29 million for manufacturing, packaging, and returns costs—but the balance, some $130 million, was its profit.

The studios, not surprisingly, consider the royalty system an essential means of preventing much of the video windfall from being transferred to the stars. Consider *Gone in 60 Seconds*, for which Nicolas Cage was contractually entitled to 10 percent of the video gross: if the actual gross receipts of $198 million had been used instead of the royalty figure to calculate his share, he would have been due $19.8 million rather than $3.9 million. "Without the royalty system," one former studio executive explained, "we would go broke."

In calculating television-licensing fees, which, after home video, are the second-largest contributor to the clearinghouses, studios are often able to gain a similar advantage by lumping together sales of individual films in a single output deal. While they cannot egregiously exclude the income from the other participants' reach as they do with 80 percent of the home-video income, they can achieve much the same effect by assigning a disproportionately low figure to those films on which other participants are owed a share and a disproportionately high figure to films on which they have no such obligations. This maneuver effectively allows the studio to reduce the payments out of the clearinghouse to other participants.

Other forms of income, such as toy-licensing and product-placement fees, may be contractually excluded from the pool for many participants. The permutations are almost endless.

After the clearinghouse determines with the help of its own rules the income and expenses assigned to individual films, it then allocates the money due to the participants. There are two basic types of deals: gross and net participation. In the former, participants are entitled to a share of the total revenues—or "rentals"—received by the studio in specified markets at various points in the film's earnings. In its richest (and rarest) form, called "dollar one," participants are entitled to a share of all the revenue received by the studio's distribution arm after the trade dues are paid. In *Saving Private Ryan*, for example, the star actor, Tom Hanks, and star director, Steven Spielberg, each got 16.75 percent of the revenues from the first dollar received (dollar one), a formula that yielded them $30 million apiece from the theatrical distribution alone.

Dollar one is usually restricted to a handful of major stars and directors. In most other cases, gross participants are entitled to a share of the film's revenues only after the film earns a specified amount or other requisites are met. For example, Michael Douglas was entitled to a 10 percent share of the revenues of *Traffic* only after the distributor's rentals exceeded $100 million. Gross participants can also be limited to income from certain markets. All gross participations are considered, under clearinghouse rules, a deferred "production cost" and, once paid, are retroactively tacked onto the budget of the film. So, when Hanks and Spielberg got their payments of $30 million apiece for *Saving Private Ryan*, the film's budget, which had been $78 million, jumped to $138 million. By treating the stars' share of the gross rentals as a production expense instead of as a distribution of the earnings, studios further push back the "breakeven" point at which less favored participants can begin to collect.

Net participants are usually entitled to a share of what remains in the clearinghouse only after the film reaches breakeven, and that point varies with participants' contracts. Indeed, in the new Hollywood, except for a few exceptional stars and producers, breakeven is more dream than reality.

Even if the clearinghouse is not built of bricks and mortar and doesn't have a precise address, it is conceptually an essential—and utterly real— part of today's studio. As owner of the clearinghouse, and the provider of management services and financing, the studio takes a hefty cut of virtually all the money that flows in and out. This service fee generally amounts to 15 percent of the total cost of each production for providing managerial "overhead"; 33 percent of the revenue the film earns for its "distribution" facilities; and an annual charge of 10 percent of the studio's budgeted outlays (until they are earned back) for "interest." Such blanket charges can sometimes exceed the cost of a film itself. Let's return, for example, to the previously discussed *Gone in 60 Seconds*, which had cost $103 million to make in 2000. Three years after its release, Disney's managerial service and financing charges on it amounted to $124.9 million—$17.2 million for overhead, $65.9 million for distribution, and $41.8 million for interest. These service charges accumulate in the clearinghouse until additional earnings manage to offset them, which only rarely happens. So *Gone in 60 Seconds*, a film Disney cited for its success, even though it had pulled in over a half billion dollars in gross sales at the box office and video stores, remained $153.3 million in deficit in 2003.

The result of these clearinghouse rules is that most films remain in deficit and the studio is therefore not required to disburse payments to many of the participants, since only a few possess the leverage to negotiate payments based on different rules, such as a straight percentage of the gross rentals.

To be sure, some extraordinary films, despite these service charges, actually manage to turn a profit, but according to industry estimates, it is less than 5 percent of all studio films—even after all the video, television, and other rights are taken into account. Even such celebrated successes as *The Blues Brothers, Ruthless People, The Untouchables, Fatal Attraction, Rain Man, Who Framed Roger Rabbit,* and *Batman* were reported in deficit.

Service charges, though perhaps arbitrary, are not entirely notional. Studios do have to maintain full-time organizations to produce, distribute, and market movies. Their myriad executives arrange with theater owners for play dates; ensure that prints, trailers, and promotional materials arrive on time; buy local and national advertising in newspapers; attend countless meetings with marketing strategists; jawbone recalcitrant exhibitors to collect money; and assess foreign opportunities. They also have to meet payrolls, contribute to pension plans, and pay rent bills, insurance premiums, and bank charges every month. They have enormous overhead. Even so, there has been no shortage of criticism of Hollywood accounting, which was described as "unconscionable" in the celebrated 1990 lawsuit *Buchwald* v. *Paramount.* Auditing of it has become a specialized field in Los Angeles, and entire books have been written about its nuances. It has been the subject of ridicule in movies such as *Hollywood Ending,* in which a director (Woody Allen) is offered—and accepts—2 percent of the profits after "quadruple breakeven," and in David

Mamet's play *Speed-the-Plow,* in which a character sums up in a sentence what he has learned about Hollywood: "There is no net."

Of course, for their part, net participants—including Art Buchwald, Woody Allen, and David Mamet—all willingly agree to the terms, including the studio's right to add service charges, in their contracts. In almost all cases, these contracts are vetted by the participants' agents and the talent agency's lawyers. So if there is a deception involved in the clearinghouse allocations, it is, like so many other aspects of Hollywood relations, a willing self-deception.

The gross participants are obviously in a more advantageous position. Since box-office figures are provided weekly by A. C. Nielsen, they have little problem in determining the approximate amount due to them from the film's theatrical release (although theaters do at times withhold, or even renegotiate, the rentals that are due the studio, and studios pay gross players only on the basis of money actually received and—in the case of foreign currencies—converted to dollars). But even the gross players have difficulty determining the money due them from other markets.

Even though they are playing with a stacked deck, the studios do not hold all the cards. Gross participants with sufficient power in Hollywood— such as Arnold Schwarzenegger, Tom Hanks, and Steven Spielberg—can negotiate better terms for themselves and, in some cases, even break through the studios' one-pocket-to-the-other-pocket royalty arrangement. In negotiating his contract for *Terminator 3,* for example, Schwarzenegger, whose identification with the Terminator robot was deemed indispensable to the movie's success, managed to get the film's video royalty for himself raised from the standard 20 percent to 35 percent. In addition, his lawyer, Jacob Bloom, inserted into his contract an extraordinary clause, stating, "For purposes of calculating Cash Breakeven only, Adjusted Gross Receipts shall include a 100% home video royalty (i.e. home video revenues less costs)." This language wiped out the studio's ability to hold back any part of the video revenues in the calculation of "cash breakeven"—the point at which Schwarzenegger was entitled to "20% of 100% of the Adjusted Gross Receipts . . . of the Picture from the first dollar" in addition to his $29.25 million fee.

Equity partners capable of investing hundreds of millions of dollars in services or cash—such as Pixar, Spyglass, and New Regency Entertainment—can also get preferred treatment in the clearinghouse. Pixar, for example, whose animated features provided Disney with over 50 percent of the entire income of its film division between 1995 and 1999, according to one Wall Street analysis, was able to negotiate a reduction of Disney's distribution charge on its films from 33 percent to 12 percent. A powerful equity partner may also be able to persuade the studio to carve out so-called "corridors" to specified geographic markets—an arrangement that entitles one participant to get a set amount of revenues from these markets before others get their share. Village Roadshow, for example, in its co-production deal on *The Matrix* with Warner Bros., was given a corridor to video, DVD, and pay-TV sales in Australia and New Zealand.

Such special dispensations often come at the expense of other participants. For example, Schwarzenegger's previously mentioned entitlements in *Terminator 3* came at a price to all of the film's less powerful participants. The enormous sums he alone would receive from his higher royalty on videos served to drive up the film's breakeven point, further distancing other participants from the point at which they were entitled to a share. Similarly, the exclusion of markets through corridors diminishes the amount left in the pool for the other participants. The insurance companies involved in the previously described relationship with J.P. Morgan Chase and other banks often blame these contractual corridors (which are typically not adequately disclosed to other investors) when participants find themselves unable to repay their bank loans.

If Lew Wasserman, in his role as an agent, had opened Pandora's box when he negotiated the deal for Jimmy Stewart to participate in the earnings of Paramount films in 1950, the modern studios, by transforming themselves into clearinghouses, have gone a long way toward resealing that box some fifty years later. Ironically, Wasserman himself laid the foundation for the clearinghouse by introducing output deals in television licensing, thereby giving studios the freedom to assign to individual films whatever values were most advantageous to them. Steve Ross and other studio chiefs then deployed the video royalty system, creating the fiction that different pockets in the same clearinghouse—the home-video unit and the movie unit—were separate entities. Michael Eisner, Sumner Redstone, and Rupert Murdoch took the concept of self-dealing even further, expanding their media empires to include the television networks, cable networks, and pay-TV channels to which they licenced their own studio products.

The clearinghouse concept provides an answer to the paradox of why, despite the apparent losses incurred on most movies even when all markets are taken into account, studios remain in business: the money that is lost comes from its less powerful partners. It also explains why studios no longer depend on tight film budgets, long theatrical runs, or even high box-office grosses as reliable measures of success. The benefit of keeping films on a tight budget, which was so important in the days of the studio system, is less important if equity partners and coproducers are contractually obliged to pay the cost overruns. (Indeed, if the added expense increases the likely return from the more profitable home-entertainment markets, a costlier film may ultimately prove advantageous for the studio.) The benefits of prolonging a film's run in the theaters are now negated by the loss that would be sustained by delaying its video opening past the point at which it can benefit from the movie's advertising campaign. And box-office grosses, which may reflect no more than expensive advertising campaigns, are clearly no longer the principal concern of the studios, although these numbers, which are reported weekly in the press, continue to dazzle the public. In light of the shift in studio priorities, it is with some justification that Paramount head Sherry Lansing said in 2002, "I'm not interested in box office and I never have been, I'm interested in profitability." Indeed, as a Paramount executive pointed out, even if a studio managed to acquire a film at little cost and, with little advertising expense, it played it for a year in theaters, and took in box-office receipts that exceeded all its costs, it might not generate enough cash in the clearinghouse to offset the studio's overhead expenses. On the other hand, a film with a huge budget, such as *Gone in 60 Seconds,* which plays in theaters for only a few weeks and fails to earn enough at the box office to pay its advertising and distribution expenses, can still be considered a major success.

The measure of success in the clearinghouse is straightforward: to maximize the amount that flows in from all sources and minimize the amount that flows out to partners and other participants. The winners are the studios and the handful of financiers and stars who can get special terms; the losers are those players who want to be included in the moviemaking game but lack the leverage to get special dispensations. What is central to the clearinghouse concept is not the art of the film but the art of the deal.

Part Two

THE ART OF DECEPTION, THE DECEPTION OF ART

Development Hell

Content is king.
—Sumner Redstone

While today's entertainment empires have become vast global enter-prises, their tentacles reaching from local video stores to satellites in outer space, they continue to rely heavily on a single product to define them-selves: movies. As Sumner Redstone once remarked, "Without content, all the cable channels, television networks, video chains, and all the other delivery systems would be totally useless. That content is movies."

The movies, which are the common feedstock for all those delivery systems, are the product of the imagination and skills of individuals who may have very different interests, and ambitions, from those of the cor-porate empires they serve. But they have a common cause: the creation of an illusion that will appeal to an audience.

Genesis

Every movie begins with an idea. It may be no more than the proverbial note scrawled on the back of an envelope, the name of a book that could be optioned, a magazine article or original story that could be adapted, or an old movie or play that could be remade with a new star. It can come from a writer, agent, actor, director, producer, studio executive, or even an industry outsider. There are five thousand dues-paying members of the Screenwriters Guild of America, two thousand agents, and thousands of directors, producers, and executives in the business of finding potential movie ideas. On almost any given day in Hollywood, at dozens of breakfast meetings in hotels or in more formal meetings in offices, a multitude of story ideas are being discussed.

Of the ideas that eventually become films, the vast majority are presented to studio executives orally in what is called a pitch. Pitches are particularly effective if they can be boiled down to a single catchphrase, a so-called high concept. This high-concept pitch is deftly parodied in the opening scenes of Robert Altman's 1992 film *The Player*, in which studio chief Griffin Mill (Tim Robbins) listens to a parade of hopeful writers rattling off shorthand descriptions such as "It's *Ghost* meets *The Manchurian Candidate*," or, in slightly more elaborate form, "It's *The Gods Must Be Crazy*, only this time 'the Coke bottle is a television actress.' "

From this plethora of possibilities, the six studios, which together in 2003 produced a grand total of only eighty movies, select those ideas that can meet their basic requirements. For their part, studio chiefs are focused on the particular elements in films that will keep money flowing into their clearinghouses. They pay particular attention to the aspects of a movie idea that are likely to attract, or repel, equity partners, cofinanciers, merchandisers, video chain stores, foreign pay-TV outlets, toy licensees, and other major contributors to their clearinghouses. When asked what elements a studio looks for, the studio chief in *The Player* answers, "Suspense, laughter, violence, hope, heart, nudity, sex, happy endings," and then adds, "Mainly happy endings." As the director Robert Altman explains in his commentary to the DVD, "Happy endings is the theme of the whole thing. Commercially, this is what the studios want."

Altman's cynicism notwithstanding, even in terms of their enlightened self-interest, studios require more than just commercially successful projects. In addition to their desire to offer a product that will appeal to financiers, merchandisers, and licensees, studio executives need to preserve and nourish their relationship with the stars, director, producers, and agents who define the Hollywood community—a community in which studio executives both work and play. If studio executives made only films that maximized the amount of money in their clearinghouses, they would do so at the serious risk of losing their standing in that community and, with it, their connection to the people, events, honors, and opportunities that brought them to Hollywood in the first place. With such a personal investment in their status and solidarity with the stars, directors, power brokers, and other doyens of Hollywood, they have concerns that go beyond that of the economic logic dictated by the balance sheet of the clearinghouse. Their decisions must also take into account a broader if less tangible consideration: the social and political axes of Hollywood. Kept constantly aware of these wheels within wheels at dinner parties, sporting events, award ceremonies, and other social functions—as well as media interviews—studio executives seek, along with strictly commercial projects, projects that are likely to attract the sort of actors, directors, awards, and media response that will help them maintain both their standing in the community and their own morale.

—

The task of developing ideas into films is generally farmed out to producers. Although they may identify themselves as "independent" producers, studios often provide them, and their production companies, with offices on their lots and money to hire writers, option books, and cover many, if not all, of their other expenses. Producers may employ literary scouts, readers, story editors, and other assistants to find the necessary material. In return for this support, studios get the right to buy those scripts that work out or at least the right of "first refusal."

Studios themselves also initiate and assign projects to these producers for further development. Some of these projects have long histories. Consider, for example, *Godzilla*. In 1952, when the studio system was tottering, Tomoyuki Tanaka, a Japanese producer, made the first Godzilla movie. In it, Gojira, a giant mutated reptile, arose out of the same waters in the Pacific where U.S. nuclear tests were then being conducted—a subject that was so sensitive in Japan, the only country to have suffered a nuclear-bomb attack, that censorship laws still prohibited any public discussion of it. Backed by Tojo Films, the largest owner of movie theaters in Japan, Tanaka produced an eighty-minute black-and-white film about the reptile destroying Japanese cities, and the movie became one of Japan's largest box-office successes. Soon after that, Embassy Pictures, an independent distributor in New York, bought the one-time foreign rights to it, deleted the antinuclear allegory, and added a quickly shot sequence depicting an American hero played by Raymond Burr. Released in the United States in 1956 as *Godzilla: King of the Monsters*, it was followed by no fewer than twenty-two sequels made in Japan by Tojo. It also established, following in the footsteps of Disney, an international franchise for selling toys and games. In 1992, when Sony was looking to create a licensing division, it decided to capitalize on the giant reptile's proven appeal and optioned the rights to make yet another sequel from Tojo.

Godzilla remained in development for another four years while Sony executives sought a formula to reinvigorate the franchise. Finally, in 1996, it turned the project over to Centropolis Films—which had just produced the immensely successful *Independence Day* for Fox—as part of a deal in which its producer-director team of Dean Devlin and Roland Emmerich would produce major films for Sony. "Spielberg's *Jurassic Park* had just made $950 million at the box office for Universal, so Sony wanted the same: a big—really big—monster that runs amuck," Devlin recalled. So he had writers Ted Elliott and Terry Rossio script a story not unlike that of *Jurassic Park*, in which a greedy entrepreneur's attempt to exhibit a monster in New York goes awry, and the monster escapes and, as Devlin put it, "tramples a lot of people and cars." Sony now immediately green-lighted the project. *Godzilla*, released on Memorial Day weekend in 1998 to poor reviews, went on to earn $180 million in rentals from the box office, considerably more from video, DVD, and other ancillary rights, and successfully established Sony's licensing division, Sony Signature.

Producers will occasionally initiate projects without studio backing. In 1998, producers Mario Kassar and Andrew Vajna, for example, bought the rights to make a second sequel of *Terminator*—to be called *Terminator 3: Rise of the Machines*—for $14.5 million from the now bankrupt Carolco Pictures, and the initial producer, Gale Anne Hurd. They then spent another $5.2 million developing a script and securing a director (Jonathan Mostow) acceptable to its intended star, Arnold Schwarzenegger. Only then did they bring the project to Warner Bros. and Sony, who agreed to provide financing and distribution guarantees (Warner Bros. in the United States; Sony elsewhere).

Such high-profile examples notwithstanding, the vast majority of scripts are financed by studios, not independent producers. Studios generally provide producers with revolving funds that are replenished when their projects reach the production stage.

Although most contracts with producers are for a number of projects, called "multipicture" deals, the studios also make countless smaller deals with producers to develop scripts for a single project. According to one estimate, in 2002 the six studios and their subsidiaries had more than twenty-five hundred ideas in some stage of development with producers. For their part, producers have little choice but to work with a major studio if they want to make Hollywood movies. The big six studios not only have the power to open a film in fifteen hundred or more multiplexes, but they also provide the legitimacy that producers may need to attract stars and directors to their projects.

The Script

Once an idea proves distinctive and attractive enough to pique a producer's and/or studio executive's interest, of course, it must then be converted into an acceptable script. "The empty page [is] everyone's terror," writes Peter Guber, who headed both the Warner Bros. and Sony studios. "Not only does the writer fear the empty page, but also the director, the producer, the financier. . . . For no matter what dazzling cyber-shots the director may have in his head, no matter what hot financing scheme the producer may conjure up, absolutely nothing happens until words start filling that empty page." A highly successful producer put it this way: "Without a script you can't make a movie." The process by which that script is gradually written, revised, polished, and often entirely reconceived to the satisfaction of all the concerned parties is called development.

Ideally, the ordeal of development leads to "green-lighting," the term used for a studio's decision to put a project into production, but most scripts never see a green light. In 2003, according to a Paramount estimate, nine out of ten projects under development at that studio were not green-lighted. Projects that fail to get green-lighted are either put in "turnaround," which gives the producers the right to sell them to another studio, or simply abandoned. To compensate for this unfavorable ratio, many producers have in some stage of development as many story ideas as they can afford to commission, option, or buy, with either studio funds or their own money. When one of these projects gets green-lighted, the producers get a fee (which can be several million dollars), a share in the future earnings of the movie, and, when completed, a credit on the film.

The people that the producers employ to work on scripts are almost always freelancers. Some are professional screenwriters, but many have other occupations, or "day jobs," as teachers, journalists, doctors, lawyers, or actors. Quite commonly, writers work in teams and produce a script on speculation, or "spec." The standard arrangement is for writers to get paid in stages—some portion on signing a contract, some portion on the completion of the first and second drafts, and the balance contingent on the story being actually filmed as a movie. For example, if a producer buys a pitch from a writer with a possible payment of, say, $500,000, installments are often scheduled as follows: $75,000 on signing, $75,000 on delivery of the first draft, and $75,000 for the second draft. This $225,000 is guaranteed, as long as he does the work. The balance of $275,000, which is part of the "production bonus," is paid *only* if the movie goes into production.

When scripts, at any stage, do not meet with the approval of the producer, either writers are instructed to rewrite them or they are given the guaranteed portion of their fees and released from the project. The producer then hires new writers. Not uncommonly, six or more writers will be retained for a single script. Sometimes a writer is hired as a "script doctor" for a flat fee of as much as $100,000 a week. If the film goes into production, all the writers with production-bonus arrangements usually get paid on the first day of principal photography. If the script has been adapted from an optioned book, the unpaid portion of the option price is also paid the writer at this point.

During this long process of development, the story idea itself frequently changes. The producer, director, or studio may change the ethnicity, sex, motivation, affiliation, and morality of characters from one script conference to another, sometimes even transforming tragedies into comedies or action films. Bruce Feirstein, who wrote the scripts for three

James Bond films, was retained in November 1999 by a movie star's production company to rewrite a script for a studio film about men who repossess airplanes for a living. The previous writer had written three drafts, but they were unacceptable to the producers. Feirstein was asked to "reconceptualize" the idea as a low-budget comedy. As is customary, he was asked to give an oral presentation at a script conference before proceeding. He came up with the idea for a "Butch and Sundance Kid repossess airplanes" buddy comedy set in contemporary America. As he tells it, "I got one minute into my pitch and the movie star said, 'Wait. Stop. You write amusement-park movies. I want a big summer movie.'" As Feirstein listened, the star continued, "I want lots of hardware. Huge action scenes. Let's blow a lot of shit up."

He added that the goal was to make "a tent-pole movie"—a movie that supports the studio's other films, like the center pole of a tent. With this new "input," Feirstein revised the story into "a giant international action film, with a climax set in China." And at the next script conference, attended by fourteen people from both the production company and the studio, the studio president apparently liked what he heard. He agreed that the climax needed to be set in China, and made one suggestion: "Do a scene where they have to repossess a trailer home instead of a plane." Eager to please the studio, Feirstein agreed to incorporate the scene. Two weeks later, a studio vice president called asking for a new set of qualities for the villain, including that he be a master of martial arts, since he believed that "kung fu" movies were "hot in Asia."

Four months later, after incorporating these changes, Feirstein turned in his script. The producer returned it to him with notes from the studio vice president's assistant. These notes, as Feirstein put it, "carpet-bombed" the entire concept, calling for a "page-one rethink" and suggesting it be turned into a thriller with a Middle East terrorist angle. There were also specific instructions to "lose" the repossession of the trailer home. During the period that Feirstein was "rethinking the movie," the president of the movie star's production company was fired, and the star appeared in an action film that was unsuccessful. Finally, after months of indecision, Feirstein met with the head of the studio, who had originally signed off on the idea. As Feirstein attempted to discuss the script with the studio president, the man admitted that he hadn't read the script but promised to "read it over the weekend" and send

Feirstein a "final, authoritative, official set of notes and instructions for a rewrite." As Feirstein recounts this story of "development hell," the notes never came, the president of the studio was fired six months later, Feirstein's contract was paid off a year after that, and several months later Feirstein learned that a new writer had been hired.

In a world in which such accounts are by no means exceptional, it should come as no surprise that dozens of writers often work on a single film. The issue of who contributed what to the project often ends in threats of lawsuits, if not actual litigation. "I did not expect that writing in Hollywood was so much about litigation and so little about imagination. I came here to dream, not to fight," the writer, actor, and lawyer Ben Stein wrote.

Such an expensive succession of writers has consequences for the movies that are ultimately made. As a former top studio executive explained, given that script costs on major projects can easily rise to $5 million for a single project, it only makes sense that studios, which are "risk-averse" to begin with, demand that such projects "be molded into star vehicles to justify their existence."

Producers also suffer through the script rewrites of development hell. Even if their expenses are fully reimbursed by the studio, the process is costly in terms of their time and patience. Each negotiation over changes in the script with writers, agents, studio executives, coproducers, potential directors, and stars risks further depleting the goodwill they need for other projects. And if these negotiations end up alienating writers (and/or their agents), as is often the case, it can complicate the task of getting other writers for future projects. On the other hand, if scripts don't conform to the expectations of the studio, producers risk losing their deal, and the status and credibility they gained from it.

Consider, for example, the decadelong odyssey of Warner Bros.' attempt to create a new Superman script. In 1993 the studio bought the rights to *Superman* from producer Alexander Salkind, who had acquired them to produce an earlier film version of the comic-book hero. Over the next ten years the studio commissioned six different writers—Jonathan Lemkin, Gregory Poirier, the team of Kevin Smith and Wesley Strick, Andrew Kevin Walker, and Akiva Goldman—to write various versions of this script, without green-lighting any of them.

The process of securing a director can be another circle of development hell. To obtain a green light, writers must fashion a script to which an acceptable director will commit himself. Unlike the days of the studio system, when directors were under contract and could be assigned to films, producers now need to recruit a director for each film. The objective is a so-called A-list director who, as veteran producer Lynda Obst explains, "has a big hit or two and a solid critical reputation." She described the difficulty of landing a director this way: "Every two-bit, second-rate script and its masters are trying to get the same fifteen [A-list directors]. These guys are payday; they are the sine qua non of a green light."

Directors, who often have competing offers and tight schedules, almost always require some control over the script. In some cases, they attach themselves to the project either as a collaborator of the producer or as the author or coauthor. Or they might join the writing process later on. In 2003, for example, over one third of the studio movies released directly credited the director as the writer or cowriter, and over half included the phrase "a film by," indirectly crediting the director as author. Even after directors agree to work on projects, they almost always reserve the right to modify the script to suit their own directorial strengths. Indeed, the rewriting, already replete with compromises and negotiations by this point, may only intensify after the director joins the project.

Even with both a satisfactory script and director in hand, producers may need to get one or more top stars to agree to act in films before the studios will consider green-lighting them for production. For example, after investing nearly $20 million in getting the rights to the story and developing a suitable script for their sequel to *Terminator 2*, Mario Kassar and Andrew Vajna still needed to secure the star of the franchise, Arnold Schwarzenegger. Even though his most recent films had done relatively poorly at the box office, and he would be in his late fifties by the time the film was released, his name had become so associated in the public's mind with the role of the robot that they considered his participation essential to the project. Consequently, they agreed to pay him fixed compensation of $29.25 million for his acting services during nineteen weeks of shooting and dubbing, and to give him 20 percent of the adjusted gross receipts once the film had earned back the cash outlays and met other conditions. His contract, which required eighteen months of negotiation, also granted him approval of not only the director and costars but also, of course, of the script. It specified that he had the right to reject any changes that "materially alter Artist's role or the story line of the Approved Screenplay."

Such rights of approval often determine the story, since stars often have their own ideas of what the audience responds to, and finds appealing, in their on-screen personas, and insist that scripts be rewritten to further their image. When the producer attempted to rewrite the character played by John Travolta in the 2003 film *Basic,* for example, to make him a more sophisticated hero, Travolta refused to accept the change, since he believed that audiences preferred him playing blue-collar underdogs. The producer had no choice but to acquiesce.

Once these essential elements are in place and brought to the studio, screenplays are scrutinized not only by the heads of the studios' motion-picture departments but by many junior executives. As producer Art Linson writes, "Those at the top can be influenced by the junior executives, because knowing 'what is good' is disturbingly subjective." In this process there frequently are, as one participant describes, "clashing egos, screaming insults, and mutual disrespect." If the project is to continue, compromises must be reached. To this end, producers and their studio liaisons negotiate with the agents, business managers, lawyers, and other representatives of the potential director and stars. "The conference calls, e-mail, and breakfasts can get very heated, and they might not leave everyone happy, but somehow the show goes on," one veteran producer explains. If a project manages to clear this last hurdle, it has finally arrived at the starting gate, and is officially green-lighted. Now the real work begins.

The Green Light

The studio's green light is the decision on which hangs the immediate fate of producers, directors, stars, writers, and others. For studios, each green light represents a commitment of enormous magnitude. For one thing, directors and stars usually have "pay or play" clauses in their contracts, requiring studios, once a film is green-lit, to pay their full fixed compensation, even if they abort the project, and this can amount to more than $30 million on a major film. Then, as the project proceeds, the costs escalate dramatically with the filming itself, the postproduction expenses, lab work (including prints), and marketing outlays. In 2003 the average commitment for a studio green light, according to the studios' own reckoning, was about $130 million.

Studios resist making such large commitments until all the elements are in place. But as directors and stars are lined up, the pressure increases from their agents (who stand to collect 10 percent of the money that will be paid out once the decision is made). If studios are not willing to commit, the directors and stars may move on to other projects.

In making this critical decision, studios usually convene summit conferences of their chiefs, who are responsible for giving the green light, and the top executives of all the divisions, who will be responsible for making, selling, and publicizing the film and its related products. According to Peter Guber and Peter Bart, who were each executives at major studios, "Most studios ask marketing and distribution executives for performance projections even before green-lighting a production, as well as a cost analysis as to how much must be committed to 'open' the movie to achieve the projected box office." The relatively easy calculation is the actual cost of shooting a film—which is estimated by the physical production department and closely vetted by the finance department. "The much tougher part is projecting how much it will cost to market it," one Paramount executive explained. These estimates require many problematic assumptions by the domestic distribution arm, which organizes films' crucial openings in the United States and Canada; the foreign distribution arm, which sells films and their rights overseas; the home-entertainment division, which sells videos and DVDs worldwide; and the marketing division, which develops the advertising and publicity for each film.

———

Every film submitted for approval has a tentative budget based on a shot-by-shot breakdown of the script. It specifies the total days of shooting and estimates all the expenses. The "above-the-line" costs, including agreed-upon payments for buying rights, developing the script, and compensating stars, directors, producers, and writers, are locked in once a film is green-lighted. The "below-the-line" expenditures, which include all the daily expenses during the actual production and postproduction periods, depend on how closely the production—including the subcontractors—adheres to the schedule. There are also "general" expenditures, which include insurance and contingency reserves.

The producer and studio then negotiate the least controllable part of the budget, the number of shooting days, in what one experienced producer describes as "a tribal dance." Producer Art Linson notes, "Each day of shooting becomes a bargaining chip. On the one hand, the studio will attempt to pull pages out of the script or reduce the complexity of a sequence or require that a series of scenes get shot in different locations, all with the good intention of saving money," and on the other hand, the producer will resist each incursion. Eventually, if the film is to get green-lighted, the dance ends in an agreement on how long and where the film will be shot. Even after the enormous commercial success of *Jaws*, Steven Spielberg had to personally meet with the treasurer and other executives of Columbia Pictures to reassure them about the production schedule before he could get final approval for his next film, *Close Encounters of the Third Kind;* as he put it, "The financiers still want to hear it right from the director's mouth, not from the producer's."

The proposed budget is then scrutinized by accountants in the studio's physical-production department, and any item that seems inconsistent with expenses incurred on similar productions is questioned. The result is a highly detailed document. Consider, for example, the $187.3 million budget of the action movie *Terminator 3: Rise of the Machines*. The 156-page document first listed $70.5 million in above-the-line expenses. These included $19.6 million for the story, which was described in the synopsis as "the adventures of Terminator and John Connor as they fight another evil nemesis"; $29.25 million for the star, Arnold Schwarzenegger; $5 million for the director, Jonathan Mostow; and $10 million to be split among four producers—Mario Kassar, Andrew Vajna, Joel Michaels, and Hal Lieberman. The balance of the above-the-line budget was allocated to supporting actors and perk packages for the star and director.

The below-the-line portion for the shooting—one hundred days for the actors' unit and sixty-seven days for the second units—came to $57.4 million. It included $12.1 million for constructing, dressing, and operating sets; $7.7 million for special effects; $2.6 million for lighting the sets; $2.4 million for the camera crew; $359,000 for sound; $566,000 for makeup, $1.6 million for wardrobe; $5.4 million for second units; $4.4 million for locations; $3.9 million for transportation; $1.5 million for stunts; $2 million for the production staff; $395,000 for extras; $1.6 million for the art department; $1.2 million for buying and processing the film; and $1.9 million for renting studio space.

The below-the-line budget for two hundred days of postproduction work amounted to $28 million. It included $20 million for digital effects; $2.5 million for editing; $691,000 for dubbing in dialogue; $1.8 million for music; and $142,000 for the opening and end titles.

The general part of the budget was $13.4 million. It included $2.4

million for the completion bond; $2 million for cast insurance; $2 million for legal and accounting; and $7 million for unforeseen contingencies.

Once the budget is vetted, studios next have to take into account a wide range of possible scenarios for marketing the film, including wide or limited openings in various markets around the world, merchandise tie-ins or solo advertising, and holiday or nonholiday release dates, involving vastly different numbers of prints and advertising budgets. At some point, a bet must be placed. In the case of *Terminator 3*, Warner Bros. assumed a year in advance (accurately, as it turned out) that it would need thirty-six hundred prints for the July 4 opening weekend (including replacement prints) at a cost of over $5 million. It set aside an additional $45 million for advertising and publicity.

The less certain part of the equation is how much money films will actually bring in to the studios' clearinghouses. In the case of so-called franchise films, such as *Lethal Weapon, Die Hard, Star Trek, Jurassic Park, Star Wars,* and *Batman,* in which similar (or the same) actors play similar roles in similar situations in movies with similar titles, studios can at least estimate on the basis of past performances. Given that *Terminator 2* had earned $52 million from its July 4 opening weekend in 1991, Warner Bros. had reason to expect that *Terminator 3,* with the same star, plot, and advertising strategy, would bear similar results when released on the July 4 weekend of 2003. (As it happened, that calculation was on target: the film grossed $64 million in its first week.)

The performance records for franchise films can be reliably consistent even when the stars change. Between 1962 and 2002, for example, MGM-UA released twenty films in the James Bond series, with five different actors playing James Bond. Because of its consistent track record, the studio could assume that *Bond 21,* the next film in the franchise, would receive favorable play dates during a holiday period in at least three thousand multiplex theaters in America; that it would enjoy prime bookings in Japan, Germany, Britain, Australia, France, Spain, and Italy—the seven markets that ordinarily account for 80 percent of a studio's foreign sales; that it would sell a minimum of 10 million DVDs and videos; and that it would serve as a locomotive in pulling other films through pay-television and other output deals. In addition, MGM could reasonably expect *Bond 21* to further earnings for some of the twenty previous Bond videos and DVDs, as well as add to the royalties on the Bond games played in arcades.

While not all franchise films replicate their past earnings as well as the Bond films have, they are often reliable enough to furnish the studios with a baseline guide to their earnings potential.

Studios also can gauge the potential of so-called genre films on the basis of the track records of similar efforts to exploit the same niche audience. Consider, for example, the genre of "ethnic films," which feature black actors in urban locales. Studios initially developed this genre between the 1930s and the 1950s, when racial segregation resulted in separate theaters for blacks in many areas of America. Even after theaters became more integrated, studio marketing executives found that they could still profitably make low-budget movies for a black urban audience. The *Shaft* movies, for example, in which Richard Roundtree plays a tough, savvy black detective, became a profitable staple for MGM in the 1970s. Cable television then made this genre even more cost-effective by allowing studios to "laser-beam their ads cheaply to high concentrations of black teens," as a Universal marketing vice president explained. Spots on such specialized media, such as the cable program *The Box*, which cost only a small fraction of what national network advertising does, enable studios to fill theaters in "ethnic areas" at a cost "of only pennies per moviegoer." In considering whether to green-light such low-budget genre films, studio executives estimate the precise number of pennies needed to create a profitable audience.

Before making a green-light decision, the studios can also usually ascertain whether or not films will qualify for advertising support from major merchandise tie-in partners. The studios all maintain liaisons, if not contractual arrangements, with fast-food chains, beverage companies, toy manufacturers, and other merchandisers willing to invest tens of millions of dollars to promote a single film in return for the attention it will bring to their own products. For example, twenty different merchandise partners for the James Bond film *Die Another Day* invested $120 million in advertisements (about triple the studios' own advertising budget). Although these ads featured the merchandisers' own products, they also helped to promote the film.

Some of the largest merchandisers enter into exclusive arrangements with a single studio to associate their products with the studio's own brand. In 1996, for example, McDonald's entered into a ten-year merchandising alliance with Disney, through which it agreed to promote

Disney's animated and other family-oriented films, and thereby greatly multiplied Disney's own marketing budget. The hamburger giant invested more than $100 million—four times Disney's own advertising budget—in just one film, *Monsters, Inc.*

By greatly amplifying the public awareness of a film, such merchandise tie-ins can help to ensure large openings during premium scheduling periods in worldwide markets as well as greatly increase the likelihood of subsequent large video and DVD sales. In addition to considering whether a film is likely to be a beneficiary of a huge marketing boost, studios assess the script for characters that might be licensed to toy, doll, game, clothing, and other manufacturers. If so, studios can count on such royalties flowing into their clearinghouses.

The contribution that stars make to a film's earnings is more difficult to predict. Two films with the same star will not necessarily enjoy similar results. Leonardo DiCaprio, for example, appeared in three films in a single year: *Titanic, The Man in the Iron Mask,* and *Celebrity. Titanic* was the highest-grossing film of all time, earning nearly $900 million in worldwide theatrical rentals, while *The Man in the Iron Mask* earned only a fraction of that—$80 million—and *Celebrity* brought in only a scant $3 million. The huge difference in the results may be accounted for by many variables—such as the differences in genres, stories, directors, roles, costars, or marketing campaigns—but the fact remains that the appearance of DiCaprio could not, on its own, guarantee a large opening audience, even for two films that followed closely in the wake of *Titanic.*

Even Julia Roberts, the highest-paid actress in 1997, could not be relied on to automatically draw a consistently large audience, as the numbers for her two consecutive romantic comedies playing in 1997 illustrate. The first, *My Best Friend's Wedding,* earned $127.5 million in theatrical rentals, and the second, *Everyone Says I Love You,* earned only $12 million. Same star actress, same genre, same romantic twist, same year—but one film drew ten times as many people to theaters as the other.

Such wide swings hold true even for most successful male stars, such as Tom Hanks, who in 1997 could command a fee of $29 million and 16.5 percent of a film's gross. He appeared in two consecutive movies with vastly different results: *That Thing You Do!* earned $14 million in theatrical rentals, and *Saving Private Ryan* earned in excess of $200 million.

Or consider the back-to-back openings of two Eddie Murphy movies in 2002, *The Adventures of Pluto Nash* and *I Spy*. Although both films cost approximately $100 million to make, and in both Murphy is cast in the role of a civilian battling criminals, more than twenty times as many people went to the opening of *I Spy* as went to *The Adventures of Pluto Nash*. "Stars can't pull in an audience by just having their names on the marquees," a Fox executive said, summing up what the numbers clearly show.

Directors are even more uncertain predictors of results. New directors entail great risks. As one producer pointed out, until directors have proven themselves on actual shoots, "there's no way to know whether they've got the emotional resilience, the drive, and the vision to hold it all together." Yet even established directors cannot guarantee that their films will consistently garner a large audience. Take, for example, Steven Spielberg, who has directed many of the highest-grossing films in history, including *Jurassic Park*, *E.T.*, and *Jaws*. Despite these successes, other of his films—including *Artificial Intelligence: A.I.*, *1941*, *Amistad*, *Always*, *The Color Purple*, and *Empire of the Sun*—have earned only a fraction of those grosses. Nevertheless, for studios, directors who have had successes, even if their track records are not consistent, are crucial elements because they attract stars to projects. Many, like Spielberg, also bring with them a talented retinue of production designers, musical coordinators, directors of photography, assistant directors, editors, and others with whom they have worked on previous productions. No matter how appealing the script may be, without such proven directors, assembling the most desirable cast and crew may prove an insurmountable problem.

Even with all the financial breakdowns and projections at his disposal, the studio head cannot rely merely on economic analyses of costs and revenues. He must also take into account the less quantifiable value of a possible "hit," which, even if it does not earn back its costs, can nevertheless generate a high level of attention for the studio within the industry, community, and press. Lew Wasserman stressed, in his discussions with a financial consultant, the need to produce what Hollywood perceived as winners—which included winning critical success and awards as well as box-office prizes—if only to provide a morale boost within the Hollywood community.

In this "winner" context cited by Wasserman, studio chiefs also must consider the costs of *not* green-lighting a film. For one thing, there is the risk of potential embarrassment if a rejected project becomes another studio's hit. For example, Universal Pictures, after spending more than three years developing the script of *Shakespeare in Love,* finally decided not to green-light it and instead put it in turnaround. Disney's subsidiary Miramax bought it and produced it, and the film went on to win seven Academy Awards, including Best Picture of 1998.

In turning down projects, there is also the risk of alienating producers, directors, and stars, all of whom a studio may need for future films. The damage can irreparably rend the social fabric. "We live in the same small universe," Steve Ross said, referring to the golf games, awards ceremonies, social parties, fund-raisers, publicity events, and other gatherings that executives, producers, directors, and stars attend. In rejecting their projects, the studios may lose the goodwill of the directors, producers, and stars who champion them.

In 1986 Ned Tanen, who then headed the Universal studio, was confronted with the decision whether to approve an additional $4.5 million to the proposed budget of *The Untouchables* so that director Brian De Palma could cast Robert De Niro in the film (whose stars already included Kevin Costner, Sean Connery, and Andy Garcia) or to reject the project. De Palma told Tanen, according to the producer who attended that meeting, "We have the opportunity to get De Niro to play Capone. I believe if we stay with the cast we have, [to] shorten the schedule and reduce the scale of the picture . . . it will not work, and I cannot afford to work on it." Tanen, rather than lose De Palma, elected to green-light the film with De Niro. As one top Hollywood agent explained, "Whatever the financial calculus, it takes a truly brave studio head to reject the movies of stars they value."

Studio heads also have a more self-interested reason for not rejecting movies that involve leading producers, directors, and stars. "There is no real price for failure," explained a studio's former chief financial officer. "If they pick the wrong pictures, studio heads don't get fired, they get multiple-picture deals from the studios." He added that as independent producers with studio deals, ex-executives can earn more money than they did at their studio jobs. In other words, a studio head who makes a mistake and loses his job often finds himself earning even more money as an independent producer. Since their success as producers will depend on their relations with directors and stars, they stand to reap the rewards they accrued in their previous careers as studio executives by not turning down the projects of these same directors and stars. So, as a rule, if the stars are of sufficient importance in the Hollywood community, their vehicles rarely fail to get green-lighted.

8

Preparing the Illusion

From the moment that films are green-lighted, they assume a new reality as official "productions." After drawing up and executing contracts with the producers, cofinanciers, directors, and other principals in the production, studios deposit the initial installment of funds in a bank account set up for the production. Then they assign a team of executives to make sure that the script is transformed into a global entertainment product that fulfills their corporate requisites.

Each production is a highly specialized, if ephemeral, enterprise, dedicated to producing a single product: roughly two hours' worth of film. To accomplish this mission, the production, usually set up as a separate corporation, retains hundreds of temporary employees, including actors, artists, technicians, construction workers, drivers, caterers, and personal assistants. Large action films such as *Godzilla*, *The Matrix*, and *Gladiator* can employ thousands of people. Even *Shakespeare in Love*, a relatively low-budget comedy, employed four hundred people.

Assembling a small army of individuals with highly specialized skills on a temporary basis is not an easy task. It requires persuading individuals to contractually commit themselves, often six months in advance, to a job that may last for only a few weeks, and to forego other opportunities. They must work long and unusual hours, often with strangers who may be unfamiliar with their methods and, in some cases, hostile to them. Then, after completing their task, they must seek other employment.

Each production needs its own executive structure. Generally, the hierarchy will include a line producer (sometimes called a production manager), who, on a day-to-day basis, makes sure that the director has the wherewithal to make the movie; a first assistant director, or AD, who, among other tasks, schedules the arrivals and departures of actors and technicians on the set so that the director can efficiently shoot the movie; a director of photography, or DP, who supervises the camera and lighting crew; a production designer, who is responsible for creating much of the visual illusion on sets and locations; a wardrobe head, who is responsible for outfitting all the actors; a location manager, responsible for the logistics of all the shooting done outside the studio; and a unit manager, whose staff tracks the expenditures, keeps the books, and makes sure the bills are paid. Before filming can begin, several months of preparation are usually required. The "prep" entails four major tasks.

First, a detailed shooting schedule is established, taking into account the stars' schedules and, after that, the most efficient use of expensive locations and other time-sensitive resources. Stars who may have other commitments are often given a "stop date," after which they will not be required to appear. In the case of *Basic*, for example, which had a shooting schedule that ran from November 26, 2001, to January 29, 2002, one of its stars, Samuel L. Jackson, had a stop date of December 11, so, to provide time for reshots, all his scenes were scheduled for the first week of principal photography. Even without stop dates, stars usually limit their availability to a specific number of weeks, called the "guaranteed period," after which they get paid a hefty increment. For example, Arnold Schwarzenegger's contract for *Terminator 3* required that he be paid $1.4 million per week—"prorated ($\frac{1}{5}$ for studio; $\frac{1}{6}$ for location) for periods of less than a week"—for any services he performed, including publicity, beyond the guaranteed period of twenty-one weeks.

Geography is another major determinant of the shooting schedule. To avoid multiple trips to a single location, all the scenes at that location may need to be shot at the same time, regardless of when they take place in the story.

In reordering the script to fit these priorities, it is rarely, if ever, possible to keep the scenes—or even all the shots in them—in their proper sequence. In the thriller *The Sum of All Fears*, for example, which ends with a tense confrontation between U.S. president Fowler (James Cromwell) and Russian president Nemerov (Ciaran Hinds), the American half of the scene was filmed four months before the Russian half.

Once the movie is reorganized for efficient shooting—and virtually all studio movies are shot out of continuity—each scene is transferred to a "day strip," a twenty-four-inch-long piece of paper that is color-coded to indicate whether the scene is an interior or exterior, day or night. White is interior day; yellow is exterior day, blue is interior night, and green is exterior night. (The job can now also be done by a computer program called "Movie Magic.") From this breakdown, the studio's physical production staff can determine which actors, technicians, extras, stunt-people, sets, locations, and other elements are required and when.

Many productions then "storyboard" the sequences. For a storyboard, an artist creates a cartoonlike rendition of each shot showing exactly how the characters and settings will be seen by the camera. Director Brian De Palma used such precisely detailed storyboards for *The Untouchables* that he was able to walk the production staff through, as the producer described it, "a sort of stick-figured playback of the final movie" months before it was ever shot. Production designers, directors of photography, set designers, casting directors, stunt coordinators, and others responsible for preparing the illusion then use the storyboards to plan and coordinate their work.

The second element of the prep process is casting the speaking roles in the film. If stars are already attached to the project, as is often the case at this point, the director now needs to find the right supporting actors. To assist him (or, more rarely, her), he employs a casting director, who acts as a specialized consultant in suggesting actors for movie parts. The casting director's principal concern is finding supporting actors with the right "chemistry"—actors who, in the words of one casting director, "visually click together on-screen." Stressing the importance of an actor's visual appearance, this casting director likens the task of finding the right actor to that of finding "models for fashion shows." She explains, "Whatever other virtues they might have, they must look the part." To this end, casting directors usually sort through thousands of head shots, either in their own files or in talent agencies' so-called "player guides." Nor is the search necessarily limited to professional actors. Depending on the part, they might also need to canvas athletes, pop singers, rap artists, or fashion models. In casting the 1999 football movie *Any Given Sunday,* casting directors Mary Vernieu and Billy Hopkins furnished director Oliver Stone with candidates that included more than a dozen professional athletes, such as Joe Schmidt, and rap artists, such as LL Cool J.

Directors also usually have their own candidates, including actors they know or with whom they have previously worked. Sometimes they will gravitate toward actors who have played similar parts in other films, especially ones that proved successful. For example, Stone chose Cameron Diaz for the part of the daughter of the sports-team owner in *Any Given Sunday* after seeing her play the part of the daughter of a sports-team owner in the 1997 film *My Best Friend's Wedding.* The script is not the only guide. If a director believes that a particular actor will add value to a movie, even if he or she does not physically fit the part as scripted, he often has the part rewritten to suit that actor.

At some point in the prep, screen tests are arranged for the most promising prospects. After the results are assessed by the director, producer, and studio executives, the director usually makes the final decision.

The selected actors are then offered contracts prepared by the production's lawyers that specify the periods they will be available both for principal photography and subsequent dubbing and reshooting sessions. Sometimes an actor is chosen who lacks a necessary attribute for the part, such as a proper accent, dancing ability, or martial-arts skills. To correct such problems, actors are assigned training coaches who work with them while the film is still in preproduction. The process of finding and training the cast can itself take several months.

The third part of the prep process involves creating the setting in which the story takes place. The production designer—who heads the art department and supervises the art director, set dresser, greens people, and construction crew—designs the sets, props, clothing, and other artifacts for every scene. These designs, often done as renderings, are then incorporated into the storyboards. Engineers, carpenters, prop buyers, and other specialists then create or find the necessary ingredients to transform these designs into three-dimensional, full-scale "reality."

At the same time, personnel must be found for the various crews that will photograph, light, record, and prepare the actors and sets. The director of photography needs to retain focus pullers, camera operators, and clapper loaders with whom he is comfortable working. The sound engineer needs to hire the appropriate boom operators, cable pullers, and audio technicians. The head electrician needs gaffers, best boys, and other lighting specialists. In addition, the producer needs to hire hairdressers, makeup artists, and wardrobe dressers.

Aside from their technical expertise, these crew members must have the social skills to work in close quarters with the director, stars, and the senior staff. They must also be willing to commit themselves well in advance of the start of principal photography.

If filming is to take place outside of the soundstages, location scouts are called on to scour the relevant area of the world and find locations that fit into the production design. When they find a place that meets the design requirements, they assess any problems it may pose to filming, in terms of noise levels, eyesores, light conditions, weather, and equipment accessibility. Then logistical arrangements must be made for the arrival of a small army of technicians and actors—a multistep task that often involves leasing hotel space; arranging for meals; renting vehicles, trailers, and portable toilets; hiring security guards, paramedics, and fire marshals; altering the landscape; installing power lines, generators, and tracks for stunt cars; repainting buildings; removing photographic obstacles; and obtaining the necessary permits.

Finally, an immense amount of paperwork has to be completed. Lawyers must draw up, and get signed, employment agreements, liability waivers, shooting permits, rental agreements, nondisclosure agreements, and insurance policies. To begin with, there must be a clear chain of control over the script, which means that everyone who has contributed to it—or to the story, property, or ideas on which it is based—must sign legal documents ceding control to the production. Then dispensations must be negotiated with various unions on locations where working conditions for the crew are problematic. Where animals, even insects, are called for in the script, arrangements must be made for animal-rights representatives to certify that no creature is harmed during filming. Where minors are involved as actors or extras, clearances are required from parents, and if it's during the school year, a studio teacher must be brought in to teach the child actor on the set.

Although some major films require as much as nine months of pre-production before shooting can begin, most are prepped in four months. This period provides studios with a further opportunity to bring film projects in line with their own priorities. In the bygone studio era, when the studio controlled every phase of preproduction, Walt Disney could, for example, personally oversee not only the frame-by-frame storyboards but also every detail concerning the production schedule. Even though today's studio executives, who have far more diverse duties, often rely on their junior executives to attend creative conferences on scripts, sets, and casting to keep the film under control, they still occasionally find time to intervene in preproduction decisions. For example, Michael Eisner, chairman of Disney, took a red pen to the script of the 2002 film *The Hot Chick*, circling twenty jokes he deemed inconsistent with Disney's image. He then e-mailed his request for changes to the studio executive in charge of the film, who passed the memo on to the producer. Of course, the changes were made.

Even if producers are not contractually obligated to make the changes suggested by studio executives, they cannot afford to disregard the people on whom they depend for the distribution and marketing of their films. With such powerful incentives, studio suggestions are rarely peremptorily rejected. Consequently, by the time the project moves toward the next phase, principal photography, it increasingly dovetails with the values of the studio.

Lights, Cameras, Action

Principal photography is a race against time. Once the stars, supporting actors, technicians, engineers, and other specialists are assembled, the clock begins running. Every day of shooting is phenomenally expensive. Even a low-budget film, such as the 2003 comedy *The Singing Detective*, which had a below-the-line production budget of $6 million, had a daily running cost of $80,000. A large-scale action film, such as *Terminator 3*, which had a below-the-line production budget of $57 million, had a daily running cost of $300,000. The average daily running cost in 2000 was $165,000.

Staying on schedule is not merely a question of money. As previously mentioned, stars, directors, and technicians often have other commitments and contractual stop dates that allow them to leave the production if the filming goes over schedule. So every delay caused by weather, illness, accidents, labor disputes, personality conflicts, and other such unexpected events is a potential disaster for the studio.

The director, although theoretically in command, must galvanize what is essentially a group of temporary employees. "The director more often than not also feels he is on alien ground," Peter Guber and Peter Bart write. "He may have previously worked with a few key members of his crew . . . but most are unknown. He's probably rehearsed the principal members of his cast for a week or two, but he also knows that their behavior is unpredictable" when filming begins.

Directors depend heavily on their first assistant directors (ADs), who act as their executive officers, making sure that every necessary person is in position when the director utters the magic word "Action." It is the AD's job to prepare the daily "call sheets" that specify the precise time at which the actors must report the next day for makeup, the electricians must rig the lighting, and everyone else must be present on the set.

Principal photography, whether on a studio soundstage or an isolated location, usually begins on a well-prepared set that is precisely lit by artificial light. Actors (or their stand-ins) take their positions behind chalk marks. Above them, a microphone on a boom must be exactly positioned to capture the actors' words without casting a telltale shadow. Technicians measure the light and sound levels around them. Prop people, set dressers, wardrobe assistants, and makeup artists make last-minute adjustments to the actors and the sets to ensure that they conform to the storyboard in place and time. The director of photography (DP) looks carefully through a viewer to make sure that no glass, mirror, or other reflective surface on the set exposes any evidence of the camera or crew. A still photographer takes pictures to map out the exact position of actors and props for future retakes, which the continuity person assiduously notes in a log.

When they all agree that the illusion is intact, the camera operator turns on the camera, a clapper loader clicks a board identifying the scene, the director yells "Action!" and the actors begin performing their parts. A few minutes (or seconds) later, the director says "Cut," the camera stops filming, and the first "take" is completed.

The director then usually views a crude digital version of the take made by a video camera. If, as is usually the case, he is not satisfied with this single take, he orders the shot redone. The camera is left in exactly the same position (or, if on a dolly or crane, is returned to its original position). The actors go back to their marks, and the makeup, hair, and wardrobe staff make them look exactly the same as they did before. The filming begins again, the clapboard signals "Take #2," and, on cue, the actors repeat their lines and actions. The takes continue, over and over again, until the director, DP, and sound engineer are satisfied.

Numerous takes are more the rule than the exception. In one not par-ticularly memorable scene from *Wall Street*, for example, Daryl Hannah, who plays the role of an interior decorator, speaks the following lines: "I want to do for furniture what Laura Ashley did for fabric. Produce a line of high-quality antiques at a low price." Not satisfied with her intonation, director Oliver Stone ordered a retake—and then proceeded to order twenty-five more. Each time, after the makeup and hair crew redid her appearance, the cameraperson rechecked the lighting, and the sound en-gineer tested the sound level, Hannah looked into the camera and re-peated the same two dozen words.

The number of takes varies with the working style of the director. Stanley Kubrick often used more than thirty takes to get the shot he wanted, while Sidney Lumet was often satisfied with fewer than five. Most studio directors average between five and ten takes for each shot.

During this process, actors may further slow things down by objecting to their scripted lines. They may argue that the lines themselves sound wrong, that they cannot say them with the proper effect, or even that the scripted lines are inconsistent with their public image. They may propose alternate lines or gestures. Major stars frequently make such suggestions. During Steven Soderbergh's remake of *Ocean's Eleven*, for example, Brad Pitt not only proposed new lines for himself but also suggested that he chew on fast food while he delivered them (ideas that Soderbergh ac-cepted).

Directors cannot ignore such requests without risking offending the actors and adding to the level of tension on the set. They generally hear them out, negotiate the alterations, and often agree to do extra takes with the modified lines. Even if these takes are not ultimately selected in the final editing (for which the actors are not present), they do consume valu-able time on the set.

The DP also may object to the shot if the action of the actors inter-feres with the reflected light captured by the camera. He may insist on redoing the take or even altering the wardrobe, props, or actor's move-ment. For example, in *Sweet Smell of Success*, DP James Wong Howe was unsatisfied with the shadows on the face of the principal character, J. J.

Hunsecker (Burt Lancaster). He delayed the take while he tested every possible position of the actor's face with a light meter. He then told the director, Alexander Mackendrick, that the only way he could get the proper shadow on the actor's face was for him to wear heavy-rimmed spectacles. Mackendrick had the prop department make the specified eyeglasses, and hours later the shooting continued. Directors rarely turn down such demands by their DP, even if they slow down the shoot.

Sound engineers have a similar veto power over shots with recorded dialogue. In order to balance the dialogue track with the background sound, which is recorded separately, the sound engineer needs absolutely pristine recordings of each actor's lines. If there are any extraneous noises on the set, the shot will need to be redone.

Producers may also make product-placement deals that can further delay shooting. In the case of *Natural Born Killers*, for example, a producer arranged for the director, Oliver Stone, and other members of the production to get two free pairs of cowboy boots in return for showing the boots' brand name, Abilene, on a passing truck. The boot truck was to make its appearance by passing the open convertible driven by the character Mallory Knox (Juliette Lewis) in a single shot. This meant that the two vehicles—Mallory's car and the Abilene boot truck—coming from opposite directions, had to arrive in front of the camera at precisely the same time. Over and over again both drivers, starting their approach a half mile apart, had to be continually cued with walkie-talkies as the camera, which was mounted on a crane, swooped down. "It's a tough shot to pull off," the coproducer wrote, "and if we didn't get it, our schedule was screwed because it was a critical establishing shot." Nevertheless, to get the free boots, Stone did the necessary retakes to get the boots' brand in the shot.

When directors put pressure on actors to speed up to compensate for delays, other problems can occur. As Jane Hamsher, a producer of *Natural Born Killers*, relates, Juliette Lewis "became so exhausted from what was being demanded of her on the set" that Hamsher would find the star "sobbing in hotel elevators"; one morning, after Lewis slept through an early call, Hamsher had to send hotel security men "to break down her door so we could get her to the set."

Directors also have to take account of the limitations imposed by insurance companies, which often have a representative on the set. The policies they issue, which are mandatory for any Hollywood production, require that the "essential elements" of the production, which usually include its principal stars, not be used in specified ways. For example, since Nicole Kidman had a chronic knee problem in 2001, insurance companies prohibited her from acting in any scenes that involved her kneeling or otherwise being in a position that risked her knee going out of joint. The director had to use either a double or a mechanical device to raise or lower her.

Adding to such delays are the issues that arise when managing unionized employees, which can include union-mandated meal breaks, equipment-safety concerns, and appropriate working conditions on location. Any dispute about the application of union rules can stop the production until a union representative is found—and satisfied. Not surprisingly, completing the takes necessary for a single shot in the script often eats up an entire day.

After a shot in the script is completed to his satisfaction, the director moves on to the next camera position or "setup." Even the simplest exchange between two actors usually requires a minimum of three setups: a "master," which establishes the basic geography of the scene, and two close-ups—one from the perspective of each actor. If there are additional actors, or the scene is more complex, the director may require many more setups. Each setup requires technicians, artisans, and laborers—often working under unionized rules—to move lights, thread high-voltage cable, lay tracks, and reposition the microphones and camera.

The intervals between setups can take up to three hours, and during these intervals stars usually return to their dressing room or trailer. During this "downtime," they are often surrounded by an entourage that can include friends, gurus, coaches, personal trainers, masseuses, beauticians, bodyguards, and personal shoppers. During the production of *Basic* in Florida in 2002, John Travolta included in his immediate entourage two pilots, a hairstylist, a makeup artist, a chef, a personal stand-in, the president of his production company, a personal driver, and five friends (who were each given, at his request, one line of dialogue in the script, which qualified them for health insurance). During this extended time-out, stars often deal with other personal or business matters—reading documents, taking conference calls, working out on treadmills, meeting friends, and engaging in other activities that have no relation to the movie being filmed. Since it is vitally important to maintain the physical and mental health of the stars during principal photography, productions also almost always keep doctors on call. During the filming of *Natural Born Killers*, for example, a full-time "Dr. Feel Good" osteopath was employed to dispense, according to the producer, various pharmaceuticals, including "B-12 shots and Vicodan."

The stars may also be visited by the unit publicist and a crew making so-called electronic press kits, or EPKs. These are essentially publicity interviews, often tightly scripted, in which stars discuss the making of the film for the benefit of publicizing it on television.

All these downtime activities may further distance and distract actors from focusing on their character and the story being filmed.

At a certain point a production assistant, usually stationed outside the dressing rooms or trailers, signals the actors that the crew has completed the next setup. The actors then have to get back "in character" while hairdressers, makeup assistants, and wardrobe personnel adjust their appearance.

When they return to the set and again take their position behind the chalk marks, the camera has to be refocused, the sound levels have to be retested, the frame has to be checked for microphone boom shadows, and, if necessary, the equipment has to be rearranged to obviate any problems. Meanwhile, a continuity person checks that everything precisely matches that of the shot in the script that precedes or follows it. A script prompter again reads them their lines, which, if this is a retake of the same scene from a different camera angle, may not differ from their lines in the previous setup, and the director again orders "Action."

At the end of each day, the director and the AD, along with the producers, the DP, the production designer, and the editor, go to a projection room to watch the unedited "dailies" from the previous day's shooting. This footage, printed on thirty-five-millimeter film by the lab, usually runs between one and two hours and consists of repetitive shots with only small variations. From this the director determines whether he has the particular shots he needs for the film (perhaps only a few minutes' worth), the DP and production designer confirm that there are no glitches in the quality of those selected shots, the editor makes sure that the shots give enough coverage and flexibility for the eventual editing of the film, and the producer makes sure that the footage meets whatever requirements are specified by the studio and its financial partners for the production.

Meanwhile, studio executives review the same footage in the privacy of their own screening room and pass on to the producer any objections they might have. If problems are found, the AD schedules a "pick-up shoot" to reshoot the scene. If not, the production moves on to new setups and eventually to the next scene, which may require new sets, props, and additional actors.

Unlike in the days of the studio system, when all or most of the shooting was done in the same studio or its back lot, films now are seldom shot in only one studio or location. *Gladiator,* for example, was filmed in five different countries: the United States (California), Britain (Surrey), Morocco (Ouarzazate), Italy (Tuscany), and Malta. The choice of different locations may proceed from a variety of considerations: tax subsidies—the tiny island republic of Malta, which provides such subsidies, has been a venue for seventy films—weather conditions, low-cost labor, and the relevance of certain landscapes to the film's plot. Moves from one location to another can be logistical nightmares, involving documenting, packing, and air-freighting vital cameras, lenses, wardrobes, makeup kits, props, special-effects material, and other equipment, as well as incorporating new crew members, drivers, guards, and caterers into an ongoing production. Provisions may also have to be made for different union and insurance regulations, clothing, food delivery, and weather conditions. If the move is to a foreign country, there may be further complications with language and customs. In each new place, there may be new actors, stunt and other doubles, and technicians. In *Gladiator,* the production used different art directors, second-unit directors, set decorators, makeup artists, property buyers, special-effects crews, electricians, animal wranglers, and camera crews in different countries.

Directors themselves need not film all the scenes or go to every location. Instead, they usually farm out to second-unit directors the task of shooting many of the scenes not requiring the appearance of the major actors. This division of labor greatly speeds up the production of a film by allowing different parts of it to be shot simultaneously. In the 1997 James Bond film *Tomorrow Never Dies,* while principal actor Pierce Brosnan was playing James Bond at the Frogmore Studio outside of London, one second unit was filming a stuntman playing James Bond driving a BMW car in the Brent Cross Shopping Centre's parking lot in Hendon, England, another second unit in Florida was shooting another stunt double playing James Bond parachuting out of a plane, a third second unit in England was shooting a swimming double playing James Bond underwater in a tank at the Pinewood Studio outside London, and a fourth second unit in Bermuda was shooting yet another Bond double piloting a speedboat. If the director, Roger Spottiswoode, had directed all these scenes himself, the production—which took five months to complete—could have dragged on for years. Moreover, Pierce Brosnan could not have played James Bond in all the scenes anyway, because risky activities such as parachuting were prohibited by the insurance policy covering the production. Indeed, since Harold Lloyd nearly lost two fingers performing his own stunts in 1920, insurance companies, which stand to lose tens of millions of dollars if a production is interrupted, almost invariably ban key actors from participating in stunts that could be injurious.

As a result, stuntpeople are commonly used for any potentially dangerous scene, such as car chases, fights, and horseback rides. The illusion is effective because the doubles' faces and other identifying features are concealed by either the costumes or camera angle. If the scene requires showing actors' faces, the principal actor's face can be subsequently digitally "attached" to the body of a double by a process called "digital masking."

Most stunts are filmed by second units, which have their own unit managers, camerapeople, and crew. Depending on the action the stunt requires, fight choreographers, martial-arts coaches, special-effects crews, stunt drivers, and other specialists may also be employed. The production of *The Matrix*, for example, flew in from Hong Kong a team of sixteen "wire men," whose job, by pulling stuntpeople on wires (which were later digitally deleted), was to make it appear that the actors were flying.

Aside from these action scenes, second units also film most of the scenes that do not include the actors. They photograph the backgrounds for shots in which actors are later added by the lab; the cutaway shots of landmarks, crowds, traffic, and other scenery that show the audience what the characters are supposedly looking at; and certain long shots, such as those used to establish the geography of a setting, in which doubles are substituted for the actors.

Directors usually control what their second units shoot by providing them with storyboards that depict each shot from the angle from which it is to be filmed. If the footage fails to meet the director's specifications, or his requirements have changed, he can also order the unit to reshoot the sequence.

The expenses of second units, especially on a major action film, can be enormous. The camera crew and other second-unit technicians for *Terminator 3* cost $5.4 million.

While the production continues, the studio keeps careful track of its expenditures, which can average hundreds of thousands of dollars a day. The unit managers and their accounting staffs forward a list of each day's expenditures to the studio's head of physical production, whose thankless mission it is to prevent the production's costs from exceeding its budget. When productions are in danger of running over their budgets, studios generally require producers, who may be contractually liable for the overage, to deal with the problem. To avoid mounting overruns, producers—who cannot often control the speed with which actors, directors, and second units complete their scenes—must sometimes resort to cutting from the script scenes yet to be filmed. When *Godzilla* began to run over budget, producer Dean Devlin, whose production company, Centropolis, would have been liable for the additional costs, deleted ten "character-development" scenes from the script. "Monster films do not really depend on character development," he explained.

Although films that run into obstacles, such as *Titanic*, can shoot for more than a year, these are rarities in the expensive universe of principal photography. Most studio productions complete their shooting within three to five months. As the shooting nears completion, studio executives review the footage from all the units to make sure that all the requisite production values have been captured on film. If they find them lacking, they may order additional shooting.

When the last actor completes his final take, principal photography is over. If there are no missing elements, the production is deemed a "wrap," the crews are dismissed, and the rented equipment and trailers are returned. The production, however, is far from complete.

Bits and Pieces

A movie is just bits and pieces.
—François Truffaut, *Day for Night*

When principal photography is completed, the financial pressure of daily shooting ends. So do concerns about unpredictable weather, set damage, and egotistical stars. The insurers relax the discipline they imposed during the days of shooting. Yet critical parts of both picture and sound are still missing. These missing pieces are created and then fused into the film in the postproduction phase.

Missing Pictures

For many films, entire sequences are subcontracted out to companies that specialize in computer graphics, or CG. These companies create scenes, or elements of scenes, not by filming them or drawing them, but by manipulating data in computers.

Walt Disney, in his early animation films in the 1930s, developed the technology of overlaid celluloid strips—"cels"—that could be mechanically combined in different ways so that artists did not have to draw an entire new frame every time a character moved. Even with this ingenious contrivance, the number of permutations were limited, and thousands of separate drawings were still needed for a single cartoon. The result, moreover, lacked an element of realism, since the characters did not appear to move in three-dimensional space. A half century later, the desktop computer revolutionized animation. Not only did it make the artwork less cumbersome to manage, but it produced a much more realistic result—called 3D animation.

Now that drawings can be scanned in digital form into a computer, the different elements in them can be combined in nearly limitless ways. All it requires are the proper keystrokes and the programs to handle repetitious tasks.

Disney's successors first used CG extensively for the space adventure *Tron* in 1980. As computing power became less expensive and computer programs more sophisticated, CG evolved into the preferred means of generating time-consuming action sequences in a variety of movies. Like conventional animation, CG can create scenes that do not require locations, sets, props, costumes, directors of photography, stuntpeople, or actors. But it can also blend computer-generated images with live actors in a far more convincing way than can conventional animation. It can, for example, fill in a completely blank "limbo set"—aptly named because the actors in it are in a sort of limbo stage—by "painting" elaborate costumes on actors, filling in ornate walls and furniture behind them, or inserting charging monsters in front of them. In the production of *The Sum of All Fears*, for example, the actor Arnold McCuller sang the national anthem in a limbo set, and months later CG technicians created around him a giant football stadium, thousands of cheering fans, and a sky full of fireworks.

CG work is no small undertaking. Action movies now often have more computer-animated scenes than lives ones and, in many cases, a larger budget for CG than for principal photography.

This part of filmmaking is generally done separately, in both time and space, from the principal photography. For each sequence, storyboards of the action—as well as still photographs of the actors, props, and settings—are sent to outside CG studios. After computerizing the material, the CG technicians, pixel by pixel, rearrange it to approximate the characters, setting, and action in the storyboards. To achieve realistic motion in these scenes, a "motion capture" unit often films people simulating the required movements. The CG house then uses its proprietary computer programs to transfer these movements to the characters.

Since the work can instantly be sent to the director by e-mail, it can be done anywhere in the world. Still, despite the advances in computer technology, CG work remains extremely expensive. For *Terminator 3,* $19.9 million was spent on such CG effects. For *Godzilla,* the monsters digitally created by CG programs cost $9.5 million. According to the producer's estimate, "CG cost more than all the live actors combined." He explained, "In effect, there are now two different productions taking place on the same project: the live-action movie shot in a studio or on location and the CG movie created on computers." This twin effort explains in large part the increased length of the credits at the end of films in recent times. (In 1977 the credits for the original *Stars Wars* listed 143 technicians; in 2003 the CG sequel, *Attack of the Clones,* listed 572 technicians.)

Even with its high price tag, CG has become an indispensable part of Hollywood filmmaking. It affords the director more control over the illusion than live-action filming does—even in nonaction sequences—since there is no limit to the way that the data can be altered in a computer. In *Titanic,* for example, James Cameron used CG to decorate and furnish entire rooms, like the ballroom, on the ship, and to add freezing breaths to those who had gone overboard. And in *Gladiator* it was used to insert into certain scenes the image of the character Proximo after Oliver Reed, the actor who had been playing him, died during filming.

Because CG work often must meet strict postproduction schedules, different sequences are usually farmed out to many different companies. *X-Men,* for example, used eight different companies for its CG work.

When the completed CG material is delivered, the director, production designer, editor, and other technicians evaluate it. If it does not satisfactorily fit in with their filmed material, it can be sent back for further work, but that will increase the cost of the film and possibly delay its release. When the completion of a film is guaranteed by an insurer, such as International Film Guarantors (IFG), the insurer usually requires directors to separate their postproduction CG work into two lists: shots that are "essential" and those on their "wish list." As a completion-bond executive explained, items on the former list are done first, and then, if the production is over budget, the director is told to cut items from the wish list.

In depicting many complex disasters—such as a ship blowing up—filmmakers usually find it less expensive to film a miniaturized model of the event than to use CG to create the scene from scratch. Since this photography uses highly specialized skills, such as pyrotechnics, puppeteering, and model making, productions often farm out the work to visual-effects companies with particular experience in the required illusion. The subcontractor then realizes the image—usually working from a director-approved storyboard and with its own crew and equipment. In the case of the destruction of a U.S. aircraft carrier in *The Sum of All Fears,* for example, the visual-effects company Rhythm & Hues Studios used pyrotechnics to blow up a twenty-foot-high scaled model of a carrier's conning tower in front of a blue screen in a studio. Meanwhile, an aerial-photography unit filmed the footage of actual U.S. ships at sea that the lab then added to the areas of the shot demarcated by the blue screen.

Productions also often use subcontractors for conventional artwork when they can do the job more cheaply or quickly than a CG firm. Artists draw images or sculpt three-dimensional models that are then photographed with special lenses to produce the desired illusion. Title sequences, for example, often use conventional animation.

Additional photography is often required for "insert shots." These may include close-ups of hands, calling cards, guns, newspaper headlines, or other objects that the director chose not to shoot during principal photography to save time while the actors were on the set. In some instances, the inserts may also be shots of branded products that the producer has agreed to put in the film in a product-placement arrangement. Since these shots require lighting that is time-consuming to set up, they are usually assigned to photographers who specialize in this work and have their own lenses and lighting apparatus for close-up work. If the inserts are of body parts, the photographer usually recruits whatever body-part doubles are necessary.

Finally, productions may require existing footage from newsreels, television programs, amateur videotapes, or other movies. For example, in his 1998 film *Saving Private Ryan,* Steven Spielberg used newsreel footage of the 1944 invasion of the beaches of Normandy; in his 1994 film *Natural Born Killers,* Oliver Stone used clips from the television series *Leave It to Beaver* and the infamous videotape of the Los Angeles police beating of Rodney King; and in his 1999 film *The Limey*, Steven Soderbergh used excerpts of Terence Stamp's performance in the 1967 film *Poor Cow* to show the aging title character, Wilson (played by Stamp), as a young man. Productions buy this material from the stock-footage libraries of movie studios, television networks, museums, and other sources.

Missing Sounds

Productions must also complete the aural illusion in postproduction. A large part of the dialogue between actors cannot be successfully recorded during principal photography because of the interference of extraneous noises. Even lines recorded under perfect conditions in studios often need to be "revoiced" to improve clarity, nuance, or humor. Or directors may need to accommodate changes in the story by having actors say lines—such as jokes, clarifications, or revelations—that were not in the filmed script. (These additions, called "wild lines," must be inserted in shots in which the speaking character's mouth is not visible to the audience.) Sometimes a character whose accent is not sufficiently clear may need to be revoiced. It was not until after the principal photography of *Goldfinger* had been completed that its director, Guy Hamilton, discovered that the German actor Gert Fröbe, playing the title role, was difficult to understand; the entire character was subsequently revoiced with an English voice double, Michael Collins, mimicking a German accent.

The voices of minor roles are also often added after principal photography. For example, the voices of characters chattering at a cocktail party are usually done in a recording studio by voice extras, called "walla-walla groups." Such background chatter can also be bought from sound-effects libraries.

In the case of feature-length animation movies, each character usually "voices" his entire part solo in a recording studio. (The top fee, even for the highest-paid stars, was only $10,000 a day in 2003—though it could be higher in sequels.)

The postproduction recording is called "looping," and actors are required to return for these looping sessions. If they are unavailable, voice doubles may take their place. The technical process by which this revoicing is done is called ADR, which stands for automatic dialogue replacement. For the actors, or their voice doubles, it is usually tedious, repetitive work. Under the supervision of the director and ADR supervisor, they must repeat their lines over and over again until they get the exact tone and inflection the director is after. These looping sessions can extend for weeks, depending on the schedules of the needed actors.

As filmmakers realized when they made the transition from silent to talkie movies, dialogue is only part of the sound illusion needed for films. They found that no matter how precisely rendered and enunciated it was, and no matter how clearly it was reproduced, the recorded human voice sounded unnatural to theater audiences. What was lacking was the background noise that exists in reality—the almost inaudible chattering in a room, the distant footfalls on a street, the murmuring of wind in the country. Without these background sounds subtly blended in with the dialogue, the entire film seemed artificial.

The problem was solved by Jack Foley, a resourceful stuntman, who developed a separate track of background noises that became known as "Foley effects." To create this track, sound engineers, now called Foley artists, begin by deleting most of the natural sound that the sound-recording engineer couldn't avoid recording on the set or location during photography, such as doors slamming, clothing rustling, and actors' breathing. Ironically, such natural effects tend to sound unnatural in movies. These sounds are then replaced by artificial sound effects created by the Foley artists who, while watching the footage in closed-off sound booths, use their own devices to create noises that will sound realistic to audiences. The sound of footsteps in snow, for example, is best replicated not by tramping through a winter landscape but by crunching cat litter. Foley artists also have their own archive of frequently used sounds, such as cars in traffic, squeals, explosions, airport crowds, and birds chirping. Sound designers can also compose original background sounds on a computerized device called a synclavier or can combine a mélange of prerecorded sounds to achieve a new effect. When the Foley effects tracks are completed, they are then mixed with the dialogue tracks.

Finally, music—what studio head Peter Guber called "the heart and soul of film"—must be created or bought. The music for a film often includes both a score (the original music created for the film) and songs, which are licensed from music companies.

The score is used to cue audiences as to how they should respond emotionally to events in the movie. If successful, it directs them to feel anxious, relieved, or threatened by what they are seeing, or about to see, on the screen. Alfred Hitchcock famously used the eerie score by Bernard Herrmann in *Psycho* to signal the knife-wielding appearances of the psychopathic Norman Bates (Anthony Perkins).

Scores for movies are composed in much the same way as operas are, which explains why many of the opera composers of the twentieth century, including Igor Stravinsky, Erich Korngold, Sergey Prokofiev, Dmitry Shostakovich, and Arthur Sullivan, also scored music for movies. Like opera composers, film composers consider the passion, conflicts, and torments associated with the protagonists and develop motifs to foreshadow and heighten them. Unlike the opera composer, they have the luxury of viewing the scenes before they compose the music to accompany them. The score is then orchestrated, recorded by an orchestra, and matched to the action of the film on a separate track.

The songs serve a different function. The works of well-known artists whom audiences are likely to associate with specific times, styles, and places can help create a context for the characters. For example, in the 2000 film *Almost Famous,* director Cameron Crowe used snatches from hit songs by Neil Young, Stevie Wonder, Cat Stevens, and Elton John to establish the rock-and-roll era of the early 1970s. Songs can be extremely expensive to license, however. Paramount reportedly paid $1 million to license the original song "I Disappear" by the group Metallica for *Mission: Impossible II,* and, according to a producer, more than $2 million was spent on rights to songs for *Natural Born Killers.*

Once licensed, songs can be inserted into the story itself (when, for example, characters are listening to their stereos, Walkmen, or car radios) or used in the title sequences, sometimes—as in the case of Madonna's song for *Die Another Day*—with great effect. The songs are then balanced with the score and recorded on a "temp" track to await the final cut.

At this point, all the pieces of the illusion have been created, and all that remains is assembling them into a convincing illusion.

Completing the Illusion

"There are actually three different movies," veteran actor Roy Scheider once explained. "The one that is written, the one that is shot, and the one that is edited." After principal photography is over, and all the material from second units, computer-graphics houses, animators, stock libraries, and other sources is sent in, that third movie must be configured from the jigsaw puzzle of possibilities. Even a single moment in the final movie may contain elements created at several different places and times by several different crews. The sequence of James Bond in a pipeline explosion in Russia in the movie *The World Is Not Enough* required close-ups of Pierce Brosnan (James Bond) shot against a blank screen in Pinewood Studio by director Michael Apted; establishing shots of a pipeline on location in Gwynedd, Wales, by a second-unit director; footage of an explosion of a miniature model shot by a special-effects crew at Hankley Common, Elstead, in Surrey, England; CG inserts of a wall of fire done by Cinesite, U.K.—all created under different lighting conditions—and sounds recorded at postproduction looping sessions at Pinewood Studio, created by Foley Artists and obtained from stock sound libraries.

Even before principal photography ends, the film editor has begun assembling the footage into a rough first cut. The computer graphics, animation, inserts, and other missing scenes are marked by blank green film or placards reading "Insert missing." The first job of the editor is to make sure that the director has enough usable shots for each scene. When he examines the raw footage after it comes back from the lab, the editor may find many technical problems. As one veteran editor wrote, the possibilities are wide-ranging: "Shots go out of focus, the director loses the light at the end of the day or doesn't get some angles he needs, the negative gets damaged in the lab." To remedy such problems, the director may have to either reshoot the sequence or rewrite the script.

The more grueling job of the editor is to reduce the plethora of daily footage—the dailies—to manageable proportions. To begin with, as all the dailies come in, a low-quality videotape of them is scanned into a computer so that every scene is time-coded and matched to the negative. This videotape is then transferred to a specialized computer called an Avid on which the editor can rearrange the shots in different combinations without actually cutting the film itself. Prior to the arrival of the Avid in the early 1980s, the editor had to physically cut and splice actual film. With the Avid, the editor can accomplish the same result with a few keystrokes—and, if unsatisfied, instantly do another version. Once the editor and the director are satisfied, the editor assembles the rough cut, which may be only a small fraction of the film that was shot.

Directors closely supervise this process. This is the point at which they are finally free of the demands imposed by actors, directors of photography, line producers, unit managers, and even the script. They can choose whatever takes they prefer, eliminating or rearranging shots, sequences, and characters as they see fit. In the editing of the 2002 film *Murder by Numbers*, for example, director Barbet Schroeder eliminated the entire opening sequence that featured the star, Sandra Bullock (using some of it in flashbacks he inserted in later parts of the movie). Working with editors, directors can view all the likely permutations until they find the order that most satisfactorily tells the story the way they want to tell it. When they achieve this combination, which can take weeks, editors cut the film accordingly, producing what is called the "director's cut."

The film lab, by matching the time codes on the Avid version with a duplicate of the negative, then cuts the actual film. The lab also creates optical transitions (such as the "dissolves" and "fade-outs"), fills in the blank spaces behind the actors with the designated CG inserts, and blends in whatever other bits and pieces are still missing from the film.

Even after all the material is "married" in the film, the lighting still needs to be corrected, especially if, as is usually the case with films shot out of order, different parts of the same scenes have been shot under different conditions. It is critically important to restore the illusion of continuity by adjusting the brightness, contrast, and color for each scene. "Color balancing," as this is called, is also extremely time-consuming. "It requires sitting both the DP and director down with the timing technician for sixteen- and twenty-four-hour sessions of intense work," a postproduction supervisor explained. "They have to eyeball the footage, color-time each piece, try different hues and contrasts, and then make test prints for each trial." The entire trial-and-error procedure must then be repeated for home video and television versions, because the color balancing does not translate between the various formats.

To avoid this tedious process, studios have recently begun to convert the entire film into a computer file, called a "digital intermediate." Although the digital conversion alone costs several hundred thousand dollars, the computerized process allows color balancing to be done almost instantaneously by a digital colorist—an occupation that only emerged in the film industry in 1999—with the help of programs that automatically match the color and lighting in scenes. If, for example, a director decides to change the color of a river in a movie from muddy brown to sparkling blue-white—as, for example, Kevin Costner did in his 2003 film *Open Range*—he simply instructs the digital colorist to make the change, and presto, the river sparkles blue-white in every scene. Not only that, but results can be translated by the same computer program for home video, television, and other formats. The downside of this further step toward computerizing the filmmaking process is a degradation of quality—"a slight bump down in resolution," as one producer put it— because less digital information is scanned in the computer than exists on the film.

Once the color balancing is completed, the sound—including the dialogue, postproduction looping, Foley effects, score, and songs, all of which have been mixed into the final soundtrack—is now perfectly synchronized to the film. The resulting product is an "answer print," which approaches the illusion that viewers will experience in theaters.

Even at this point, however, the odyssey from an idea to a finished movie is not quite complete. The studio almost always retains the right to make the final cut. Usually, that is specified in the production contract, but even in cases where it is not, producers and directors have a powerful incentive to acquiesce to this demand: they need the backing of the studio's marketing machine for the film to succeed both commercially and critically.

So, studio executives now review the edited products to make sure that nothing in them will lessen the chances of a successful theatrical release. Not surprisingly, these issues often are the subject of intense negotiations among the studio, producer, and director. From the inception of ideas to the final cut, filmmaking almost invariably requires a series of such accommodations. The process demands that authors, screenwriters, producers, production designers, actors, composers, and directors, however much they prize their artistic integrity, make the adjustments and compromises necessary for the film to move ahead. The more time and effort they have invested in the project, the more powerful their incentive to compromise, especially if the problem is one that, if unresolved, would prevent the timely release of the film. If a dispute cannot be resolved, and the film is guaranteed by a completion bond, the issuer of the bond may step in and make the cuts and additions necessary to resolve the issue. In any case, the studio's final requirements are almost always met.

Once these changes have been made, and the studio has given its approval, negative cutters in the film lab cut the negative and make a duplicate for producing copies for theaters. The accountants, meanwhile, complete their final tally of the "negative cost." The lawyers then make sure all the necessary waivers, releases, and other legal documents have been signed by the producers, director, and other relevant parties.

At this point the movie moves into the studio's inventory, where, along with as many as twenty to thirty other unreleased films, it awaits distribution to the public. This wait can last for months, with the studio's clearinghouse adding interest onto the production's debt at the rate of 10 percent a year. During this holding period, if real events, such as wars, touch on the movie's plot in a way that might affect public reception, the studio might ask for even further changes.

By the time of the release, most of the film's participants, including the writers, producers, actors, and directors, have long since gone on to other things. The bitter and sweet experiences of the production, and the relationships they may have formed with one another—including friendships, romances, and enmities—if they are remembered at all, have by now faded. But the players, along with their video clips, press kits, and still photographs, are recalled to service once more at this point: to publicize the movie on television programs, in newspaper interviews, at trade shows, and, if all goes particularly well, at awards ceremonies.

☆ Part Three ☆

THE CREATION OF AUDIENCES

12

The Awareness Mission

In the era of the studio system, when Hollywood produced just a single product, movies, most Americans went to their neighborhood theater once a week and happily saw whatever was playing there. The studios then needed no advertising other than that of the movie title's on the theater's marquee, the likeness of the movie's stars on posters in the theater's lobby, a trailer of coming-attraction scenes from the movie shown on the theater's screens (all of which were free for the studios), and listings in local newspapers (for which theaters paid part of the cost).

But in the system that has replaced it, studios have to manufacture not only the movies but the audiences to watch them. In a world dominated by home-entertainment choices, including free television, the studios have to persuade millions of people each week to leave their homes, go to theaters several miles away, and buy tickets for a movie that they may have heard little, if anything, about. This feat, which in many ways is as challenging as producing the movie, is accomplished through the marketing campaign. "These days we supply multiplexes with two different products, movies and marketing campaigns," a top Sony executive explained. "And most large theater owners consider the latter one more important."

If a marketing campaign does not produce the expected opening-weekend audience, multiplexes will tend not to keep showing a film in their larger auditoriums—a move that, in turn, can further diminish the film's chances of success. Even more important to the studios, a film's success on opening weekend helps to determine its fate in video stores, since the video-chain buyers usually base the size of their orders on the size of the opening weekend's audience (assuming that a marketing campaign that worked for the theater audience will carry over to pull in video renters).

Consequently, studios spend a large proportion of their resources on marketing campaigns. In 2002 they invested nearly as much in world-wide advertising and prints as they did in making the movies themselves.

Such campaigns differ from those of branded products, such as Coca-Cola, Kellogg's Corn Flakes, and Colgate toothpaste, in that the campaigns for branded products do not need to succeed immediately; they can gradually condition people to respond to the brand name over years, and as time goes by, their message can be refined with the help of consumers' feedback. But film advertising has one shot at success: opening weekend at the multiplexes. The advertising message for a movie has to motivate people to leave their home, travel a substantial distance to a multiplex—the national average was fifteen miles in 2002—and, once there, select a particular movie from all the competing offerings. Since it is aimed at the opening weekend, the message cannot be refined based on consumer behavior. It either works on a given weekend or it fails.

As one studio executive explained it, "Movie marketing campaigns are like election campaigns. They not only have to get people to favor their candidates, they have to get them to do it on Election Day." To accomplish this feat, studios first have to identify a potential audience for each film. The initial categories they use, which coincide with those used by television stations and networks, are under or over twenty-five years old, male or female, and white or nonwhite. From these groups, a film's primary target audience is roughly defined—for example, white males under twenty-five. The studio's marketing division then works through focus groups and other surveys to further refine the group to which the film is most likely to appeal. Each film is assumed to have its own distinct potential audience. "If we release twenty-eight films, we need to create twenty-eight different audiences," a Sony marketing executive explained, which necessitates "twenty-eight different marketing campaigns."

The studio begins its marketing effort as soon as a project receives a green light. The marketing department then usually appoints a task force to superintend the creation of an audience for this film that does not yet exist. Its first job is to identify the composition of the film's most likely audience based on an analysis of the story, stars, and locales. Often the target audience is identified months before the actors arrive on the set.

The task force's next goal is to make a significant portion of the target audience aware of the future film. "First studios have to prepare the battlefields," a studio marketing vice president explained. "Even multi-million-dollar blitzkriegs of television ads can totally fail if those being bombarded are not already familiar with their existence." The preparation of these "battlefields" usually requires building some level of awareness, even if it is vague, of the film's title or its stars well before the paid advertising campaign emerges. This task is greatly facilitated if the audience is already familiar with the title or characters from another context. For example, because of their immense success as children's books, the Harry Potter films enjoyed high awareness among their targeted audience of males under eighteen even before they had been green-lighted. Similarly, as previously mentioned, productions that are part of a successful franchise series—such as *Spider-Man 2, X-Men 2, Die Hard 2, Austin Powers: The Spy Who Shagged Me*, the *Star Wars* sequels, and *James Bond* films—benefit from being well known to their intended audience. Even in these cases, the audience must be made aware that the characters will appear again in a new movie; but in the case of most other productions, in which the characters are nearly or completely unknown to potential moviegoers, the studio's publicity machines must create the awareness from scratch.

The studio's critical consciousness-raising exercise is usually accomplished with little, if any, paid advertising. As films go into production, studios assign publicity strategists the mission of obtaining free publicity for them. The principal means of doing this is planting stories in entertainment-news outlets—including *Entertainment Weekly, People, TV Guide,* and the E! channel, all of which are owned by the studios' corporate parents—which rely on gossip about celebrity stars to fill their pages or airtime. "The easy part is generating publicity about stars," a studio executive explained. "The hard part is focusing it on the production." Since stars often appear in competing films in the same period—Julia

Roberts, for example, starred in films made by Sony, Warner Bros., and DreamWorks in 2001—it is not sufficient merely to publicize the stars themselves; the publicity must be directly linked to the upcoming movie. To get these stories, therefore, entertainment reporters often have to agree simply to include references to the title or stars in ways that increase awareness of the upcoming production (and to omit references to competing movies that use the same stars).

Many magazines also need photographs of stars for their covers. The studios generally allocate photo opportunities with them to magazines that agree to conform to their conditions about the timing and content of the stories that accompany them. Not uncommonly, publicity staffs vet the resulting stories to make sure they do not mention any items, such as competitors' films, that might undermine the awareness mission. In accepting these conditions, these publications are regarded by the studios as "complicitous partners," as one studio executive described them.

The principal awareness instrument that the publicists have at their disposal, obviously, is the public reputation of the film's stars. As part of their arrangement with the studios, the stars effectively allow the studios to use their reputations to publicize their films. To this end, the studios script "back stories" that merge the stars' activities, real or invented, with those of the characters they play in the films. To limit the risk that any members of the cast might spread dissonant information that could undermine the scripted back stories, unit publicists are attached to the production to control actors' contacts with the media. All the crew and cast are also routinely required to sign nondisclosure agreements, or, as lawyers term it, they are "NDA-ed." The publicity back stories, meanwhile, are systematically planted in fan magazines, wire services, syndicated gossip columns, and other selected media. If successful, these items accumulate in the media's collective memory—now the electronic clip file—and can be reinforced in interviews, during which the stars themselves refer to them.

Consider *Mission: Impossible II*, for example, which was distributed by Paramount. Based on a television series that ran for more than ten years and on the prior movie *Mission: Impossible*, the title had high audience awareness even before it was green-lighted. So did the star, Tom Cruise. The strategy of Paramount's marketing campaign was to ineluctably link the star to the title so that all the publicity Cruise received in the months leading up to the release would remind people of the film. A back story was then scripted in which Cruise was seen to be indistinguishable from Ethan Hunt, the acrobatic hero he played, via the claim that he, and not a stunt double, had done the free falls, fire walks, motorcycle leaps, and other perilous stunts that Hunt did in the movie.

This back story was keynoted in a publicity short, *Mission Incredible,* shown on MTV and other cable channels owned by Paramount's corporate parent. Made in the style of a documentary in which the crew and cast of *Mission Impossible* are interviewed, it has the director, John Woo, expressing great fear that Tom Cruise would plunge to his death in leaps across mountaintops or be incinerated in fire scenes. Woo states, at one point, "Tom has no fear. I prayed for him." In another publicity short, Woo says, "Tom Cruise does most of his own stunts, so we did not need a stunt double."

In the actual production, there were at least six stunt doubles for Tom Cruise's part. Even if Cruise had possessed the skills and training to do the stunts himself, and even if the studio was not to object to the delays in shooting this conceit might cause, the insurance company, which insured Cruise as an "essential element" of the production, would not have allowed him to risk so much as an ankle sprain, much less his life. As far as this publicity script diverged from reality, however, it served its purpose by providing a plausible story for the entertainment media—"Tom Cruise is Ethan Hunt," and a tag line, "Expect the impossible again."

If successful, a solid back-story campaign increases the general awareness among those viewers who pay attention to the entertainment media. But for some movies, especially those looking to recruit children, a much wider audience is needed. Studios often seek this wider audience through tie-ins with mass merchandisers. As part of this arrangement, fast-food chains, such as McDonald's, Burger King, and Domino's Pizza, often give away toys, games, and souvenirs based on characters from future movies and advertise these gifts to potential customers. Although this publicity is not tied directly to the release date of the film, it serves, as one executive put it, "to alert millions of people that the film is coming." It has the added advantage of being fully paid for by the merchandising partner.

The problem for studios is that the number of films that qualify for these tie-in deals is limited by the merchandisers' strict requisites. From the merchandiser's perspective, tie-ins work by associating their businesses with the movie or its characters. Any film that would detract from their corporate image—such as ones with violence, sex, perceived perversity, controversial politics, or an irreverent worldview—is likely to be excluded from consideration. Those that qualify, such as Disney's animated films, usually appeal to a family audience and provide characters that are easy to admire.

Another means of raising awareness of a film is the teaser trailer. Unlike conventional coming-attractions trailers for movies that are already booked in the theaters, teasers, with tags such as "Coming this summer," are shown months before films are even scheduled (or in some cases even completed) and often shown in theaters that will not show the film when it is released. Usually no longer than three minutes, they are, for studios, a form of free advertising.

In the 1930s, coming-attraction trailers always followed the first movie of a double feature—hence the name "trailers"—and simply informed the weekly audience, usually with a few shots of the stars, about movies scheduled to arrive at theaters the following week. When the weekly audience began to wane, and movies had to compete with other media for the audience's attention, the trailer evolved into a more sophisticated marketing tool, one whose images, music, and words were designed to whet a specific audience's appetite for a particular movie: the coming attraction.

The marketing staff often begins work on the trailer even before production has been completed. They cull through the script, storyboards, and rough cut to find provocative images and words. Since their purpose is capturing the attention of a potential future audience, they have no compunction about using footage that might not actually be in the final film itself.

After arriving at the teaser theme, they usually contract out the job of creating a series of short teasers and the coming-attraction trailer to firms who specialize in promotional films. In 2001 the trailers for a single film generally cost somewhere between $300,000 and $800,000 to produce.

The trailers are then shown to focus groups and sample audiences to, as an audience-research executive explained it, "determine how well a given title sticks in the memory of moviegoers." If they do not have the requisite "stickiness," he added, the teasers are "tuned" or even "redone from scratch." When the studio is satisfied with the results from test audiences, it orders the necessary number of teaser prints, which can be costly if thousands of theaters are involved. It then has to persuade chain owners to use their limited preview time to show studio advertisements for future films that may ultimately be booked in competitors' theaters. "Getting multiplex chains to run our teasers for the right demographic audiences at the right time is a tricky business," one studio distribution chief explained. "It may involve leveraging our goodwill." Such "leveraging" may include denying theaters highly sought-after films unless they agree to run the studio's teasers. For example, when Warner Bros. released *Harry Potter and the Sorcerer's Stone,* which theaters believed would generate huge audiences, it required that the chains agree to play teaser trailers for other Warner Bros. movies. And even though theater owners often complain about the "pressure" to place teaser trailers long in advance of the release of the movies, they usually acquiesce to the big studios.

While this process is under way, the studio measures the results of its awareness campaign on a weekly basis via telephone polls of some twelve hundred "frequent moviegoers" supplied to them by the National Research Group (NRG). As has been previously discussed, NRG determines the age, sex, and, in some studies, ethnic background of the respondent. NRG's analysts then break the results for each film into four principal groups, or "quadrants": moviegoers under twenty-five, over twenty-five, male, and female. (The respondents are also divided by race in some cases.) The NRG then furnishes each studio with constant reports about awareness levels of particular upcoming movies in these different quadrants, as well as other data. When Peter Bart, the editor of *Variety,* was allowed to observe this process in 1999, he found that "the key players were awash in data on overall audience awareness plus the reaction of various demographic groups to the campaign, subject matter, even the ending and every other imaginable iteration that research could conjure up."

At a certain point, even though a release date has not yet been decided on, the studio's marketing staff decides that a large enough percentage of the target audience—usually over 60 percent—is aware of a film to justify going to the next phase of the marketing campaign: the audience drive.

The Drive

The last stage of the marketing campaign—the "drive"—is an advertising blitzkrieg whose full force comes in the two weeks preceding opening weekend. Unlike the leisurely awareness mission that takes advantage of free publicity opportunities, the audience drive is short and intense, and relies primarily on television ads, which are extremely expensive. Taking its name from the cattle drives of the American West, it requires getting herds of potential moviegoers, already primed by the awareness campaign, to leave the comfort of their homes on a particular weekend and head for a movie.

This final act in the marketing scenario is a relatively recent development. When studios were first finding it necessary to create audiences, they limited their marketing efforts to using the stars, and items about the stars, to generate free publicity. Even up until the mid-1980s, according to one top marketing executive, "the business was basically publicity-driven." But with multiplexes narrowing the window of opportunity for a movie to succeed to its opening weeks, and video buyers pegging their advance orders to turnouts in an even shorter period, studios can no longer hope to find their audience solely through fortuitous publicity and favorable word-of-mouth reports. Instead, as one executive said, studios now rely on purchased advertising spots that can be "directed to desired audiences."

The studios have found that the single most effective medium for reaching potential moviegoers is network television. Geoffrey Ammer, the president of marketing for Sony Pictures, explained, "When you do research and try to figure out why people came to a movie, the main source [of information] is always television."

Since broadcast networks, with their affiliates, can blanket nationwide audiences with bursts of commercial messages on any given date, they are now, as one studio executive described it, the "key driver" of all the studios' national campaigns. In 2003 the studios spent $3.4 billion on television advertising. About two thirds of that sum went to the six networks—NBC, CBS, ABC, FOX, UPN, and Warner Bros.—and stations owned by the studios' parent companies. Although this network and spot advertising is extremely expensive, it allows the studios' marketing arms to meticulously orchestrate their campaigns.

Depending on the audience sought, television ads on cable networks can also be a good bet. Cable television is more "laser-beamed," as one executive put it, to specific audiences and is therefore used by studios when movies mainly appeal to an identifiable group, such as teenage males. In 2003 the studios spent $720 million on cable-television ads.

To make these ads cost-effective, the marketing task force must devise a suitable "hook" that, when encapsulated in a brief commercial, will make the television viewer not only want to see this movie but choose to see it as soon as it opens. The graphic icon must also be memorable enough to trigger impulse buyers, as, for example, the image of Arnold Schwarzenegger cocking a rocket launcher and saying "Hasta la vista, baby" proved in selling *Terminator 2*. "The trick is to hit the right button at the right time," one executive explained.

The search for the hook requires elaborate testing of the most promising images on the targeted audience through interviews, focus groups, and even test screenings in which individuals are hooked into polygraph machines to measure their involuntary responses. Once a satisfactory "hook" is found, the studio has its ad agency design television commercials, usually thirty seconds long.

Next, the head of marketing and other top studio executives assemble in a "war council," as one marketing vice president called it, to decide on the amount of money that will be committed to the drive, a decision that will determine the proportion of the targeted audience that will be covered, called the "reach," and the number of times the ads will be played, called the "frequency." Since a single thirty-second commercial on a network program with a reach that covers a nationwide audience can cost as much as $300,000—and, to be effective, studios reckon that the ad must have a frequency of at least eight times—this can be an extremely expensive decision.

To help the war council determine the reach and frequency of the ads, the marketing task force gets tracking data from the NRG on their effectiveness in test markets. If it finds that a significant portion of those aware of the film say they do not intend to see it, they assume the hook in the test ad is not working. The war council may then decide to "triage" the movie by cutting the advertising budget and reducing the number of screens on which it will open, as Warner Bros. did in 2002 with *The Adventures of Pluto Nash.* As a result, even though the film had major star Eddie Murphy in it, it earned less than $2.5 million in worldwide rentals.

If the results show the hook is effective with test audiences, however, the war council may authorize a full "blitz." With eight times the coverage of a target audience for a wide-opening film, advertising costs for a blitz ran between $15 million and $20 million in 2002.

Television advertising is also used to support television talk shows, notably *The Tonight Show with Jay Leno* and the *Late Show with David Letterman,* that show clips and interview stars about their newly opened films. This noncommercial exposure is considered particularly valuable for attracting young adult viewers. "Letterman and Leno act for us as highly effective prods, especially with young adult audiences," a Viacom executive explained, "so we are happy to support them."

Similarly, studios advertise heavily on MTV and other music-video channels to encourage them to play videos from the movie during its opening week.

In all, the drive can cost the studio upward of $30 million. Before it can be launched, the war council must pick the all-important opening date.

D Day

The most critical decision that the studio's distribution arm makes is the date on which a film will open. "That is D day for us," said a top Fox distribution executive. "It can make or break a movie."

The reality that all the studios' distribution arms must confront is that not all opening dates are equal. Those nine months between September and May when schools are in session generally promise only a fraction of the audience possible during the three months in the summer, when a large population of children and teenagers are free to go to the movies every day. (The only exceptions to this rule are Christmas, Thanksgiving, and other extended holidays.) The difference in box-office receipts between summer and the rest of the year can be enormous. Films released over Memorial Day weekend, for example, usually have at least three times the opening-weekend audience of those released in October.

Studios also may have films in their inventories that it is advantageous to open only during certain weeks. Children's films, for example, are assumed to do best during holiday periods, such as Christmas and Thanksgiving, when both children and parents are free to attend movies. Films may be geared to specific holidays, such as *Independence Day, The Santa Clause,* and

Halloween, or to entire seasons, such as the summer surfing movie *Blue Crush* and winter skiing movie *Aspen Extreme.* Studios may also be obligated to open films with merchandise tie-ins at a particular time that coincides with the merchandiser's sales schedule. Warner Bros., for example, had made deals with merchandisers to open *Terminator 3* on July 4, 2003. "Our job is to find the optimum slot in the calender for each film," a distribution executive from Warner Bros. explained, "although we might not get it."

The reason that a studio may not get the optimum opening slots for a given film is that another studio may want the same slot for a film that is competing for an audience of the same age, sex, and ethnic composition. "What are we fighting about," the joke among distributors goes, "if we all want the same thing?" The answer, of course, is that if two studios schedule competing movies on the same opening dates, and want the same audience, their television ads may run on the same programs at the same time and confuse, or "cross-pressure," their targeted audience. As a result, both films might get only part of a smaller total audience. "In a head-on collision," one Disney executive said, "no one wins."

To win, it will be recalled, studios often avoid such conflicts, yielding to one another. Since direct discussions among the studios that result in dividing up the opening slots might risk violating the antitrust consent decrees, each studio largely relies on the weekly "competitive positioning" report it gets from the NRG to coordinate openings of competitive films. From the report's breakdown of upcoming movies' relative appeal to different age, sex, and ethnic groups, studios can see how their films would fare against competing films appealing to the same audience groups. In addition, they have advance intelligence from theater chains and trade newspapers as to when competing films are planning to open.

When two studios see that their competing films are headed for opening on the same weekend, both have to reconsider that date, since, as a Sony executive said, "there is no longer a clear path for the advertising drive." The studio whose film has the weaker appeal to the target audience has a strong incentive to change its slot, since if the NRG numbers prove correct, it stands to get a smaller share of a confused and cross-pressured audience and will probably fail. By moving such films to another weekend, even if it is a less optimal one for audience size, they give their marketing campaigns a better chance to succeed in getting a large part of that smaller audience to turn out.

To avoid such a collision, usually, but not always, the studio with the weaker film yields. In some cases, the executives of competing studios may meet socially to reach an accommodation. For example, in 2002, Disney's subsidiary Miramax had a direct conflict with DreamWorks SKG concerning the openings of their two competing films, *Gangs of New York* and *Catch Me If You Can*, both starring Leonardo DiCaprio and both scheduled to open on December 25. Even though the Miramax film *Gangs* had a slightly higher "awareness" level in the targeted "males-over-twenty-five" quadrant in the competitive positioning report, DreamWorks refused to yield. At that point, Harvey Weinstein, the president of Miramax, and Jeffrey Katzenberg, a founding partner of DreamWorks SKG, had breakfast in New York to discuss their movies' "release dates," as Katzenberg later explained in an interview with *The New York Times*. "[Weinstein] and I had many conversations about why releasing the movies on the same day was in none of our interest . . . as both companies have a big investment in Leo DiCaprio." A few days later Miramax moved *Gangs of New York* to a different, and less favorable, opening date. Whatever means of persuasion are employed, the result is that films that directly compete against each other rarely open on the same weekend.

Once an opening date is decided upon, the final elements in the scenario are rapidly nailed into place. To begin with, the distribution division lines up the theaters in which the film will open. This is no small task. Openings generally require booking between 1,500 and 3,500 screens, depending on how "wide" they are. To minimize competition for the same audiences, the studios divide the country into geographic zones, which contain anywhere between 100,000 and 400,000 people each. In each zone, a theater, which may have many screens, is given an exclusive license to show each film.

Distributors deal mainly with chains. In 2002 over two thirds of the multiplexes at which studio movies premiered were owned by five national chains—Cineplex Odeon, KKR Regal, Carmel, AMC, and United Artist Cinemas—which fiercely negotiate, among other things, the division of box-office revenue; the "house allowance," which is the fixed sum that will be paid to the theaters regardless of ticket sales; and the minimum length of the run. Although distributors are prevented by the consent decree of the antitrust settlement from connecting these negotiations with the promise of future films, they have considerable tacit leverage, since the theater chains depend on them to favor them with major blockbusters. As a result, the big studios almost always get the screens they need for their openings.

Meanwhile, the theater-relations staff in the distribution division swings into action, providing each theater with lobby posters, press kits for local reporters, and other paraphernalia that might help the film. It dispatches dozens of representatives, who spend time cultivating theater managers, to make sure the theaters are carrying out these promotions, including playing the coming-attraction trailer at prominent times.

The studio also has to make the requisite number of prints for theaters in time for the opening. The cost of the prints depends on the length of the film, but the average in 2003 was $1,500 a film. The prints are then shipped to the studio's film exchanges across the country to be transferred to reels, checked for defects, and await D day.

As this is taking place, the studio's media buyers are feverishly buying space on network programs and cable channels that reach a large part of the targeted demographic audience. If, for example, they are seeking a middle-class teenage audience, they will buy time on network programs such as *The O.C.;* if they are looking for a male audience, they will advertise on sports programs such as *SportsCenter;* if a black youth audience is what they are after, they will buy time on cable programs such as *Music Box Videos.*

Finally, to support the blitz, studios spend heavily on newspaper advertisements just prior to opening. Such ads often carry, aside from the location and times of the showings, quotes from critics and entertainment reporters that the publicists have culled from reviews. The largest beneficiaries of this advertising are two newspapers: *The New York Times,* which in 2001 received $156 million from the studios, and the *Los Angeles Times,* which received $106 million. Even though display ads in these two newspapers may reach only a small part of the targeted audience, especially for youth-oriented films, the papers are important to Hollywood because of the prestige their special Sunday entertainment sections can confer on movies. They can, as a Sony marketing executive noted, "not only establish movies as events, but New York and L.A. is where the stars and directors live." For those reasons, studios are often obliged, sometimes in contractual form, to place ads in, and cultivate goodwill with, these newspapers.

As D day approaches, the studio's marketing department does whatever it can to further increase audience awareness. Such measures include creating individual websites for films, renting billboards, and distributing T-shirts. To get advance news stories and reviews, studios often fly dozens of entertainment reporters on junkets to hotels or specially chosen locations where they are granted brief "revolving-door" interviews with the stars and other notables of the film. Before the extraterrestrial fantasy film *Independence Day* opened in 1996, for example, Twentieth Century–Fox publicists bussed more than one hundred journalists to Rachel, Nevada, to Area 51 on Highway 375—a place where the U.S. military had conducted a "top secret alien study project," according to a Twentieth Century–Fox newsletter. In fact, there is no such project, but as part of the "news event," the publicists arranged for the governor of Nevada, Bob Miller, to dedicate Highway 375 as an "Extraterrestrial Highway," where aliens would be granted safe haven. The studio also unveiled for the press a monument intended to serve as a beacon to guide aliens to Nevada. The press junket may have been an absurd exercise, but it was also successful, resulting in more than one hundred news stories prior to the film's release.

Publicists also arrange hundreds of screenings for film critics and distribute electronic press kits to television stations. If they have succeeded in their mission, the stars will appear on magazine covers and in entertainment-news reports, as well as on television talk shows.

Just prior to D day, the targeted audience is blanketed over and over again with the same spot ads on television programs. Then, the night before the film opens, the reels are sent by UPS trucks to thousands of multiplexes across the country.

Whether the drive has succeeded or failed is decided by one thing: how many "voters" elect to see the movie on its opening weekend.

Part Four

THE ECONOMIC LOGIC OF HOLLYWOOD

The Popcorn Economy

Once the studios open their films in theaters across the United States and Canada, they have little control over how their products will be exhibited, since the chains that operate the multiplexes have their own economic considerations.

Back in the era of the studio system, the theaters, owned or controlled by studios, had a single purpose: to harvest admissions for studio films. To this end, they were vast palaces capable of seating several thousand ticket buyers at a single showing—the Paramount in New York, for example, could seat four thousand people—and to lure audiences to these films, they also featured on their stages live performances of famous singers like Frank Sinatra, big-name bands like Duke Ellington's, and chorus lines like the Roxy Ice Show. They could also extend the tenure of a film for as long as it generated money for the studio—sometimes nine months or more. Even the neighborhood theater, under this arrangement, acted as an outlet for studio products.

The multiplexes that replaced these theaters, most of which are owned by a handful of national chains, have a very different relationship with the studios. They are in three different, and sometimes conflicting, businesses. First, they are in the concession business, keeping for themselves all the proceeds from the sale of popcorn, soda, and other snacks. Second, they are in the movie-exhibition business, showing movies and paying out a large share of the admission proceeds to the films' distributors. Finally, they are in the advertising business, selling time on their screens prior to movie showings.

Their principal profit comes not from selling tickets or screen advertising but from selling refreshments. Popcorn, because of the immense amount of popped bulk produced from a relatively small amount of corn kernels—the ratio is as high as sixty to one—yields more than ninety cents of profit on every dollar's worth sold. It also makes customers thirsty for sodas, another high-margin product, especially if it is heavily laden with salt. As one theater executive pointed out, adding extra salt to the topping is the "secret" to running a successful multiplex chain.

It is no accident that most theaters are designed to shepherd ticket buyers past the concession stand on their way to the auditorium. "We are really in the business of people moving," one theater owner explained. "The more people we move past the popcorn, the more money we make." He described the cup holder mounted on each seat, which allows customers to park their soda while returning to the concession stand for more popcorn, as "the most important technological innovation since sound."

This lucrative popcorn traffic is threatened whenever ticket sales decline. No matter what other merits a movie may have, or how favorable its reviews, multiplexes cannot afford to keep it in a premium auditorium if it does not generate enough traffic. Multiplexes usually move such movies to smaller auditoriums (if they are contractually bound to play them), reduce the number of showing times, or cancel them entirely. Here the interest of theater chains in maximizing their popcorn traffic and the interest of the studios (which do not share in the popcorn business) often conflict. Studios, who have already spent tens of millions of dollars in prints and advertising, want to keep their films in the larger auditoriums as long as possible so that they can earn back this investment. Even having their films and trailers shown in partly filled auditoriums is better than having them replaced by those of their competitors.

Studios therefore provide theaters a monetary incentive to extend films' showings, giving theater owners a progressively larger share of the box-office take for every week the film plays. The usual arrangement is for theaters to keep only 10 percent of the box office the opening week in addition to a "house allowance," which amounts to a flat rental fee for their theater. With the house allowance factored in, the studio generally winds up with between 70 and 80 percent of the box-office revenue for the first two weeks. The theaters' percentage then increases, often by 10 percent per week, until by the fourth or fifth week the theaters are getting most of the box office.

Despite their smaller share of the opening-week's box office, multiplex chains generally stand to make much more money during that week because the studios' television advertising tends to attract a larger proportion of the main popcorn consumers: teenagers. After the advertising blitz stops—usually after the opening week—popcorn sales often begin to diminish. As a consequence, theater chains often move films out soon after the opening. In 2001 the average time a studio film remained in multiplexes was only three weeks.

No matter how strong—or weak—the opening, if the audience declines substantially by a film's second weekend, multiplex owners assume that the word of mouth is not sufficiently positive, and move quickly to either switch those movies to smaller auditoriums or replace them with newly opening films. This harsh fate applies even to films that had near-record openings—as was the case with *Godzilla*—and is even harsher for films that don't open well. Even when studios contractually mandate a minimum number of weekends, multiplexes can usually manage to cancel showings without any legal consequences, especially given that studios need to maintain good relations with them for the sake of their future films. (Occasionally, as with the movie *My Big Fat Greek Wedding*, the word of mouth continues to create an audience even after the publicity and talk-show interviews have petered out. But in most cases the audience wanes, and the multiplexes arrange to return the prints to the studios' film exchanges. For such films, it is the beginning of the end of their domestic distribution.)

For their audience-maximizing strategy to work, multiplexes require many auditoriums, or "screens," of different seating capacities. A film that generates a high volume of traffic can be shown on multiple screens at staggered times to produce a constant stream of consumers past the popcorn stand. *The Lost World: Jurassic Park*, for example, opened at many multiplexes on four adjacent screens, with a starting time of every half hour.

Many multiplexes now have twenty or more "screens" of relatively small seating capacity. This development was greatly influenced by the Americans with Disabilities Act of 1990, which requires that theaters with more than three hundred seats provide wheelchair access to all the seats. Since providing such access requires about one-third more space for the necessary ramps, theater owners usually do not build auditoriums with more than three hundred seats. The minimum size is determined by the distance between the projection booth and the screen. Because this usually requires at least ten rows of ten seats, multiplex theaters rarely have fewer than one hundred seats.

Even with multiple screens, theaters are able to keep costs down by using a single projectionist for a number of films. Not uncommonly, one projectionist services up to eight movies, an economy of scale that saves seven salaries. While these projectionists are able to change reels for one film while other movies go unattended, in doing so they run the risk that the other films might momentarily snag in the projector and get burnt by the projector lamp. To prevent such costly mishaps, multiplexes frequently have their projectionists slightly expand the gap between the gate that supports the film and the lamp. As a result of providing this margin of safety, films are often shown slightly out of focus. "Efficiency requires trade-offs," in the words of one multiplex owner, who found in the case of his eight hundred screens that "audiences of teenagers don't care about blurry pictures so long as films are action-packed and loaded with special effects." The same assumption often leads multiplex managers to delay changing projector-lamp bulbs that do not produce the specified level of brightness on screens. By less frequently changing these bulbs, which cost over $1,000 apiece, multiplex chains can save hundreds of thousands of dollars a year. The result, of course, is that movies are darker than the directors intended.

While these "efficiencies" benefit the theaters, they can harm the studios, which depend heavily on positive word of mouth once a film opens. If the picture quality is degraded by out-of-focus and darkened projection, audience enjoyment—and therefore word of mouth—may suffer, and the movie will be less "playable" as a result. Studios, however, are dependent on theaters' cooperation and their standards when it comes to the quality of projection.

The theaters' advertising business also presents a potential conflict with the studios. Theaters earn substantial profits by selling screen ads that are shown during the twenty or so minutes between movies. A single firm, such as Coca-Cola, may pay chains more than $50,000 a screen annually to advertise its products. Since there are virtually no costs involved in showing ads, the proceeds go directly to the theaters' bottom line.

For their part, studios also have an obvious interest in advertising their upcoming films on the screens of theaters during that same brief period between showings. Since the studios do not pay the theaters to play trailers—an arrangement that dates back to the time when studios owned theaters—they are "free advertising," as one chain owner termed it.

Some of these trailers directly benefit the chains, since they promote films that are scheduled to open in their theaters, but others may not. For example, as noted earlier, teaser trailers may be for films that will open in rival theaters. Not only do such trailers potentially put theaters in a position of giving free screen time to advertising a film that they will not show, but they take up time that might otherwise be profitably sold to paying advertisers.

In any event, most films at the multiplexes produce rapidly diminishing returns as far as the studios are concerned. Not only does their share of box-office receipts decrease with every succeeding week, while the cost of repairing and servicing prints increases, but it becomes progressively more difficult for studios to collect their rental fees. Not uncommonly, theater owners, claiming grievances—real or imagined—withhold payments and ask the studios to renegotiate the deal. Since legal redress is generally impractical, and the chains' screens are needed for trailers to advertise future films, a settlement is usually reached or the debts just remain on the studios' books. As one former Fox executive noted, "At some point, it's cheaper simply to recall the prints."

Since theaters owners operate according to their own, popcorn-based economic logic, studios have to take this into account in making their movies. One concern is running time. If a movie's length exceeds 128 minutes, theater owners will lose one show an evening. On weekends this reduces the number of their evening audience "turns" from three to two, which means 33 percent fewer customers. Aside from losing revenue from the box office (which they divide with the studios), the theaters also risk losing a significant portion of the popcorn-and-beverage sales on which they depend for their profits. In the case of a major "event" film, such as Disney's *Pearl Harbor*, which is accompanied by massive publicity, multiplex theater owners may willingly take this risk, but in other cases they may elect to show films longer than 128 minutes in their smaller auditoriums, thereby reducing the chance that these films will draw a large opening-weekend audience. Consequently, studios often ask the director to cut the film so it will not exceed 128 minutes.

Another concern is ratings. For virtually every film, the MPAA issues a rating that theaters must abide by. Its G ("general audiences") and PG or PG-13 ("parental guidance") ratings permit anyone to buy a ticket to theaters. Its restricted ratings—R (for "restricted"), which excludes all children and younger teenagers who are not accompanied by an adult, and its NC-17 (no children), which excludes anyone under the age of seventeen—are usually assigned to a film if the rating board deems that the nudity in it is too graphic, the violence excessive, or the language too profane.

Restricted ratings can present a major problem for multiplex theaters, because they are legally responsible for excluding part of the audience. In practice, this means that some number of theater employees, who might otherwise be selling popcorn and soda, are required to check the identity documents of the teenage audience. These restrictions not only reduce the size of the theater's audience but can cause disputes with its regular patrons. To avoid this loss of business and the attendant inconvenience, especially during holiday periods when the audience is at its peak, many theater owners resist booking such films—at least in their larger auditoriums. In addition, if a film receives a PG-13, R, or NC-17 rating, Nickelodeon, Disney, and the other children-oriented cable networks will not accept TV ads for it. As a result, studios have found that the more restrictive the rating, the less money a film is likely to generate in the theaters.

So, before approving the release, studio executives consult with the rating board. Through negotiations that can be prolonged and arduous, they determine the words, images, or even entire scenes that may have to be deleted to get the rating they want. They then demand that the director or producer make the necessary cuts. Even directors who claim the right to make the "final cut," such as Oliver Stone, often comply. In the case of *Natural Born Killers*, for example, the producers received a detailed memorandum from the studio, Warner Bros., specifying objectionable material. Stone made the specified cuts, and the film was resubmitted, but the MPAA board then had further complaints. "In the end we had to go back to the MPAA five times and make a hundred and fifty cuts in the film in order to get the R rating that we were obligated to deliver," producer Jane Hamsher noted. "It completely destroyed the whole pace and rhythm of the film." In some cases these modifications are extremely expensive. To get an R rating for Stanley Kubrick's *Eyes Wide Shut*, Warner Bros. had to pay for a CG studio to digitally insert figures that obscured the full frontal nudity in an orgy scene. The bill for these digital fig leaves was anything but modest: it reportedly ran to more than $500,000.

A third concern for the studios is ensuring that films aimed at the critically important teenage male audience have enough action sequences not to disappoint it. Part of the studio's "mission," as one Universal executive put it, is to provide multiplexes "with movies, when school is out, that deliver the teenage male audience they need for their concession stands." Since the observation of test audiences of youth over many years has demonstrated that this particular audience heavily prefers action to dialogue, studios may require that directors add dialogue-free sequences to summer movies that lack the requisite quota of pure action. For example, after Universal had scheduled *The Bourne Identity* to open in June 2002, its executives discovered from test-group results that the film lacked the number of action scenes necessary to pull in a young, male summer audience, so they ordered director Doug Liman to reassemble the cast in Paris and shoot additional scenes, including a taut confrontation on a bridge, a blazing fire, and a gun battle on a digitally created five-story staircase. The additional studio-mandated scenes, which took two weeks to shoot, replaced almost twenty minutes of more cerebral scenes and gave the film the action-packed finale necessary to qualify it, at least in the view of multiplex owners, as a summer film.

Finally, beyond the goal of accommodating theater owners, studios also have a concern in creating a favorable perception of their products with moviegoers themselves, since the successful launching of a film depends not only on recruiting an initial audience through advertising but on its word of mouth once the initial audience leaves the theater. Studios find negative word of mouth greatly diminishes future audiences, even the next night of opening weekends—a falloff that is especially pronounced with critical teenage audiences. Moreover, audience studies show that much of the negative reaction traces directly back to moviegoers' dissatisfaction with the way the story resolves itself at the end—for example, whether the hero's fate is life or death, love or rejection, capture or freedom. To avoid such potential badmouthing, studios test-screen early versions of their movies, often with different endings, among their target audiences. *Fatal Attraction*, for example, was test-screened with no fewer than four different endings. When a test-screen audience shows appreciably more dissatisfaction with the original ending than alternative endings, studio executives often require that directors change the ending.

———

For all its tensions, the popcorn economy is a reality studios have learned to live with. Indeed, in accommodating multiplexes, studios largely serve their own interests—especially if they manage to get the large opening-weekend numbers they've been hoping for: a large audience turnout is widely reported in the trade press and manages to impress the gatekeepers of foreign, video, and other ancillary markets.

Alien Territory

Since a film's earnings from the domestic market are largely offset by the massive cost of the initial advertising campaign, studios have to look abroad to begin to earn back their immense investments. While they distribute their films in more than one hundred countries, just a few of those account for the lion's share of their overseas earnings. In 2003, eight countries—Japan, Britain, Germany, France, Spain, Mexico, Italy, and Australia—provided most of the foreign revenues for the major studios (Table 4). Consequently, the studios' principal focus is on these eight countries.

To ensure that their films are well situated in these markets, studios rely on distribution arms under their control. Two studios, Paramount and Universal, jointly control the largest overseas distributor, United International Pictures (UIP). This joint venture distributes, aside from the two studios' own films, the films of DreamWorks, USA, Lion's Gate, and other independent producers. The other studios have their own distributors—Disney's Buena Vista International, Sony's Columbia TriStar Film Distributors International, News Corporation's Fox International, and Time Warner's Warner Bros. Pictures International (which also distrib-

TABLE 4. MAJOR STUDIO REVENUE FROM 8 TOP FOREIGN MARKETS, 2003
(MILLIONS OF U.S. DOLLARS)

Country	Theater Rentals
Japan	450
Germany	392
Britain	344
Spain	248
France	242
Australia	166
Italy	154
Mexico	124
Total, 8 Countries	2,120
Total, All Overseas Markets (Excluding Canada)	3,272

utes New Line and HBO films). These five international distributors, working either alone or through local companies, distribute almost all American films abroad. The only exceptions are so-called presales, instances in which a particular market is sold to raise financing. For example, the producers of *Terminator 3* sold the Japanese market to Tojo Films for $12 million, while the rest of foreign distribution went to Sony.

Like their domestic-distribution arms, the studios' international distributors book theaters, organize marketing campaigns, circulate prints, and collect money abroad. But unlike their domestic counterparts, they must design separate campaigns for each of the eight major markets. These markets, while potentially lucrative, are also far more complicated to service. For one thing, the distributors have to make sure that their films meet local standards. For example, in Germany, where American films accounted for over 85 percent of the box office in 2003, local censorship laws restrict theaters from showing realistic violence, though not nudity. In Italy, on the other hand, local censorship laws allow violence but not graphic nudity. Aside from attending to government censorship, distributors also have to make sure that no parts of the film conflict with religious, social, or political taboos in any of the cultures in which they will be shown. Not uncommonly, the studios custom-edit films for different markets. In some cases, they may also add material—for example, Fox added a scene of a Japanese press conference for the Japanese version of *Independence Day*—but usually the reediting involves no more than deleting scenes that may possibly offend moviegoers in a particular country.

The distributors also have to deal with language barriers in most foreign countries. Not only do they have to dub or subtitle the films, but they must have the publicity material translated as well. These translations must be carefully vetted to make sure that the words or idioms do not carry any unintended meanings. The soundtracks then have to be remixed for each version.

Next the distributors need to make hundreds of new prints for all the major markets (with the possible exception of English-speaking countries, such as Britain and Australia). They need to insure them, ship them via air freight, and clear them through customs. This involves a huge advance investment. For *Gone in 60 Seconds*, the cost of foreign prints, shipping, translations, and customs clearance was $12.7 million.

Scheduling is also complex. Distributors have to take into account weather, holidays, and other particulars of different parts of the world. For example, in countries in Asia, Africa, and Latin America, which have many open-air theaters, rainy seasons can create what one executive termed seasonal "wastelands." Even in Japan, which has the highest admission prices in the world, many theaters lack air-conditioning, making them inhospitable venues in the torrid summers. As a result, distributors in Japan aim their films with the largest potential at dates in the holiday periods that occur during the cooler months, such as the winter New Year and the springtime Golden Week.

To get the choicest play dates, distributors often have to deal with theater chains that have a near monopoly in their region. In Japan, for example—which in 2003 provided American studios with one seventh of their total foreign revenues—two theater chains, Tojo and Schokeda, control about 90 percent of the theaters suitable for international films. Not only do they have what amounts to a duopoly of theater ownership, but they both also produce films for their own theaters. To persuade them to yield the better holiday dates to Hollywood films, the international distributors must offer them films with proven appeal to their principal audience, which is teenagers. (To provide an alternative to the terms offered by the duopoly, one distributor, UIP, began building its own theaters in Japan in the 1990s.)

Finally, once the films are booked, the distributors have the Herculean task of organizing separate advertising campaigns in Europe, Asia, and Latin America. In each country, media buyers, advertising agencies, publicists, and a message or "hook" must be found for each film. Moreover, distributors have only limited resources for this job. Studios generally budget to foreign marketing only a fraction of the amount they budget for the United States and Canada. For one thing, advertising is less efficient at reaching foreign audiences than it is at reaching American audiences. "To get the same coverage of an audience abroad as America by television," one Fox executive said, "we would have to spend an extra fifty million a picture, and that would wipe out our profits overseas."

Consider again the instructive example of *Gone in 60 Seconds*. For North America, Disney spent $42 million on advertising and publicity. For the rest of the world, it spent $25.2 million. This latter sum included $6.5 million for Japan, $3.1 million for Germany, $2.5 million for Britain, $1.4 million for France, $1.1 million for Australia, $997,000 for Spain, $915,000 for Italy, $820,000 for South Korea, $769,000 for Brazil, $648,000 for Mexico, and $520,000 for Taiwan. The remaining $6 million was spent in sixty other markets. To increase these foreign expenditures to the level of American coverage, Disney would have to have spent, according to a producer's estimate, another $60 million.

Even in the most important markets, like Japan, Germany, and Britain, distributors rarely have enough money to blanket their target television audience the way they do in the United States. Overseas, even on their most promising films, studios usually cannot afford such exposures.

Consequently, the international distributors have little choice but to rely on unpaid publicity to supplement their paid advertising. The most effective vehicle for this is the fame of—and, ideally, appearances by— the films' stars. Not surprisingly, if films do not have major stars with international appeal, they often do not receive favorable play dates and consequently lose money abroad. Consider, for example, the 1997 drama *Midnight in the Garden of Good and Evil*, directed by Clint Eastwood. The film's principal actors—John Cusack, Jude Law, and Kevin Spacey—

had only limited recognition in a number of foreign markets. The $39 million film opened in only a handful of theaters in Japan, Australia, Korea, Italy, Brazil, and other major markets; and even though the distributor, Warner Bros. International, spent $6 million for foreign advertising and prints, it produced only $3.1 million at foreign box offices, leaving Warner Bros. with a $2.9 million loss on its foreign distribution.

Stars with name recognition are the principal means by which studios can increase their share of revenues from abroad, especially if the stars are willing to make personal appearances. Often such appearances are stipulated in a star's contract. Arnold Schwarzenegger's contract for *Terminator 3*, for example, required that he "shall make himself available for at least ten days, including travel days (a minimum of seven days for foreign and three days for domestic) of publicity and promotional activities in coordination with the initial theatrical release of the Picture in both the domestic and foreign territories." The contract further specified that these promotional appearances would include "television and radio appearances, photo sessions, interviews, appearances at premieres, Internet appearances (i.e. online interviews and chat room sessions), and similar activities." (Even when contracts stipulate "without limitation," stars usually have the right, as Schwarzenegger did, to approve "the selection and scheduling of all promotion and publicity activities," a provision that gives them considerable discretion over when and where they will satisfy their contractual obligations.)

When studios cannot exert contractual pressure on stars to make foreign appearances, they must resort to an appeal to the stars' self-interest. Stars who have a share of the gross rentals, or even of the net profits, obviously stand to make more money if the film does well worldwide. In trying to make the case for stars' participation in foreign publicity, a senior executive at Fox used a PowerPoint presentation to demonstrate to stars' agents why studios could not afford to buy the same eightfold coverage of target audiences overseas that it bought in the United States. His message was that if stars did not cooperate by supplementing this limited advertising budget with their own free appearances, their earnings, and those of their agents, would be greatly diminished.

Whether or not this logic is accepted by stars, studios have been increasingly successful in recruiting them for publicity tours in some, if not all, foreign countries. "Studios now expect that for the twenty million dollars they pay stars, the stars will help them open their films abroad," the head of a major talent agency explained. "Even if it's not written in the contract, it's part of the deal." When stars commit themselves in advance to such trips abroad, it helps not only with the publicity but also with distribution, since star attendance is an inducement for getting better opening dates.

A further wrinkle in the foreign-marketing game plan is that overseas publicity trips often occur a year or more after films have been completed, and overseas openings may occur many months apart. For stars, this usually means interrupting their work on newer productions to travel to far-flung parts of the world to publicize characters that may be no more than a distant memory to them. Even when they are supplied with private jets, large hotel suites, and other travel amenities, many stars find this aspect of their work "onerous," as one agency head put it.

Even with the strenuous demands of today's foreign markets, with all their particular requirements—not the least of which is finding stars who are willing and able to cooperate in complex marketing schemes in a half dozen countries—the benefits are deemed well worth the costs. Not only do successful foreign openings bring revenue into a studio's clearinghouse—indeed, in 2003 foreign revenue exceeded domestic revenue—but they also constitute a crucial part of the groundwork for the global video, television, and other licensing sales that follow the theatrical release.

The DVD Revolution

In the days of the studio system, movies would play in first-run theaters and then, months later, migrate to neighborhood theaters. In the present system, movies play in multiplexes for only a few weeks and reopen months later in video stores. In an average week in 2002, some 50 million Americans—more than twice the weekly movie audience—went to one of the country's more than thirty thousand local video stores to rent a movie, spending some $24 billion, approximately four times what they spent on movie tickets. (The ratio was even higher abroad.) In addition, videos are now sold in supermarkets and other retail outlets. Sumner Redstone described it as "the bonanza that saved Hollywood from bankruptcy."

Although few would now dispute Redstone's assessment, initially the major studios did not view videos in such a favorable light. Indeed, when videocassettes were introduced in the mid-1970s, it will be recalled, the studios, led by Lew Wasserman at Universal, viewed the home video player (VCR) as a threat to theater attendance, which had fallen from 90 million a week in 1948 to less than 22 million a week in 1978. Concerned that home videos would further divert potential moviegoers from theaters, the studios attempted to strangle the new medium with litigation. They still failed to appreciate that the shift in the audience from theaters to home viewing was irreversible and consequently their future was in home entertainment. In 1979 Fox sold the video rights to its library for a mere $8 million to a company called Magnafilm (which it then had to buy back); Columbia, after rejecting a proposal to create a video division after its president, Fay Vincent, equated the video business with "pornography," assigned the video rights to its library to RCA; MGM sold the video rights to its library to Ted Turner; and Disney put its library of animated features off-limits to video.

If not for the iron-willed determination of Sony's Akio Morita, who fought the studios through the American courts and won, the VCR might not have become a ubiquitous part of American homes and there might not now exist a massive video market to support the very studios that tried to kill it.

The Video Revolution

Before that 1984 Supreme Court decision, less than 10 percent of Americans owned VCRs, and a large proportion of the videos they watched were either pornography or exercise tapes sold by small stores (often located in low-rent areas, which did not concern themselves with the legal nuances of the appellate process). As the video business developed over the next two decades, the studios adapted their marketing strategies to accommodate it. Initially, the studios had little choice but to accept the fact that most Americans preferred to rent videos for a night from neighborhood stores rather than buy them. Nor could they exercise any real control over the pricing policies of the stores, since the first-sales doctrine, which had been upheld by American courts, gave buyers the right to rent, share, or resell goods they had bought. The studios therefore priced their titles so high—often $100 or more—that, although few individuals could afford them, stores could buy them as rental copies and make back their investment by renting them over and over again to consumers. Typically, stores would order titles only once from wholesalers, which would buy large quantities of titles soon after the openings at a discounted price of between $60 and $85 a copy. Since it cost only a few dollars to manufacture and package a video, and orders for popular films could amount to hundreds of thousands of copies, the rental business, despite Steve Ross's early doubts about a business in which studios had little if any control over the renting of its products, proved highly profitable for the studios.

By the late 1980s, Paramount experimented with an alternative strategy for selling videos by pricing them low enough for consumers to buy rather than rent them. Its first success, *Top Gun*, was priced wholesale at only $12—about one sixth of the price that rental stores usually paid for rental videos. To make up for the lower price, Paramount obviously had to sell at least six times as many copies of *Top Gun* as the 200,000 or so it would have sold in rental copies priced at $72. As it turned out, the gamble paid off: *Top Gun* sold 3 million copies. This "sell-through" strategy, as it came to be known, was usually reserved only for enormously popular films, which held the prospect of selling millions of copies. Even though the right title could sell more than 5 million copies, studios preferred not to take such a risk on most of their films. (The exception was Disney, which found it could sell enough copies of its children's films in its theme parks, Disney stores, and other outlets to justify the risk.) As a result, except for a handful of films priced as sell throughs, video stores continued to buy movies at the higher price, and they seldom bought enough copies to service the huge demand when titles were first released.

By the late 1990s, it will be recalled, Sumner Redstone introduced yet another strategy, called revenue sharing, to address this bottleneck in supply. Under this new system, in which the studios license—or, in effect, lend—large numbers of copies to video stores for a cut of the rental fees. Redstone's innovation, which he persuaded all the other studios to implement, finally gave the studios a large measure of control over the rental business.

Enter the DVD

The digitized version of the video, or DVD, was the result of a happy marriage between American studios and Japanese electronics manufacturers. The same laser technology that Sony and Philips had developed in 1982 to read indentations and nonindentations on a CD as either a 1 or a 0 was not limited to music. It provided the high-tech equivalent of a cooking recipe to store any information in a way that it could be used over and over again without diminishing its quality. Although Sony had succeeded in digitizing images on tape by the mid-1980s (marketing a professional digital video recorder in 1986), it confronted a formidable stumbling block in putting a full-length movie on a CD-size optical disc: storage space. To get the huge amount of information to fit in digital form on a six-inch disc, it had to be compressed through a technology called digital signal processing in such a way that there would not be a noticeable loss in picture quality. This digital wizardry, in turn, required powerful computer chips and circuitry that in the mid-1980s was still too expensive to be incorporated in products for the consumer market. So while Norio Ohga, Morita's brilliant protégé and successor, recognized the "limitless possibilities" of video digital technology—and even moved to acquire content for it in the late 1980s—its full implementation would have to wait until the 1990s, when the exponential growth in computer power— and falling prices of chips—made practical a home player for the audio-video digital disc or, as it would eventually be called, the DVD.

Even though Sony (with its partner Philips) held the crucial patents on the digital audio portion of the CD, it was not alone in pursuing the DVD. Sony's rival Toshiba was on a similar track. Its research engineering team had envisioned the possibility of the DVD as early as 1982, and in the early 1990s, Toshiba entered into negotiations to buy part of Time Warner Entertainment for $1 billion. Such a "strategic partnership" would give Toshiba access to one of the largest libraries of Hollywood movies, which would greatly facilitate the successful launch of a new video product. To further this alliance, Toshiba dispatched Koji Hase, the executive who had been largely responsible for Toshiba's huge success with a similar optical disc for computers, the CD-ROM. Hase then met with Warren Lieberfarb, the president of Time Warner Home Entertainment, in his office in Los Angeles.

Fortunately for Hase, his proposed disc answered a concern that Lieberfarb had independently identified: the inferior picture quality of VHS compared to the new digital satellite broadcasting that had recently been introduced in the United States. Hase explained that the digital disc not only could produce as good a picture as satellite television but that it would contain features that satellite broadcasting could not offer, such as pausing the film, skipping to scenes, and replaying. Lieberfarb recounts, "I asked if they could get 135 digital minutes [on a disc]?" When Hase answered affirmatively, Lieberfarb extended the meeting by nearly five hours and invited Hase for dinner. By the time Hase returned to Tokyo, he had managed to get Lieberfarb's commitment to put the full weight of Warner Bros. behind the project.

Toshiba still had to meet Lieberfarb's requisite of squeezing an entire movie on a two-sided six-inch disc, which took until 1993. By this time, however, Sony and Phillips had also developed a six-inch digital disc for video that, although it had less storage capacity, had the advantage for personal computers of being single-sided. Meanwhile, another Japanese electronic giant, Matsushita, which had bought Universal (and therefore also had access to a large library of movies), likewise had plans to launch a version of the DVD.

Lieberfarb concluded that a digital format war between Japanese hardware manufacturers would be disastrous. Not only would it confuse consumers but stores would resist carrying two versions of the same movies. If the DVD was to succeed, it had to have a common format. So he personally called the heads of the home entertainment divisions of the major studios and asked them to join Time Warner in a common front called the Ad Hoc Studio Committee. All accepted, although Fox declined to meet with the other studios because, as one executive later explained, "it could be considered an antitrust violation." Such concerns did not stop Lieberfarb. He had the group not only demand a single format but issue a "wish list" that favored the Toshiba format. He then warned Sony that the U.S. Department of Justice might intervene if Sony used its control of its CD audio patents to block acceptance of a common format. Under this pressure, Sony and Toshiba (as well as other Japanese manufacturers) convened in Hawaii in August 1995 and agreed on a single format for the digital versatile disc, or DVD, on which they would all share the patents.

The introduction of the DVD in 1996 was, as one studio executive put it, "the beginning of the end of the video rental system"—a system that had dominated the home video business since its inception. The appeal of renting a DVD is diminished both by its vulnerability to dirt particles and scratches from mishandling (since, unlike videos, it is not contained in a cartridge) and its relatively low retail price (which a consumer can weigh against the hassle of returning rentals as well as the cost incurred by late fees). In addition, unlike VHS tapes, which must be recorded, DVDs are stamped out, allowing them to achieve much greater economies of scale if millions of copies are sold for the global market. To get this volume, Time Warner and Sony, which together supplied almost all the titles during the initial year, elected to price DVDs as a "sell-through"—typically $14 to $18 apiece—and that strategy was adopted by the industry. The studios therefore now earn all their money on DVDs from sell-through sales (although video stores can still rent the DVDs they buy at this price).

At Viacom, this DVD-pricing strategy created a direct conflict between its Blockbuster Entertainment division and its Paramount division. Blockbuster executives, fearing that the sell-through policy threatened the viability of its ten thousand video stores, opposed Paramount issuing any titles on DVD. Consequently, Paramount movies did not appear on DVD for over two years.

In 1999, DVDs represented 11 percent of the studios' home entertainment revenues, and video rentals represented 30 percent. By 2003, DVDs represented 76 percent of the studios' home entertainment revenues, and video rentals represented only 6 percent. As Table 5 demonstrates, the video rental business was rapidly eroding (though it still produced more than $1 billion in revenue for the studios in 2003).

With home entertainment now mainly a sell-through business, the video (either DVD or VHS) is usually announced only a month or so after the film ends its run in theaters, with the release scheduled some three to six months later. Aside from the posters and other paraphernalia provided to video stores, the studios spend little money advertising videos, and stars are rarely, if ever, called on to publicize them. Instead, the studios rely on the lingering awareness created by the theatrical advertising campaign. Since studios assume that this residual awareness will diminish over time, they have a powerful incentive to get movies into video stores while some residue of the television advertisements and publicity appearances still exists in the public's memory. "It may seem perverse," a studio marketing executive said, "but the more successful the marketing campaign, and the bigger the opening-weekend gross at theaters, the greater the pressure to move the movies to video." *Terminator 3*, for example, opened in theaters in early July 2003 in the United States and Canada and in other major markets around the world in July and August—and was released on video and DVD on November 4, 2003.

The quick move to video is, if anything, even more pronounced with less successful films. Warner Bros., after spending $27.6 million on television advertising for *Midnight in the Garden of Good and Evil*, truncated

TABLE 5. THE STUDIOS' VIDEO INCOME, 1999-2003
(BILLIONS OF DOLLARS)

Year	DVD	VHS Sell-through	VHS Rental	% Rental
1999	1	5.2	3.4	35
2001	5.7	4.1	2.6	21
2002	10.4	4.1	1.8	11
2003	14.9	2.7	1.3	7

the theatrical run of the film—which produced only $10.3 million in ticket sales—to move it speedily into video stores, where it brought in $24 million. Unlike in the bygone studio system, when a film's success could be measured by the length of its run in theaters, now a film depends for success on its video release, which often benefits from following close on the heels of the theatrical release. Thus, both the studios and theater-chain owners, who, it will be recalled, seek to improve popcorn sales by getting new films, benefit from shorter theater runs for movies.

The international market for videos works much like the domestic market, with the video released in foreign countries keyed to the theatrical release. Since translations, dubbing, subtitles, reediting, and customs clearance usually have already been done for the theatrical release, there is little additional expense entailed in preparing the foreign videos; advertising is mainly left to the stores.

Although DVD players are still establishing themselves in American households, they have already proved the most successful new consumer product since television (see Table 6). Even before the DVD had completed its penetration of American homes, it had "radically changed the equation of the movie business," as one Viacom executive put it. Although less than a decade earlier Sumner Redstone had made the case that the Hollywood studios depended for their survival on the video business of Blockbuster Entertainment, Viacom moved in 2004 to divest itself of that business. With fewer potential buyers coming into video shops to rent and return videos, they were becoming far less important than mass

TABLE 6. DVD PENETRATION, 1998–2003

Year	TV Households (millions)	DVD Households (millions)	Penetration (%)
1998	99.4	1.2	1.2
1999	100.8	4.6	4.5
2000	102.2	13	12.7
2001	105.2	24.8	23.6
2002	106.7	38.8	36.4
2003	108.4	46.7	43.1

merchandisers for studio sale of DVDs. The studios now needed sought-after shelf space from retailers such as Wal-Mart, Best Buy, and Circuit City.

These retailers have different interests than video shops, however. They often use DVD sales not as an end in themselves but a means to an end: building "traffic" for other items in their stores. Indeed, DVDs are often sold for less than their wholesale price as "loss leaders." For this strategy to work, retailers select titles that they think will attract shoppers likely to buy other, more profitable store offerings. For example, Wal-Mart makes it a policy to vet DVDs, videos, and CDs according to its own standards with regard to profanity, sexual imagery, or anything else that it deems potentially offensive to "family values." If studios want the premium shelf space at Wal-Mart—which sold over $5 billion worth of DVDs and videos in 2003, making it the studios' single largest source of revenue—they have to take into account its standards. According to a top executive at Warner Bros.' home-entertainment division, these standards sometimes can be accommodated by simple changes in scripts, such as "substituting bloodless kung fu fights for more realistic ones" or, in some cases, "slightly modifying the story line." Still, this means that studios are now altering their products not just for theater chains but for retail chains as well. As the Warner Bros. executive further explained, "Movie producing can no longer be directed solely at theater audiences."

The immense storage capability of a DVD disc has further changed the home entertainment business. For one thing, studios can include on a

DVD material not in the movie itself, including music videos, trailers for other movies, games, deleted scenes, and director's commentaries. (Some "extras" are now shot just for the DVD.) By adding such features to past releases, studios can label them "special editions" and sell them as new products. In 2003, Disney, for example, added to the DVD "special edition" of its 1994 film *The Lion King* two hours of new material, including a second version of the film (only one minute longer than the original), an "all-new song," four animated games, deleted scenes, a director's commentary, and the music video "Can You Feel the Love Tonight," performed by Elton John. The DVD sold 11 million copies (and brought over $200 million in new revenue into Disney's clearinghouse).

The DVD also gave new value to the studio library. Initially, when studios controlled the theaters, their libraries made their money by redistributing major movies in theaters. Television largely put an end to reruns in movie theaters and, by the 1960s, the studio library's main business was licensing old movies—and later the television programs they produced or acquired—to local television stations. The VCR then provided studio libraries with another source of income: selling older titles to video stores. But since video stores bought very few copies of older movies (which they then could rent out thousands of times without any additional payments), it provided little profit.

The DVD proved to be a very different story. Because of the ease with which a viewer can navigate to any part of the disc, they provided studios with a ready market for collections from their libraries. Paramount, for example, combined its 1972 film *The Godfather*, its 1974 film *The Godfather Part II*, its 1990 film *The Godfather Part III*, and a 1971 promotional documentary entitled *The Godfather Family: A Look Inside* into a new DVD boxed set. The permutations for combining such material—including sequels, publicity interviews, featurettes, trailers, screen tests, and deleted scenes—provides endless possibilities for finding new profits from library titles. One top studio executive explained to *The Wall Street Journal*, "We realized we could drive the value of the library by constantly repromoting and repackaging titles in new ways."

The DVD format also offers studios a new means for mining new gold from their television libraries. The "season-in-a-box" DVD sets have allowed them to extract huge profits from both recent seasons of series, such as *The Sopranos*, as well as from decades-old material, such as the

1966 season of *Star Trek*. As a result, library sales have surged, accounting for nearly one third of the enormous stream of DVD revenues by 2003. "It is found money," one executive explained, especially because "older titles don't generally have big talent payments."

The dawning of the DVD format greatly brightened Hollywood's big picture. Although the now ineluctable transition from videotape to DVD was still only barely past the halfway point in 2004, it had already enhanced the fortunes of the studios by generating a raft of lucrative new products repackaged from bygone movies, television series, and other intellectual properties they had amassed in their libraries. Indeed, since the introduction of the DVD, Time Warner's library had appreciated by an estimated $7 billion by 2004, according to an executive of its HBO unit. Other studios with large libraries have presumably enjoyed a similar windfall. That this multibillion-dollar enrichment may be less visible to the outside world than the highly publicized losses proceeding from box-office failures does not detract from the increasingly important role it plays in the new Hollywood.

18

The Television Windfall

The fact that studios invest substantially more money in advertising films on average than they recoup from the tickets sold to see them may be less a defiance of economic logic than it appears. As Steve Ross pointed out, "We are not just in the movie business, we are in the intellectual-property business." Huge marketing investments usually pay off only if they succeed in creating some form of intellectual property—whether it be a continuing saga like *Star Trek*, an animated character like Mickey Mouse or the T. rex dinosaurs in *Jurassic Park*, or a music soundtrack such as that of *Snow White and the Seven Dwarfs*—that can be sold over and over again to other media. The largest—and, for the studios, most profitable—of these other media is television.

Initially, it will be recalled, Hollywood viewed television more as a menace than a boon. Even though only 2 million or so households owned a television set by the late 1940s, TV had an indisputable advantage over movie theaters: it was free.

To counter this perceived threat, the studios relied on two principal tactics. The first was denial of their products. Even though licensing movies from their libraries to the networks would have provided the financially weakened studios with much-needed revenues in the early 1950s, all the major studios refused. They even refused to allow the television networks to rent their soundstages, equipment, and contract employees to make their own television programs.

This tactic proved disastrous when smaller production companies rushed in to fill the programming void. Walt Disney opened the floodgates, as noted earlier, when he negotiated a seven-year contract to produce an hour-long weekly show called *Disneyland* for the ABC network. Lew Wasserman followed suit, having MCA churn out made-for-television movies. Before long, other independent producers were providing the networks with wrestling matches, game shows, cartoons, baseball games, and serials. By the mid-1950s, it was clear that the studio boycott had not only failed to impede the growth of television, it had further eroded the studios' control over the movie business.

The studios' other tactic aimed at differentiating their product from what could be seen on television. Instead of continuing to supply theaters with a program of news, sports, and fashion shows, all of which could now be seen on television, the studios closed their newsreel divisions and concentrated on producing spectacular sagas in wide-screen formats that the television sets of the 1950s could not match. Instead of the 4:3 format used in television, the studios introduced a wider format called CinemaScope. There were other innovative systems, including Cinerama, which employed triple projectors to show panoramic travelogues on split screens; 3D, which furnished moviegoers with polarized eye wear that made objects seem to pop out of the screen; and Smell-O-Vision, which provided viewers with time-released aromas to go with their visual feasts.

Aside from heightening the theater experience by expanding the format and adding six or more channels of sound, these technological innovations failed to restore the audience. The studios then strove to produce movies that would be seen as events in and of themselves. While this effort led to some extraordinary epics—including *The Bridge on the River Kwai* (in CinemaScope), *How the West Was Won* (in three-screen Cinerama), and *Lawrence of Arabia* (in Super Panavision 70)—it could not change the basic facts that the number of television homes had grown from fewer than 1 million in 1948 to 55 million in 1962 and that Hollywood had lost over this same period half its weekly audience.

Confronted with this massive defection, the studios had little choice but to reverse their strategy. One by one, they began both using their own studios to produce original television programming and licensing their film libraries to television.

The former move proved especially profitable for studios because of the FCC regulation instituted in 1970 called the Financial Interest and Syndication Rule, or "fin-syn," which prohibited television networks, but *not* movie studios, from having a financial interest in television programs broadcast by networks and then sold in syndication to local stations. By effectively removing the three networks from the syndication business, the FCC radically changed the economic landscape of television. Since it was not profitable to produce television series for their original run without owning the rights to sell them in syndication, the networks simply withdrew from television production. The movie studios were then able to dominate the business of making and owning television programs, which they then licensed to the networks for their original runs and afterward, not restricted by the fin-syn rule, sold in syndication to local as well as foreign stations.

As this lucrative business developed, studios were increasingly willing to accept a per-episode license fee that was somewhat less than their production costs, since once a series was established in the public's mind, and eventually ended its run on the network, the studio could license it, over and over again, to local and foreign stations at an immense profit. And by the 1990s, when broadcast-television revenues were fifteen times those earned by movie theaters, stations could afford to spend lavishly to buy programs in syndication. A single episode of *ER* could sell for as much as 1.5 million. Sony Pictures, which owns no fewer than 350 television series—including the international hits *Fantasy Island, Starsky and Hutch, Charlie's Angels, Maude, All in the Family,* and *Designing Women*—made over two thirds of its money in the 1990s from licensing these programs to television stations and cable networks throughout the world. Sumner Redstone reported that the 125 episodes of *The Cosby Show* that Viacom owned earned a half billion dollars during this period.

The studios discovered an even more prolific cash cow in licensing their own theatrical movies to television. If they could not pry most viewers from their television sets, they could more than make up for lost ticket sales by licensing their movies to television. In 2003 the six studios earned some $2.9 billion this way.

To maximize their television profits, studios divide the licensing of their movies into discreet time periods, called "windows." The first window (after the video release) is pay-per-view, which allows subscribers to cable and satellite television to order movies directly through a joint venture that licenses the films from all the major studios. Initially this window was timed to open about 210 days after the theatrical release to avoid delaying or competing with the video release, but when studios began releasing the more lucrative DVDs in the late 1990s, the window had to be moved up and made briefer. Despite claims that pay-per-view would provide another cash cow, the six studios' earnings from it have remained relatively modest. In 2003 the studios earned a total of only $367 million from it.

The second window, which opens one year after the film is released in theaters, is subscription pay TV. There are three buyers: HBO, which is owned by Time Warner; Showtime, which is owned by Viacom; and Starz, which is owned by Liberty Media (a company in a strategic alliance with News Corporation). This window remains open for a year. The licensing fee to show the film an unlimited number of times over a one-year period averaged about $13 million for major studio releases in 2003. That year, the six studios earned a total of $1.5 billion from pay TV in the United States.

The third window, network television, opens two years after the theatrical release. Since networks also make their own movies, they buy only a handful of studio films. In 2003, for example, they collectively bought only twenty studio films, which meant that approximately two hundred other studio films were passed over for this market. For those films that do get licensed, however, the networks pay relatively large fees. In 2003 these networks paid between $20 and $45 million per movie, typically for three "bites," or showings, of each over a three-year period, which amounted to a total paycheck to the studios of $750 million.

The next window is the rest of television. If there has been a network sale, it opens one year after network television (otherwise, it usually opens right after the pay-TV window). A studio usually licenses to a cable network the right to show the film as often as it wants for seven years. The average price paid by cable networks was about $5 million a title in 2003.

With local television stations, the price per showing is relatively modest—often only a few thousand dollars. Titles can be licensed to hundreds of television stations every year, separately and in multifilm combinations, over and over again. Studios that have thousands of titles profit handsomely from these continuing sales. In 2003 the studios' total from it was $426 million.

Television licensing is equally profitable abroad. Unrestricted by American antitrust regulations, studios can sell their films in packages of six to ten films to foreign television networks. As noted earlier, the license fee for the package is then allocated among the titles at the studio's discretion—an arrangement that allows the studio to shift earnings in its clearinghouse from titles in the black (for which future proceeds might have to be shared with outside parties) to films still in the red (for which there is, as yet, no profit distribution). Each studio produces only a few locomotives each year, but a single locomotive can earn more than $100 million from foreign pay and public television. The principal buyers of studio movies for foreign pay TV are pay-television channels controlled by the News Corporation, Vivendi (Canal Plus), and Sony. As Table 7 indicates, these three companies accounted for over two thirds of the $1.76 billion pie in 2003.

In addition, the six studios earned $1.8 billion in 2003 from their sales to conventional broadcast stations and networks in more than one hundred foreign countries.

What makes licensing, both at home and abroad, especially profitable for the studios is that, unlike the income gleaned from their movie business, almost all the expenses required to market a television program are paid by the broadcaster or network. To be sure, in many cases actors, directors, and writers get a portion of these fees as "residuals," but almost all the rest remains in the studio's clearinghouse. Consider the division of licensing fees for pay television for *Gone in 60 Seconds*. Pay TV provided Disney with a fee of $18.2 million to show the movie for two years. From that, Disney set aside $2.7 million for those entitled to residuals and a total of $149,000 for insurance, taxes, reediting, still photos, and publicity. The remaining $15,351,000 was studio profit.

In the 1990s, as studios became increasingly dependent on television for their profits, they also sought more access to its principal gateways: the broadcast networks. So when in 1995 the FCC lifted its fin-syn rule, the studios' corporate parents moved to take control of major networks. (Rupert Murdoch, who had secured an exemption from fin-syn because

TABLE 7. STUDIO SALES TO FOREIGN PAY TV, 2003

Country	Revenue (millions)	Major Interest
Britain	$468	News Corp.
Japan	$228	Sony, News Corp.
Spain	$179	News Corp., Canal Plus
France	$148	Canal Plus
Germany	$118	Kirch, News Corp.
Italy	$91	News Corp.
Venezuela	$66	News Corp.
Australia	$58	News Corp.
Brazil	$56	News Corp.
Total International	$1,760	

the FCC did not consider that his Metromedia stations constituted a network, had already created the Fox Network.) Disney bought the ABC network in 1995; Time Warner created the Warner Bros. network in 1995 (and the following year added Turner Broadcasting); Viacom bought full control of the UPN network in 1996 and the CBS network in 1999; and General Electric merged Universal with the NBC network in 2003. (As a foreign company, Sony, the only studio parent not owning a network, is prohibited by U.S. law from owning one.) This corporate strategy of vertical integration was also extended by the studios' parents, both in the United States and abroad, to cable television, pay TV, and satellite television. The medium that Hollywood had initially tried to starve had not only survived but thrived—and Hollywood has now largely consumed it.

License to Merchandise

Studios license merchandise in many peripheral markets in which their films and television programs create interest. From the days of Walt Disney, the principal recipients of these kinds of licenses have been enterprises that make products aimed at amusing and diverting children, preteens, and teenagers.

Walt Disney, it will be recalled, was the first studio to exploit such licensing opportunities. In 1930, when it was still a small animation company, Disney began licensing the Mickey Mouse image, first to watchmakers and then to publications, clothing companies, and toy manufacturers. By 1935, the royalties from animated characters were providing more profits than the movies in which they starred, and over the next twenty years, as Disney created more characters and more licensing channels, this stream of revenue, which was almost pure profit, continued to expand. Today, aside from this licensing income, Disney also directly sells to consumers billions of dollars' worth of its own merchandise at its theme parks, retail stores, and Internet site; in these venues, profit margins run as high as 80 percent.

The theme parks Disney began opening in the mid-1950s—first in

California, then in Florida, Japan, and France—have served to greatly expand the audience of children for the studio's branded merchandise. In 2000, for example, some 80 million people paid admission fees to spend the day in what amounts to not just an enclosed shopping mall but one that exclusively sells goods exclusively licensed—and often manufactured—by a single company: Disney. Another 250 million people shopped in the seven hundred strategically located Disney Stores, which, that year, sold $13 billion in merchandise (more than was spent at the box office worldwide). Just the licensing fees—about 6 to 8 percent of retail sales—on apparel, books, toys, and games add an estimated $500 million to Disney's profits every year. One film alone, *The Lion King*, produced more than $1 billion in retail sales.

The major studios followed Disney into the licensing business, but only after the collapse of the studio system. Indeed, in some cases the licensing business came about more by chance than by design. MGM, for example, licensed the Pink Panther cartoon character popularized by the movie's opening credits only reluctantly in 1964, and then found that the licensing rights made more money than the film itself. Other studios initially used characters for promoting the films rather than to earn licensing income (since they often did not own the licensing rights to characters that had originated in, for example, comic strips, magazines, and children's books). When Twentieth Century–Fox released *Star Wars* in 1977, it gave away the licensing rights to merchandisers who would commit themselves to advertising campaigns for the products. This "merchandising tie-in" strategy, while it may have increased the size of the movie audience for *Stars Wars*, missed the potential licensing income that might have been made on the movie's characters. As one Fox executive explained, "No one had any idea how lucrative they would be."

As it turned out, more than $4 billion worth of *Star Wars*–related merchandise was sold, which, at a 6 percent royalty on the wholesale price, would have produced $120 million in licensing fees. After the success of *Star Wars* merchandise, the major studios learned their lesson and changed their strategy to take fuller advantage of the potential of movies to sell toys, T-shirts, and other goods. Not surprisingly, when George Lucas decided to revive the *Stars Wars* franchise in the late-1990s with prequels, he retained the licensing rights for the merchandise.

In the case of Warner Bros., Steve Ross, it will be recalled, positioned the studio to take full advantage of this licensing strategy in the 1980s by acquiring the National Licensing Corporation, as well as DC Comics, which owned the rights to Batman, Superman, and other cartoon heroes. The other studios gradually followed suit, either buying or creating characters. By 1990, all the major studios had licensing divisions, but Disney still had a unique advantage among retailers by virtue of its theme parks. With millions of children passing through these parks, it could credibly guarantee the manufacturers that toys based on its characters would get such enormous exposure that retail stores would undoubtedly give them prominent shelf space during the crucial Christmas season. No other studio could make such assurances, and without them, toy manufacturers have little incentive to make major commitments in advance to toys without proven appeal.

Consequently, Disney films are the one exception to the general rule among toy manufacturers to license characters only after a film has successfully established itself. This barrier provides another powerful reason for the studios to make franchise films—such as *Batman, Superman, Star Trek,* and the prequels to *Star Wars*—since, after the initial one establishes the franchise, the studios are able to get advance commitments from toy manufacturers for sequels.

While only a small portion of studio films contain licensable characters, those few characters exert enormous influence over retail sales. In 2000, for example, movie-based characters brought in $40 billion in worldwide global sales and accounted for over one third of sales for the entire licensing industry. Since these characters almost invariably outlive the movies that spawn them, the stream of licensing fees from them can enrich the studios' clearinghouses for many decades.

Electronic games provide a further licensing niche for studios. Since Sony's PlayStation 2 and Microsoft's Xbox serve as DVD as well as game players, games based on movie characters can be combined with the movies themselves, as Sony did, for example, on the DVD of *Final Fantasy*. Through such technology, movies become marketing agents for games, whose retail sales not only approach that of the global box office for movies but whose life, especially among teenage game players, long exceeds the life of the movies from which they are derived.

Studios also license the original music on their films' soundtracks to music companies. After it became possible to record sound directly on film, the studios began orchestrating "mood music," as it was called, to enhance the illusion on-screen. Much of this material was initially taken from the public domain and assembled in canned "track" libraries, to minimize the royalties owed to composers under the ASCAP regime that then dominated the sale of music.

Although at that time each studio owned its own music-publishing house, the movie soundtracks were sent to radio stations and record companies principally to promote interest in the movies themselves rather than to earn money from the sale of the music. This strategy worked as long as movies enjoyed extended runs in theaters.

After the studio system was replaced by a more competitive environment, producers began using original music, such as the catchy "Lara's Theme" from *Dr. Zhivago,* to help establish their movies. In 1967 *The Graduate* became the first film to incorporate into a soundtrack songs that had already been released—including Simon and Garfunkel's "The Sound of Silence." Then, in the late 1970s, with the innovation of the audiocassette, which made mobile music possible for automobile travelers and pedestrians, the studios suddenly found a massive audience for their soundtracks. Whereas previously sales of soundtrack LPs had rarely exceeded ten thousand copies, now the soundtrack cassettes (and later CDs) of scores from films like *Grease, Saturday Night Fever,* and *Dirty Dancing* were selling millions of copies. By 2000, even though soundtracks had far less value in attracting audiences to theaters (especially since films now rarely play for more than a few weeks), the studios were making substantial sums in licensing them to record companies. The soundtrack of the Coen brothers' film *O Brother, Where Art Thou?,* for example, sold $72 million worth of records, exceeding the film's global box-office gross of $55 million in 2002. Admittedly, such successes are rare. It is estimated that only ten to fifteen films in any year produce a "gold" album that sells more than a million copies. Still, those few do provide the studio with a cash flow long after the film itself has vanished from the screen.

The Learning Imperative

Studios are finely tuned learning networks. Faced with a constant stream of reports on how relevant audiences in different markets are reacting to their films and other products, they analyze the various elements including marketing, stars, and music—and, along this learning curve, adjust their subsequent decisions accordingly.

Shortly after films are released to theaters, studios learn approximately how many people went to see it on the opening weekend. (To make sure theaters are not misreporting the number of tickets sold, they employ undercover checkers, who buy numbered tickets at the first and last shows at randomly selected theaters.) They also learn a great deal about the makeup of the audience by conducting exit polls, similar to those used in elections, to determine the age, sex, and race of audiences in different geographic regions. From just those data, their marketing departments can determine the extent to which their targeted television advertising succeeded in recruiting particular moviegoers. (Their information on the size and demographics of the television audience they blanketed with ads comes from the A. C. Nielsen rating service, which installs meters in viewers' television sets.)

If a large percentage of the people who show up at the theaters demographically match the group the studio targeted in their television ads, the studio judges that the film has high "marketability," which means only that the advertising has worked to activate a particular audience and will presumably work in other markets. If a film continues to draw a large audience after the blitz of television advertising ends, which is usually after the opening weekend, it is judged to have high "playability," meaning that moviegoers are recommending it to their peers. When films produce large opening turnouts and then the audience rapidly disappears, they have, in the lingo of the marketing department, "high marketability, low playability," which, as one marketing vice president explained, "is a feather in our hat, since it shows we did a good job with a bad movie."

Conversely, if the ads do not create a large initial audience, no matter what other virtues the film might possess, it has little chance of success in other markets, such as video, because it will be assumed to lack "marketability." Marketability, then, is critically important to the future earning stream.

If the television-advertising campaign is judged to have drawn a satisfactory percentage of the intended audience to the opening weekend, studios assume that the elements in the ads—such as two stars in conflict, particular lines of dialogue, snatches of music, et cetera—worked together and can be used in similar combinations in future movies. For example, when the Disney subsidiary Dimension Films released *Scary Movie* in July 2000, it found that its thirty-second ads on cable television, which visually combined horror with comic spoofing, succeeded in recruiting a white female audience under twenty-five that produced a large opening-weekend gross. Even though the tag line in the ads had been "No mercy. No shame. No sequel," Dimension made two sequels based on the same marketing concept, *Scary Movie 2* and *Scary Movie 3*.

When a film fails to find the expected audience at its opening, studio executives tend to the blame not the film itself but the way it was advertised in the crucial weeks immediately preceding the weekend. They reason that word of mouth cannot be a significant factor, since almost no one has seen the film prior to its opening, and assume that reviews have only a limited effect on audience turnout at this point, especially on films aimed at youth audiences—an assumption usually confirmed by exit polls. So the initial suspect is the television ads. For example, when Disney's animated *Treasure Planet* finished fourth at the box office on Thanksgiving weekend, 2002, Richard Cook, the studio's chairman, explained the failure in the following terms: "All it says is that for this particular Thanksgiving weekend . . . for whatever reasons, we did not make it look appealing enough."

Even the appearance of top stars in television advertising does not guarantee a large audience. Indeed, with the preeminence of teenage moviegoers, stars' images often prove far less effective than exploding cars or other special effects. Consider the fate of two action movies, Sony's *Hollywood Homicide* and Universal's *2 Fast 2 Furious*, released the same week in June 2003. The ads for *Hollywood Homicide* featured images of the star, Harrison Ford, while the ads for *2 Fast 2 Furious*—a film without any stars—featured images of cars crashing. Even though similar-sized budgets were expended on the ads, and they were placed on similar TV programs, *2 Fast 2 Furious* had an enormously successful opening ($50 million) and *Hollywood Homicide* had a poor one ($11.1 million).

When a film fails to draw the anticipated opening-weekend audience, studios then conduct, as one marketing executive termed it, an "agonizing reappraisal" to determine the reason a particular campaign failed. They review the ads themselves, the results of the focus groups and other prerelease tests, and the competing advertising campaigns. Comparing them with successful ones for similar films that appealed to similar audiences, they ask, as one Sony marketing executive put it: "What is wrong with the bait?" In the case of *Hollywood Homicide*, the marketing executive concluded, "Teens are more excited by car crashes than big-name stars—even one who gets a twenty-million-dollar paycheck."

Studios also learn at an early stage whether the music videos derived from films have succeeded in reaching their intended audience. With many films, especially those based on urban conflict, producers cast popular singers—such as Puff Daddy (P. Diddy), Ice Cube, and DMX—in supporting roles so that they can then incorporate shots of them in music videos, which can be distributed to music-video channels, such as MTV, VH1, and The Box. This free publicity can generate audiences among the teenagers who watch these shows. For example, the constant playing of the Eminem video from the 2002 movie *8 Mile* was credited by the distributor, Universal, with producing a large opening-weekend audience. About 10 million people bought tickets at 2,450 theaters that weekend, and according to exit-polling samples, most of them were drawn to the movie by the music videos on cable television. The frequency with which music videos are being played, therefore, constitutes important feedback and in many cases is reported back to the marketing departments on a daily basis. Depending on how often they get aired, the videos themselves are judged to be successes or failures.

The studios also learn about the relative appeal of their products in key foreign markets before they are released. Their overseas-distribution arms usually book films abroad well in advance of their opening on little more than their most salient elements. For example, *Minority Report* was described as a "Spielberg science-fiction thriller with Tom Cruise," *Runaway Bride* as a "romantic feel-good comedy with Julia Roberts and Richard Gere," and *I Spy* as a "black-white buddy movie with Eddie Murphy and Owen Wilson, based on the internationally syndicated TV series." These presentations also often specify which stars will visit foreign countries for publicity purposes, the marketing budget, and, if the film has already opened in America, the opening-weekend box-office grosses. The overseas distributors generally maintain close relations with foreign theater chains and learn from the chains' executives which factors—such as cast members, plot elements, or the genre—weigh most heavily in their decisions to give films favorable or unfavorable bookings.

Through the previously discussed partnership with Blockbuster and other major video-store chains, studios' home-entertainment divisions have access to the daily computerized tabulations from many video stores. These results allow them to determine how well rental videos perform in neighborhoods that vary demographically and to make educated guesses about the waxing—or waning—appeal of different stars. For example, since videos starring Eddie Murphy had poor rentals in urban locales in two consecutive films, 2002's *I Spy* and *The Adventures of Pluto Nash*, the studio might deduce that Murphy was losing his appeal with black audiences. By testing such declining rentals against other videos in the same genre, the division can draw further conclusions about whether the results proceed from idiosyncratic factors or a more general phenomenon.

Further feedback comes from the small audience of executives at the television networks, cable networks, and pay-TV channels whose licensing fees account for a major share of the studios' profits. The studios have ongoing relations with them—a connection that in many cases proceeds from their being part of a common corporate family. Such a relationship exists, for example, between Disney and ABC, Paramount and MTV, Fox and B-Sky Television, and Warner Bros. and HBO.

These television-network and pay-TV executives closely monitor their own audiences (including their advertisers) and, after determining what types of movies will best satisfy them, pass this information on to their counterparts at the studios. Their requests concern not only specific movies but also genres of movies. Fox, for example, was asked by Star pay TV, which is owned by its corporate parent, for "action-based films, under two hours in length, with little dialogue and universally understood heroes and villains." Such requests are understandably assigned great weight.

Studios also receive constant information from national and regional chains of multiplexes in the United States and Canada. In addition to getting the box-office tallies, distribution executives are in almost daily telephone communication with theaters' film bookers to deal with their complaints and customary requests to renegotiate the agreed-upon division of box-office revenues. They also receive them in their hotel suites at exhibitors' conventions, such as ShoWest and ShowEast, where, over drinks and snacks, they hear highly specific criticisms of their movies. During the 1998 ShoWest in Las Vegas, for example, Buena Vista executives heard complaints that Disney's nonanimated films were not appealing to males aged fifteen to nineteen because they were, as one theater owner put it, "overly verbose," "too slow in getting to the action," and "lacked blood and gore."

The studios' marketing departments also hear from other outside professionals—such as their advertising agencies, media buyers, publicists, consultants, financial analysts, merchandising partners, and audience-measurement services—who also employ polls, focus groups, and statistical models to develop theories about why particular films, or whole classes of films, succeed or fail in various markets. Fox, for example, originally produced its 2002 animation feature *Ice Age* as a young-adult drama, but after it tested poorly with that targeted audience, Fox executives ordered it reedited and rerecorded to convert it into a children's comedy.

Finally, of course, there is no shortage of critics, pundits, and Monday-morning quarterbacks in the media, trade organizations such as the MPAA, actors guilds, and other peer groups whose opinions are taken into account by studio executives.

All this feedback from these myriad sources, in both anecdotal and statistical form, is then filtered through numerous meetings, phone calls, and other communications among studio executives. Much of what is then judged relevant is relayed through the green-lighting process back to those involved in developing new products. It may seep down in many forms. It may be explicit, in the form of a strategic memorandum from the studio head, or implicit, such as the passing along of snippets of proverbial wisdom attributed to unnamed corporate "suits." In some cases, it may be no more than an unverified rumor that a person of authority in the studio has low regard for a star, director, writer, or other person under consideration. This information is then passed on to producers, directors, writers, and talent agents as they go about consummating their next deals.

Positive feedback often facilitates the financing for sequels. Consider, for example, *Terminator 3: Rise of the Machines,* which, with a projected budget for direct costs of $166 million, was the most expensive film in history when it went into production in 2002. Toho-Towa of Tokyo was willing to invest $12 million in the project in return for the rights to the Japanese market because the previous *Terminator* with Arnold Schwarzenegger had become such a dependable brand name in electronic games that the Japanese distributor was confident it could earn back its money from the ancillary rights alone. For its part, Sony was willing to pay $77.4 million for the right to distribute the film in almost all other foreign markets because of the immense box-office success of the previous *Terminator* in eight particular markets—Germany, Britain, France, Australia, Italy, Spain, Brazil, and Hong Kong—and the continued name recognition of the product in these markets, as measured by polls. Time Warner was willing to pay $51.6 million for the right to distribute the film in the United States and Canada because, among other reasons, the continued sale of the previous *Terminator* on DVD had persuaded its home-entertainment division that the product had such a following that the ancillary rights could guarantee the return of the investment regardless of how well the film did in theaters. The director, producers, and other participants agreed to defer $10 million of their fees on the promise that these sums would eventually be paid out of funds provided by advertisers placing products in the film, who, in turn, had committed themselves because of the established brand name *Terminator*. Finally, Intermedia Entertainment, which had assembled the deal, provided the balance from its own funds based on its confidence in the franchise. In the case of an initial film, in which there could be no such feedback, the investments, if made at all, would be far more risky.

Feedback also often shapes future productions by encouraging or discouraging certain casting choices, plot lines, ethnic settings, or endings. For example, *The General's Daughter* was initially formulated as a mystery-drama involving the investigation by warrant officer Paul Brenner (John Travolta) into the death of a commanding general's daughter, but when Paramount executives made the producers aware that a previous Travolta action film, *Face/Off*, was enjoying extraordinary success in foreign and video markets, the producers added to the script a pretitle sequence—in which Travolta, as an undercover agent, engages in an extended shoot-out with arms smugglers—that contained enough explosions and other special effects to allow Paramount to present the film as an "action thriller."

Such feedback, when effectively conveyed, completes the connection between the studios' clearinghouses, which are engaged in measuring profitability, and the studios' creative processes. It makes the economic logic, at least at that point in time, glaringly visible to those selecting new productions. They can act on it—or, as will be seen, disregard it to achieve noneconomic goals.

21

The Midas Formula

Enter the numbers men—the corporate financial officers, accountants, auditors, and bookkeepers—who, at some point, tally up all the monies received by or due the studios' clearinghouses. When this reckoning is made, a less-than-comforting reality is usually revealed: even with the studios' elaborate marketing strategies, tight production controls, and so-phisticated research, only a very few films account for the lion's share of a studio's earnings. To be sure, blockbusters—a term used to denote a hit movie with explosive impact, resulting in long lines of customers—are not new, but their twenty-first-century equivalents, which cross the boundaries of myriad global markets, are capable of generating such tsunamis of earnings that a single one can keep an entire studio afloat for years. "If it were not for a single [Sony] film in 2002, *Spider-Man*," a top executive of a rival studio noted, "Sony would have had the second-worst year in its history." *Spider-Man*, by channeling $1.1 billion into the Sony clearinghouse, had joined what one Sony executive called "the billion-dollar club." It also could be expected to continue earning substantial sums for decades to come.

The movies that qualify for club membership, though extremely few

TABLE 8: BILLION-DOLLAR-EARNING MOVIES, 1999-2004

Film	U.S. Rentals (Millions)	Foreign Rentals (Millions)	World Video and DVD (Millions)	U.S. TV (Millions)	Foreign TV (Millions)	Other Rights (Millions)	Total
Harry Potter 1 (2001)	$259	$329	$436	$87	$86	$52	$1,249
Spider-Man	$202	$209	$464	$80	$82	$60	$1,097
The Two Towers	$170	$298	$484	$84	$90	$84	$1,210
The Fellowship of the Ring	$157	$276	$396	$88	$90	$86	$1,093
The Return of the King	$183	$176	$500	$80	$80	$110	$1,129
Harry Potter 2	$131	$304	$496	$90	$95	$88	$1,204
Finding Nemo	$170	$182	$500	$80	$80	$110	$1,122
Pirates of the Caribbean	$155	$180	$510	$85	$80	$112	$1,122
Attack of the Clones	$155	$172	$480	$85	$95	$100	$1,087
The Phantom Menace	$220	$240	$440	$90	$95	$100	$1,185

in number, are remarkably similar in several respects. Consider the $10 billion films since 1999 (Table 8).

These films follow a similar formula. All of them:

1. are based on children's stories, comic books, serials, cartoons, or, in the case of *Pirates of the Caribbean,* a theme-park ride.
2. feature a child or adolescent protagonist.

3. have a fairy-tale-like plot in which a weak or ineffectual youth is transformed into a powerful and purposeful hero.

4. contain only chaste, if not strictly platonic, relationships between the sexes, with no suggestive nudity, sexual foreplay, provocative language, or even hints of consummated passion.

5. feature bizarre-looking and eccentric supporting characters that are appropriate for toy and game licensing.

6. depict conflict—though it may be dazzling, large-scale, and noisy—in ways that are sufficiently nonrealistic, and bloodless, for a rating no more restrictive than PG-13.

7. end happily, with the hero prevailing over powerful villains and supernatural forces (most of which remain available for potential sequels).

8. use conventional or digital animation to artificially create action sequences, supernatural forces, and elaborate settings.

9. cast actors who are not ranking stars—at least in the sense that they do not command gross-revenue shares. For his role in *Spider-Man*, Tobey Maguire, for example, though he was a well-established actor, received only $4 million and a share of only "net profits" (which, it will be recalled, do not divert from the revenues flowing into the clearinghouses).

Even though the Midas formula has been greatly enriched in recent years by the advent of the DVD, pay TV, and computer games, it has been generating large earnings for Hollywood—and especially post-studio-system Hollywood—ever since Walt Disney's *Snow White and the Seven Dwarfs* was released in the 1930s. The Disney empire is in fact largely the result of Disney's successors having closely hewed to this formula. Indeed, the studio's 1994 movie *The Lion King*, released even before the dawn of the DVD, was the founding member of the billion-dollar club.

While the other studios were initially slow to follow Disney's lead, directors and entrepreneurs of the postwar generation, many of whom were brought up on Disney products, seized on and greatly advanced the formula. Among them was George Lucas. Born in 1944 and raised on a walnut farm in Modesto, California, he had initially planned to be a race-car driver—an ambition squelched by a near-fatal accident in 1962. He went to film school at University of Southern California, won a

$3,000 Warner Bros. scholarship to apprentice on the studio's production of the fantasy-musical *Finian's Rainbow* in 1967, and then wrote and directed *American Graffiti*—a coming-of-age movie that was nominated for the Oscar for Best Picture in 1974. Following that success, he began writing the treatment of a science-fiction film to fill what he perceived was a glaring void in Hollywood: nonviolent and nonsexual fantasy sagas. The result was *Star Wars* (1977), two sequels and three prequels (1980–2004), thirty-two different video games, and more than $3 billion in licensed merchandise. Lucas used the proceeds from the *Star Wars* franchise to build his computer-graphics arm, Industrial Light & Magic, into the dominant visual-effects company in the film industry and establish THX, his branded surround-sound system, in multiplex theaters.

Another director who brilliantly developed the formula was Steven Spielberg. Born in Cincinnati in 1946, he dropped out of Long Beach University to work in Hollywood, apprenticing in television at the Universal studio. After achieving spectacular successes directing *Jaws* (1975), *Close Encounters of the Third Kind* (1977), and *Raiders of the Lost Ark* (1981), he turned to a project that he termed his "personal resurrection"— a fantasy film through the eyes of a child about befriending an alien: *E.T.: The Extra-Terrestrial*. Modeled partly on Disney's Mother Night in *Fantasia*—"a whisper of my own childhood," as he termed it—the film, which proved a phenomenal box-office—and licensing—success, further demonstrated the enormous potential of children-oriented movies.

Steve Jobs, though not a filmmaker, also contributed to the formula. Born in 1955, Jobs grew up on an apricot orchard in Los Altos, California. He cofounded the Apple Computer company at the age of twenty-one and, ten years later, cofounded Pixar Animation Studios, which then pioneered computer animation. The cumulative earnings of its first five films—*Toy Story 1* and *2; A Bug's Life; Monsters, Inc.;* and *Finding Nemo*—exceeded $2 billion, and the success of the concept resulted in the company's market value rising to $3.7 billion.

While the movies that follow the Midas formula are costly to make— production costs for the films in Table 8 averaged $105 million—the making of star-driven action movies that do not follow this formula can be equally expensive. Among the recent R-rated films in this category are *Bad Boys 2* ($130 million), *The Last Samurai* ($100 million), *Gangs of New York* ($100 million), *Pearl Harbor* ($135 million), *The Patriot*

($110 million), *Windtalkers* ($115 million), *Basic* ($105 million), and *Terminator 3* ($176 million). The R ratings of these films limited not only the theatrical audiences that could see them but also the television channels that could show them or even their ads, and the merchandisers who were willing to associate their products with them; as a result, they had far less chance to reach their break-even point than films adhering to the Midas formula. And even if they reached that point, the revenues would have to be divided with those stars, like Arnold Schwarzenegger, whose contracts entitle them to a share of the gross, further diminishing the studios' take. Given these constraints, nonformula films have little, if any, possibility of becoming billion-dollar-club members.

Despite the overwhelming economic arguments in its favor, studios often deviate from the Midas formula, and when this digression results in faltering profits, it can cause tension at the highest corporate level. When Walt Disney's nephew Roy—then Disney's vice chairman, the head of its feature animation division, and its largest individual shareholder—and his longtime business associate Stanley Gold resigned from the Disney board in December 2003, they bitterly criticized Disney's chairman, Michael Eisner, for departing from the company's traditional strategies in ways that produced "dismal results." One of their concerns was Disney's huge investment in expensive, R-rated films—such as *Gangs of New York*, *Kill Bill*, and *Cold Mountain*—that did not fit the formula.

The noneconomic logic that accounted for this digression was succinctly summarized by Harvey Weinstein, head of the Disney subsidiary Miramax—the division that had spent $100 million to produce *Cold Mountain* and another $30 million to market it. He took a broader view of the company's investments in non-"comic-book" movies. "The problem with American business today is we don't allow ourselves to take the kind of risks we should in the arts," he said. If he had been making "a comic-book movie," he acknowledged that "the only impetus would have been to make money." But *Cold Mountain*, a nonformulaic film, as he put it, "wasn't about making money."

This willingness to take risks with more artistic movies is reinforced by a practical consideration: obtaining desirable filmmakers. "You can't get directors of the caliber of Anthony Minghella [*Cold Mountain*], Martin Scorsese [*Gangs of New York*], and Quentin Tarantino [*Kill Bill*] to work on movies designed to get kids to buy toys and drag their parents to theme parks," one top Disney executive explained. "And these are the directors who win the Academy Awards." Such prestigious films—and directors—also help give a studio its standing in the Hollywood community. Deviating from the formula thus has its benefits, along with its risks. As persuasive as the formula is from a moneymaking standpoint, it doesn't satisfy the community members' appetite for prestige, recognition, and creative expression. These are among the needs that drive the less visible but surprisingly powerful noneconomic logic of Hollywood.

☆ Part Five ☆

THE SOCIAL LOGIC
OF HOLLYWOOD

22

Homo Ludens

I don't make pictures just to make money. I make money to make more pictures.

—Walt Disney

A principal construct of classical economics is *Homo economicus,* or economic man. This creature was conceived as a sort of human calculator. He adds up the monetary gain or loss of each choice at his disposal and then chooses the one that provides him with the maximum return. While such a creature is not assumed to be anything other than an "ideal type," he still gives economists a convenient means to quantify human behavior. They need only to calculate the monetary outcomes for various alternatives to predict what choices economic man will make. As the Austrian economic theorist Ludwig von Mises writes, "The much talked about *Homo Economicus* of the classical theory is the personification of the principles of the businessman. The businessman wants to conduct every business with the highest possible profit: he wants to buy as cheaply as possible and sell as dearly as possible."

Homo economicus also provides a simple explanation for the workings of Hollywood's earlier studio system: making as much money as possible. In his book *An Empire of Their Own*, Neal Gabler describes how "the Jews that invented Hollywood" were all personally concerned with money. For studio founders Jack Warner, Harry Warner, Louis B. Mayer, Marcus Loew, Adolph Zukor, Harry Cohen, William Fox, and Carl Laemmle, all of whom came from desperately poor families, this concern was of course well grounded. If they were to escape their lot of destitution, they had to make their own money. As Jews, moreover, they had to accomplish this feat in a highly competitive world where anti-Semitism limited their access to more traditional economic opportunities, such as finance, industry, and communications.

In pursuing their dream of economic betterment, they could not afford to concern themselves with social opprobrium. Although movie exhibition was considered by more established businessmen as little more than a tawdry peep show, they saw in it an opportunity to apply the merchandising skills they had honed hawking rags, furs, and other goods to a new mass market. It required little capital—only a few hundred dollars to open a theater—and served a potentially vast demand: the thirst of a largely illiterate population for visual entertainment. Unlike vaudeville or live theater, in which actors had to be paid for each performance, movies could be shown over and over again at little additional cost. Since they could sell tens of thousands of tickets for the same product, their profit depended on keeping the product cheap and the audience plentiful.

Moving their production facilities to Hollywood was another economic-based decision. In Hollywood, where courts were lax and labor unions were not yet established, these men could both evade the Edison Trust's efforts to collect royalties and cut their labor costs to the bone. They organized highly efficient film factories, which they called studios to lessen the industrial stigma of the enterprise, and began manufacturing products for their own theaters.

The image of the Hollywood moguls was further reinforced by the extravagant salaries they took home from their studios. In the Great Depression of the 1930s, MGM's Louis Mayer was the highest-paid executive in the world; even more significant, of the next twenty-five highest-paid executives in the world, nineteen were from the Hollywood studios. Such compensation rates fed anti-Semitic screeds that Jewish entrepreneurs, motivated only by their love of gold, were demeaning American values. Henry Ford's newspaper the *Dearborn Independent,* which had previously published the fraudulent "Elders of Zion" document describing a global Jewish conspiracy to control the world, blamed Jewish businessmen for "the trivializing and demoralizing influences" found in movies. It ranted in a 1921 editorial, "As soon as the Jews gained control of the movies, we had a movie problem. . . . It is the genius of that race to create problems of a moral character in whatever business they achieve a majority."

Many business historians, while not sharing these anti-Semitic views, also argued that Hollywood's product was determined by the profit calculation of the moguls. In his classic study of the movie industry in the 1930s, Tino Balio describes how financial executives in New York, not studio executives in Hollywood, made most of the major decisions concerning the selection, casting, and design of movies, "because they were closest to the principal source of income—theater admissions." He also notes that "the presence of outside bankers and businessmen on boards of directors reflected the fact that the assets of the major [studios] consisted chiefly of theaters."

Since these corporate executives could count on a weekly audience to buy tickets at their theaters, their main concern was making sure the cost of their productions didn't exceed the proceeds they expected to collect from their box offices. According to Balio, these executives controlled the costs by specifying not only the cast, set, location, and other production elements but also the number of script pages directors were to shoot per day. By such measures, the *Homo economicus* that ran the studios reduced entertainment to a product based not on aesthetics but on the abacus of cost efficiency.

The concern that economic man, in the form of the Hollywood moguls and their corporate henchmen, would trample out the art of the cinema was not limited to critics. In 1919, actors Charlie Chaplin, Douglas Fairbanks, and Mary Pickford—along with director D. W. Griffith—founded United Artists as an artistic alternative to the plutocratic studios. As Tino Balio writes in his history of that enterprise, "United Artists was not expected to generate profits but to function as a service organization that operated at cost." The creative talent—Griffith, Chaplin, Fairbanks, and Pickford—would act as their own producers so they could control the artistic aspects of their films. United Artists would then distribute them, as well as other high-quality independent films, to theaters. The problem with this attempt to escape economic constraints was that the studio, with its few stars, could not produce a high-enough volume of films to persuade theaters, which booked blocks of major studio films months in advance, to give them favorable play dates. By 1924, verging on bankruptcy, United Artists had to be reorganized into a more conventional business.

Even in the days of the most money-conscious studio system, not all the financiers in the film industry could be cast as *Homo economicus*, however. Even then, some came to Hollywood in pursuit not of money but of fun, status, power, and even art. Consider, for example, William Randolph Hearst and Howard Hughes, both of whom inherited huge fortunes before they entered the film business. If they are represented by any ideal type, it is not *Homo economicus* but *Homo ludens*, or man at play.

William Randolph Hearst, who inherited his silver-mining fortune when he was still a child and then built out of it the Hearst newspaper empire, came to Hollywood in 1918. Then fifty-four, he wanted to advance the acting career of his mistress, Marion Davies. With his enormous wealth, he created a film company, Cosmopolitan Pictures, which coproduced and released its films through Paramount, MGM, Warner Bros., and 20th Century–Fox. Since the gossip columnists on Hearst newspapers held enormous sway in Hollywood, the studios accommodated him during his Hollywood adventure for the next twenty years. It was an extraordinary exchange of intangible benefits. Hearst wanted to please his mistress and enjoy the benefits that came with producing films, including stars' attendance at his banquets, house parties, and yachting expeditions. The studio moguls—including Adolph Zukor, Louis Mayer, and Jack Warner—who were still insecure about their status in American society, in turn got favorable publicity in Hearst's newspapers. As a result of this collaboration, Hearst's Cosmopolitan Pictures produced more than one hundred major films, including *Perils of Pauline, Janice Meredith, The Five O'Clock Girl,* and *Going Hollywood.* He also created a newsreel company, Hearst-Metronome News, that invented the format of news, sports, and fashion segments that was later adopted by much of television news.

Howard Hughes came to Hollywood in 1926 when he was only twenty. Like Hearst, Hughes had inherited his vast fortune from his father (whose company, Hughes Tool, had a veritable monopoly on oil-drilling bits), and like Hearst, he entered filmmaking as a means of pursuing his passions. In 1926 he formed an independent company, Caddo Productions, signed a distribution deal with United Artists, and began producing films that—thanks to his great personal wealth—were unhampered by the financial restraints with which the major studios had to contend. One of Hughes's passions was daredevil flying. In *Hell's Angels* (1930), he himself flew the stunt planes, disregarding the budget so he could fly more daredevil scenes. He also enjoyed ridiculing the pomposity of establishment institutions, and his film *The Front Page* (1931) gave him a chance to mock both journalists and politicians. Yet another passion Hollywood enabled him to indulge was passion itself; he was able to use his productions to further his romances with comely starlets. In his film *The Outlaw* (1943), he cast his romantic interest Jane Russell in sex scenes that challenged the entire Hollywood censorship system.

Hughes's ability to finance films without any concern for their economic return also allowed him to indulge his friends. One such friend was the director Preston Sturges, who, like Hughes, had been an aviator. He had made his money by inventing kiss-proof lipstick before becoming a filmmaker. After Sturges had pleased Hughes by using him as a model for the Hollywood character Sully Sullivan (Joel McCrea) in *Sullivan's Travels* (1941), Hughes created an entire film company for him, called California Films, and provided him with financing for his comedies.

Throughout his long involvement with Hollywood, Hughes consistently paid little attention to economic considerations. As Preston Sturges once noted, "The deal on which we shook hands was that I would make movies for the company . . . and that he would put up the money for the pictures." Although Hughes subsequently became dissatisfied with Sturges and terminated their deal, the issues were personal, not financial. The motive that drew Hughes to Hollywood was not profits; the rewards he sought—and earned—were nonmonetary ones, such as prestige, status in Hollywood, and fun.

Hughes further expanded his playground in 1948 by buying David Sarnoff's discarded studio, RKO. Not surprisingly, since he proceeded to run RKO to satisfy his own personal interests, not those of the company's bottom line, it lost large sums of money. By 1955, his enjoyment of Hollywood had finally flagged, and he sold RKO to the General Tire and Rubber Company (which presided over its liquidation).

Hearst and Hughes, even if men at play, had no small effect on Hollywood. They produced between them a large share of the independent films in the era of the studio system and, equally important, provided a precedent for the many millionaires who later came to Hollywood for its nonmonetary rewards. Consider the purchasers of MGM after the collapse of the studio system. First there was Edgar Bronfman, Sr., who became chairman after his whiskey company, Seagram, bought $40 million worth of MGM stock in 1969. According to the family biography, *King of the Castle, the Making of a Dynasty: Seagram's and the Bronfman Empire,* Samuel Bronfman asked his son Edgar, "Are we buying all this stock in MGM just so you can get laid?" (To which Edgar Senior, who by then was chairman of MGM, replied, "It doesn't cost forty million to get laid.") Subsequently, in 1990, Italian financier Giancarlo Parretti bought MGM for $1.6 billion and told Alan Ladd, Jr., the studio's head, "You just make the films, I just want to make the actresses."

After Parretti went bankrupt, MGM was taken over by the huge French bank Crédit Lyonnais. In considering the claims that proceeded from this takeover, California Superior Court judge Irving Shimer suggested that the bankers who lent MGM money weren't "interested in making movies. They were interested in getting girls. . . . That's why bankers come to Hollywood." While Judge Shimer may have been using "girls" as a metaphor for pleasure more generally, the evidence he reviewed showed that the Crédit Lyonnais bankers, like Parretti before them and Bronfman Senior before him, had indeed provided little proof that their investment in MGM was motivated by an interest in monetary profits.

A long procession of parabillionaires from other businesses followed in the footsteps of Hearst and Hughes in investing in Hollywood companies. These included commodity speculator Marc Rich, wildcatter Marvin Davis, Australian media tycoon Kerry Packer, shopping-mall operator Mel Simon, financier Ronald Perelman, hedge-fund operator Michael Steinhardt, real-estate mogul Sam Belzberg, and Microsoft cofounder Paul Allen. Part of their enjoyment no doubt came from being what Ben Stein called mere "voyeurs" in Hollywood, part came from playing a role in the creation of filmed fantasies, and part came from a desire to make money as they had in other businesses. Whatever the exact proportions, their mixed motives seemed to more closely fit the profile of *Homo luden* than *Homo economicus.*

Wealthy outsiders are not the only ones who view the movie business as a playground. The insiders at the heart of today's Hollywood establishment also make many of their work decisions to maximize their pleasure, not their monetary rewards. As a result, the choices to green-light or reject a film are often made for reasons that are very different from the ones that studio executives retrospectively use to rationalize their successes and failures to stockholders, financial analysts, and, in many cases, entertainment journalists.

Even decisions that define the future of studios may proceed from noneconomical considerations. Consider, for example, Walt Disney's decision to turn his studio into an international distributor in 1953. Up until that point, RKO had distributed all of Disney's films. Instead of paying the overhead of a large organization to get his films into theaters, Disney paid RKO a percentage of the theater receipts for that service. While this deal had proven highly profitable for Disney on most of his films, RKO was unable to keep the Disney nature documentary *The Living Desert* (1953) in theaters for an extended run. RKO had determined that such documentaries were commercially unprofitable because they did not attract sufficient audience interest.

Disney, however, did not view his documentaries merely as commercial ventures. He sometimes ordered camera crews to remain on location for years, at immense cost, in a personal quest to record the often slow process of fauna performing their humanlike actions. To him, *The Living Desert* and the subsequent *Vanishing Prairie* (1954) were works of art and, as such, deserved to be seen by wide audiences, even if the distributor lost money advertising and marketing them. To make sure that his future documentaries enjoyed a better fate at theaters, Disney abruptly terminated his profitable arrangement with RKO and created his own distribution arm, Buena Vista Distribution, even though it meant that his company would have to produce many more films a year to amortize the increased overhead cost. This crucial decision, which reshaped the entire studio, proceeded not from economic calculation but from Disney's own passion to realize his art.

Even the original Jewish moguls, who had so many attributes of economic man, at times acted out of their concern with social status. In an effort to shed their ethnic roots, they used their new positions to recast their images as American plutocrats. As Neal Gabler points out, "They lived in large palatial homes, they became members of a lavish new country club called Hillcrest that mimicked the gentile clubs that barred them." They also used their studios' publicity machines to portray them as men of wealth.

For its community members, the Hollywood that replaced the studio system has even more ambiguous measures of success and, along with them, a more nuanced blend of incentives, including not only increasing monetary wealth, but also tightening communal bonds, enhancing social status, and extending celebrity standing, as well as pursuing enjoyment and artistic respect, and pleasing intellectual and spiritual gurus. Working sometimes at odds with one another, and sometimes in concert, these motives drive the surprisingly powerful social logic of Hollywood.

The Communal Instinct

Ever since Hollywood was first colonized in the early twentieth century by movie entrepreneurs and their supporting casts, it has been far more than a geographical entity. It represents, at least in the popular culture, an elite society that shares not just an art form but sensibilities, political values, philanthropic causes, and friendships; it is a magic circle of celebrated studio executives, stars, directors, and other insiders.

Steven Spielberg, in discussing the community in 1978, explained, "We see each other when it is convenient and we exchange screenplays, make comments of each other's rough cuts. . . . We spend a lot of time gossiping, speculating what the business is going to be like twenty years from now."

A top European executive stationed in Hollywood in 2001 described it in terms of a "feudal system": "A small number of princes, completely obsessed with personal loyalty, enter into temporary alliances to control territories, including stars and sequel rights," and then each "recruits mercenaries to do battle for them." Even those on the less glamorous side of Hollywood, by virtue of working for a studio and their presumed proximity to acclaimed stars, can claim to be part of the universe that creates the world's entertainment—a benefit unique to Hollywood.

As peripatetic and informal as this social intercourse appears, it has profound consequences for the movie business. Hollywood studio executives are often guided in their decisions of which movies to make not just by financial considerations but also by a desire to solidify their standing in this community of celebrities.

The boundaries of the Hollywood community, real or imagined, were shaped partly in response to the outsiders who besieged it during its first half century. Some outsiders, such as the lawyers for the Edison Trust, wanted to garner a share of its profits, while others, such as the Catholic Legion of Decency, wanted to regulate the morality reflected in its movies. There were also politicians who attempted to limit the studios' power over independent theaters; government agencies, such as the Office of War Information, who wanted to use its films for propaganda; and union leaders who wanted to control its work practices.

Many of these intrusions were laced with anti-Semitism. Congressman Martin Dies, who would later steer the House Un-American Activities Committee (HUAC) to investigate a "hotbed of communism" in the movie industry, called for scrutiny of Hollywood on the grounds that "most of the producers were Jewish." Nor were the references to the religion of the leaders of the Hollywood community limited to demagogic politicians. Intellectuals also carped about the fact that the Jewish moguls, through their control of studios, were determining a large part of American culture. F. Scott Fitzgerald, in this regard, once proclaimed Hollywood "a Jewish holiday, a Gentile's tragedy."

The nascent Hollywood studio owners, under siege, sought ways to shield themselves against outside intrusions on their new domain. One of their strategies was to place family members and cronies from their old neighborhoods in positions of power in their studios. (Nepotism had some great advantages: if relatives and friends failed to meet the test of personal loyalty, they could be disposed of with the same arbitrariness with which they had been hired.) At Columbia Pictures, for example, mogul Harry Cohn employed his three brothers, Jack, Max, and Nathan, and a neighborhood friend, Sam Briskin, to run the company. Briskin in turn hired his brother, Irving, and his two brothers-in-law, Abe Schneider and Leo Jaffe. When Cohn departed, Schneider became president and hired his own son, Bert Schneider, as a production executive. Jaffe became chairman and hired his sons, Ira and Stanley, as top executives.

At Warner Bros., the four original Warner brothers hired more than a dozen relatives, many of them in-laws, such as Mervyn LeRoy, who at the age of twenty-four became the "boy wonder" of the studio and went on to direct more than seventy Warners movies. At Universal, Carl Laemmle appointed his son, Junior, to run the studio on his twenty-first birthday; and at MGM, Louis B. Mayer turned over much of the production to his son-in-law David O. Selznick—leading *Variety* to pen the irresistible headline "The Son-in-Law Also Rises"—and later helped another son-in-law, William Goetz, become head of the newly merged Universal International studio. When producer-financier Joseph M. Schenck took over United Artists in 1924, he had only three stars under contract: Norma Talmadge, his wife; Constance Talmadge, his wife's sister; and Buster Keaton, his brother-in-law.

The studio owners also tended to rely on kin and cronies to deal discreetly with recalcitrant unions, congressional investigations, government agencies, and other behind-the-scenes problems. Lawyers such as Sidney Korshak, bankers such as Serge Semenenko, and rabbis such as Edgar Magnin became part of their extended community.

To the extent that nepotism became—and continues to be—an accepted part of the Hollywood community, it served to strengthen the value of personal loyalty. Even Rupert Murdoch, who dedicated himself to building a highly efficient company on three continents, has been quoted as saying, "I am a great believer in nepotism." But it also exacts a cost. As a consequence of appointing people on the basis of personal relationships, the community depreciates the value placed on pure merit. Actors, directors, and writers often assume that their getting assignments depends more on personal liaisons than on talent. Failure to be chosen can then be explained, as it was in David Lynch's movie about Hollywood, *Mulholland Drive,* as the result of the sexual, drug-dealing, or other hidden connections a rival has with studio executives. Nepotism, to the extent that it is accepted, leads aspirants to seek to cultivate helpful connections rather than to depend on developing their talent.

To deal with attacks on its legitimacy as an arbiter of popular culture, the community adopted a strategy of self-celebration that continues to flourish. In 1928 Louis B. Mayer suggested that the studios set up a prestigious-sounding unit, called the Motion Picture Academy of Arts and Science, to bestow annual awards on films and thereby "establish the industry in the public's mind as a respectable institution." The result was the first Academy Awards presentation, in which statuettes called Oscars were handed out to the stars, directors, and other representatives under contract to the studios. The subsequently annual black-tie show—replete with scripted speeches by stars, tearful acceptances, promotional clips from movies, and eulogies—has been successful enough to become one of the televised highlights of the year and has spawned numerous other award ceremonies, such as the Golden Globe Awards, New York Film Critics Circle Awards, and the Hollywood Film Festival Awards.

Indeed, the value of public self-congratulation has become so inculcated in the Hollywood culture that one producer carpingly complained, "These ceremonies have taken over our social life. Almost every week we get into our formal gear, push through a gauntlet of paparazzi to get to some ballroom, give ourselves awards for everything from movies to lifetime achievements, and then applaud ourselves." Even the greenlighting process has been affected by the spirit of self-celebration, as studio executives find themselves looking for projects that—by touching on social, political, environmental, or cultural issues—have the potential to be award magnets, even if the films lack the potential for making great financial profits.

The community also sanctions, and often lobbies for, movies that express artistic values rather than purely commercial ones. The community's penchant for seeing itself as engaged in a serious art form took on great momentum during World War II with the influx of refugees to Hollywood from European film and art centers. Unlike the industry's pioneers, who had little formal education or artistic training, the new arrivals—such as Michael Curtiz, Billy Wilder, Fritz Lang, Anatole Litvak, and Otto Preminger—had cosmopolitan backgrounds and substantial cultural credentials, having already made impressive films in Europe. Many of these exiles found Hollywood, if not entirely devoid of culture, at least a far cry from paradise. To bon vivant producer Sam Spiegel, it was merely "a factory in the sun"; to socialist Bertolt Brecht, it was the "marketplace of lies." Whatever their misgivings, many not only retained their confidence in themselves as artists but brought this confidence to the community. They had been schooled in techniques that mirrored avant-garde movements in the art world, such as expressionism and surrealism, and the value they placed on "cinema" as a legitimate art form gradually became part of the Hollywood vocabulary. The most common explanation given by publicity people for almost any Hollywood decision is "artistic reasons." For example, when Tom Cruise turned down a starring role in *Cold Mountain,* he said through a spokeperson that he had decided against the film for artistic reasons, not financial ones.

The collapse of the studio system also radically changed the social landscape of the community. As has been noted earlier, a large portion of the wealth that had formerly gone to the studios now began flowing to the stars, directors, writers, and musicians. Their multimillion-dollar paychecks for a single movie now often exceed the annual compensation top studio executives receive. This radical redistribution of wealth in Hollywood has resulted in new elites whose values form a critical part of the new system's social logic.

The New Elites

The Stars

The Hollywood community has long drawn much of its allure from star actors. Initially, before the movie industry moved to the sunnier and less litiginous environment of Southern California, lead actors did not necessarily have public personas; indeed, their names often were not even mentioned in the introductory credits of films. Instead of attempting to brand the actors in the public mind, the studios of the early 1900s branded their products with their own names. The first celebrated movie actress, Florence Lawrence, was referred to in press releases as "the Biograph Girl" while she worked for Biograph Pictures; after she was hired in 1909 by Carl Laemmle for his company, IMP (Independent Motion Pictures), she became "the IMP Girl."

The creation of stars with names, albeit often invented names, was partly undertaken by the studios themselves as a tactic to defend against the lawsuits that had been filed by the Edison Trust. In disputing the Trust's claim that the value of movies proceeded from the recording devices that Thomas Edison had patented, filmmakers argued that their movies achieved their commercial value from the actors who starred in them. To advance their position in the court of public opinion, they began featuring named actors on posters, ads, and marquees—and, by doing so, conferring instant celebrity status on them. Mary Pickford, for example, quickly became "Little Mary," and other such star brand names followed.

By the time the moguls organized their studios in California, the star system was in full force. Under this arrangement, the studios helped create public personas for their stars by typecasting them in roles and publicizing their on-screen personalities. By establishing stars as brands in the popular imagination, studios enhanced their own position (and profit), since the stars remained bound by long-term contracts, no matter how popular they became.

Under this arrangement, brand-name actors were effectively the property of the studios, just as Mickey Mouse, Pluto, and the other created characters in Disney's cartoons were the property of his animation studio. Despite the conceptual similarity, and their legal bondage, however, actors did have at least one advantage over cartoon characters: they could use their celebrity status to empower themselves within the Hollywood community, even if it was only by attending dinners, picnics, and other social functions given by those with power, such as William Randolph Hearst.

The advent of sound movies in the late 1920s changed the pool from which stars were drawn. With silent movies, stars had only to look the part. They could be ex–rodeo cowboys, ex-stuntmen, ex-models, or ex–vaudeville hoofers. With talkies, stars had to sound as well as look the part, both on and off the screen. For the studios, this requisite meant that new stars had to be recruited with vocal abilities, and that meant drawing largely from the legitimate theater in New York, Chicago, and London.

The new technology, by giving actors voices rather than captions, also elevated their status. Their screen characters, which the public was encouraged to take for their own characters, could now be witty, sassy, coquettish, moving, and, with the aid of the right script, politically rousing. So could their off-screen personas display these attributes on at least two other voice-driven media: radio—which by the 1930s had an immensely powerful hold on the American imagination—and newsreels, which then had a captive audience of over half the population in theaters. Though much of this entertainment news was a scripted product of the studios' own publicity machines, it nevertheless gave the stars themselves tremendous exposure, as did their sought-after appearances at charity events, political rallies, and society parties. They became the public face of Hollywood.

Unlike the ex-cowboys, ex-stuntmen, mimes, and other silent-screen stars whom they replaced, the voiced actors were also in a position to exert more control over their public personas—and, with their public acclaim, were increasingly motivated to take advantage of their public voices. Studio executives still had the power to edit what their stars said both in their films and in their publicity appearances, but the resentment engendered among the stars, who were becoming furious in their own right, became increasingly taxing to the goodwill on which the community relied. For example, in 1936, when Academy Award–winning actress Bette Davis rejected a role, her studio successfully sued her for breach of contract, arguing, as Jack Warner testified at the trial, that the studio had created her out of "almost obscurity." Davis had no choice but to go back to work for Warner Bros., but the studio's Dr. Frankenstein–like claim of creation did not sit well with Hollywood actors. Nor did the clause in their contracts that automatically extended the length of their term of service to the studio if they failed to work for any reason. If a star rebelled, as Olivia De Havilland did at one point, refusing to work on a film at Warner Bros., no other studio would employ her, out of concern that it would be sued for abetting contractual evasion. In 1944 a California court, finding in De Havilland's favor, declared the extension clause in the studio contract invalid on the grounds that it constituted "involuntary servitude." This decision spelled the beginning of the end of the stars' chattel status.

After the studio system ended and its moguls were replaced by corporate conglomerates, stars became the dominant force in the Hollywood community. Their compensation, spurred on by bidding wars between studios and independent producers, rose astronomically. By 2003, the ranking stars were not only receiving fees of more than $20 million per film and multimillion-dollar perk packages but a substantial percentage of the rental income from film, video, DVD, television, product placements, and licensing rights when the film's earnings exceeded their guaranteed fee. Arnold Schwarzenegger, it will be recalled, got for *Terminator 3* a fixed fee of $29.25 million, $1.25 million for his perks, and 20 percent of all the gross revenues produced by the film worldwide after it reached its cash breakeven point. Such contracts can take months to negotiate, with the legal bill for a film often exceeding $800,000.

The average earnings per film for the top ten stars of 2003 was roughly thirty times what the equivalent stars had earned in 1948 under the studio system (even *after* correcting for inflation). To be sure, less than 1 percent of the eight thousand actors in the Screen Actors Guild received multimillion-dollar fees, but for those few who do—and for the many others who aspire to such compensation—the size of those paychecks helps establish their place at the top of the community's hierarchy.

With these enormous fees, stars began creating their own personal production companies, which became their fiefdoms. Tom Cruise's production company, Cruise-Wagner Productions, for example, has coproduced not only several of Cruise's own movies—such as *Vanilla Sky*, *Mission: Impossible,* and *The Last Samurai*—but some of the movies made by his former wife, Nicole Kidman, such as *The Others.* Many of these companies resemble miniature versions of the mogul-era studios. Just as studios frequently rented out their stars to other studios, these companies rent out their stars to other production companies. Oak Productions, owned by Arnold Schwarzenegger, for example, acted as the "lender" of the star's services to the film production of *Terminator 3.* The studios then contractually arranged to pay the lender rather than the star for Schwarzenegger's acting and publicity services. Through this arrangement, a star can delay paying his state and federal personal taxes if the lender delays disbursing the money. Typically, stars use these corporate vehicles to pay a large part of their personal retinue, which may include lawyers, accountants, business managers, script readers, body trainers, masseuses, bodyguards, pilots, and chefs. Not uncommonly, friends, wives, and relatives are listed on the corporation's payroll as producers, writers, and consultants.

Even when not acting as coproducers, stars often have the contractual power to choose, or block, many of the people who will work on a production. In *Terminator 3,* for example, Schwarzenegger had the right to "preapprove" not only the director (Jonathan Mostow) and principal cast, but his hairdresser (Peter Toothbal), his makeup man (Jeff Dawn), his driver (Howard Valesco), his stand-in (Dieter Rauter), his stunt double (Billy Lucas), the unit publicist (Sheryl Merin), his personal physician (Dr. Graham Waring), and his cook (Steve Hunter).

Stars can also lend their prestige to independent filmmakers as, for example, Tom Hanks did by acting as nominal producer of *My Big Fat Greek Wedding* and Robert Redford did in helping to found and sponsor the Sundance Film Festival (earning "special thanks" for numerous independent films such as *The Brothers McMullen*). Just the use of their names can put rising actors, directors, and technicians in the thrall of stars.

Stars generally expect allegiance and fealty in return for their support. They also often demand that those under their protection exercise extreme discretion, especially where their legend might be damaged by disclosures. Everyone involved in their movies, production companies, or employ is usually "NDA-ed," that is, required to sign a binding nondisclosure agreement that rivals in strictness anything that existed at the height of the studio system—or in the CIA, for that matter. The producers, distributors, and even insurers are likewise required not to release unauthorized information. The producers of *Terminator 3*, for example, had to agree not to "release, disseminate, divulge, publish, or authorize or cause to be released, disseminated, divulged, or published (including, without limitation, by means of articles in newspapers or magazines or in books, whether fiction or nonfiction) any medical information or other material information that becomes available to their authorized representatives" about the star, Arnold Schwarzenegger. To ensure the stars' control over their biographies, their contracts frequently prohibit any behind-the-scenes filming of them without their advance approval and give them effective veto power over the use of their photographs in advertisements and any publicity releases involving them.

Stars seek such protection over their public personas because, even if they may be skilled actors capable of playing many different parts, their earning power is largely predicated on their ability to fit a single image both on and off the screen. For example, after it was reported that his father, Charles Voyde Harrelson, had been imprisoned for multiple murders, including the contract killing of a federal judge, studios began casting Woody Harrelson—who had first made his name playing a genial TV bartender—in movies in which he played a prisoner or criminal (including *Natural Born Killers, Palmetto, Wag the Dog, The People vs. Larry Flynt, Scorched,* and *Money Train*).

Despite the history of nepotism in other parts of Hollywood, the top stars usually achieve their standing entirely by dint of their own efforts. Few, if any, of today's stars receiving fees of $20 million—which in agents' lingo qualifies them as "superstars"—came from privileged backgrounds, inherited wealth, or attended elite schools.

Most of these top stars also have had only limited formal education, having dropped out of college and even high school to pursue their careers. "What it does mean is this: early entry," screenwriter William Goldman points out in his memoir of Hollywood. "And when you come into show business early, there is one simple truth that applies to one and all: the business takes over your life."

Consider, for example, the careers of the ranking male superstars of the last decade of the twentieth century: Tom Hanks, Tom Cruise, Arnold Schwarzenegger, Harrison Ford, Mel Gibson, and John Travolta. They were all born to parents of only modest means. Their childhoods tended to be nomadic. None completed a four-year college. Thomas Cruise Mapother attended no fewer than fifteen different schools before dropping out of a Catholic seminary at the age of fifteen, and a public high school at eighteen. He then sought work as an actor and was cast as a teenager in *Endless Love*. Tom Hanks had a succession of stepparents and attended a series of grammar schools during his childhood. Dropping out of the California State University system, he took various bit acting parts before being cast in the television series *Bosom Buddies*. Harrison Ford, after being expelled from Ripon College in California, worked on a number of television series before a casting director chose him to be in *American Graffiti*.

As a teenager, Mel Gibson moved from Peekskill, New York, to New South Wales, Australia, because his father, who had won prize money on the quiz show *Jeopardy*, did not want Gibson to be drafted to fight in the war in Vietnam. In Australia, Gibson enrolled in Sydney's National Institute of Dramatic Art and, after some minor roles, was cast because of his striking physical appearance as the lead in *Mad Max*.

Arnold Schwarzenegger, the son of an Austrian policeman, became through a highly disciplined exercise regime a world-champion bodybuilder, repeatedly winning the Mr. World title. In 1970 his physical as-

sets won him the title role in *Hercules in New York*, a low-budget exploitation film, under the pseudonym Arnold Strong. He then played
himself in the documentary *Pumping Iron*, and finally, after five years of
bit parts as muscle men and gym instructors, he landed the starring role
in *Conan the Barbarian*, and, demonstrating a willingness to work
through the night, if necessary, to help complete a shot, he became a favorite of such top action directors as James Cameron, Richard Fleischer,
and John McTiernan.

The obvious importance of their looks notwithstanding, these actors
succeeded in achieving stardom in the community not just because they
looked the part—there exists at any given time in Hollywood a plethora
of actors and models capable of fitting similar stereotypes—but also because they readily adopted the values of the community.

Paramount among these values is the "show-must-go-on" work ethic.
"Superstars do not get where they are by throwing temperamental fits,
malingering on the set, or not following direction," explained the head of
a top Hollywood talent agency. "Popular misconceptions notwithstanding, they succeeded by being hardworking, highly disciplined professionals." For one thing, almost all films that use outside financing or equity
partners need to obtain "essential-element" insurance on stars. This allows the producers the legal right to abandon the entire project if, for any
reason, the stars are unable to complete the shooting of their parts and to
get fully reimbursed for all the direct costs of the production from the insurer. If, for example, Arnold Schwarzenegger had been unable to finish
shooting *Terminator 3*, the insurers would have had to pay $168 million
to the producers. Insurers will only provide such an essential-element
policy if they are confident that the stars themselves have no history of
medical, drug-taking, or psychological problems that might result in an
inability to perform. To get insurance from Fireman's Fund, Brad Pitt
had to submit to independent drug testing during principal photography
of *Confessions of a Dangerous Mind* (which he passed). The insurers also
insist that productions agree to use doubles to film any action scenes that
might result in even a sprained ankle, and even when not filming, stars
must agree not to engage in any hazardous activity, such as piloting an
airplane, riding a motorcycle, or water-skiing. While insurers cannot
guard against all contingencies, they attempt to minimize their risk by

refusing to insure actors who have a history of temperamental behavior, depression, risk taking, or other problems.

If productions are unable to get such star insurance, they cannot get the completion bonds that banks and outside financiers require. If actors are not deemed insurable, then no matter how many honors they receive, they cannot be stars in films that require outside financing or coproducers. Nicole Kidman is a case in point. In 2000 she injured her knee during the filming of *Moulin Rouge!* in Australia, resulting in a $3 million insurance loss, and then quit *Panic Room* in 2001, which led to the insurer having to pay $7 million for the replacement actress (Jodie Foster). As a result, her public and critical acclaim notwithstanding, Miramax was initially unable to get insurance on her for its film *Cold Mountain*, which had a budget approaching $100 million. To get such a policy, Kidman agreed to put $1 million of her own salary in an escrow account that would be forfeited if she failed to maintain the production schedule and to use a stunt double for all scenes that the insurer considered potentially threatening to her knee. Insurers finally agreed to grant the policy only after a coproducer added another $500,000 to the escrow account, and after the completion-bond company, International Film Guarantors, certified that "Kidman is fully aware that she must get through this picture without a problem. She fully understands this and will not allow anything to get in the way of her finishing this picture."

Even when films are made without outside financing—and therefore do not require essential-element insurance—studios tend to put a high value on those stars who demonstrate by their actions that they "will not allow anything to get in the way" of completing films on time. Since it usually costs between $100,000 and $250,000 for every extra day of principal photography on a major film, studios have a powerful incentive to select performers who demonstrate early, and consistently, an ability to arrive punctually on the set whenever they are needed for makeup and other preparations, and remain as long as necessary, even under adverse conditions, to complete the day's shooting. Reese Witherspoon, who began her acting career when she was fifteen, prided herself on arriving on the set of *Legally Blonde* at 6 A.M. to give makeup crews two and a half hours to prepare her look and remaining, if necessary, late into the night.

Producers, by the same logic, avoid using stars with a history of causing delays. Such a concern was dramatized in the 2002 movie *Simone,* which concerns the modern filmmaker's problem of relying on the cooperation of stars who may be tempestuous, capricious, or egocentric. When the narcissistic star of the movie within the movie, Nicola (Winona Ryder), delays shooting with her demands for a better trailer, producer-director Victor Taransky (Al Pacino) fires her. He ruefully explains to the studio head (Catherine Keener) that it used to be better in the old days of the studio system: "We always had stars, but they used to be our stars. We would tell them what to do, what to wear, who to date. They were under contract to us." While agreeing, the studio head demands that he either find a new star or quit the movie. Taransky solves the dilemma by creating a computer-generated composite of a star that incorporates the best features of such bygone luminaries as Marlene Dietrich, Audrey Hepburn, and Lauren Bacall.

The creation, named Simone, is then programmed to do whatever Taransky requires. By substituting a computer image for an actress, he is able to keep to the studio's production schedule, and as a result, the studio head suggests that they consider replacing all the other stars with simulations.

While the idea of computer-generated actors may seem like the answer to a studio prayer, in fact the studios (and their insurers) manage fairly well by finding stars who can be counted on to cooperate with them in avoiding delays on sets and locations. With the tacit help of the talent agencies, the studios weed out at an early stage those people, whatever their other acting virtues, who do not share the community's work ethic.

A second requisite for stardom is a willingness to "stay in character"—on television talk shows, in magazine interviews, during ceremonial hosting and award duties, and at all other public appearances. As a top Sony marketing executive said, "The consistency between their on-screen and offscreen image is what makes stars uniquely marketable." To accomplish this feat, stars often follow either scripts or talking points prepared by the studios' publicists to reinforce their movie personas. If they play romantic heroes on-screen, for example, they may have to find occasion to allude to liaisons that did not occur, perhaps even with a person whose sex they do not have a preference for.

Not only may they be called on in their scripted interviews to display the false, but, to make it credible, they usually also have to conceal the real. It is no coincidence that the sly terms of art—for example, "twilight tandems" and "lavender marriages"—used to denote the phony personal relationships devised by the studios' publicists to conceal stars' homosexuality came in fashion during the era of the studio system. A prime example is Rock Hudson (born Roy Scherer), who died from AIDS in 1985. For more than thirty years, to preserve his image as a romantic lead in films such as *Pillow Talk, Magnificent Obsession,* and *Lover Come Back,* Hudson had—and was able—to conceal the homosexual relations of his private life, even though they were well known in the Hollywood community. By this public disguise he managed to stay in character as a strong, silent type of romantic hero. When unavoidable public circumstances, such as arrests or lawsuits, prevent actors from staying in character, their careers as stars are often severely damaged, if not destroyed. Winona Ryder's conviction for shoplifting in 2002 conflicted with the "innocent" persona that had been developed for her, and as a result, it became difficult to cast her in the roles that she had been playing up to that point.

A third requisite for stardom is a willingness to compromise to further the underlying business of Hollywood: deals. Talent agencies, independent production companies, and studios all act as "rainmakers" for these deals. To facilitate them, they often need actors to make concessions on their "quote," as agents call their established fee, or on their objections to the script, director, cast, or locations. If actors resist such accommodations, talent agencies can't put other clients in the "package," the production companies can't get the green light that frees them to develop other projects, and studio executives cannot fill their pipeline with future films. "If stars aren't players, this business simply does not work," the head of a talent agency explained. Talent agents consequently favor among their clients those they deem "team players," who will do what is required to advance projects, even if it means accepting unfavorable terms for themselves, over those who are rigid in their standards. Producers and studio executives also have a mutual interest in advancing "pragmatists," as one studio president termed them. Such stars frequently can be counted on in adverse circumstances. For example, when the budget of *Terminator 3* got into difficulties, Arnold Schwarzenegger offered to help finance the cost of reshooting scenes by deferring $3 million of his own salary.

The performers who advance to the top rank of stardom therefore tend to have qualities that go far beyond their acting skills and physical appearance, foremost among these an ability to identify with the values of the Hollywood community. This virtue is often described in Academy Award presentations and other ceremonial testimonials as "professionalism." So long as studios can recruit stars with this virtue, they need not resort to *Simone*-like simulations.

In return, stars introduce their own values to the Hollywood community. Consider, for example, the almost iconic value placed on private jets. Tom Wolfe's description in his essay "The Ultimate Power" of private jets as "one of the last big objects that symbolize power" applies aptly to their use by movie stars. Tom Cruise's Gulfstream IV jet, which cost $28 million, is configured with three cabins and a Jacuzzi. John Travolta has not only a private jet but his own pilot's license. Describing what is virtually a private airline, he said, "We always fly the Gulfstream with three pilots, including myself," as well as "a flight engineer and one or two flight attendants. Most commercial airlines don't have the flight-deck crew we have." Stars who do not own jets frequently insist on having film productions charter them for their exclusive use during the filming of their movies. Schwarzenegger's contract for *Terminator 3*, for example, specified that he "be provided with exclusive private jet transportation on a G-4SP for travel in North America and on a G-5 for travel overseas."

Even when they are not filming, stars often get access to studio jets as a goodwill gesture. Gwyneth Paltrow explained that the New Line subsidiary of Time Warner gained favor with her by giving her and her dog a ride from New York to Los Angeles in its corporate jet in June 2002, saying, "It was just after September [11] and I had trepidation about flying out there and I wanted to bring my dog. So Bob Shay, who is the head of New Line who I love, sent me a plane, which made me feel very excited. So that was my payment [for *Goldmember*]. I got a one-way trip on a private plane."

Studio executives quickly came to realize that private jets could be used to enhance their standing with the stars. For example, Robert Evans, who in 1972 was the head of Paramount, attempted to get Marlon Brando to attend the opening of *The Godfather* by making, as he put it, "an offer that even Marlon couldn't refuse—a private jet for him and [his son] Christian." (As it turned out, Brando did refuse it.) Steve Ross applied the same logic to justify purchasing a small fleet of private jets for Warner Bros. so they could be lent out to such stars as Clint Eastwood, Steven Spielberg, Barbra Streisand, and Madonna. David Wolper, a close business associate of Ross's, explained, "Steve discovered the one perk you can give Madonna [is] not jewelry, limos, or grand hotel suites. That's all peanuts. It is your corporate jet. That's a business thing that glues [stars] to Time Warner." He added, "The first thing those [former Warner Bros.] producers Peter Guber and Jon Peters did when they went to Columbia-Sony was to get a corporate jet."

Once the stars established private jets as a totem of success, the symbol percolated down through the community to directors and others. For example, Barry Sonnenfeld, one of the top directors in Hollywood, brought the subject up when he appeared on David Letterman's show in 2003, claiming that he spends a large part of his income chartering private jets to commute between his homes in East Hampton, New York, and Telluride, Colorado.

The now-central position of the stars in the Hollywood hierarchy ensures that whatever objects or causes they value will assume importance to the community at large. The stars' gravitational pull, which in no small part stems from their shrewd appreciation of the who-gets-what-from-whom interdependence of Hollywood, helps determine the relative position of the directors, producers, writers, agents, and other key members in the community.

Directors

Today directors, even more than stars, are crucial to the traffic in film production that energizes the Hollywood community. A movie can be made without a star—indeed, many of the most profitable movies do not have stars—but without a director, no production can get a green light from a studio. It will be recalled that directors did not always have such a pivotal role. In the studio-system era, directors were often no more than employees—and even the most celebrated directors of their day were often treated accordingly. At MGM, Louis B. Mayer had no compunction about punching directors like Erich von Stroheim and Charlie Chaplin in the face when they said things to him of which he disapproved. They were also part-time employees, generally arriving at the beginning of principal photography, after the scripts had been developed, the parts cast, the technicians hired, the sets approved, and the musical numbers choreographed and rehearsed. They generally left at the conclusion of principal photography, which was often before the footage was edited, the soundtracks mixed, and the musical score created. The director's main job during principal photography was to keep the production on schedule by getting the actors to complete a fixed portion of the shooting script each day. The footage was then screened daily for the supervising studio executives, who ordered the directors to reshoot any scenes they were not satisfied with. If at any point studio executives assessed that the production was falling behind schedule, they ordered directors to speed up the process. And if directors were unable or unwilling to conform, which seldom happened, they were replaced.

There were, to be sure, notable exceptions, such as Orson Welles, who not only directed his first film, *Citizen Kane*, but cowrote, coproduced, coedited, and starred in it in 1941. But even such a phenomenon as Welles, who had his own acting and production company, the Mercury Players, was unable to retain control over his next film, *The Magnificent Ambersons* (1942). The studio, RKO, removed him after principal photography, bringing in new writers to rewrite his script, three new directors to reshoot scenes, and two new editors to cut the film according to the studio's dictates.

Directors in Europe, meanwhile, were enjoying a very different position, assuming authorship of the entire product from its initial concept to its final editing. In the European tradition, films were considered a work of art inseparable from their directors or, as the Paris journal *Cahier du Cinéma* called them, "auteurs." In the auteur theory that developed around them, directors, not the writers or actors, were alone responsible for the artistic achievement—or failure—of movies. When many of these auteur directors fled Europe to escape Hitler, they brought that concept with them to Hollywood.

After the collapse of the studio system, Hollywood directors greatly increased their role in the filmmaking process. The reorganized studios ceded them a much larger measure of control over the creative content of films, not because they were sudden converts to the European auteur theory, but because they had little choice. The stars, now emancipated from their contracts, insisted on prior approval of directors—as did outside financiers, on whom the studios now heavily depended, and completion-bond guarantors, on whom the financiers depended. To get stars and money, studios now had to commit themselves to a particular director. Directors, making the most of their new leverage, began insisting on approval of the script and casting. The result was that studios could no longer replace directors, or any elements over which they had approval, without courting disaster. Even though studios reserved the right to make the final cut, by the mid-1950s directors such as John Ford, Howard Hawks, and George Stevens had a hand in the entire creative process, from script development in preproduction to editing, visual effects, and musical scoring in postproduction editing.

Like their European counterparts, today's directors also often act as both cowriters and coproducers. Even when writers receive full credit for the story and screenplay, directors often find ways of asserting their de facto authorship. Consider, for example, the 2002 movie *The Bourne Identity*. Robert Ludlum, the author of the 1980 novel of the same title and the 1988 television movie *The Bourne Identity*, as well as screenwriters Tony Gilroy and W. Blake Herron, received the official screenplay credit. But director Doug Liman took the even grander "A film by" credit for himself. In his DVD director's commentary, Liman asserted that while he "loved the book in high school" and spent more than two years acquiring Ludlum's rights to it, he "jettisoned pretty much everything in the book except the premise, not only to modernize it but to bring it in line with my politics, which are definitely left of center."

With the exception of screenwriters and book authors, most Hollywood participants have little reason to dispute the artistic conceit of directorial "authorship." Studios, for their part, find it convenient to have directors publicly credited with creative authorship, even when the credit rightfully belongs to someone else. Not only do directors serve as the effective lynchpin in organizing the cast and script, but they form a helpful buffer between the stars and the studio (and handy scapegoats if the film fails or receives poor notices). Talent agencies have a similar interest in promoting the concept of directorial authorship, as they can now use their director clients as the building blocks of "packages" that can include their stars, literary properties, writers, and other talent. For production companies, the notion of directorial authorship can lend further credence to the significance of a director's track record and become an additional means of persuading investors to participate. Finally, reviewers find in directorial authorship a focus for their criticism and commentary. All these parties thus have independent but complementary reasons for lending their support to the cult of the director.

Directors themselves, of course, greatly profit from the idea of film authorship. Whereas in the studio system they rarely received more than $80,000 for a film, salaries of more than $4 million were common by 2003. Director John McTiernan was paid $5.3 million for his work on the film *Basic,* Roger Donaldson received $4.4 million for directing *The Recruit,* and Jonathan Mostow received almost $5 million for directing *Terminator 3* (part of which was to be paid out of the fees for product placements in the movie).

In addition to earning more money, directors get bragging rights, especially with the advent of the director's commentary on the DVD. In many of these commentaries, directors impute to themselves Pygmalian-like powers to physically transform and control actors. Director Alan Pakula, for example, tells how after Meryl Streep had "literally" begged him on her hands and knees for the part of Sophie in *Sophie's Choice,* he had her go on a liquid diet until she lost ten pounds, undergo dental work to change her teeth, wear a wig, and speak her part in German, a language she did not understand. For *Against All Odds,* director Taylor Hackford claims that he physically transformed both Jeff Bridges, who was "a real porker," and his costar Rachel Ward, who looked "too soft." He had Bridges "lose thirty pounds" and wear eye pads and made Ward "cut her hair short." Conversely, director Adrian Lyne relates how, for his version of *Lolita,* he ordered his two stars, Jeremy Irons and Melanie Griffith, to gain weight and Irons to give up his smoking habit. For *The Bourne Identity,* Doug Liman claims that he directed his star Matt Damon to "bulk up" his body by undergoing a rigorous daily muscle-building regime for "three or four months." For *Eye of the Beholder,* director Stephan Elliott claims that he got his star Ewan McGregor "drunk on Cognac" to get a more intoxicated performance.

Hair, or the lack of it, is another way that directors now demonstrate their absolute power over their performers. Director Michael Caton-Jones said in his DVD commentary that he ordered Richard Gere to remove all his "facial hair" for *The Jackal.* For *Anna and the King,* director Andy Tennant had Chinese costar Ling Bai, who had been wearing her beautiful hair down to her waist since she first arrived in America, "completely shave her head" for the purpose of a single scene. For *High Crimes*, director Carl Franklin asked the book's author, Joe Finder, to shave his head to earn a nonspeaking part in the film. And director Betty Thomas explains that she had all the black extras in *I Spy* shave their heads "because I thought it would be fun."

While directors may indeed exercise a great deal of puppeteering power and credit themselves in DVDs and television interviews with singular authorship, they also confront a tacit reality on the set: they need the cooperation of others—and, in particular, their stars—to complete their films on schedule. For the most part, they do not have the power to compel this cooperation. For example, they cannot fire their stars if they do not follow instructions. Nor, in practice, can they force them to do endless rehearsals and reshoots. The typical contract limits a star's services to a finite number of weeks of principal photography, and usually only a week or so for preproduction rehearsals and postproduction reshoots. Arnold Schwarzenegger's contract for *Terminator 3* provided that he would make himself available for one week on a nonexclusive basis for rehearsals and five days for reshooting. Even attempting to press stars to perform in ways that they consider to be wrong or inappropriate can pose a great risk for directors' careers, since they depend on stars' prior approval of them for future projects.

There are also limits to what directors can demand from their other coworkers, such as their second-unit directors, who independently shoot their action sequences, and digital-effects subcontractors, who independently create many of their missing scenes. In theory they can order such sequences redone, but in practice any substantial reshooting of second-unit scenes and re-creation of digital material risks running up the budget, which, in turn, requires the approval of studio executives. As a result, the creation of a movie is very much a group effort.

Alexander Mackendrick, who directed the classic films *Sweet Smell of Success* and *The Ladykillers* in succession, made this point with great force. He explains that he could make movies as different as these two because "each was the product of its ensemble. Different writers: William Rose for 'Ladykillers,' Clifford Odets on 'Success'; different directors of photography, Otto Heller and James Wong Howe; different music, Boccherini and Bernstein; different actors, different locations." The fact of two such disparate films, shot back-to-back by the same director, may not quite demonstrate, as Mackendrick provocatively concludes, that "the director makes no difference," but it effectively debunks the claim of sole authorship by the director. Even a perfectionist like Stanley Kubrick, who can spend several years personally supervising every element of every shot of a film and ordering as many as sixty retakes, had ultimately to conform to stars Tom Cruise and Nicole Kidman in *Eyes Wide Shut*, and even a director as powerful as Steven Spielberg, who effectively controls his own studio, acknowledges that his films are a "collaborative effort."

For most directors, success depends on the ability to engineer the consent of others. For this task, directors' skills must include the sort of diplomacy that allows them to get the participants to compromise their own views and collaborate as an ensemble for the duration of the production. Directors here are generally greatly aided if they can persuade writers, actors, and others in the production that their own vision is inalienably associated with the artistic integrity of the product and will be perceived as such by audiences, critics, and award presenters. "If actors believe we can win awards for them, they are much more likely to defer to our judgment," one director explained. "The trick is building confidence." In this sense, the projection of artistic integrity is essential to a director's control.

To enhance this perception of directing as an art form with a distinct tradition, today's directors frequently include in their films "homages" to past directors—such as Alfred Hitchcock, Federico Fellini, and John Ford—and discuss their films in interviews, at award ceremonies, and in film-studies lectures in the context of past classics. Indeed, at almost every turn, inside and outside the community, they work to lend an aura of aesthetic dignity to the community's own perception of itself.

Agents

With the disintegration of the studio system, a new player, the talent agent, moved from the community's periphery to its center stage. Once studios no longer had actors under long-term contracts and had to competitively bid for their services, agents became vital intermediaries in the community. By the 1950s, agents such as Lew Wasserman were bundling their star actors together with directors, producers, and writers into packages for studios. Hollywood, by then in desperate competition with television, needed stars with name recognition, even if it meant delegating a large part of their casting to these agents. So the agents became not only stars' representatives but their deal makers. They effectively took over from the studios the task of managing the careers of their star clients.

Some agents parlayed these prized relationships into high positions at studios. Agent Ted Ashley, for example, became Warner Bros.' studio chief, agent David Begelman became president of Columbia Pictures, agent Ron Meyers took over as Universal's head, and agent Michael Ovitz became Disney's president. Other agents, meanwhile, became the executives of independent production companies, such as Paula Wagner at Cruise-Wagner Productions, Jack Rapke at Image Movers, and Gareth Wigan at the Ladd Company. Whether at talent agencies, studios, or independent production companies, these professionals performed essentially the same job: brokering an accommodation between a small group of star actors who were needed in movies for their name recognition and the directors who were necessary to arrange the movies' financing and distribution. Whatever the title on their doors, they were essentially facilitators who met a basic need in the community: knitting together the services of powerful, idiosyncratic, and often temperamental individuals. To succeed at this delicate task, they had to maintain the confidence not only of the "talent" but also of the talent's lawyers, business managers, insurers, and, in many cases, spouses and gurus.

By the end of the twentieth century, agents had established themselves as a formidable force in the Hollywood community. "In terms of sheer numbers, they not only dominate deal making, they dominate the press in Hollywood," the former head of one studio said. In 2003 an estimated 6,000 agents were employed, representing some 120,000 clients.

Most of the profession's fees are generated by a few dozen top agents who represent almost all the major stars. These "superagents," as they are called in the trade press, are almost all partners at five major agencies—Creative Artists Agency (CAA), International Creative Management (ICM), William Morris, United Talent Agency (UTA), and Endeavor. CAA, which has the largest number of stars and directors, was alone involved in the negotiations of over half of all the movies produced by the studios in 2003.

The very nature of these agencies' work, liaising between providers and buyers of creative services, makes their agents the unofficial gate-keepers to the Hollywood community. It is the agents who customarily arrange their clients' agendas, setting up personal meetings, conference calls, business dinners, and other encounters. They provide convenient meeting places, sometimes offering their own offices and homes as well as selecting restaurants and clubs. They extend invitations to social events, such as screenings, cocktail parties, art openings, and philanthropic benefits.

Agents also act as confidants to their clients. Since they negotiate their clients' contracts, they are often privy to their financial situation, time commitments, and—if they require cast insurance—medical problems. Lew Wasserman, when he presided over MCA, provided a full-service ministry for clients. According to Peter Bart and Peter Guber, he even "mediated divorce settlements for superstar clients."

In fulfilling their various responsibilities, agents frequently maintain working relationships with their clients' personal attorneys, business managers, tax consultants, real-estate agents, and other advisors. They often discreetly listen in on conference calls. And they are charged with getting informal dispensations for their clients on productions—special requests that can include accommodations and other benefits for their clients' lovers, trainers, gurus, personal dieticians, pet handlers, and other members of their entourage. As one top agent at Creative Artists Agency said, "There are very few secrets our clients have from us."

Agents also often double as tacit public-relations representatives for their clients, supplying off-the-record items to *Variety* or *The Hollywood Reporter*. As a former studio head explained, "They are constantly whispering in the ear of the media whatever stories, true or false, best serve their clients." Some agents also claim to hold particular sway over entertainment journalists thanks to their secret weapon: the power to reward with tempting screenwriter assignments. Michael Ovitz, when he headed CAA, was reported to have said: "I'm not worried about the press. All those guys want to write screenplays for Robert Redford." Even if such conceits rarely have a basis in fact, to the extent that they give their clients a sense of protection from a hostile press, they serve to enhance agents' power in the community.

In their role as facilitators, agents may also help clients obtain services that only peripherally relate to their professional careers. Consider, for example, Jay Moloney, a CAA agent who came to represent such star directors as Steven Spielberg and Martin Scorsese before he committed suicide in 1999. In 1986 Moloney, the son of screenwriter James Moloney, was hired at the age of twenty-one by CAA, where he worked for its chief executive, Michael Ovitz. Ovitz assigned him, among other things, the task of arranging table reservations for stars at Spago and other Hollywood restaurants owned by Wolfgang Puck. According to writer Nikki Finke, who spent thirty hours interviewing Moloney for her book on CAA, Moloney became "Puck's unofficial reservations vetter, verifying for Spago's maître d' who was deserving of an A table on any given night." When he was eventually made an agent at CAA, he and his guests, Finke writes, "hung out at Morton's or Spago at dinner, the Peninsula Hotel for drinks, Matsuhisa for sushi," they went "to Hawaii for golf or Colorado for white-water rafting or the Bahamas for a tan," and he "rented a house in Santa Barbara where they would party when they tired of his Hollywood Hills and Malibu pads." The services Moloney provided at these parties reportedly included obtaining cocaine and other drugs. Finke writes, "Moloney wasn't just doing drugs but flaunting them in every hip club and restaurant from coast to coast . . . snorting cocaine out of glass vials." According to a screenwriter who was a CAA client during this period, Moloney's drug exchanges, however "dark," also had a business function: they were part of the agent-client "bonding." "Since all agents charge their clients the same ten percent fee, the unique incentive they can offer is their personal dedication to their clients," this writer explains. "By bonding with them, they demonstrate that they identify their clients' ambitions and problems as their own."

Whatever its basis in reality, agents help mitigate the intrinsic uncertainties of the film business by projecting an awesome power. During a 1989 panel discussion entitled "What Does an Agent Really Do?" Jeremy Zimmer, then a top executive at ICM, said, "The big agencies are like animals, raping and pillaging one another day in and day out. We're all out there doing business. It's very competitive. And at the end of the day the question is always who's doing what to whom, how much are they doing it for, and when are they going to do it to me." Hyperbolic or not, Zimmer's remarks made the front page of *Daily Variety* because they fit in with the general belief in Hollywood: that agents exercise predatory power on behalf of the talent in the community.

Agents' standing in the community is directly related to the way their clients are perceived by the studios. When that perception weakens for any reason, such as the disappointing performance of their clients' films, their status in the community also declines. "Agents dwell in their own sociopathic cocoon," according to former studio executives Peter Bart and Peter Guber. "They dedicate themselves to the proposition that perception is reality." This makes them especially valued in a community largely dedicated to much the same proposition.

Writers

Writers have always occupied a special, if vexed, place in the Hollywood community. The talking movies brought a new class of them to Hollywood in the 1930s, many of whom—like Nathanael West, F. Scott Fitzgerald, William Faulkner, Raymond Chandler, Dorothy Parker, Aldous Huxley, and Ben Hecht—were already established in the literary world. Others were struggling novelists, essayists, and playwrights from New York, Chicago, Boston, and other intellectual centers. The lure that brought most of them westward was pecuniary. They generally assumed that, in the Depression, they could earn more money writing film scripts, or even added dialogue, than they could writing articles, magazines, or books.

Often they were disappointed. Studio writers were paid by the week, in some cases by the day. If they failed to write enough script pages to satisfy the studio's story departments, they were often summarily fired. In the mid-1930s, as the Depression deepened, the studios substantially cut writers' wages and simply replaced any writer who balked. One studio fired all its writers the day before Thanksgiving and rehired them the day after the holiday to save one day's pay.

Nor was there much glory for writers. For script doctoring, they often got no credit, and for screenplays they often shared the credit. They could hardly consider their product to be an extension of their literary art, since it was commonly rewritten by other hands, including producers, directors, and actors. The disparaging atmosphere was perhaps best summed up by Irving Thalberg, the creative head of MGM, who once asked, "What's all this business about being a writer? It's just putting one word after another."

Writers also derived little satisfaction from their attempts to insert political content in their scripts. In many cases their political agendas, if anything, served to further isolate them from the wider community. Consider, for example, John Howard Lawson, who, after writing for the Marxist journal *New Masses,* sought a wider audience in Hollywood. He made no secret of his political convictions, openly declaring himself a Communist Party member and becoming the first president of the left-leaning Screen Writers Guild. Although he tried to insert Marxist messages into his own scripts and asked other writers in the SWG to do the same, he succeeded in slipping only a few token images, such as a character whistling "La Marseillaise," into his movies. He found, as did other writers, that almost all politically controversial material was rewritten by studio producers or, if filmed, cut by editors or censored by the Hays Office. When the House Un-American Activities Committee intensified its investigation of subversives in Hollywood, Lawson and many other Guild writers were blacklisted from further studio employment.

With few exceptions, writers in those days remained on the periphery of the Hollywood colony. In most cases they found themselves the low man on the social totem pole, shunned by stars and directors and treated like necessary nuisances by studio executives. Nathanael West describes the grim conditions this way: "All the writers sit in cells in a row and the minute a typewriter stops someone pokes his head in the door to see if you are thinking."

Under such circumstances, whatever their original motivation, writers eventually came to see themselves as poorly treated pawns in a money-driven system. Their writing about Hollywood—such as Budd Schulberg's *What Makes Sammy Run,* F. Scott Fitzgerald's *The Last Tycoon,* Nathanael West's *The Day of the Locust,* and William Faulkner's "Golden Land"—often expressed contempt, if not outright loathing, for the values of the studios. A principal theme of such works is that financial calculation was systematically destroying the artistic integrity of movies. The same contempt, it should be noted, has also pervaded movies about Hollywood over the years; in *The Big Knife, The Bad and the Beautiful, Barton Fink, The Player,* and *State and Main,* the studio is constantly portrayed as run by philistines maximizing their earnings on the back of the writer's integrity. In Jean-Luc Godard's *Contempt* (1963), insult is heaped on injury: the heroine, Camille (Brigitte Bardot), holds her screenwriter husband (Michel Piccoli) in such contempt for writing a movie for a Hollywood producer that she can no longer bear to be in his company.

With the collapse of the studio system in the 1950s, the financial situation of writers—though not necessarily their low esteem of the process—improved. Independent producers largely replaced the studio's story departments and assumed much of the job of initiating studio projects by optioning and developing scripts that could attract the stars and directors that the studios required. They therefore began to seek writers who had demonstrated an ability to provide scripts that were acceptable to stars and directors.

Although there has never been a shortage of screenwriters, only a very select few—such as Robert Towne, who wrote *Chinatown*, Ernest Lehman, who wrote *North by Northwest*, William Goldman, who wrote *Butch Cassidy and the Sundance Kid*, and Shane Black, who wrote *Lethal Weapon*—have the track records to persuade stars and directors to sign on to particular projects. Since the writers with the credentials to do so almost always auction off their services through talent agencies—often the very ones who represent the stars and directors their scripts are meant to attract—the prices paid for their scripts can be astronomically high. For example, Shane Black's script fee, which was $250,000 in 1987 for *Lethal Weapon* and $1.75 million in 1991 for *The Last Boy Scout*, had climbed to $4 million in 1996 for *The Long Kiss Goodnight*. With paychecks like these, Hollywood's top writers can afford the accouterments of the community, including beach houses, ski chalets, and Ferraris. In addition to their million-dollar-plus fees for scripts, they get so-called residual payments from the licensing of movies to television and video. They can also earn up to $150,000 a week as "script doctors," rewriting the work of other writers. Robert Towne, for example, has doctored without credit the scripts of such screenwriters as William Goldman (*Marathon Man*), David Newman and Robert Benton (*Bonnie and Clyde*), Elaine May (*Heaven Can Wait*), Oliver Stone (*8 Million Ways to Die*), Norman Mailer (*Tough Guys Don't Dance*), and Stirling Silliphant (*The New Centurions*). Even though producers have to pay in advance only a portion of a writer's fees to secure a script, the rising costs of scripts do strain the limited resources of most producers, especially those who want to have a portfolio of different projects. So producers often attempt to get writers to accept smaller advances on their options by cultivating them as friends, offering them social solidarity and prestige in the community.

Screenwriter John Gregory Dunne describes the "social tapestry" in Hollywood this way: "The executive mantra goes: I don't just work with these guys . . . they're my friends." Dale Launer recalled that after his script of *Ruthless People* was made into a successful film in 1986, "producers rushed to bring me into their social orbit with invitations to dinner parties and home screenings," adding, "They seek to align themselves with any writer who can get a movie made."

Producers also frequently offer writers credits as executive producer, associate producer, or even coproducer. Since, among other things, this serves to elevate a writer's status in the community, many writers become, at least nominally, producers. In 2002, for example, over two thirds of screenwriters whose movies were nominated for Academy Awards also had producer credits on these movies.

Even though they may enjoy the joint benefits of substantial monetary rewards and social inclusion, writers still have to deal with an "alienation problem," as one highly successful writer put it. They often perceive of themselves as alienated from their product in a way that runs counter to their creative self-image. After their optioned screenplays are fully purchased, which usually occurs when productions are green-lighted by studios, the writers lose control over them. This is a reality even the top writers must learn to live with. If rewriting is necessary, directors often prefer to hire uncredited writers, who will make the changes they dictate, or do it themselves. By doing so, they not only avoid any objections that the original writer may have to changes that damage the integrity of his story but they strengthen their own claim of authorship. In many cases, directors do not even allow credited screenwriters to visit the set during shooting or to view the rough cut during postproduction. On *Chinatown*, for example, the writer Robert Towne was barred from the set and not allowed to see the dailies.

Alienation, to be sure, can have benefits. One of these is that screenwriters—unlike directors, actors, set designers, stunt coordinators, editors, and others involved in the actual group effort to complete a film under the pressure of a schedule—need not conform to the same standard of compliance and accommodation that is normally highly valued in the community. Instead, writers are allowed to be idiosyncratic and even antisocial in their behavior. Robert Towne, for example, has been known to arrive barefoot for meetings with executives. Paramount studio head Robert Evans has described him as "lethargic, scattered, perpetually late."

As it does with these displays of individualism, the community also tolerates screenwriters deprecating the accepted artistic values of Hollywood. Even after screenwriter Joe Ezterhas wrote (and published in *Premiere*) an open letter to Michael Ovitz, attacking the heavy-handed practices of Hollywood, he nevertheless continued to receive major writing assignments. Writers are allowed such latitude because their abuse is usually rationalized as little more than an outburst of intellectual vanity. Even in its apparent tolerance of writers' protest, the community effectively points to its futility, and thereby reinforces the value it places on pragmatic accommodation.

The writer's peculiar situation—at once an insider and outsider in the community—is explained by Peter Guber, who, before he founded his own production company, Mandalay, headed first Warner Bros. and then Sony, and Peter Bart, former vice president of MGM and editor of *Variety*. "The writer is at once lionized and scorned," they observe. "He is treated like the lord of the manor, yet required to eat at the servants' table. He may sell a spec script for $5 million, then have trouble getting his agent on the phone." Treated as such, writers share a "persecution complex" that "has a basis in reality."

But while the writer's position may be ambiguous in the community, it is not without consequence. Aside from their work in movies, writers also script much of the content of the awards ceremonies and other events—including speeches, self-deprecating jokes, and nostalgic commentaries. At the end of the day, they are still the ones who write the lines that others speak. And these lines help establish the values of the Hollywood community.

Producers

The producer is the community's primary rainmaker. Through skilled manipulation of personal funds, civilian investors, social connections, talent agents, and other resources, the producer can cause the swirling elements of Hollywood—including stars, directors, writers, and studio interests—to coalesce into a project.

Instead of claiming a single producer, as they did in the days of the studio system, today's movies boast a half dozen or more producers in their credits. Many of these individuals, whatever else their accomplishments, have had little, if anything, to do with producing the film—at least in the rainmaker sense. The category of "producer," in fact, is now broad enough to require subcategories: line producers (who are in fact production managers for the day-to-day shooting), coproducers (who may simply be investors), executive producers (who may have demanded this credit in return for some right they held), and associate producers (whose relation to the production may be marginal at best). While the distinctions between these types of producer may be lost on the general public, they signal defined, if subtle, gradations of power within the community.

In the David Mamet movie *State and Main,* when the character of the writer (Philip Seymour Hoffman) asks, "What exactly is an associate producer?" the director (William Macy) answers, "It is a title you offer your secretary when you can't afford to give her a raise." Even the vaunted credit of producer may reflect little more than a favor being repaid. For this reason, *Reversal of Fortune* producer Edward R. Pressman agreed to give a producer credit to Oliver Stone, even though Stone had little to do with the production, because Stone had done him the favor of calling Glenn Close to act in the film. On the other hand, Stone refused to share the producer's credit on *Nixon* with Eric Hamburg, who had developed the script. Hamburg, who had to settle for a coproducer credit, later complained, "It was inevitable that it would turn into one of his sick and twisted power games, and that he would withhold it simply because I wanted it. In the real world, nobody knows or cares about the difference [between "producer" and "coproducer"], and in fact there is no real difference in most cases. It is just a question of who has more power in Hollywood and can grab the best credit for himself (or for his wife, mistresses, agent, or hairdresser)."

The inflation in notional "producers" notwithstanding, there are still a fairly large number of legitimate producers in the Hollywood community. In 2003 the Producers Guild of America, which has exacting standards, counted some eighteen hundred producers in its membership.

Producers are paid a sizable lump-sum fee—usually ranging between $2 million and $5 million—when, and if, movies are green-lighted. But if that fee is divided among multiple producers, each one may earn considerably less than the screenwriter on a production, and once they repay their expenses for script development, they may be left with little profit. Even so, better-established producers, either from their studio deals or private funds, usually have ample resources to fund a fairly extravagant standard of living. The mogul-like lifestyle is, of course, not unrelated to their rainmaking function. In hosting dinners, brunches, screenings, and other gatherings in the community, they can bring together the people they need in relaxed settings to forge workable alliances for future deals. By fostering these social networks, producers work to strengthen the bonds that cement the community.

Suits

The major studios employ between 150 and 250 senior executives—or "suits" as they are derisively called by writers, directors, and producers— to manage their far-flung operations. Only a small proportion of these executives are part of the Hollywood community, and paradoxically, that contingent is rarely drawn from those divisions—home entertainment, television production, international distribution, and licensing—that contribute the most to the studio's profits. One reason for the disparity between community membership and generating studio profits is simply geography. The executives from the most profitable divisions tend to live not in Hollywood but New York, and those who commute from New York do not always find the place socially amenable. For example, when Warner Bros. moved its home-entertainment division from New York to Los Angeles, the head of that unit, Morton Fink, resigned from the company because he—and his fiancée—considered the prospect of life in Hollywood "too isolating."

Physical distance is just part of the answer. The real divide between the executives in the studios and those in home-entertainment, television, and foreign-licensing divisions is caused by the mental distance of the latter executives from what most interests the community: the creation and celebration of movies and movie stars. Although they may enrich the studios and their corporate parents, they do not make the deals for the movies on which producers, stars, writers, directors, agents, and other community members thrive. Neither do the suits who manage the studios' finances, accounting, legal work, research, merchandising deals, theater relations, and physical properties. On the other hand, the suits directly involved in the "creative meetings," as well as those who liaison with the production, are accepted as communal partners. So are their studio chiefs and anyone in their organization who is viewed as capable of, as one producer put it, "getting our movies made." William Goldman spoke from the perspective of the community when he wrote that the ultimate importance of the studio executive is his ability to give the "go decision"—or green light.

The suits who do belong to the community get there by various routes. Some are literally born and bred into the Hollywood culture as the children or grandchildren of movie actors, directors, producers, or others involved in the business. They attend the same high schools, acting classes, film courses, and social events. Others come to Hollywood to make their mark as cinematic artists and intellectuals and spend the early years of their careers pitching ideas, auditioning for bit parts, or working on friends' films. Still others begin as "gofers," working their way up from the proverbial mail rooms of talent agencies or as associates at entertainment-law firms. Finally, many come from unrelated professions, such as investment banking, that, though they may provide high annual earnings, can't promise the kind of personal satisfaction that Hollywood can offer. Despite their different backgrounds, and the different proportions of economic man or man at play that motivate them, they often share a common objective: associating themselves with the celebrity culture of Hollywood.

Consider the account Robert Evans gives of his achievements as Paramount's head of production from 1967 to 1974: "I was a big man in the industry, living in a big home," and married to a movie star, Ali MacGraw, but "I couldn't afford to pay my taxes." He remained committed to the industry even though his struggles in it had reduced him to borrowing money from his brother to maintain his lifestyle in the community, which included socializing with such celebrated "pals" as Warren Beatty, Marlon Brando, Jack Nicholson, Al Pacino, and Sir Laurence Olivier. He sums up his career by saying: "You name 'em, I've met 'em . . . either worked with 'em, fought with 'em, hired 'em, fired 'em, laughed with 'em, cried with 'em, figuratively f*cked by 'em, literally f*cked 'em." As far as Evans is concerned, these are the satisfactions that only the culture of Hollywood can provide.

Nor does the social intercourse and professional standing within the community necessarily end when top executives leave, or are fired from, their studio positions. They often maintain their role in the community by continuing to buy scripts, recruit stars, and produce movies for their own companies. After he left Paramount, Robert Evans produced films under the aegis of the Robert J. Evans Company. Similarly, when Sidney Sheinberg, who succeeded Lew Wasserman, left Universal, he created the Bubble Factory; when Ray Stark left Columbia, he set up Rastar Films; when Daniel Melnick left MGM, he set up IndieProd; when Peter Guber left Sony, he set up, it will be recalled, Mandalay Films; and when Joe Roth left Disney he set up Revolution Studios. These top executives can also expect fulsome praise on their departure. When John Goldwyn— whose grandfather Samuel Goldwyn had been the original *G* in MGM— did not have his contract as Paramount's head of production renewed in 2003, he candidly admitted, "It would be disingenuous to say that [Paramount's disappointing box-office record] wasn't a factor." Nevertheless, Paramount's cochairman Sherry Lansing, upon awarding the departing Goldwyn a multiyear producer's contract, generously told the trade press, "John is a brilliant executive. I really couldn't have done this job without him. . . . I'm thrilled that I'm still going to be able to work with him [as a producer]."

In making the switch to producers, ex–studio heads can take personal advantage of whatever goodwill they have earned with stars (and their agencies) through their previous green-lighting activity. Since the ability of these executives to consummate deals and make films generally proceeds less from their acumen in administrating corporate activities at studios than from their ability to build relationships with stars and directors, they often find their solidarity with the community to be a more valuable asset than their studio title. As one former executive of Paramount wrote, "Once your membership was assured, you could glide from one studio job to the next as the regimes changed. You still played golf at Hillcrest, ate dinner at Ma Maison, and screened movies in your private theater at home."

Gurus

The Hollywood community, although a celebrity-driven culture, has always relied on less visible advisors to shape it in mind, body, and image. Consider, for example, Edgar Magnin, who served both literally and figuratively as a rabbi to the MGM studio chief at the height of the studio system. He eventually became so influential in organizing Jewish religious, country-club, and fund-raising networks that helped bind together the community that Louis B. Mayer even offered him a top position at MGM (which he promptly turned down). As Neal Gabler writes, "By the mid-thirties, when his power was unchallenged, Rabbi Magnin had come to serve many functions among the Hollywood Jews: legitimizer of assimilation, safe bond to the past, fund-raiser, advocate with the larger Jewish community, friend." As the community's spiritual orientation grew more complex with the waning of the studio system, its "rabbis" transcended the traditional religious qualification and began to include other figures of authority, people who could convincingly promise to improve, enrich, or even extend the lives of community members in a variety of less orthodox ways. These new gurus included not only religious and cult leaders but yoga masters, astrologers, nutritionists, plastic surgeons, political theorists, and other holders of special knowledge.

Well-connected "éminences grises" often fill the guru role by giving community members, especially those who already consider themselves outside the ordinary boundaries (and rules) of society, an increased sense of entitlement, whether that involves helping to get children into elite schools, obtaining green cards for their servants, or quashing unsavory drug charges. Community members often invest their confidence in facilitators, such as lawyers like Mendel Silberberg, who was reputed to have had a hand in the appointment of judges in California; Greg Bautzer, who was reputed to have influence in the 1980s with the Reagan White House; and Sidney Korshak, who exercised immense leverage over business and labor relations in Hollywood.

Some community members revel in the imputed power of their advisors. In his autobiography, Robert Evans describes his "consigliere," Sidney Korshak, in the following terms: "He was a lawyer living in California without an office. Who were his clients? Well, let's just say that a nod from Korshak, and the Teamsters change management. A nod from Korshak, and Santa Anita closes. . . . A nod from Korshak, and Las Vegas shuts down." Not uncommonly, the community maintains its faith in an éminence grise even if the perception of the guru's power proves inconsistent with reality. Evans, for example, kept his faith in Korshak even though Korshak proved unable to extend his employment at Paramount, intervene in an unfavorable divorce settlement with Ali MacGraw, or help him avoid having to plead guilty to a cocaine-possession charge.

The community is also susceptible to gurus who offer enlightenment rather than power. The Hollywood career of Steven Seagal is a case in point. Born to Jewish middle-class parents in Lansing, Michigan, in 1951, Seagal moved in 1975 to Osaka, Japan, where he married Miyako Fujitani, whose family owned a martial-arts studio, and earned a black belt in aikido, taking the name Master Take Shigemichi. After his return to the United States in 1982, he opened up an aikido dojo in West Hollywood and taught martial arts to a number of actors, including Sean Connery, Elke Sommer, and James Coburn. "People come here [to Hollywood] for a need to be adored and a need to be loved," he subsequently explained on *The Larry King Show.* "When that veil is pierced, [actors] see that illusions are in fact illusions and the only thing that we have is the mind and the heart. . . . Once people find their respective path, it [aikido] becomes, you know, a method for them to perfect themselves."

In the mid-1980s, while providing such spiritual guidance to actors, Seagal met Michael Ovitz, then the head of CAA. As Seagal tells it, "Michael was somebody that I was teaching the martial arts to," but subsequently Seagal became his guru. In 1986 Ovitz arranged for Seagal, dressed in baggy black pants and white robes, to demonstrate his aikido skills to Terry Semel, then cohead of the Warner Bros. studio, and Mark Canton, the studio's head of production. As a result of this exhibition, Semel and Canton offered Seagal a role as an action star, saying, as Seagal recalled, "We'd like to make you part of the family here." Seagal thus made the leap from being a spiritual guru to playing one on-screen in the film *Above the Law,* directed by Andrew Davis, who was also an aikido student of Seagal's. In discussing the film that portrays Seagal as an ex–CIA assassin teaching martial arts in Japan, Davis told an interviewer, "What we're really doing here with Steven is making a documentary." (After making the transition from guru to movie character, Seagal, though he continued as an aikido advisor in his Hollywood dojo, acted in another seventeen Hollywood films, as well as in a television documentary on his career as a *sensei* at his mother-in-law's dojo in Osaka.)

Other gurus have a more materialistic appeal. Dana Giacchetto, a financial advisor whose Cassandra Investment Fund was based in New York, claimed the special knowledge to make community members great fortunes in the stock market. His reputation as an advisor grew in the 1990s after CAA agent Jay Moloney introduced him to his boss, Michael Ovitz. By 1998, in addition to Ovitz, Giacchetto had such disciples, or at least investors, as Leonardo DiCaprio, Matt Damon, Ben Affleck, Courteney Cox, Ben Stiller, and Cameron Diaz. Giacchetto not only managed their money but traveled with them. DiCaprio, for example, reportedly stayed in Giacchetto's SoHo loft in Manhattan and brought him as his guest to Thailand in 1999 (while he was working on the film *The Beach*). The constant flow of celebrity clients through the loft left at least one guest agog: "You'd be standing there talking with Leo [DiCaprio], and Alanis Morissette would ask you to hold her drink for a minute so she could sing, then you turn around, and Mark Wahlberg is asking you to dance."

Giacchetto's guru status ended with his arrest for misappropriating clients' funds. On February 7, 2001, a U.S. district court sentenced Giacchetto to serve fifty-seven months in a federal prison and pay a total of $9.87 million in restitution to his victims, including some of his Hollywood clients.

Whether intellectual, spiritual, or financial, gurus are only transient members of the community. Their acceptance lasts only as long as their claims to specialized knowledge remain credible. Even so, as long as their tenure lasts, they serve to enhance not only the comfort level of community members but also their sense of empowerment.

Hollywood at Work and Play

It is not uncommon for Hollywood community members, like most other people, to view work as the price that must be paid so one can play. When asked in a television interview what he intended to do with his eight-figure salary, George Clooney, perhaps the quintessential combination of a man at work and a man at play, answered, "Buy more toys for myself." But while for Clooney and many others in the Hollywood community multimillion-dollar compensations are undeniably a part of the equation, if only as markers of their relative standing in the hierarchy, another part of it is the psychic value they get from the caprices of Hollywood's celebrity culture and the glitter that accompanies it. The calculation often takes the form of a Jekyll-Hyde balance between *Homo economicus* and *Homo ludens,* with the films one does to make money on one side, and the films one does for fun or personal gratification on the other.

Steven Soderbergh, for example, between directing the remake of *Ocean's Eleven* for Warner Bros.——which earned more than $90 million in rentals——and its equally commercial sequel, *Ocean's Twelve,* decided to make "an experimental art film" called *Full Frontal.* He conceptualized it as part of a "two pack with *Ocean's Eleven,*" explaining in his DVD commentary that since he had had some guilty feelings about the commercial success of *Ocean's Eleven*, which he considered "the least threatening film I've ever made," he wanted to "immediately follow it with something more provocative." He also decided to do it on a low budget to give himself more "creative freedom." For *Full Frontal* he raised $2 million from Miramax and filmed it in eighteen days in a shaky style he called "faux vérité." To achieve the look of an amateur movie, he not only filmed it without any artificial lighting and purposely shot scenes out of focus, but he had the film lab further darken portions of it to add graininess. As a result, many elements, including the actors' faces, are often unrecognizable. He accepted such "visual degradation," as he called it, because it helped him make the point that movies, no matter their "aesthetic style," are "all fake."

The film's actors who included Julia Roberts, David Duchovny, and Nicky Katt—agreed to work for $630 a day (the union-mandated minimum wage, or scale) because, in addition to their token compensation, Soderbergh offered them, as he put it, "fun whether you want to or not." He allowed Julia Roberts, for example, to purposely "act badly" in her role as the Hollywood actress and the romantic lead in the movie-within-the-movie, called "Rendezvous." He allowed Nicky Katt to improvise his dialogue for Adolf Hitler, the romantic lead in the play-within-the-movie, called "The Sound and the Führer." And he allowed David Duchovny to toy with a plastic bag while playing the part of a film producer getting masturbated by an attractive masseuse, after Duchovny told him, "I'm into plastic bags." (The image of this character, found nude with the plastic bag over his head, gives the film its title, *Full Frontal*.) Although the film predictably lost money in its brief theatrical release, Soderbergh considered his education in video art, as well as the fun he had making it, "worth the two-million-dollar" loss.

Harvey Weinstein, who heads Disney's subsidiary Miramax (which also, as it happens, paid for *Full Frontal*), applied a similar logic—or at least a similar justification—on a far grander scale to the making of *Gangs of New York*. When the historical drama, directed by Martin Scorsese, ran over its $94 million budget in its third year of production, Weinstein, who had personally become deeply involved in the venture, argued that any losses it suffered would be offset by other, more commercially successful films produced by his brother, Bob Weinstein, at his company,

Dimension Films (another Disney subsidiary). Harvey Weinstein explained: "There's no gamble [with *Gangs of New York*] as long as there's *Halloween* and *Spy Kids* and whatever other shit he [Bob Weinstein] does."

Harvey Weinstein claimed that he was willing to incur potentially large losses on the Scorsese film because it fulfilled his passion for "movies," as he told a writer for *The New Yorker.* "The most enriching thing that happened to me with Marty Scorsese is that, when making *Gangs of New York,* Marty would give me a movie to watch every Saturday night, a movie that influenced him in the making of the movie. So in three years, I saw eighty films." The making of *Gangs* thus provided a way—admittedly an expensive one—by which Weinstein indulged his love of movies.

Movie stars are also sometimes willing to sacrifice monetary gain for the psychic satisfaction of directing a personally gratifying film. Consider, for example, Mel Gibson, who, as an actor, earns well over $20 million for a single movie. In 2002, he decided to forego lucrative acting offers and instead direct, for no cash compensation, *The Passion of the Christ,* a story about the last forty-four hours in the life of Jesus, based on the eighteenth-century diaries of Saint Anne Catherine Emmerich. Considering it a labor of love, he personally scouted the locations in Italy, had the script translated by a Jesuit scholar into Aramaic and Latin, and cast the parts with actors who were willing to act in these ancient languages without subtitles. Because none of the studios would fund the project, he invested $25 million of his own money, explaining: "They think I'm crazy. Maybe I am. But maybe I'm a genius. I want to show the film without subtitles. Hopefully it'll be able to transcend the language barriers with visual storytelling." When asked by an Italian journalist if he expected the film to make a profit, he answered, in Italian, *"Sarà un film buono per l'anima ma non per il portafoglio"*—this film is good for the soul, not good for the wallet. His reward, he said, would be *anima,* or spiritual uplift. "I have a deep need to tell this story," he told reporters for *Time.* "The Gospels tell you what basically happened; I want to know what really went down." Ironically, just before it opened, *The Passion* set off a huge brouhaha in the media after Abraham H. Foxman, the head of the Anti-Defamation League (ADL), suggested the film "could fuel hatred, bigotry and anti-Semitism." In the midst of the massive publicity generated by theses charges, the film became an unexpectedly huge moneymaker for Gibson.

Director Stephan Elliott also substituted the pleasure principle for the cash nexus when, in 1994, he proposed to Jeffrey Katzenberg at Dream-Works a film called *Eye of the Beholder*, in which the two protagonists are a serial murderer and a voyeur who watches her commit her crimes. Even though Elliott had previously directed the successful *Adventures of Priscilla, Queen of the Desert*, Katzenberg turned down *Eye of the Beholder*, telling Elliott, "You can't make an immoral movie." Fully expecting that the film would not be profitable, Elliott went ahead and spent the next six years making it, drawing no backing and financing it largely with his own money. As predicted, the film, which was released in only a few theaters in the United States, lost money. Despite this disappointing outcome—"Never put your own money in a film," he later advised—Elliott was gratified by the "fun" of what he called "guerrilla filmmaking." He explained in his DVD commentary, "Where else but in the movies can you decide you would like to see a Rolls-Royce demolished by a truck, so you write it in the script, and it happens," adding, "I bashed it up with a sledgehammer."

During the production of *Nixon*, director Oliver Stone similarly shot at least part of the footage for his personal enjoyment. According to his co-producer, Eric Hamburg, Stone, after completing the filming of one scene of hippie protesters at the Lincoln Memorial, offered the women extras an additional $100 apiece "to take off their tops," so that he could shoot nude scenes that were not used—and were never intended for use—in the movie. Hamburg concluded that Stone "probably did it just for fun."

Community members also sometimes participate for fun in their colleagues' projects, even if they are competitive with their own. Consider, for example, the willingness of Steven Spielberg, Gwyneth Paltrow, and Tom Cruise to play cameo roles in New Line's 2002 film *Goldmember*, a spoof of the James Bond film *Goldfinger*, starring Mike Myers as Austin Powers. Even though the film would directly compete for box-office share with two of his own films—*Jurassic Park III* and *Minority Report*—Spielberg had no compunctions about appearing (unpaid) in *Goldmember*. The only compensation he got was the gratification of playing himself, Oscar in hand, and being called by Austin Powers (Mike Myers) "the grooviest filmmaker in the history of cinema."

Spielberg said he agreed to appear in the movie gratis after reading the "hysterical" script. "I normally wouldn't say yes, but Mike [Myers] is a very close friend of mine, and the scene was really funny," he explained in an interview. "He also had written a part for Gwyneth Paltrow, who's like one of my kids. I knew Gwynnie before she was born, actually . . . I sent the pages to Tom [Cruise] and Gwynnie, and they both agreed to do it."

Paltrow's unpaid role involved getting off a motorcycle wearing a skintight leather suit, introducing herself as "Dixie Normous" to a character played by Tom Cruise, and passionately kissing him. "It was so much fun," she later explained. "I never get to do stuff like that. Mike Myers and his wife, Robin, are good friends of mine. When they asked me to do it, I was like, 'Of course! I'll do whatever you want me to do.' Then the costume designer came over for a fitting, and she was like, 'Now, you're going to be in a leather catsuit,' and I was like, 'Whoa, okay. This is not my normal Wednesday afternoon,' but it was so much fun. I couldn't believe that everybody said that they would do it. It was just a great day, you know, making out with Tom Cruise."

Tom Cruise, who ordinarily makes well in excess of $20 million for lending his name to a movie, also participated gratis, playing an actor. "It was a blast," he said, "and really fun."

These psychic incentives—having "a blast," "making out" with a star, wearing a cat suit, pleasing a close friend, acting in a "really funny" scene, and being flattered on-screen by being called "the grooviest filmmaker in history"—can offset financial considerations for star actors and directors. Cruise and Spielberg, for example, each had a share of the gross revenues of *Minority Report*, a movie that, as previously mentioned, would compete for audiences with *Goldmember*. The success of *Goldmember* could conceivably cost each of them substantial sums of money. Yet they evidently believed such a monetary risk was outweighed by the fun and gratification they would enjoy on the set of a friend's film.

Nor is it uncommon for stars to waive multimillion-dollar fees to play roles in movies they consider artistically satisfying. The list of stars who have acted in Woody Allen movies for the minimum union rate—or scale—is long and impressive: Alan Alda, Dan Aykroyd, Alec Baldwin, Drew Barrymore, Elizabeth Berkley, Jason Biggs, Helena Bonham Carter, Kenneth Branagh, Michael Caine, Stockard Channing, Billy Crystal, John Cusack, Danny DeVito, Leonardo DiCaprio, José Ferrer, Hugh

Grant, Melanie Griffith, George Hamilton, Goldie Hawn, Mariel Hemingway, Helen Hunt, Téa Leoni, Madonna, Tobey Maguire, John Malkovich, Demi Moore, Edward Norton, Sean Penn, Christina Ricci, Julia Roberts, Winona Ryder, Cybill Shepherd, Mira Sorvino, Meryl Streep, Charlize Theron, and Robin Williams.

Not all of Hollywood, to be sure, indulges in this play culture. Consider, for example, television production, which constitutes a substantial part of the remuneration of the corporate owners. The TV-production system more closely resembles the bygone studio system than it does the modern celebrity-driven movie business. Like other industrial occupations, it requires performing repetitive tasks, hewing to precise schedules, and working grueling hours. The TV actors generally work under long-term studio contracts; the directors work under the studios' direct supervision and may be replaced if they fail to maintain the studios' schedules; the episodes are mainly shot on the studios' own soundstages so the production accountants can closely control costs; postproduction expenses, such as digital additions, are kept to a minimum; censors and lawyers carefully vet all the footage to make sure it conforms to the networks' standards; and the final product is edited to meet time requisites. "Unlike movies, TV episodes never run a second longer than contracted for—or get a restrictive rating," a Fox executive explained. "It is a very disciplined business." It also produces a rich source of profit—a single animated television series, *The Simpsons*, had earned over $2 billion in merchandising and licensing and syndication income for Fox by 2004.

Despite their immense contribution to the corporate bottom line, those who work in the less dazzling parts of the Hollywood archipelago, which includes the home-entertainment division as well as television production and syndication operations, tend to be distanced, if not entirely isolated, from the celebrity culture. They work, like most other people, mainly to pay the bills, with fun and pleasure an incidental consideration. For those working in the more glamorous areas of selecting and making movies, where the benefits of recognition, camaraderie, and enjoyment of the celebrity culture weigh against the economic considerations of creating a $100 million product, it is not always easy to distinguish the incentives—or pressures—of the playhouse of *Homo ludens* from those of the countinghouse of *Homo economicus*.

The Culture of Deception

INTERVIEWER: *What attracted you to the* Jaws *project?*

SPIELBERG: *I can tell the truth?*

INTERVIEWER: *Go ahead, tell the truth.*

SPIELBERG: *I could get in trouble if I tell the truth.*

—Steven Spielberg interviewed by David Helpern

The principal product that Hollywood depends on—and has almost since its inception—is the celebritized star. To transform their stars into celebrities, the early studio owners took advantage of the emerging concept of public relations. In the latter half of the nineteenth century, the publicity business was generally limited to the relatively modest objective of getting newspapers to mention products that already existed. To this end, freelance press agents, paid by the number of "mentions," would provide editors of local newspapers with items to fill their pages or, in a few extreme cases, such as the ballyhoo of P. T. Barnum, would stage pseudoevents to attract reporters to products.

In the early twentieth century, however, public relations began to assume the far more ambitious aim of shaping a newly defined product:

public opinion—or at least what then would appear to be the public's opinion—on particular subjects. The studio moguls greatly advanced this new idea by employing staffs of publicists to help organize, if not wholly create, the public's perception of their movie stars. These operations, as has been discussed earlier, involved inventing fictional biographies for their stars and scripting interviews and speeches for them in keeping with those biographies. Public relations, as practiced by the studios, thus became a euphemism for public deception. By the time sound was added to films in the late 1920s, every studio had a well-organized publicity department to systematically carry out this function.

The studios' newly created publicity departments had three formidable assets at their disposal. First, the studios produced their own newsreels, seen by weekly audiences of as many as 80 million people, into which they could insert flattering clips of the stars whose images they wanted to burnish in the public mind. The studios also owned or controlled major fan magazines, in which they could place well-vetted stories about their stars. By the 1930s, these magazines were reaching tens of millions of moviegoers. Finally, the publicists had symbiotic relationships with the leading columnists, such as Hedda Hopper and Louella Parsons, through whose columns they were able to maintain a constant flow of items that advanced the image of their stars.

For their part, the stars fully accepted the fictionalization of their lives, on and off the screen—and that fictionalization could be dramatic. For example, the Jewish-American vaudeville actress Theodosia Goodman, from Cincinnati, was transformed into Theda Bara, the Egyptian-born daughter of an Arab princess and a French artist. This license to lie about their lives for the good of the show was cleverly portrayed in one of the classic movies about Hollywood: Gene Kelly and Stanley Donen's *Singin' in the Rain*. This film begins in Hollywood in 1927 at the height of the silent-film era, with Don Lockwood (Gene Kelly), the reigning film idol, telling a newspaper reporter the story of his rise to stardom and his romance with his costar Lina Lamont (Jean Hagen). His story, however, is a legend fabricated by the studio's publicity machine. While Lockwood gives the official version, the film itself shows his true story.

While the disparity between real and fictive lives may be less dramatic off the screen, the license to insert false data in their biographies to make their images more credible has not been revoked. For example,

Raymond Burr, who was unmarried, invented two dead wives and a dead child, according to *The Encyclopedia of Gay Culture*, claiming that his first wife had died in a plane crash and his second wife and his (imaginary) son had died of cancer.

As the public-relations system was perfected over the decades, and the studios achieved near-dominion over the entertainment-media outlets, stars' reputations became an increasingly valuable currency for the stars as well as the studios. Today the lives and experiences of stars—real or scripted—can be packaged, sold, licensed, and promoted, to a dizzying extent. Even the paparazzi rights to the events in their private lives can be sold for substantial sums. Michael Douglas and Catherine Zeta-Jones, for example, sold the rights to photograph their November 2000 wedding for $1.55 million to *OK!* magazine (and successfully sued a rival magazine who took unauthorized photographs of the ceremony).

Since they derive much of their fortune, fame, and emotional connection from their public personas, stars have an obvious interest in sustaining them. So do the agents, actors, directors, producers, writers, gurus, studio executives, and other community members who benefit from the star's aura. Indeed, maintaining the star's public-relations inventions, and the values they project, is now—and always has been—one of the ways Hollywood controls the outside world's view of it.

The Value of Pseudoheroes

Stars become far more valuable if their audience perceives them not just as actors in movies but as heroes who transcend their movies. The studios began to realize the value of stars assuming the mantle of real-life heroes during World War II when many stars joined the armed forces, with some, such as Jimmy Stewart, volunteering for dangerous combat missions. The government's Office of War Information, by putting the picture of stars in uniform on posters, literally made them poster boys for patriotism. Not only did stars in the war years rise, as Leo Rosten writes, "to the apogee" of their glory, but studios encouraged the blurring of the lines between on-screen and offscreen heroism by giving acting contracts to war heroes, such as Audie Murphy, the most decorated soldier in World War II (who starred in more than twenty movies between 1948 and 1960).

Today, with the vast expansion of licensing rights, the public perception of stars as real-life heroes is, if anything, even more important. When stars achieve such heroic status, their value as a licensable product can be maintained even if their movies fail to draw large audiences. Arnold Schwarzenegger is a case in point. Despite three consecutive box-office disappointments—*End of Days* (1999), *The Sixth Day* (2000), and *Collateral Damage* (2002)—he remained an action hero in the public's mind and consequently could not only command huge fees in 2003— $29.25 million for *Terminator 3*—but be elected governor of California. Even after he had assumed political office, his holding company protected his image rights by suing a small toy maker selling a Schwarzenegger-like bobblehead doll on the grounds that "Schwarzenegger is an instantly recognizable global celebrity whose name and likeness are worth millions of dollars and are solely his property."

The establishment of such a heroic image for an action star requires some offscreen blurring of the line between fiction and reality. These stars must publicly present themselves as more than mere movie actors who memorize their lines, wear extensive makeup, and follow the instructions of directors. They must suggest through their words and demeanor that they possess extraordinary virtues in their own right. They must appear not only in control of their lives but undaunted by the concerns of ordinary people. On television, for example, Tom Cruise describes his leaping from a mountaintop, crashing a motorcycle, and coolly walking through blazing fire during the filming of *Mission: Impossible II*. With such colorful accounts of their physical powers, they "stay in character" offscreen as heroes.

They must also avoid any discussion on these television programs of the realities of moviemaking that would jeopardize their heroic auras. Action stars could hardly maintain the illusion of control and fearlessness if they told how stunt doubles, disguised as them or even wearing digital masks on which the stars' faces are later superimposed, stood in for them in many action scenes. Nor can they talk about how insurance companies actually prohibit them from performing scenes that entail any risk of injury, how many of the action scenes in which their characters appear are shot by second units when they are elsewhere, and how computer-graphic companies insert, in postproduction, the fires and hazards their characters are supposedly passing through. (Meanwhile, they can rely on stuntpeople, insurers, and other professional colleagues not to demystify these illusions because, aside from their contractual restrictions on disclosures, they generally accept that such offscreen fictionalizing serves the industry.)

Male stars may even deny wearing makeup out of the concern that it is not consistent with their macho image. George Clooney, for example, claimed that he had achieved his grimy look in the Coen brothers' film *O Brother, Where Art Thou?* naturally. "I would just take dirt, Mississippi dirt, and rub it on my face before we'd go and do the scene. Makeup chairs make me crazy and I don't really like them, plus you wanna just look dirty anyway." He claimed he also avoided makeup in *Three Kings,* explaining, "I'd just pick up dust and rub it in my face and just go [in front of the camera]. . . . I get to roll around in the dirt and it's pretty fun not having to grow up so you don't have to spend time in the makeup chair." While Clooney may indeed have rubbed dirt on himself, that would not obviate the need for professional makeup, which is essential to facilitate the lighting and photographing of scenes and to provide consistency to scenes that are shot out of continuity. To that end (and not to accommodate the vanity of the stars), *Three Kings* employed fifteen makeup technicians, and the lower-budget *O Brother, Where Art Thou?* employed eight—including Waldo Sanchez, who had worked on that and eight other films as Clooney's personal hairstylist.

A star may also be imputed to possess the real-life skills of a character he plays, even if the claim has no basis in reality. Consider, for example, the pretense in the publicity for the 2002 film *I Spy* that its star, Eddie Murphy, who plays a boxer in the film, was also a boxer in real life. Asked whether Murphy was an "experienced boxer," the director, Betty Thomas, replied: "Yes. Eddie grew up with a father who was a boxer. He learned to box when he was a kid." This realistic touch required considerable license, since in fact Murphy's father, who died when Murphy was a toddler, was a New York City policeman, not a boxer, and his stepfather and brothers worked in an ice-cream plant. In any case, a stuntman, Austin Priester, doubled for Murphy in the boxing scenes.

For the most part, stars do not exercise this license out of personal dishonesty, vanity, or egotism. The subterfuge is part of the system by which studios, talent agencies, music publishers, licensees, and others create, maintain, and profitably exploit the stars' public personalities.

The Value of Pseudorealism

Hollywood places great value on stories that go beyond fictive entertainment and appear to reveal the truth about important people and events. Directors sometimes achieve this illusion by making parts of their movies look like documentaries. Steven Spielberg spliced in actual newsreel footage in *Saving Private Ryan;* Warren Beatty inserted interviews with actual participants in the Russian Revolution in *Reds;* and Constantin Costa-Gavras used jerky camera motion, grainy film, and other cinema-vérité techniques in *Missing.* Through such techniques and choices, directors can achieve a high degree of verisimilitude, or the appearance of being real, with the result that the distinction between fiction and nonfiction is purposely blurred for audiences. Audiences are sometimes even duped into believing that fictional works depict true events. In his first film, *Citizen Kane* (1941), Orson Welles so effectively used a newsreel style to render the biography of the fictional press lord Charles Foster Kane that part of the audience was misled into accepting it as the actual biography of the press lord William Randolph Hearst.

In present-day Hollywood, directors sometimes go to great lengths to achieve the appearance of realism. Consider, for example, David O. Russell, who aspired, with his movie *Three Kings,* not just to provide an entertaining story about the 1991 war with Iraq but to provide his audience with an insight into, as he put it on his DVD commentary, "what really happened." He sought verisimilitude by having his film meticulously duplicate actual television footage and still photographs of the war. He then bleached some of the footage he shot to create the visual effect of a desert and used Iraqi refugees as extras on location in Casa Grande, Arizona. Even though the story itself was entirely a work of fiction, Russell so succeeded in creating a realistic-looking film that when he screened it in the White House in 1999, President Bill Clinton told him, according to Russell, that the movie had "confirmed" Pentagon reports about Iraq. If so, art had informed a president.

Russell further advanced the perceived realism of his film through media interviews, telling *Newsweek,* for example, that a close-up that graphically showed a bullet pass through the organs of a body was really done on a dead extra. "We filmed a bullet through a cadaver," he said to the reporter, adding, "The studio was concerned." After *Newsweek* published the "news" that a real corpse had been shot by Russell, Casa Grande police became concerned that Arizona laws had been violated. At this point, Russell admitted that the story he had given *Newsweek* was nothing more than false PR meant to bolster the realism of the film. In fact, a constructed dummy had been used for the special effect.

Oliver Stone also puts a high premium on achieving realism in his films. In *JFK*, Stone blended together the footage of his actors with actual shots of the Kennedy assassination in Dallas taken by amateur photographers and a pseudodocumentary he shot in a cinema-vérité style with look-alikes (Steve Reed doubled for John F. Kennedy). To further reinforce the film's verisimilitude, Stone dramatically announced, at a press conference at the National Press Club in Washington, D.C., that the mystery man, "Mr. X" (played by Donald Sutherland), who in the film reveals the inner workings of the plot to kill President Kennedy to New Orleans district attorney Jim Garrison (Kevin Costner) at a mysterious meeting at the Washington Mall, was not only a real person but was actually present in the room. He then proceeded to identify Mr. X as Fletcher Prouty, who he said had been a liaison between the Pentagon and the CIA at the time of the assassination. In fact, the character of Mr. X had been a fictional invention in the script, and Prouty had not in real life made any such disclosure to Garrison; Prouty had been retained—and paid—by Stone as a technical advisor. "Oliver considered this to be acceptable dramatic license to get his point across in the film," one of his executives explained.

Realism is also valued in a movie even if it is taken from a work of fiction. In his film *The Bourne Identity*, for example, director Doug Liman wove into the fictional plot about a U.S. assassination bureau that murders an African leader a "back story" about a rogue U.S. intelligence operation, including scenes in Washington, D.C., that he claimed in the publicity for the film was based on revelations made to him by his deceased father, Arthur Liman, who had served as counsel to the Senate Iran-Contra hearings. So, even though the novel *The Bourne Identity* makes no pretense of representing a historical event, the movie, through its director, finds it necessary to add this claim of realism.

The Value of Pseudoyouth

In Hollywood, as writer-actor Ben Stein puts it, "the only real value is youth, the only meaningful coin of life." Hollywood is, he suggests, "high school with money." The preoccupation with youth emerges in almost every Hollywood movie about Hollywood. Consider Alan Cumming and Jennifer Jason Leigh's *The Anniversary Party*, a film that concerns the ambitions of a group of aging actors to find roles for themselves in a youth-dominated community. Joe Therrian (Cumming), a writer-director, is about to make a romantic movie based on his own novel about his celebrated actress-wife, Sally Nash (Leigh), but, since Sally is forty years old, he casts Skye Davidson (Gwyneth Paltrow), a twenty-seven-year-old actress, to play her character. After Skye tells Sally, "You are my icon. I have been watching your movies since I was a little girl," Sally bursts into tears. "You have no idea how humiliating it is for me," she tells her husband. "I am an actress." To this he replies, "I have never considered you for the part because you are too old—and if you think any differently, you are out of touch with reality. Even if somehow we could strip ten years off your face, there is still no way I could have got this film made."

The "reality" referred to in the fictional *Anniversary Party* proceeds from a perception shared by producers, executives, agents, and actors that in Hollywood, youthful appearance counts above almost everything else. Even in the early days of Hollywood, it was a business with young faces: Darryl F. Zanuck was Warner's head producer at twenty-six, Irving Thalberg became MGM's head of production when he was twenty-eight, David O. Selznick was RKO's vice president in charge of production at twenty-nine, and Hal B. Wallis became Warner's studio head at twenty-nine. Even as the moguls got older, they recognized the value of having their studios led by men with the appearance, and energy, of youth; by 1940, most studio producers were still under forty-five.

By the 1990s, when their financial health, if not their absolute survival, became dependent on licensing products to people under twenty-five, the studios had even more reason to be concerned with making movies that appealed to youth. Their ability to reach a young audience was the basis on which merchandisers predicated their lucrative tie-in deals, multiplex theaters provided the choice holiday play dates, video chains placed massive advance orders for videos and DVDs, and toy and game manufacturers licensed their characters. To maintain this connection, studios now concentrate over 80 percent of their cable and broadcast-network advertisements on programs watched primarily by people under twenty-five. They are careful to incorporate in their soundtracks hip-hop, rap, and other music that is bought mainly by teenagers, and whenever possible, they cast youthful-looking stars (including children) as principal characters in the movies.

For their part, adult actors and others in the community often seek to conceal visible signs of their increasing age. Not only do they commonly wear youthful clothing in their publicity engagements, but they disguise their true age with hair dyes, hair transplants, wigs, Botox and collagen injections, and face-lifts. The constant effort to maintain the illusion of youth requires a veritable army of specialists, such as colorists, facialists, personal trainers, plastic surgeons, and others.

The Value of Pseudoacting

In Hollywood, it is no coincidence that a distinction is made between "legitimate" acting, as performed in the theater, and movie acting. Indeed, such a high value is placed on acting in the legitimate theater that movie actors sometimes forego multimillion-dollar fees to do it. In 2000, for example, Patrick Stewart interrupted his lucrative film career as Captain Jean-Luc Picard in the *Star Trek* movies to act in Arthur Miller's play *The Ride Down Mt. Morgan* on Broadway for a token fee (which did not cover his rent and living expenses in New York). Stewart, his Hollywood success notwithstanding, described himself as first and foremost a stage actor and explained that he is willing to sacrifice the material benefits of movie opportunities for the "personal satisfaction that comes from acting in front of a live audience."

Acting in movies is, as François Truffaut demonstrates in his film *Day for Night*, a frustrating process, involving the eventual amalgamation of many "bits and pieces" filmed at different times, in different places and circumstances. Each "bit" in the mosaic may only be a few minutes long, with dialogue, background sounds, and visual effects added later. Further, when these brief performances are filmed out of order—as they usually are—the actor must continually alter his appearance and character to maintain the illusion of continuity. Unlike stage actors who stay in character as the play unfolds, film actors must closely follow the instructions of the director and the continuity person to "get in character" anew for each shot. Such out-of-order shooting can be frustrating, unsatisfying, and exhausting. They have to deal with interruptions from camera, lighting, sound, and makeup technicians to remedy conditions they have no control over—such as noise on the set—and do numerous retakes from different angles merely to provide "coverage" for the future editing of the film. The delays and repetitious "takes" tend to further distance a film actor from the spontaneity a stage actor might experience. Yet no matter how ungratifying the work may be, actors, in their videotaped interviews, publicity appearances, and acceptance speeches at award ceremonies, are expected to portray their acting as a form of spontaneous art.

The Value of Pseudopraise

Flattery, already the coin of the realm, is further institutionalized in Hollywood in the interviews that are conducted with actors, directors, producers, and writers during every major production for inclusion in the "The Making of" featurettes that are furnished to the media. In these interviews, participants are not expected to divulge their actual evaluations of the performances of their coworkers. "Everyone in the cast understands that their job in these interviews is to lavish unqualified praise on whoever they are asked about," a producer of these featurettes explained. "There is usually a publicity person around, and if he finds the praise lacking in any way, he orders another take." An actress who worked on *Titanic* recalled, "The last thing publicists want is any sort of accurate descriptions of behind-the-scenes events. They asked for congratulatory praise." It is therefore common in these interviews for the stars, producer, director, and writer to describe one another, over and over again, as a "brilliant" performer, "consummately talented," and "a genius."

Many of the superlatives employed in these interviews also find their way into the media through the electronic press kits, or EPKs, which are edited by publicists into virtual praise-fests. "EPKs provide stars with their templates for their interview shows," a studio marketing head explained.

Nor are the songs of praise last heard in the scripted interviews and press kits. They continue to be sung at the many award ceremonies and festivals around the world, notably the annual Academy Awards presentations, when stars and other community members celebrate their colleagues.

This systematic praise—aside from pleasing the actors, directors, producers, and other recipients—reinforces the idea that the enterprise of the Hollywood community is based on unique and extraordinary talent.

The Value of Pseudocredits

Community members have always valued the public credit they receive for films. Up until the 1950s, however, relatively few individuals, aside from the actors, were actually listed in the film's credits. In 1948 the typical major production listed about twenty-four people in addition to the actors. With the end of the studio system, the demand for credits increased to the point that, by 2002, the typical major production listed several hundred people in addition to actors. Instead of a single producer, as there had been in the studio system, movies commonly had a half dozen or more. As one top producer observed, "Nobody regulates the producers' credit, so therefore it can go to anyone."

The credits for writing Hollywood movies also do not necessarily identify the film's true authorship. The assignment of such labels as "Written by," "Story by," "Screenplay by," and "Adaptation by" is usually made by the Writers Guild of America (WGA), often as the result of a contentious arbitration. The stakes are not merely recognition and reputation, but often a six-figure "credit bonus" for those who prevail in the arbitration. After the studio submits a "proposed credit" to the WGA, every writer with a claim to it has a chance to challenge the credit, and if that credit includes a director or producer, arbitration is mandatory. Because scripts may pass through many stages of development and rewriting over the years and then be rewritten again by script doctors and directors in production, the claims of authorship often require the arbitration panel appointed by the WGA to evaluate statements submitted by claimants, which can run forty pages with all the various drafts of the scripts and treatments. Even the seemingly small matter of whether members of a writing team are joined in the credit by "&" or "and" turns out to be significant in the community (since "&" means they wrote as a team and "and" that they individually wrote separate drafts). No matter how dissatisfied claimants are with the results, they must accept them, since the arbitration is binding.

Directors, it will be recalled, often preempt the authorship issue by taking for themselves the credit "A Film by." Even in the face of a threatened writers' strike in 2001, directors insisted on maintaining their right to this credit of authorship, arguing that writers' objections were, as one representative of the Directors Guild of America put it, "an unwanted invasion on [directors'] creative turf."

Conversely, directors who decide that the films they directed do not meet their standards or will detract from their standing in the community are allowed by their contract and the Directors Guild to remove their own name from the film and substitute the false name Alan Smithee. As a result, since 1955, "Alan Smithee" has received credit for movies made by more than forty directors, including Dennis Hopper, Arthur Hiller, Don Siegel, and John Frankenheimer.

Studio executives also value credit, even if it is unofficial, because it adds to the legend of their accomplishments. Robert Evans, for example, when he was head of production at Paramount in 1971, claimed credit for the idea for (and even the editing of) *The Godfather*, even though it was based on a bestselling book by Mario Puzo, who also cowrote the screenplay with Francis Ford Coppola, and it was directed by Coppola. For more than a decade Coppola elected to remain silent about this credit appropriation (as did Puzo). Then, in 1983, he finally telegraphed Evans: "I've been a real gentleman regarding your claims of involvement on *The Godfather* . . . but continually your stupid *blabbing* about cutting *The Godfather* comes back to me and angers me for its ridiculous pomposity. You did nothing on *The Godfather* other than annoy me and slow it down."

As to his claim that the idea behind the movie was his, Evans maintains that he had a meeting with Mario Puzo in 1968, when the book was not yet completed, and, after charming him with expensive wine and cigars, optioned the book and had its title changed from *The Mafia* to *The Godfather*. According to Puzo, such a meeting never took place. He recalled that he had his agent, William Morris, sell the option to Paramount without any personal participation on his part, and he then selected the title himself, without any help from Evans.

Frank Yablans, who was the president of Paramount when *The Godfather* was made, had this to say about Evans: "He had everybody believing Coppola had nothing to do with the movie. He created a myth that he produced *The Godfather....* That is a total figment of his imagination." Nevertheless, Evans's ability to maintain mythic credit for *The Godfather* over a decade is a testimony to his standing (and power) in Hollywood.

Even if credits do not correspond to reality, they are highly valued by the community, since they serve to establish, as one producer put it, the "who's who" of Hollywood. The Internet database known as IMDb, which is now widely consulted for credits of record by the community, acts as the official scorekeeper.

The Value of Pseudonews

The culture of deception thrives in Hollywood because not only do participants find it in their interest to obscure the distinction between fictional films and the envelope of publicity in which they are delivered, but they can count on not being exposed by the entertainment media. In many cases, the studio's publicity department works in complicitous partnership with them. For example, before major stars appear on a television program, there is almost always a "preinterview" conference between the star's publicist and the show segment's producer and writer (who are often the same person). "The invariable rule," a producer of CBS Late Night Television explains, "is the segment producer works with the publicist and then interviews the scheduled guest. The publicist makes it clear what he or she wants out of the whole thing. If stars do not do preinterviews, the segment producer scripts the interview on his conversations with the publicist and possibly clips from magazine articles. The segment producer then gives an outline of the interview to the publicist or guest. When the guest arrives, the segment producer goes over it again. The host has the structure of the interview outlined on a blue index card. Guests are never sandbagged."

The "talking points" publicists suggest are designed to burnish possible weak points in a star's image. "If a publicist wants to add to the guest's status as a global force," the CBS producer continued, "he suggests an early question about the guest's encounters with some international personage like the queen of England. No one ever checks with the queen."

The entertainment media's cooperation in the enhancement of stars' images also helps the reporters. It gives their interviews more presumptive import and helps maintain their access to the publicists, who can supply them with other celebrity stories.

The shared interest in promoting a star's favored image may also require diverting attention from sensitive data such as stars' ages, divorces, cult affiliations, and whatever else might undermine the illusions from which both the community and the entertainment media benefit. This tacit relationship between the Hollywood community and the entertainment media was dramatized by Joe Roth, the head of Revolution Studios, in the 1999 comedy *America's Sweethearts*. The hero of the farce is publicist Lee Phillips (Billy Crystal), whose job is to fabricate a romantic relationship between the film-within-the-film's costars, Eddie Thomas (John Cusack) and Gwen Harrison (Catherine Zeta-Jones). To get the cooperation of entertainment reporters, he bribes them with free trips, hotel rooms, gift bags, and interviews with the stars, as well as leaking to them fake footage of the stars' activities.

Hollywood's real-life relationship with the media, while at times approaching the farce of *America's Sweethearts*, proceeds from a serious commonality of interests, and as Tad Friend notes in *The New Yorker*, one of the interests all the players have is in not revealing that commonality. "It is in everyone's interest (except, perhaps, the reader's) to pretend that P.R. consultants are not involved in stories," Friend writes. "It behooves the journalist, because it suggests that he has penetrated a rarefied realm; it behooves the star, because he looks fearless and unattended by handlers; and it behooves the publicist, because it always behooves the publicist if the star is behooved."

In some cases, the cooperation between the celebrity's handlers and reporters may involve more material benefits. According to a profile of him in *The New Yorker* by Ken Auletta, Harvey Weinstein went so far as to make offers of writing assignments to journalists, even, at one point, getting "Richard Johnson, the editor of the *Post*'s Page Six [gossip column], to write a script for a movie, *Jet Set*." These efforts are not always successful. But they do measure the enormous value that the studios place on controlling the image of their stars—and themselves.

Nor is it surprising that the culture of deception is so deeply entrenched in Hollywood. The industry, after all, derives much of its wealth and power from its ability to create convincing illusions in the form of movies and television programs—even so-called reality shows—that entertain audiences worldwide. Furthermore, to realize their full profitability, these illusions must be sustained in other products—such as videos, games, theme-park rides, and toys—for years, if not decades. As far as the Hollywood community is concerned, keeping the stars—and other elements—in character offscreen as well as on-screen is now seen as just part of that extended process.

Part Six

THE POLITICAL LOGIC
OF HOLLYWOOD

The Pictures in Our Heads

The people here in the White House think they have power. That's wrong.
The people who make these [pictures] have power.... They can get inside
your head. They can completely take control of everything you see and do,
change the way you feel, everything that happens to you, and that's power.

—Ben Stein, *Her Only Sin*

Politics, in its broadest sense, involves a great deal more than winning elections, appointing officials, or influencing legislation. In Harold Lasswell's classic definition, it involves "who gets what, when and how." The "what" is both material goods, which create wealth, and favorable images, which create honor. In this sense of politics, motion pictures, which have the ability to establish honorific or pejorative images for whole classes of people, represent political power.

In his 1922 study of public opinion, Walter Lippmann described such defining images as "stereotypes," coining the term from the static molds then used by printers to set type. "We define the world around us according to preexisting stereotypes" or "pictures inside our head," he wrote, even if "they do not automatically correspond with the world outside."

Motion pictures, when they came on the scene, proved the most powerful carrier of such mental pictures to date, since they provided a far more convincing illusion of reality than the static representations of photographs and paintings that had preceded them. By transcending the bounds of literacy, and being much more accessible than books, they gave filmmakers an unprecedented power to shape people's perceptions of the world around them.

In the 1890s, before the feature film had been devised or Hollywood incorporated, early filmmakers were creating their own versions of reality, called "actualities." They began by "re-creating" past events—such as the assassination of President William McKinley—and quickly moved on to staging current events. In 1894 a film producer paid boxers James Corbett and Peter Courtney to stage a prizefight in which each of the rounds would last precisely ninety seconds (the duration of the film in the camera), culminating in a final round in which Corbett would knock out Courtney. Filmed prizefights proved so appealing to audiences that a single one in 1897 earned $750,000 (the equivalent of $25 million in 2003).

Once they realized that they did not have to limit their illusions to reconstructed events (or staged contemporary ones), producers rapidly began expanding the medium to fictional subjects, such as the twelve-minute-long *Great Train Robbery*, produced in 1903. By 1915, producers were churning out more than four hundred feature-length films a year.

These early movies, often relying on crude stereotypes, depicted different groups of people at work and play and in doing so informed a large part of the population, especially the new arrivals in cities, about accepted social conventions, behavior, and fashion. Some also provided graphic interpretation of events that had shaped the nation. For example, D. W. Griffith, who directed more than four hundred films, created an epic reconstruction of the Civil War, *The Birth of a Nation*, that served to define both Afro-Americans (played by white actors in black makeup) and the white Southerners (shown in Klu Klux Klan robes). After the 190-minute film was screened for President Woodrow Wilson (the first White House screening of a movie), Wilson was apparently so impressed with the fictional imagery that he said, "It is like writing history in lightning, my only regret is that it is all so terribly true."

The political issue now became a matter of deciding who would control a medium that could produce images so powerful that they could make fiction appear to be truth. Even before the film colony of Hollywood had established itself, government bodies were seeking to control the new medium. As early as 1907, Chicago passed a law allowing censorship of movies. In 1915 the U.S. Supreme Court ruled on the issue and upheld the right of local government to censor movies, specifically excluding them, as "entertainment," from First Amendment protection.

The federal government asserted its interest in the control of filmed images at the start of World War I, when President Wilson made an arrangement with Hollywood studios for their movies to promulgate pro-American views. Movies were subsequently required, if they were exported abroad, to contain such views—called euphemistically "educational material"—and they had to be approved by Wilson's Committee on Public Information. George Creel, who headed the new censorship body, explained: "What we wanted to get into foreign countries were pictures that presented the wholesome life in America, giving fair ideas of our people and institutions." Since at that point all major movies were made for export as well as domestic consumption, this gave the government immense power over the pictures of America received by people at home as well as abroad.

During the Second World War, Roosevelt set up the Motion Picture Bureau of the Office of War Information (OWI) to both censor and use movies to mobilize American public opinion in support of the war effort. Made up of State Department diplomats, White House officials, and military officers, and headed by former journalist Elmer Davis, the OWI went to great lengths to make sure that Hollywood's images vilified the nation's declared enemies—Germans and Japanese. As Davis candidly explained, "The easiest way to inject a propaganda idea into most people's minds is to let it go through a medium of an entertainment picture when they do not realize that they are being propagandized." To this end, his staff reviewed all scripts in advance and proposed changes in dialogue, characterizations, and plots that would demonize the German and Japanese enemies. In the case of a Tarzan film, for example, they insisted that the wild animals react violently whenever the Germans appeared.

In the late 1940s and early 1950s, the House Un-American Activities Committee (HUAC) shifted the political focus from a concern with the values of the images to a concern with the values of the people who made them, launching what amounted in Hollywood to a full-scale cultural inquisition. The congressional inquisitors gave writers, directors, and actors accused of subversion the choice of demonstrating repentance by naming others who had engaged in subversive activity. If they refused to name names, they were threatened with criminal contempt charges and possible imprisonment. As noted earlier, the studios, far from taking this opportunity to support their creative workforce, greatly amplified the power of the inquisitors by declaring that anyone who refused to cooperate, even by invoking their constitutional right against self-incrimination, would be fired. To spare themselves public embarrassment, studios also hired ex–FBI agents to weed out those with suspected ties to the Communist Party or even the groups that were suspected of having connections to it. As a result, many writers and directors were blacklisted or otherwise prevented from contributing to American movies (at least under their own names). Although these investigations produced little, if any, evidence that writers, directors, and actors had actually inserted identifiable Communist positions or propaganda in Hollywood's movies, the fear they engendered led the studios to vet scripts well into the 1950s to make sure that they did not contain elements that could be construed by these political investigators as subversive to the American way of life.

Nor was the federal government, with its war-and-peacetime concerns over the political power of celluloid images, the only party that had vied for control over Hollywood's content. Throughout the 1920s and 1930s, local politicians, religious organizations, and self-styled custodians of public morality—such as the Catholic League of Decency, the Daughters of the American Revolution, and the National Congress of Parents and Teachers—all claimed a right to censor movies.

For their part, the studio moguls of the time were not yet secure enough in their new position to fully resist such pressures. Part of this insecurity proceeded from their rapid rise, in less than a generation, from immigrant outsiders to captains of industry—and from their pursuit of the social status that accompanied such a rise. As Neal Gabler writes in *An Empire of Their Own*, "While the Hollywood Jews were being assailed by know-nothings for conspiring against traditional American values and the power structure that maintained them, they were desperately embracing those values, and working to enter the power structure." They also had to take into account their economic vulnerability. Most of the

major studios—Paramount, MGM-Loews, Warner Bros., Fox, and RKO—
made most of their profits, it will be recalled, not from producing movies
or licensing their rights but from the box-office receipts of their own
first-run theaters. And these theaters, the fount of their profits, were especially vulnerable to local laws and selective boycotts.

To ensure that their products met the accepted standards of decency,
the moguls collectively decided to give up much of their individual power
to select what stereotypes and other images of American society appeared
in their movies. In 1924 they agreed to acquiesce to a common censor,
William Hays, a former postmaster general. Hays was given the job of
negotiating with all the relevant civic, religious, and government authorities to arrive at an acceptable formula, or "production code," that the studios would then impose on all the movies that would be shown in
American theaters. The result, it will be recalled, was the Hays Office,
which worked under the auspices of the studios' trade association, the
MPAA. This in-house censorship went further than merely banning nudity, profanity, and graphic violence. It proscribed certain entire subjects
(such as interracial marriage) and limited the way that particular types of
characters (such as policemen) could be portrayed. It even required plots
on controversial subjects to have approved endings.

By 1927, the code governed every aspect of production and editing
and was circulated among studio executives in the form of a list of
"don'ts and be carefuls." The initial proscribed list included "disrespect
for military forces, vilification of the clergy, misuse of the flag, sedition,
licentiousness, suggestive nudity, cruelty to children or animals, illegal
drug traffic, prostitution, sexual perversion, profanity, rape, miscegena-
tion, man and woman in bed, sex hygiene, childbirth, institution of marriage, sympathy with criminals, and excessive kissing."

When sound replaced silent pictures a few years later, censorship became more complex. The addition of synchronized sound made it far
more difficult to alter movies after they were completed by simply deleting offensive images or written words. So the Hays Office began censoring not just films but proposed scripts, a move that required a larger and
more intrusive organization. At the height of its power, this censorship
office mandated that every story about law enforcement be one in which
lawbreakers never escaped justice and that every picture of marital relations be one in which any form of divorce led ineluctably to tragedy.

When in the 1930s the Hays Office looked askance at movies that focused on social problems such as poverty, studios responded accommodatingly with lighter fare, such as screwball comedies. The pressure on directors to avoid seriously treating the problems arising from the Depression is the subject of Preston Sturges's 1941 comedy *Sullivan's Travels,* which tells the story of a successful Hollywood director, John Sullivan (Joel McCrea), who rejects his studio's demands that he direct another moneymaking slapstick comedy. Instead, he decides to make pictures on a political issue: abject poverty in America. Sullivan's attempt at substituting a social-content film for a comedy meets with disaster: not only does his film, entitled *O Brother, Where Art Thou?,* not get made, but he ends up in prison (for a murder he did not commit), where he discovers that poor people do not, in fact, want to see movies about poverty; they want to laugh at slapstick comedies. So, on getting his metaphoric freedom, Sullivan returns to making what the studio wants: noncontroversial comedies. Like the fictional Sullivan, most mainstream filmmakers in Hollywood accepted, if not rationalized, the political limitations within which they were working.

After the studio system ended, the Hays Office and official forms of censorship gradually faded away. (The government had also by this time disbanded the Office of War Information.) Yet politicians, interest groups, and other parties concerned with influencing public opinion have not entirely abandoned their efforts to shape the pictures in people's heads. And the studios, although free of formal censorship restrictions (at least in the U.S.), are ever mindful of the power the government wields, if not over them directly, over the farflung interests of their corporate parents.

28

The Rules of the Game

Hollywood cannot escape its political orbit. Indeed, the new studio system is itself a product of three government interventions. The first came in 1948, when the Justice Department offered the studios a deal they could not refuse: either give up their control over major retail outlets or face the consequences of a criminal antitrust investigation. The studios, one by one, signed the Justice Department's consent decree and, by doing so, relinquished their lucrative system of manufacturing filmed products for captive theaters. This left them little choice but to move into the riskier business of creating content that could be licensed and sold in competitive arenas. Their profits, which were now problematic at best, depended not on box-office sales at theaters they controlled but on their long-term exploitation of intellectual properties in different markets.

The second government intervention came in 1970. By the early 1960s, the television audience had grown to nearly ten times the size of the movie audience and, as Walt Disney—and then Lew Wasserman—had demonstrated, production companies could make enormous profits by making game shows, series, and other programs for the three networks and then syndicating them to local stations. By the time the major studios realized that they needed access to this market, they faced a significant barrier: the networks. CBS, NBC, and ABC effectively controlled access to the prime-time viewing audience, owned most of the major stations in the most important markets, decided which programs got aired, and owned subsidiaries that produced their programs. As long as the television networks could produce, air, and syndicate their own shows, the movie studios' opportunities were limited.

But unlike the movie business, television broadcasting is regulated by the government. The Federal Communications Commission (FCC), whose seven members are appointed by the president, grants six-year licenses for stations to broadcast over the public airwaves and issues the rules that they have to follow to get them renewed. In 1970, after much lobbying in Washington by MCA's Lew Wasserman and other studio heads, the government intervened on the studios' behalf and the FCC passed the previously discussed fin-syn rule, which gave Hollywood studios such an insurmountable advantage over the networks in this business that they took most of it over. The six major studios—which already had underused soundstages, large staffs of technicians, and substantial lines of credit at banks—further gained dominance in television by acquiring the libraries and production facilities of the leading independent television producers, such as Aaron Spelling Productions, Norman Lear-Tandem Productions, Desilu, Lorimar, and Merv Griffin Productions. As a result, the studios' cash cow became television, not movies. Columbia TriStar Pictures, for example, came to depend on the syndication rights of just three series—*Who's the Boss?*, *Married with Children*, and *Designing Women*—to yield over a half billion dollars in licensing income in the 1990s.

The third government intervention paved the way for the studios to merge with the television networks. The FCC weakened the fin-syn rule in the early 1990s and in 1995 abolished it altogether. This move allowed the studios and networks to become part of vertically integrated conglomerates that now control production, distribution, stations, networks, cables, satellites, and other means by which not only the American public but a large part of the world sees television.

Equally important, if less visible, are governmental decisions not to intervene in cartel-like arrangements. In the case of the DVD Consortium, for example, the U.S. Department of Justice not only permitted the arrangement between American studios and Japanese and European manufacturers, it tacitly encouraged it. It will be recalled that in 1994 Time Warner and its Japanese partner, Toshiba, approached Sony and Philips, who jointly controlled the patents for the digital encoding of sound, and, concerned that Sony and Philips might use these patents to gain an advantage in the codevelopment arrangement, asked the Justice Department to issue guidelines concerning "the misuse and abuse of a dominant patent portfolio to restrict competition." Relayed to them by Time Warner, the guidelines were taken by Sony and Philips officials as a clear warning that the American government expected them to cooperate with Time Warner, and on December 12, 1995, along with Time Warner, Toshiba, and Matsushita (which then owned both Panasonic and Universal Pictures), Sony and Philips pooled their patents into a single DVD Consortium. The patent agreement that emerged from this cartel effectively gave the Hollywood studios crucial control over where and when their movies were shown on DVD.

Because their principal profit centers were now located in areas that either were directly regulated by government, such as the ownership of television stations, or benefited from governmental assistance, such as their control over the DVD, the studios' corporate parents had to concern themselves with not offending the governments that set the ground rules. For one thing, the studios had to take into account the government's views of what benefited the public interest. For example, in the early 1970s, in the wake of the beneficial fin-syn rule, the Nixon administration convened a series of White House conferences with television producers and studio executives aimed at reshaping the image the public was getting of the drug issue in America. According to Egil Krogh, who then served as a Nixon strategist on domestic issues, Nixon and his attorney general, John Mitchell, believed that the administration's "war" on drugs would be helped if drug users were portrayed in movies and television not as mere "victims of addiction" but as "an integral part of the urban crime problem." Instead of portraying drug abusers as merely self-destructive—as they appeared to be, for example, in Otto Preminger's *Man with the Golden Arm* (1955)—the studios were asked by officials in the Nixon administration to portray them as menaces to the entire society. To this end, Krogh helped organize for the top producers and studio executives "dog and pony" shows in which law-enforcement officials demonstrated how drug dealers, acting as modern-day versions of evil vampires, infect their clients with an insatiable need to commit robberies and murders to get their ration of drugs and, in doing so, create a nation-wide crime wave.

The production executives for these shows got the message. As one Warner Bros. vice president who attended the White House conference in 1971 explained: "These White House people made it clear that they wanted to see a lot more narco-villains, and that was okay with us." Numerous memos were dutifully written by these executives to writers, advising them of ways in which they could use drug addicts as the villains in series. As a result, perpetrators of crime—ranging from robbery and rape to bank embezzlement—were now commonly depicted as addicts.

Two decades later, the government provided a more direct financial incentive to television stations to deliver its antidrug messages. In 1997 Congress passed a law allowing networks effectively to get paid, through a complicated formula, for integrating in the plots of television series antidrug messages that were approved by the White House Office of National Drug Control Policy. To qualify, television executives often had to negotiate plot points in scripts with officials from this agency. As one Warner Bros. television executive explained, "The White House did view scripts. They did sign off on them." Of course, even if it were not for such financial payments, television and studio executives have ample reason not to offend the government regulators.

The studios' deepening dependence on television requires that they take into account not only the desires of government officials but the influence that various interest groups have on Congress, the White House, and the FCC. After all, the local stations that show the programs, movies, and other material they produce are required to serve the "public interest" of their particular community. In theory, at least, stations could be denied licenses if the FCC found that their programming was a disservice to their community.

In practice, television stations have rarely, if ever, failed to have their licenses renewed, but the FCC requisite has opened the door to challenges from organizations claiming to represent offended community interests. One of the earliest challenges came from the National Association for Advancement of Colored People (NAACP), an organization with whom the studios had already dealt. In 1942 the NAACP had successfully persuaded Disney to modify racial images of blacks used in its animated movie *Song of the South* and then established a "Hollywood Bureau" to liaise with top studio executives—including David O. Selznick, Darryl Zanuck, and Louis B. Mayer—about avoiding derogatory stereotypes of blacks in movies. This apparent victory notwithstanding, the NAACP's influence with the studios was limited, because it rarely had the opportunity to review scripts before movies were made—and afterward it was too late. So the organization decided to focus its efforts on television.

As it happened, the television networks were ripe to respond to the NAACP's concerns. After the National Advisory Commission on Civil Disorders concluded, in 1968, that America was "moving toward two societies, one black, one white—separate and unequal," due in some part to the misrepresentation of Afro-American life in the media, the networks were especially sensitive to charges that their programs contained stereotypes that contributed to the racial divide. In response to pressure from the NAACP and other concerned groups, each network, as well as the studios producing the programming, began using unofficial "gatekeepers" to negotiate script problems with the NAACP and other minority representatives. As a result of this effort, the formulaic stereotypes of blacks gradually faded from television and most movies. Instead of black actors being cast as servants, athletes, entertainers, and petty criminals, as they had been in the past, they were now being cast as scientists, judges, presidents, and CIA directors. Conversely, and ironically, producers now found themselves typecasting a new stereotype: white petty criminals. When asked by Ben Stein why virtually all criminals in television series in the 1970s were white, David Begelman, who had been president of Columbia during this period, explained that it was the direct result of pressure from lobbyists to exclude blacks from these roles.

Other interest groups have also attempted to alter the messages conveyed in movies and television on subjects ranging from homosexual relations to seat-belt use in cars. In many cases, the studios assign a producer or writer to review scripts and characters with representatives from these groups, evaluate their complaints, and attempt to resolve any disagreements. DreamWorks, for example, has an "outreach" office that contacts relevant advocacy groups even while films are in preproduction to determine if scripts might offend their members.

The Pentagon, even if not a conventional interest group, has a clear interest in shaping the American public perception of its activities—if only to help it recruit soldiers. When it comes to movie companies using its facilities—planes, ships, bases, weapons, and personnel—it lays down strict ground rules enforced by its Film Liaison Office. Studios can, of course, reject this free access and rent their own military, as, for example, Coppola did at great cost for the making of *Apocalypse Now*, but if they accept it, as they usually do, they must also give this Pentagon office some control over the resulting images. "If you want to use the military's toys," a consultant on such military films explained, "you've got to play by their rules." This accommodation can be seen at work in the terms Disney agreed to in exchange for the warships, planes, and other military assistance for the film *Pearl Harbor*. Not only did the producers have to submit the script to the Pentagon, but they made changes proposed by the Pentagon's designated historical advisor, Jack Greene. Such changes included replacing the depiction of American pilots as sassy, disdainful, and rebellious toward their superior officers with one that showed them as polite, respectful, and submissive to orders.

Recently, the CIA, following the Pentagon's lead, created its own liaison office with Hollywood. By supplying films—including *The Recruit*, *The Sum of All Fears*, *Enemy of the State*, and *Bad Company*—with technical consultants, briefings, and even guided tours of its headquarters in Langley, Virginia, the CIA attempts to shape a more "realistic," and presumably favorable, image of itself.

Similarly, foreign governments also often insist that movies filmed in their country—and that benefit from its locations, facilities, and, in some cases, subsidies—depict their country, culture, and, most important, leadership in a favorable light. To ensure this cooperation, they often require filmmakers to submit the script for approval. To be sure, some filmmakers are not willing to accept these conditions and find less politically sensitive countries to "double" for their subjects. For example, films about China and Vietnam, both of which require script approval, can be shot in Thailand or the Philippines (though usually at a much higher price). But if filmmakers require the authenticity (or budget savings) of shooting in a politically sensitive country, they have to play by its rules. In addition, when it comes to showing a film, the studios must respect the censorship regime that exists in many countries—including France, Germany, China, Japan, Italy, Mexico, Korea, and Brazil. Depending on the country, restrictions can apply regarding the portrayal of political, cultural, or religious movements. Even the depiction of particular kinds of violence can be proscribed—Britain, for example, has banned head butts in fight scenes. If they want to sell their movies, videos, DVDs, and television programs in these markets—and in some cases, such as *Terminator 3,* foreign markets are presold to help finance the production—studios have to accommodate the government either by changing the script prior to filming it or by making an alternate version of it for foreign release.

Finally, even if there are no foreign censors, the studios—or their corporate parents—may impose their own ground rules on filmmakers to maintain good relations with the host government. Sony, the only corporate parent that does not—and is not allowed to—own a television network in the United States, hews closely to the political ground rules of Japan (where it does have television interests as well as insurance, banking, and other regulated businesses). Or consider the remarkable range of considerations that must come into play for News Corporation, whose chairman, Rupert Murdoch, in 2002–2003 was lobbying the Chinese government to expand the reach of his Star TV's satellite service; the Italian government to facilitate his acquisition of the Telepiu, which pioneered pay television in Italy, and Sky Italia, his satellite service for Italy; the U.S. government to formally approve his company's acquisition of DirecTV, the largest satellite company in America, as well as to loosen FCC restrictions on ownership of television stations; the Russian government to sell the satellite service of NTV, one of Russia's largest television networks; the German government to waive restrictions blocking him from buying part of bankrupt KirchMedia; and the British government to reduce support for the BBC's News 24, which directly competed with his Sky News. To pursue their worldwide objectives, the corporate parents often are in need of allies abroad—a political consideration their studios must at least be aware of in producing movies or television programs that might embarrass or offend officials whose goodwill is critical.

The ground rules for filmmakers are not always uniformly enforced. Nor are they set in stone. They are essentially opportunistic, changing with political developments, legal decisions, cultural climates, and other circumstances. Nevertheless, they are an indispensable, if not always visible, part of the force field that shapes the logic of Hollywood.

The six major studios need the acquiescence of those who can change the laws to accommodate their interests. Their corporate parents need the U.S. government's permission to complete their acquisition of all the television networks, cable networks, satellite broadcasters, pay-television channels, and stations in major cities to dominate the portals to their home-entertainment audience. They need laws mandating encryption devices on television sets to control consumer home use of their content. They need laws, such as the Digital Millennium Copyright Act of 2000, to prevent video pirates and other poachers from providing their content without their authorization, or altering their regional restrictions on DVDs. They need a censorship regime to guard against competitors fragmenting their market by offering more explicit material. They need exemption from antitrust laws and other regulations so that they can reach agreement with one another on the standards, formats, and market protection for their content. A singular reality confronts the six corporate giants: they need the support of governments in key countries to protect and expand their entertainment domains. Even if the strategies for fulfilling these political requisites are confined to only the top echelons of the sexopoly, carrying them out affects decisions made at every level of the creative process.

The World According to Hollywood

Taken together, the selection of images from Hollywood, both in movies and on television, creates a vision of how the world works. When David Puttnam took over the management of the Columbia Studio in 1986, he wrote in a memo to the chairman of Coca-Cola, which then owned the studio: "Movies are powerful. Good or bad, they tinker around inside your brain. They steal up on you in the darkness of the cinema to inform or confirm social attitudes." Even if it is an ephemeral worldview, it reflects the values of the people who create those images, the studios that back them, and the community of peers that reinforces and gratifies them.

Directors

Unlike the fictive Sullivan working under the studio system, today's directors are free to insert their own vision of society in their films without penalty. And many do. For example, Oliver Stone portrayed police as sadists and murderers in *Natural Born Killers* (including footage taken from the now famous video of the police beating of Rodney King in Los

Angeles); American soldiers as sadists and murderers in *Heaven and Earth, Platoon,* and *Salvador;* and government leaders as murderers and conspirators in *JFK* and *Nixon.* Kathryn Bigelow portrayed the Los Angeles police officers as racist murderers in *Strange Days.* And Francis Ford Coppola portrayed the cardinals of the Vatican as the Mafia's partners in assassination in *The Godfather: Part III.*

At least part of a director's determination to render such powerful pictures of society proceeds from his or her own politics. John Wayne, for example, undertook to produce, direct, and star in *The Green Berets* because he wanted to establish a positive, humanitarian image of American soldiers in the Vietnam War. To this end, he personally wrote President Lyndon Baines Johnson in December 1965 that he intended to make "the kind of picture that will help our cause throughout the world.... We want to do it in a manner that will inspire a patriotic attitude on the part of fellow Americans." After the White House endorsed the idea, Wayne bought Robin Moore's bestseller *The Green Berets*—a novel that showed the American forces humanely saving the people of Vietnam from the atrocities of the Communists—and made it into a movie in 1968. Although the film barely earned back its $7 million budget, it achieved Wayne's political objective.

Coppola used this power to present a very different picture of the Vietnam War in *Apocalypse Now.* Since it focused on American atrocities against the people of Vietnam and the bizarre behavior of the American military—a depiction of the war as, in his words, "essentially a Los Angeles export, like acid rock"—Coppola concluded the project was "something no one [else] dared touch." To get the financing, he had to risk financial ruin by personally guaranteeing to pay the budget overruns himself. As it turned out, the budget deficit amounted to more than $20 million, which *Apocalypse Now* barely earned back.

Tim Robbins forewent almost all of his compensation to direct *Cradle Will Rock.* He was willing to risk a possible monetary loss because, as he explained it, he wanted to show a vision of the ruthlessness of capitalism that included Nelson Rockefeller's minions using sledgehammers to destroy Diego Rivera's mural in Rockefeller Center. For him, such a "cinematic metaphor" represented "capitalism corrupting art."

Barry Levinson also deferred most of his fee to make the 1997 movie *Wag the Dog.* He explained that the topic of manipulation of the media by politicians "fascinated" him. With the help of playwright David Mamet, he changed a script loosely based on the novel *American Hero*, about the 1991 Gulf War, into a satiric story in which a president, faced with a sex scandal, employs a Washington spin doctor (Robert De Niro) and a Hollywood producer (Dustin Hoffman) to fabricate a nuclear threat by Muslim extremists to divert attention from his domestic problems. The film succeeded so well in establishing a picture of White House manipulation that when, following the attack on American embassies in Africa in 1998, President Clinton ordered reprisal bombings of al-Qaeda facilities in Sudan, many journalistic enterprises—including *The New Yorker*, *Vanity Fair*, and CNN—characterized the actions as "wag-the-dog" manipulations.

Filmmakers also work from the images that have been planted in their own heads, at least some of which are the recycled stereotypes from an earlier generation of directors, writers, and producers. Consider, for example, the stereotypical images of financiers as criminal conspirators that emerged from Hollywood in the 1990s. In his still-relevant study of the values that shaped television series in the 1970s, Ben Stein found that most of the producers and writers responsible for a large portion of those series shared the conspiratorial view that "businessmen are bad, evil persons and that big businessmen are the worst of all," since "they are often involved with the Mafia." As a result of this shared Hollywood belief, Stein observed, "the murderous, duplicitous, cynical businessman is about the only kind of businessman there is on TV adventure shows." On programs such as *Columbo, Baretta, Starsky and Hutch, Kojak, Harry-O, Ironside*, and *Hawaii Five-O*, a three-piece suit, or even a tie, became, Stein notes, "the inevitable badge of crime."

Since episodes from these 1970s series were syndicated for decades on local stations and cable television, they entered, as one producer put it, "the food chain of what future writers watched and consumed." So it is not surprising that the generation of filmmakers brought up on such television fare may have willy-nilly adopted the iconic well-dressed criminal businessman as part of their perceived reality. In any case, by the 1990s, the murderous businessman, whose killings were not figurative, become almost a staple of movies, such as (just to name a few) *A Perfect Murder, Enough, The Devil's Advocate, Blue Steel, Ghost, The Player, Hudsucker Proxy*, and *The China Syndrome*. Even if the businessman-murderer was not originally scripted wearing an expensively cut suit, silk tie, and groomed hair, production designers commonly drew him in this emblematic style on storyboards that were in turn used by costumer designers and casting directors.

The image was then further recycled when studios sold the rights to use brief scenes from their films to television-news networks to illustrate their stories in the late 1990s. Warner Bros., for example, made such an arrangement with CNN (which was owned by their common corporate parent, Time Warner), with the result that the scene from Oliver Stone's movie *Wall Street* in which the immaculately dressed character Gordon Gekko (Michael Douglas) intones "Greed is good" was repeatedly used by CNN to illustrate news reports of corporate corruption. Through this fluid boundary between movies and television news, fictional images come to stand for real events and, if repeated consistently enough, shape the pictures in the public's head.

Even the work of directors who eschew using films to make political statements and strive to entertain the widest possible audience may contain—and powerfully project—a particular worldview. Consider, for example, the 1977 film *Close Encounters of the Third Kind*, which was both written and directed by Steven Spielberg. The story, whose appeal to a vast audience worldwide made it one of the most commercially successful films in history, concerned the arrival in America of benevolent space aliens in circular spaceships. Part of Spielberg's premise is that the government systematically lies about disturbing phenomena to avoid panicking its citizenry. The culminating scene is one in which aliens exchange a dozen or so humans whom they had abducted to experiment on for a busload of American astronauts who volunteer to accompany them back to their galaxy. To hide its transactions with extraterrestrials, the government stages an elaborate deception, including a fake nerve-gas attack.

The same idea of using well-orchestrated cover-ups to hide alien activities appears in a number of other successful movies produced by Spielberg's personal production company, Amblin Entertainment, including *E.T.: The Extra-Terrestrial, Men in Black,* and *Men in Black II* (in which government agents employ a handheld device that erases the memory of any civilian who sees alien visitors). Such films promote a view of governments as paternalistic institutions that create elaborate illusions to shield citizens from developments with which they cannot cope by—not unlike the strategies of filmmakers themselves—creating convincing illusions for them. Variations on this theme of governmental concealment are not only a commonplace of movies but provided Twentieth Century–Fox with one of its most successful television series, *The X-Files* (which also became a movie), and ABC with its hit series *Alias.*

Pictures from Organizations

As I point out in *News from Nowhere,* television networks perpetuate their values by hiring, promoting, and rewarding people who tend to identify with them. Movie studios similarly have—and advance—their own particular values. In the older era, when studio moguls showed little subtlety in impressing their values on underlings, each studio tended to make films with a distinctive narrative style that the audiences came to associate, like a branded product, with the logo of that studio. MGM was known for films that exuded the unrestrained lyrical optimism best exemplified by its musical fantasies, Warner Bros. for films that grimly depicted crime and punishment, Universal for its Gothic horror films, Twentieth Century–Fox for social realism, and Paramount for its biblical epics.

Today's studios also make films that reflect their underlying values— even if the distinction is not always obvious to moviegoers. Disney, for example, relies heavily on its wholesome family-entertainment image to attract parents to its theme parks, cruises, Disney Channel, and licensed products. "Ever since Walt Disney created the company, its image has been sacred," a Disney executive said. "Films and filmmakers are expendable, its children-friendly brand is not." To sustain this value, its executives routinely excise out of the films any scenes that might damage the reputation of the Disney brand. It even prohibits its subsidiary Miramax, though it has a separate brand, from distributing films—such as *Kids,* which depicted young teenage boys as sexual predators—that might damage its image. (In 1995 Miramax executives created a nominally independent distribution company, Shining Excalibur Pictures, to distribute *Kids.*) "Everyone here at Disney knows what the company's franchise is and always has been," a top executive at its distribution arm said. "It is the world of kids."

Universal has also defined a studio image for its executives. When Steven Spielberg was a new director at the studio in the seventies, Sidney Sheinberg, who was then running Universal for Lew Wasserman, told him, "We don't make art films at Universal, we make films like *Jaws*." Wasserman had already moved MCA into the theme-park business in Burbank, California, and would soon open an even larger park in Orlando, Florida. To serve them, Universal needed "event movies," as one MCA executive put it—films that, in addition to bringing moviegoers to theaters, would spawn attractions at theme parks and launch a flotilla of toys, games, and other licensable products. Spielberg gave Universal the product it required not only in the case of *Jaws* but with *E.T.: The Extra-Terrestrial, The Lost World: Jurassic Park,* and *Jurassic Park III*—event films that proved among the most successful licensing franchises and theme-park attractions in history.

Steve Ross, it will be recalled, had a similar formula in mind for Warner Communication. Since he had already put the conglomerate in the toy, game, and theme-park business, he directed the Warner Bros. studio to concentrate its resources on movies based on comic-book heroes from its DC Comics division, such as Batman and Superman, that could create a raft of products for these businesses.

Sony executives also knew the type of films they wanted its newly acquired studio to make when they recruited to run it the Warner Bros. executives Peter Guber and Jon Peters, who had developed the highly successful *Batman* franchise for Steve Ross, and then subsequently recruited the team of Dean Devlin and Roland Emmerich to remake *Godzilla.* They wanted movies that featured "action figures," as Devlin tells it, and particularly action figures that could lend themselves to electronic games played by teenagers.

Sumner Redstone, though he professed a "long-standing love" of the more adult movies of the past, recognized that Paramount needed to produce fare that resonated with the younger audience to which its Nickelodeon, MTV, and other cable channels had dedicated themselves. These films and television programs required, as one top Paramount executive explained, characters who require a minimum of explanation—"simple characters in exciting situations, like Indiana Jones in *Raiders of the Lost Ark.*"

News Corporation, for its part, needed event films with sufficiently broad appeal to attract subscribers to its satellite services in Britain, Europe, Latin America, Australia, and Asia—"truly global films," in the words of Rupert Murdoch. The Twentieth Century–Fox studio filled this requisite with eight of the ten most internationally successful films of the twentieth century in terms of box-office receipts, including *Titanic, Star Wars,* and *Independence Day.*

There are minor distinctions between these organizational products—Disney's animation, for example, tends to be less realistic than that of Paramount—but they pale in comparison with the overriding value that they all place on a common requisite: characters who communicate principally not through words but through visually understood actions to a universal—and younger—audience. It is no accident that a movie like *Terminator 3* features as both its heroes and villains nearly mute robotic killers blasting one another to smithereens; these are truly global action figures understandable in any language or culture, able to provide the basis for an endless variation of toys, theme-park rides, and electronic games. Even in their less fantastic versions, the heroes tend to be characters who can dispatch adversaries without the intervention of police, officials, or any other legal authority.

The most immediate casualty of this simplification is the revealing picture it paints of the legal process. It will be recalled that under the Hays Office's rules, all Hollywood movies had an embedded value: the inviolability of the law. Those who violated the law, whether bank robbers in crime movies, lynch mobs in westerns, or corrupt politicians in social dramas, had to be punished for their transgression. In *Touch of Evil* (1958), the police officer, Captain Hank Quinlan (Orson Welles), plants evidence that will lead to the conviction of a terrorist bomber; nevertheless, in keeping with the code, he is a villain who must die by a bullet at the end. Today's studio movies, in search of action heroes, often portray a different picture of justice. Legal processes are not only expendable, but they are often obstacles that heroes must overcome. With this value of the end justifying the means, police heroes need not bother with complicated forensic issues, they simply kill the villain—as do, for example, Detective Leland (Frank Sinatra) in *The Detective,* Inspector Harry Callahan (Clint Eastwood) in *Dirty Harry,* Sergeant Martin Riggs (Mel Gibson) in *Lethal Weapon,* Special Agent Eliot Ness (Kevin Costner) in *The Untouchables,* and Detective Keller (Al Pacino) in *Sea of Love,* all of whom commit premeditated homicide and go unpunished. In Curtis Hanson's *L.A. Confidential*, which was nominated for no fewer than nine Oscars in 1998, the hero, Detective Lieutenant Ed Exley (Guy Pearce), initially believes in following the law; but once he sees that rule-abiding behavior will not bring his corrupt superior, Captain Smith (James Cromwell), to justice, he takes matters into his own hands and shoots the captain in the back. After he confesses to the district attorney, police chief, and other officials, the murder is duly covered up, and Exley emerges a hero and man of action.

The same value of direct justice also gave rise to the killer cop's mirror image: the private vigilante. Just as police are seen taking justice into their own hands, so are citizens. Some of these heroic civilians were drawn from comic books, such as *Batman, The Incredible Hulk, Superman,* and *Spider-Man*. These heroes often were masked men, who had to cloak their true identity from the law (a useful feature for the studios, who were thus able to add sequences to the franchise with different actors—George Clooney, Michael Keaton, and Val Kilmer all played Batman, for example). Ordinary citizens, without special powers, were also regularly transformed by Hollywood into vigilantes who hunted down criminals to remedy the failure of the criminal system. For example, in the five *Death Wish* movies (1974–94), liberal New York architect Paul Kersey (Charles Bronson), after realizing that the police are incapable of catching the man who murdered his wife and raped his daughter, buys an arsenal of guns and operates outside the law. Over the next twenty years he murders dozens of rapists, muggers, mobsters, youth gang members, and drug dealers.

Similarly, women in the movies of the new era often turn to action rather than the courts to right the wrongs they have suffered. In *Lipstick*, Chris McCormick (Margaux Hemingway), a fashion model, is raped by a well-known music composer. Since the court acquits him, Chris must shoot him to death herself with a shotgun. In *Enough*, Slim Hiller (Jennifer Lopez), finding no legal remedy for a rich, abusive husband, trains herself in martial arts and then, with careful planning, kills him. And in *Sleeping with the Enemy*, Laura Burney (Julia Roberts), unable to divorce herself from an abusive husband, fakes her own death by drowning and, when her husband discovers the deception, calls 911 to report a "burglar," then shoots and kills him.

Lawyers are often depicted as being, if not merely unhelpful or incapable, downright corrupt. In *The Firm*, Mitch McDeere (Tom Cruise) discovers that his high-powered law firm is actually a criminal enterprise engaged in money laundering, extortion, and murder. In *Runaway Jury*, the law firm, which represents gun manufacturers, is engaged not in the practice of law but in jury fixing and bribery. And in *The Devil's Advocate*, the law firm is owned by Satan incarnate, John Milton (Al Pacino).

Intelligence services have also been redefined in movies. Up until the late 1950s, Hollywood depicted America's intelligence services as legitimate, if shadowy, parts of the national-security apparatus. In Hitchcock's 1959 classic *North by Northwest*, for example, after the CIA accidentally entangles Roger Thornhill (Cary Grant) in a diversion, he joins forces with them to help prevent an enemy agent from stealing secrets and murdering a CIA counterspy. By the 1960s, however, this picture gradually came more in line with the studio's need for action figures: the intelligence officer, like the hero policeman, became a law unto himself—an executioner. In the twenty James Bond movies, beginning with *Dr. No* (1962), the hero is not only an assassin but one licensed by the British government, which works in partnership with the American CIA, to kill. The CIA also frequently employs its own assassins—witness *The Assignment, Conspiracy Theory, The Pelican Brief, True Lies, Point of No Return, The Bourne Identity, Ronin, Confessions of a Dangerous Mind, The Recruit,* and *Three Days of the Condor.* In *Apocalypse Now*, for example, the CIA assassin-hero, Captain Willard (Martin Sheen), is dispatched to kill American colonel Walter Kurtz (Marlon Brando). Nor is the CIA necessarily acting in America's interest any longer—a plot shift that may better conform to the studio's value of global interest. Indeed, in *The Long Kiss Goodnight*, for example, CIA assassins are terrorists, planning to kill four thousand innocent people on Christmas Eve with a truck bomb and falsely blame it on Arab terrorists; in a scene that distances the CIA from America's welfare even further, the CIA officer in charge of this operation, Leland Perkins (Patrick Malahide), suggests that the CIA was similarly involved in organizing the 1993 bombing of the World Trade Center.

In creating more international villains—a function once served by cold-war enemies—the studios need to avoid gratuitously offending officials in countries whose markets they now rely on for a large share of their profits. Among the candidates that neatly fit this bill are the greedy executives of multinational corporations who can be cast, in their expensive suits, as corporate terrorists. In *Mission: Impossible II*, the villain is Sean Ambrose (Dougray Scott), who controls the multinational Biocyte Corporation, creator of the Chimera virus, which can cause a horrifically disfiguring global plague. If the virus is released—which is just what Ambrose plans to do—the corporation will reap enormous profits from selling the antidote, which it also exclusively manufactures. Similarly, in the James Bond movie *Tomorrow Never Dies*, the owner of a global media conglomerate, Elliot Carver (Jonathan Pryce), plans to start a nuclear war between China and Britain to increase the circulation of his newspapers and secure valuable television rights in China. In *The Fifth Element*, Jean-Baptiste Zorg (Gary Oldman), head of an armament corporation, arranges for an alien to destroy civilization on earth so he can profit from the chaos. In *The Phantom*, Xander Drax (Treat Williams), the head of a huge industrial conglomerate, attempts to enslave the world. In *Rising Sun*, a Tokyo conglomerate corrupts American politicians and police to gain control of digital video technology. In *The Insider*, cigarette companies purposely conceal the findings that their products cause cancer. In *The Formula*, an oil cartel headed by Adam Steiffel (Marlon Brando) conspires, and murders, to raise global energy prices by suppressing a German formula that would make cheaper synthetic fuel abundant. In *Erin Brockovich*, a power company deliberately hides its pollution of the water supply to avoid paying insurance claims. In *Johnny Mnemonic*, the Pharmakon drug company suppresses the cure for degenerative diseases so it can maintain its sales of medicines for them. Even in the increasingly rare case that a corporation does not intend evil consequences, it may cause them inadvertently—as it does in such films as *The Lost World: Jurassic Park* and *Deep Blue Sea*—through its greed.

Extraterrestrials, or at least nonhuman beings, also fill this villain bill by providing universally acceptable bad guys. In *The Matrix* series, the battle rages between humans and machines; in *Star Wars: Episode II—The Attack of the Clones*, it is humans and clones; in *Starship Troopers*, it is humans versus alien bugs. Alien villains are also important to the movie-based action-toy and electronic-game licensing business, which had $16 billion in retail sales in 2003, since a large part of the appeal of these toys and games to children is, as one toy analyst put it, "confrontation" between good and evil characters. The bestselling action toy derived from *Star Wars* was, for example, not the movie's heroes but its antihero, Darth Vader. In citing the appeal its supernatural monsters would have for toy buyers, Universal described *Van Helsing* as being "totally about good and evil."

The hero in these apocalyptic films is often a messiah figure: a single action figure who will save humankind. In George Lucas's *Star Wars* sextet (1977–2005), a simple farm boy named Luke Skywalker (Mark Hamill) is the messiah who has to be found and made to realize his power. In David Lynch's *Dune*, Paul Atreides (Kyle MacLachlan) is the messiah on whom the fate of the universe hinges. In the Wachowski brothers' *Matrix* trilogy (1999–2003), Neo (Keanu Reeves) is the "one" capable of saving human civilization by believing in his own designation, suggested by an anagram of his name Neo, as the One. The narrative advantage of messiahs in films is that they require little, if any, political context other than faith in a mystical salvation.

To enhance their perceived gravity, event movies often depict imminent global destruction. In some cases, such as *The Matrix Reloaded* and *Terminator 3*, human civilization is totally annihilated (at least until their sequels, *The Matrix Revolution* and *Terminator 4*, redress the disaster). Usually, however—as in *Armageddon*, *Deep Impact*, *The Fifth Element*, and *The Abyss*—the disaster is narrowly averted by the intervention of the hero. The postapocalyptic world envisioned by Hollywood tends to be dark, violent, and totalitarian—as in *Escape from New York*, *Waterworld*, *Mad Max*, *Artificial Intelligence*, and *Twelve Monkeys*.

Whatever their relation to reality, these studio products powerfully represent the world—past, present, and future—according to Hollywood.

The Once and Future Hollywood

*Walking at dawn in the deserted Hollywood streets in 1951 with David
[Selznick], I listened to my favorite movie boss topple the town he had
helped to build. The movies, said David, were over and done with.*

—Ben Hecht, 1954

The idea of progress is relatively new. At the end of the eighteenth century, the remarkable French mathematician and philosophe Marquis de Condorcet advanced the novel idea of human progress. He believed that man was a rational animal, uniquely capable of "making new combinations" and learning from the mistakes of others. Condorcet recognized that there would be sporadic setbacks on this noble road—he himself died on the guillotine—but, since history would provide a cumulative record of the missteps that led to them, such mistakes would be corrected over time and human enterprises would ineluctably better themselves.

While the concept of progress may help to explain many social inventions, the incarnation of contemporary Hollywood is not one of them. Even though today's system of filmed entertainment shares much of the same physical geography, nomenclature, and mythology as the studio system that preceded it, it did not evolve out of it. Like the alien pods in its sci-fi movies, it appeared with surprising suddenness and replaced it.

The original studio system has been the subject of countless books by cultural anthropologists, economists, political scientists, historians, and industry insiders, most of whom recount that the system evolved in response to the need for a constant stream of filmed entertainment to penny arcades, nickelodeons, theater halls, and other exhibition venues—resulting, less than a generation later, in the most commercially successful form of mass entertainment the world had ever seen. By 1929, just a few years after the talking movie was invented, over two thirds of the ambulatory population was going to the movies every week. No form of centrally produced entertainment had ever before captured such a large proportion of the population.

Virtually all their money, prestige, and power came from selling tickets at the box office; and the studios were able to keep this mass audience their private preserve, it will be recalled, through an elementary strategy: control over the booking of America's theaters.

Notwithstanding its near-total domination of the moviegoing public, the studio system was not the only game in town. Even at the height of its dominance, there were other moviemaking enterprises on the fringes of Hollywood whose products ran the gamut from art films and social documentaries to the pornographic movies shown at stag parties, college fraternities, and private clubs. Among these niches that the studios chose not to concern themselves with was the children's cartoon business, which, by 1932, was dominated by a single company: the Walt Disney Animation Studio.

In the 1930s the Hollywood studios saw no great benefit in catering to children. Not only was their admission price, if collected at all, only a third of the adult price, but they required specially designated theater sections and, often, theater matrons to look after them (to keep them from disturbing the adult audience). But Disney saw the boon that children represented: not only would they repeatedly see movies (with their parents in tow), but they would be eager consumers of products based on characters whose images excited them in movies. Disney saw the opportunity to open up a vast new realm of children's branded products that would eventually grow to include everything from wallpaper, books, clothing, toys, and music to rides and entertainment in enclosed playgrounds or, as they would come to be called, theme parks. To this end, he realized that movie companies could form alliances with other parts of corporate America interested in attracting youth to their products. It was no coincidence that the first "merchandising tie-in" was with the children's animated film *Snow White and the Seven Dwarfs*.

Despite the success of his Pied Piper strategy of splintering off the young audience, Disney remained an outsider in the world of the studios. But by the mid-1950s, that world was gone, and it was Disney's concept that replaced it.

Even though the continuum was broken, the studio system's legend was so powerfully ingrained in the popular imagination by this point that it persisted in dominating much of the writing on Hollywood for more than a half century. This legacy can still be seen in the persistence of a largely outdated vocabulary that includes such terms as "B-picture," "first run," "marquee name," "long run," "bomb," "blockbuster," and "box-office gross"—terms from an era in which the paramount measure of success was the performance and duration of movies in theaters. Even those insiders who, in the early 1950s, were already viewing Hollywood as little more than (as David O. Selznick put it) a "ghost town making foolish efforts to seem alive," appreciated only dimly if at all how fully it was being replaced by its rival twin, the Disney system, wrongly assuming instead that there must be a logical continuum between the old and new Hollywood.

There were an enterprising few, however, who, in F. Scott Fitzgerald's words, largely had "the whole equation of pictures in their heads" and saw what was happening. These savvy men—including Lew Wasserman, Steve Ross, Akio Morita, Sumner Redstone, and Rupert Murdoch—whose stories are told here, gradually took charge and developed the new Hollywood in ways that fully exploited the global potential of Disney's children-driven licensing system. As this new Hollywood took shape, the concept was further extended by a number of innovative entrepreneurs—including Steven Spielberg, Jeffrey Katzenberg, and David Geffen, who joined forces to create DreamWorks SKG; Haim Saban, who, with Murdoch, built Fox Family Entertainment partly by Americanizing Japanese animation; and Robert Shay, who used a licensing windfall from *Teenage Mutant Ninja Turtles* to build New Line Cinema.

The economic logic of such youth-directed entertainment made compelling sense to financiers, since children between the ages of four and twelve provide an immensely rich market. According to one leading authority on youth marketing in 2002, children influenced consumer sales of $630 billion in America alone. By that year, what was once deemed Walt Disney's folly had become a fountain of profits for most of the studios in ways that not even Walt Disney could have envisioned. In 2002 Sumner Redstone made the profitability of Paramount's animation production one of the key points of his presentation to financial analysts at the Morgan Stanley Global Communications Conference, pointing out that Paramount's 1998 movie *Rugrats* was "the first non-Disney animated film to gross over $100 million domestically." He did not even mention Paramount's nonanimated features at that presentation. That year Viacom similarly earned more from its Nickelodeon channel than from its Paramount studio. Fox's top-earning film for the year was the animated *Ice Age*. Time Warner had also created a feature-animation division to, as its studio cochairman Terry Semel explained in a board meeting, "put merchandise on the studio store shelves," and the Cartoon Channel it had acquired from Turner earned more profits in 2002 than the Warner Bros. movie studio. Sony meanwhile earned more from its PlayStation than from all its movies and television programming combined.

While the business of hooking youth on their characters provided them with monetary rewards, it did not necessarily give those who worked for the studios all the psychic and social satisfaction, or status, they sought. Just as Sumner Redstone, as a moviegoing teenager, had dreamed of running a Hollywood studio, many of the top studio executives of the 1990s had been nurtured on the adult fare of the studio system or their reruns on television. Their ambitions often involved more than generating an endless cycle of licensable characters to entertain children, no matter how profitable the results. They wanted to help produce movies that would measure up to the ones they and those around them admired—such as the classic films directed by Frank Capra, Howard Hawks, John Ford, Michael Curtiz, and Alfred Hitchcock.

Unfortunately, as these studio executives learned from their liaisons with the multiplex chains, the theaters, which they no longer controlled, now wanted a very different product. As one multiplex owner told a Fox distribution chief in 1997, "The less dialogue the better. The teens that come to our theaters want car chases, bombs, a few beautiful bodies, and mind-bending special effects." The executives further learned that even if a mass audience still existed for such adult fare, their marketing departments did not have the resources to efficiently mobilize it for a given opening weekend or to establish it in the crucial television, home-video, and other ancillary markets. Simply—if cynically—put, these films lacked the "numbers" that Wasserman once observed made "the world go round." Nevertheless, that almost romantic attachment—what Redstone described in his autobiography as "a love affair"—to the old Hollywood could not be entirely extinguished by the argument of the numbers. With such considerations at stake, profitable or unprofitable, studio executives remained determined not to be completely governed by the dictates of the children's and teen market.

So these executives, while recognizing the disconnect between the prior and present systems, looked to their own specialty film units— Miramax Pictures, Sony Classics, Fox Searchlight, Paramount Classics, and Warner Independent Pictures—oxymoronically referred to as "independent subsidiaries," to give them the awards, media recognition, artistic bragging rights, and other noneconomic rewards they sought in Hollywood. In doing so, they were returning conceptually not so much to the studio system as to the art-house system, which had at one time coexisted alongside the Hollywood studios. By 2003, these "independent" arms, either via acquiring the American distribution rights to independently made films (often at film festivals such as Sundance) or producing films themselves, were distributing more titles than the studios themselves. Although these subsidiaries often obtained these films for relatively small cash outlays, overhead and marketing costs had pushed up the average cost of each film to an astounding $61.6 million in 2003, nearly two thirds of that of studio movies. Further, since many of the more adult films produced by the independent subsidiaries did not appeal to the youth-oriented toy, game, and other ancillary markets, they often resulted in huge losses for the studios.

If producing more sophisticated films would seem to defy the economic logic of the new Hollywood, the practice—at least until now—has been accepted by studio executives because, in addition to the prestige these films bestow on them, the making of them has the backing of the stars, directors, writers, agents, and gurus whose goodwill still carries weight with studios and even their corporate owners. In the near future, however, the power of the Hollywood community may be directly challenged by another form of progress: technology.

Throughout the twentieth century, Hollywood has had an uneasy relationship with technology. Synchronous sound threatened to undermine an industry built on silent movies in the 1920s, television threatened to lure away the mass movie-theater audience in the 1940s, and the home video recorder threatened to further erode that audience in the late 1970s. Eventually, however, these latter technologies provided the Hollywood studios with its salvation: the home audience. Now, in the twenty-first century, another technological breakthrough, digitization, presents Hollywood studios with a similar dilemma. On one hand, the ability to transform movies into a formula of digits—"ones" and "zeros"—that can be easily manipulated by computers allows studios to make products that appeal to large global audiences and deliver them in a multitude of forms including DVDs, video on demand (VOD), and high-definition television. On the other hand, that same ease of replication and transmission invites video pirates, hackers, and other unauthorized copiers to usurp the studios' own control over their movies.

The continued value of digital assets, like any other intellectual property, depends on the studios' ability to protect them from unauthorized copying and exploitation. Since such protection on a global scale requires the cooperation of governments in America, Europe, and Asia, the studios share a powerful interest in achieving a political solution that results in government regulations requiring TV, DVD, cable-box, and computer manufacturers to embed circuits in their products that would make it impossible for consumers to see unauthorized versions of their entertainments. Once such unauthorized viewing can be prevented, the studios will enjoy the full economic benefits of the digital revolution.

The marriage of movies and the computer has been greatly facilitated, if not made irresistible, by rapid advances in the power of computer processing. In 1970 a one-inch chip had etched on it a thousand circuits; in 2000 the same size chip contained 42 million circuits. Since this exponential increase in capacity was not accompanied by a commensurate increase in price, the cost of using computers to generate images for movies has fallen dramatically over the last thirty years. In 1977, for example, computer processing was still so prohibitively expensive that when George Lucas made the original *Star Wars*, he could afford to use computer graphics for only a single ninety-second sequence. That sequence—a diagram of the enemy Death Star—took a battery of computers three months to complete. By 1982, computer processing cost only one eighth as much, allowing Disney to make *Tron*, a large portion of which featured live actors wearing black-and-white costumes combined with backgrounds generated by computers. By the mid-1990s, the further thirty-two-fold decrease in computer-processing costs made it feasible for Pixar Animation Studios (in partnership with Disney) to make entire computer-generated movies, such as *Toy Story*. Sony demonstrated that realistic-looking computer-generated stars could also appeal to older audiences in *Final Fantasy: The Spirits Within*. In this futuristic movie based on an electronic game, Sony's digital animators created de novo an extremely lifelike heroine, Dr. Aki Ross, whose physical beauty and sex appeal were sufficient to earn her a slot on *Maxim* magazine's 2001 "Hot 100" list—the only nonexistent person (to date) to appear on that list. By 2004, as its cost continued to fall, computer-drawn imagery of 3D animation, as it was called, had all but replaced conventional animation, with even Disney shutting down a large part of its artist-drawn 2D animation studio in Florida.

The digital revolution has also changed the way live-action movies are made. By the 1990s, all the studios were using so-called digital compositing to blend together computer-generated images and actors. This computer technology allows shots to be composed of different "layers," some of which may be filmed by a camera and some of which are created in a computer. In the "live" layer, an actor can perform his scene in an empty room, called a limbo set, while holding imaginary objects and reacting to imaginary presences. After this acting "layer" is completed, computer-graphic artists create the other layers. These computer-generated images may include the room's decor, the actor's costume, the missing objects, crowds of nonexistent people, exotic settings, and visual effects, such as fires, explosions, and floods. The digital compositors then fuse these layers together, pixel by pixel, into a single shot.

By 1999, this computer technology had advanced to the point whereby the heads of stars could be digitally composited on their stunt doubles. In *Gladiator*, for example, an image of Russell Crowe's face was scanned into a computer and converted to a transferable "digital mask."

This mask was then substituted for the green-painted faces of the stunt-men who played Crowe's character, the gladiator Maximus—a feat of identity theft that took digital operatives more than eight months to complete. (The production of *Gladiator* used seventy-nine stuntmen, more than twice the number of actors in the credited cast.)

The technology that greatly facilitates digital substitution is called "motion capture." First a film is made of a person in a green body stocking—a so-called motion-capture suit—making the necessary physical movements; the captured motion is then digitally scanned into a high-speed computer and substituted, frame by frame, for the movements of the computer-generated character. In motion capture, humans serve as mere models for animators.

By 2003, the technology had made another leap forward: computer-generated copies of actual stars—not just digital masks of their faces—could now be substituted for them. In the making of *Terminator 3*, for example, after Arnold Schwarzenegger had his facial expressions, body, and skin textures precisely scanned via laser beams into a computer file, a computer-generated clone of the actor was created for dangerous action scenes, such as the one in which his character is supposedly hanging off a giant crane as it smashes through buildings. (A computer-generated clone of actress Kristanna Loken was similarly used for the female *Terminator* character, T-X.) While those digital doubles were only used for stunts, director Robert Zemeckis took the process a step further in *The Polar Express* (2004) by using computer-generated characters to substitute for stars, including Tom Hanks, in their speaking roles, and at various ages. Zemeckis shot these scenes with acting doubles in motion-capture suits, covered with miniature sensors so that each facial and body movement could be more realistically captured. Digital animators then converted the sequences to computer files, and digital compositors blended them with the computer-generated settings, props, and visual effects.

Many others stars—including Jim Carrey, Natasha Henstridge, Tom Cruise, and Denzel Washington—have been laser-scanned, or "gone under the beam," to create digital files that can be used to generate their clones for future scenes that they may be unable or unwilling to perform (or that a cast insurer may prohibit them from performing). These digital files can also offer them—and their heirs—Dorian Gray–like opportunities, even after aging takes its physical toll, to extend their tenure as stars.

By 2004, the "holy grail" of studios that was satirized in the 2002 movie *Simone*—studios creating compliant actors out of whole cloth via proprietary computer programs—was rapidly becoming a technological possibility. George Lucas, whose computer-graphics company, Industrial Light & Magic, had spearheaded the digital revolution, noted even before the technology was fully perfected that the distinction between live-action films and animation was gradually being erased. "We can make an animal," he pointed out, "and if you do that, you can make a human." As was demonstrated by the computer-created Gollum in *The Lord of the Rings: The Two Towers*, we are already at a point where such a character can interact seamlessly with live characters in entire scenes.

The ultimate step, of course, would be making not just a colorful supporting character but a Simone-like star. Though only a small technological leap from the digital animation in *Terminator 3* and *The Polar Express*, such computer-generated stars would constitute a giant leap for the Hollywood studios in terms of licensing potential for DVDs, videos, electronic games, toys, advertising, and other products, since their ownership would be total and permanent (just as Disney's is over its animated cartoon characters).

To be sure, such de novo digital creations would lack existing stars' audience recognition, but the appearance of relatively unknown "real-life" actors in starring roles has not prevented major Hollywood action movies from succeeding at the box office. First-time movie actor Mark Hamill, for example, played the hero Luke Skywalker in *Star Wars*. And unlike humans, a digital star has the advantage of being designed with elements that are consciously chosen to appeal to moviegoers. At that point, as Lucas suggests, the distinction between movies and cartoons will be largely eliminated.

As far as the ever-important global youth market is concerned, the future may already be dawning, with digital technology transforming two-dimensional comic-book fantasy content into more realistic illusions, thereby completing the three-generation-long odyssey that began with the doll-like quasi humans in Disney's *Snow White and the Seven Dwarfs*. By establishing more realistic fantasy characters, such as the elves, orcs, and monsters in *The Lord of the Rings: The Return of the King*, digitizing further offers the prospect of a licensing cornucopia of heroes (and anti-heroes) for toys, interactive games, and amusement-park rides.

The falling cost of digitization will almost inevitably challenge the very medium that made Hollywood possible in the first place: celluloid film. In the *Lord of the Rings* trilogy, for example, more than three quarters of the film, including some 200,000 soldiers, was created on computers. This material then had to be precisely timed to fit in with the quarter of the film that was shot by cameras—a process of integration that took over a year and added enormously to the cost. As more and more of the illusions in movies are created by computers, the pressure will increase to shoot the remaining live-action sequences with filmless digital cameras, as George Lucas did in *Stars Wars: Episode II–The Attack of the Clones* and Robert Rodriguez did in *Once Upon a Time in Mexico* and *Spy Kids 2*. Live action can be shot digitally much more quickly, since it can easily and seamlessly be altered in postproduction and combined with the computer-generated parts of the movie at little extra expense. Even though the quality of digital cameras may currently be inferior to that of conventional cameras, the advantages the new technology offers in terms of lower cost and greater speed can be expected in time to prove irresistible to studios.

The final step in filmless movies is digital projection in theaters. Currently, all movies—even those entirely made by a computer and recorded on digital tape—have to be converted into a thirty-five-millimeter celluloid negative, from which reels of film are printed, sent to film exchanges, trucked to theaters, and projected on the screen with the aid of a powerful lamp. The thirty-five-millimeter prints that are distributed to theaters around the world are expensive to make and cumbersome to distribute, and they require constant repair to remedy the scratches, burns, and other damage incurred during projection. Aside from the expense and burden of making thousands of copies of each film, studios must maintain strategically located film exchanges around the world to service them.

In the late 1990s, the once radical idea of filmless projection began to emerge as an alternative. The technology, based on a digital light projector in which several million on-or-off microscopic mirrors—each representing a single pixel—are embedded on a one-inch chip, allows movies to be projected by theaters from a digital file that can be directly relayed to a theater. With this digital technology, there are no reels to be rewound by projectionists, no marred prints to be repaired, no heavy cans to pick up and return to studio exchanges, and no film to be stored and preserved. By 1999, George Lucas was testing audience reactions to the technology by using digital projections for *Star Wars: Episode I—The Phantom Menace* in a couple of theaters—without moviegoers being able to discern an appreciable difference. By 2003, 171 theaters had been outfitted for digital projection, and the major studios were working on a plan to turn digital delivery of their movies over to a telecommunications company, Qualcomm, which would provide satellite feeds of movies for theaters, just as television networks provide prime-time feeds for affiliated stations.

The most obvious advantage for studios in eliminating film would be cutting distribution costs. In 2003 the average cost to make prints for the distribution of a studio film just in America was $4.2 million. In addition, the average cost for prints for their "independent" subsidiaries was $1.87 million a film. The studios also had to bear the cost of maintaining film exchanges with hundreds of full-time employees and, if the film was shot digitally, the expense of converting it to a celluloid negative. The six studios therefore had a print bill of more than $1 billion in 2003.

The issue for the studios goes beyond merely cutting expenses, though. According to the studios' current plan, each multiplex digital projector would need a studio-supplied authorization code for a particular showing, which would give the studios power over what is shown, and precisely when, on movie screens.

Before film can be eliminated, however, studios have to overcome a formidable issue: who will pay the cost of converting the world's theaters to filmless projectors. Since the economic benefit of filmless projection would go to the studios, theater owners could hardly be expected to pay for the new projectors, which in 2003 cost approximately $80,000 apiece. The studios, although recognizing that they would have to fully subsidize the conversion, are seeking an arrangement that would assure them that the theaters would actually use the digital projectors and that the conversion would not raise antitrust concerns by excluding independently produced nondigital movies. If, and when, the studios and the major chain owners come to terms, as it seems they eventually must, the screens at the multiplexes will become another link in the digital chain that extends from the computer cyberspace where the products are created, edited, colored, and converted into different formats to the DVD players, game consoles, satellite receivers, cable boxes, video-on-demand servers, TiVo-type recorders, and other devices that serve the studios' largest and most profitable consumers: the home audience.

The digital magic that allows the New Hollywood to achieve this potential may have somewhat less salutary consequences for the community that has in the past so powerfully defined Hollywood. The division of a movie into computer-generated layers tends to change artistic relations. Although *Terminator 3* director Jonathan Mostow conceded that "digital animation is the future of Hollywood" and expressed awe at the realistic way that the technology replicated live action, he also had reservations about its further alienation of the actors from their product.

Mostow's reservations are well founded. The actor, after all, is central to filmmaking, the person whom the director directs, the cameraperson lights, the sound engineer records, the wardrobe crew dresses, and, eventually, the publicist peddles to the entertainment media. The actor's relation to his work therefore affects not only his product—movies—but the integrity and identity of the entire Hollywood community.

Admittedly, the actor on a movie set has always had a more distant relationship to his product than his counterpart on the stage. Unlike stage actors who develop a character, scene by scene, as the play unfolds, film actors typically perform their part over and over again in brief, truncated scenes that lack any continuity with what precedes or follows them. Nevertheless, no matter how frustrating, unsatisfying, and exhausting out-of-order shooting might be, the star still remains in the picture.

With the advancement of digital technologies for manipulating images, the actor's relation to the movie has become more tenuous. We are already at the point where an actor can stand in an empty room, wearing a green spandex jumpsuit, and mouth lines of dialogue—which will later be filled in at a looping session—while holding imaginary objects and reacting to imaginary visual effects and nonexistent people. Indeed, sometimes, as was the case for Russell Crowe in parts of *Gladiator*, he may be reduced to being just a grimacing digital face mask worn by a second-unit stuntman.

In filming *Terminator 3*, director Jonathan Mostow recognized the enormous strain it places on actors to perform in such unreal circumstances. "Certain actors can't do it—they have to have the physical circumstances in front of them to deliver a performance," he commented. "So it is very important in a film like this that you look for actors that have the imaginative ability to visualize in their mind things that are not there yet." The alienation only deepens when computer-generated human characters interact with live characters.

In addition to further separating actors from the reality of their work, the digitization process also makes it much more difficult for the director to retain control. Since it often takes much longer than the filming itself for digital-animation companies to create the layers of computer-generated settings, characters, and visual effects, directors generally have to complete the live shooting, and sometimes even the editing, before they receive the missing layers of the movie. Consider Jonathan Mostow's situation in directing *Terminator 3*, which began shooting in Los Angeles in July 2002 and had to be delivered to Warner Bros. eleven months later for its scheduled July 4, 2003, release. Since just the digitally created layers of the film would take the subcontractor at least eight months to create—and cost a staggering $19.9 million—Mostow had no choice but to have the subcontractor, Industrial Light & Magic, create the computer-generated layers of the sequences *before* he had finished shooting, looping in the sound, or editing the live portions of the sequences. In effect, as he points out, these were two separate projects—one taking place on soundstages and locations in Los Angeles, the other on computer consoles in Silicon Valley. The schizoid nature of this production is eerily reflected in the dividing of Schwarzenegger's face: the right side with conventional makeup, the left side bright green. Mostow directed the right side on a set in Los Angeles; then, over the next eight months, a digital-animation supervisor in San Rafael directed the manipulation of the metallic robot that became the left side of the face, which then had to be matched frame by frame by other computer technicians to the movements in the right side. By the time the computer technicians finished their work in the late spring of 2003, there was neither time nor money to substantively redo the digital layers. "For a filmmaker that is the worst thing you can imagine," Mostow recalled. "In the regular rhythm of making movies you shoot, you edit, you hone the editing, and then you add the finishing touches," he said. "Computer graphics turns the normal procedures of filmmaking upside down."

The digital divide involves a conflict of culture as well as a division of labor. Most of the contingent on the movie set—including actors, camera crew, sound engineers, assistant directors, makeup artists, wardrobe fitters, script supervisors, and set dressers—is handpicked by the director (or may even be specified by the star). They tend to identify themselves with the traditions, values, nostalgia, and perceptions of the Hollywood community. Meanwhile, the computer-graphics contingent—including digital compositors, digital timers, rotoscope artists, and inferno artists—has little, if any, contact with those on the set. They work from cartoon strips, hunched over computers in scattered cubicles. They are usually hired not by the director, the producer, or the studio but by a subcontractor who usually has submitted the lowest bid for a particular digital-animation shot. The digital-animation shots that precede and follow the one that they are working on often are done by different subcontractors. Cost, not consistency, tends to be the criterion in doling out this work. As one experienced producer described the process, "It is like asking for the lowest plumber bid on each bathroom in your house."

Since these technicians depend for future assignments on the subcontractors, not the productions, they tend to conform to a methodical, can-do work ethic of completing assignments on time. They also tend to identify more with the values and activities of the computer "geek"—which may include hacking computer programs, file sharing, and electronic-game playing—than with those of Hollywood. They are primarily computer guys, not film buffs.

Not all movies make use of digital effects, to be sure, but those that do already produce most, if not all, of the profits on which Hollywood now relies. With the geometric increases in computer power that will be available to Hollywood in the near future—the number of circuits etched on a one-inch chip already exceeds 100 million—the trend will no doubt continue, with much, if not all, of conventional moviemaking increasingly replaced by digital animation. As that happens, much of Hollywood's traditional culture will likely also find itself replaced by the computer culture. This will undoubtedly have an ineluctable impact on Hollywood's product, since, if nothing else, the Hollywood culture—with the high value it places on prestige, acclaim, and awards—serves as the only remaining, and still surprisingly potent, lobby for films that transcend the economic logic of Hollywood.

If content remains king in the emerging New Hollywood, as Sumner Redstone holds, it will increasingly enthrall as its vassals those consumers, especially among the global population of youth, who have come to depend on its blend of heroic figures, exotic settings, and audiovisual effects for its fantasy gratification. As film itself becomes obsolete in the new digital era, and much of the movie culture based on it fades away, the distinction will further blur between animated cartoons, live action, and interactive computer games in movies, television programs, and reality shows—as will the boundaries between conventional advertising, which carries a label, and product-placement inserts, which can be seamlessly fused in the content itself to stoke the appetites for licensable merchandise. Further, in this new economy of illusions, digital delivery systems—including TiVo-like personal recorders, video-on-demand feeds, interactive cable boxes, Internet modems, and DVD players—will allow authorized viewers to receive their chosen content in their homes any time of the day or night. To be sure, there still may be movies made for grown-up audiences to see in theaters, but they will play an ever-smaller part in the big picture.

Afterword

THE RISE OF THE TUBE MOGULS

Since I completed this book, all six Hollywood studios have come under new management. In each case, the old guard was replaced by newcomers who had little, if any experience in the art of studio film production. This new Hollywood ascendency did, however, have a common thread: television.

Sir Howard Stringer, a former president of CBS, succeeded Nobuyuki Idei as chairman and chief executive officer of Sony. The appointment of a Welsh-born British-American citizen who had never lived in Japan and did not even speak Japanese to head a Japanese corporation that was closely identified in the public's mind with Japanese technological innovation came as a wake-up call. It served notice that Sony would have to adapt itself to the global digital revolution. While Idei had called on Sony to revolutionize itself, and formulated a blueprint for re-inventing the company, he had failed to execute it. Now it is Sir Howard's mission.

I spoke with Sir Howard, in his elegant thirty-fourth-floor executive suite on top of Sony's headquarters in New York City, soon after he took the helm. He explained to me that the digital revolution had forced competing manufacturers to use the exact same standards, if not the identical computer chip, in products such as DVD players, CD players, and digital television sets. So competitors in countries with lower labor costs, such as China, could sell products with the same performance specifications (and digital chips) as Sony, but at lower prices. For example, during the Christmas season of 2004, a Chinese-made DVD player sold at Wal-Mart for $25, one-quarter of the price of a similar Sony player. Digitalization, which Sony had helped pioneer, had the unanticipated consequence of turning the consumer products—the foundation of Sony's initial success—into commodities, and their marketing into a rat race. Since its founding as the Tokyo Telecommunications Engineering Corporation by inventors Akio Morita and Masaru Ibuka in 1946, Sony had been dominated by an engineering culture dedicated to developing new proprietary products such as the CD, the Trinitron color TV, and the Walkman. Recognizing that this focus on proprietary products is incompatible with the universally standardized plug-and-play products of the digital age, Sir Howard is moving the company, as he puts it, "from an analog culture to a digital culture." In the emerging digital world, Sony will still manufacture things—including DVD players, high-definition televisions, game consoles, computers, CD players, and digital projectors—but it will make most of its profits not from the hardware itself but from the digital data played on it. The PlayStation 3, for example, is not just a game console; it plays digital movies, music, television programs, and offerings from the Internet.

Sony hardly lacks the means to participate in the digital revolution— indeed, it had augmented its massive library of movies and television programs by acquiring 4,100 titles from MGM, and the digital equipment it has brought to market includes a blue-laser high-definition DVD player, a digital recorder that can store thirty movies, and a 6-million pixel television display. The challenge, as Sir Howard frames it, is to "optimize" the release of the digital content across a raft of platforms, including movies, games, video-on-demand, television programs, and interactive DVDs. Before digitalization made replication inexpensive, Hollywood had released movies into different markets sequentially during so-called "windows." Each window separated markets by between four months and one year from the next market. First is the theatrical window, when the movies play in theaters, which is followed by the video window, when DVDs are sold and rented in stores. Next is the video-on-demand window, when pay-per-view is made available in homes, followed by the pay-TV window release, when it is released on HBO and other subscription channels. Finally, there is the free-TV window, when networks and stations air the movie. The window system had worked reasonably well before the digital age lowered the cost of replication to the point that mass retailers such as Wal-Mart used DVDs as a traffic builder in their stores and video pirates took advantage of the time delays between windows to effectively compete with the studios. Now, however, with more than 85 percent of the studios' revenues coming from people watching DVDs, television, or playing games at home, Sir Howard has to find better ways of releasing digital products.

The alternative permutations are endless. A property may be established in the public's mind first as an interactive game on the super-realistic PlayStation 3, and then be made available as a DVD, a TV series, through video-on-demand, and, finally, as a motion picture. It can also be established directly on DVD via a massive advertising campaign and then be moved to other platforms or become a cable TV series. Whatever the theoretical possibilities of optimization, Sir Howard sees a chicken-and-egg dilemma. The chicken is the movie; the egg is the other valuable digital rights, including DVD, game, and television licensing. The dilemma: the chicken that had traditionally produced these eggs could be killed by laying an egg larger than itself.

At Disney, Robert A. Iger, the former president of ABC Television, was formulating an even more radical strategy for optimizing profits. He had replaced Michael Eisner as CEO in October of 2005. During Eisner's twenty-one-year reign at Disney, he transformed the company in ways that not even Walt Disney could have envisioned. The concept of Disneyland was globalized, with 11 theme parks now open worldwide, including in Paris, Tokyo, and Hong Kong. A fleet of Disney Cruise ships was launched. Disney acquired the ABC network, along with the ABC Family Channel on cable. The Disney Channel became part of a children's cable empire that had twelve overseas Disney Channels, three Toon Disney channels, twelve Kids channels in Europe (called Jetix) and four Playhouse Disney channels. Also on cable, Disney now controlled the world's most powerful sports network, ESPN, with its twenty-nine channels, and the Soap network. Its home video division, which did not exist in 1984, produced 6 billion dollars in revenue in 2004, and the stage play division that Eisner created, which converted such Disney cinematic hits as *The Lion King*, *Beauty and the Beast*, *Mary Poppins*, and *Tarzan* into musicals, now earned more money each year than the entire company did in 1984. Even though Eisner had increased the company's value nearly thirty fold, the institutions that own two thirds of Disney's shares were dissatisfied with his inability to deliver a better stock market payoff, and so the Disney board selected Iger to succeed Eisner.

Iger immediately raised the hot-button issue: windows. "We have to look at window changes . . . across the board," Iger told a meeting of Wall Street analysts, adding, "Windows need to compress. I don't think it's out of the question that a DVD can be released, in effect, in the same window as a theatrical release." While studios had been privately debating for months about how to change the window system, Iger's public broaching of the issue so unsettled theater owners that the head of their trade association, the National Association of Theatre Owners, termed it a "death threat" to the industry.

Iger meant it more as a wake-up call to a new reality in which theater owners will have much less of a protective window against digital competition. His background is in the television industry and, from this vantage point, movie theaters are a declining business. Since the availability of television in 1946, the American weekly moviegoing audience had dropped from 90 million to 29 million, even though the general population nearly doubled during this time period. The relevant fact for Iger is that over 90 percent of Disney's profits in 2004 came not from movie theaters but from the "back end"—DVDs, TV movies, and product licensing to the home audience. By doing away with fixed intervals, or at least compressing them, Iger looks to increasing profits by substituting more lucrative DVD, TV, and video-on-demand sales for less profitable box-office ticket sales. Even if this ruffles the feathers of theater owners, or of others of the old guard in the industry, his more relevant audience is Disney's institutional investors who forced Eisner out.

The story is much the same at the other Hollywood studios.

At Time Warner, pay-TV executive Jeffrey Bewkes is now chairman of the entire entertainment division, which includes two movie studios (Warner Bros. and New Line Cinema), HBO itself, and all the Turner cable networks and the Warner Bros. Television Network. Bewkes, to be sure, had a brilliant success story at HBO, launching a slew of original series, such as *Sex and the City*, and *The Sopranos*. Their success showed that HBO's less than 30 million subscribers could create enough word-of-mouth to establish huge DVD hits without the benefit of either movie theater openings or multimillion-dollar ad campaigns on network television. In 2005, according to Bewkes, Warner Bros.' DVD revenue from TV shows alone will far exceed $1 billion. Instead of following artificial window delays, Bewkes has sought the optimal release date to maximize profits. In light of these successes, Bewkes can be expected to search for new ways, if not reinvent, the sequence in which other products, including movies, are released.

At Viacom, Thomas Freston, one of the creators of MTV, is now in charge of both the Paramount studio and the cable networks. The previous regime at Paramount was led by Jonathan Dolgen, Sherry Lansing, and Thomas McGrath, all of whom had grown up in the movie business and who focused their efforts on rationalizing Paramount's movie business. They created two highly successful film labels (MTV Films and Nickelodeon Films), built their foreign arm, United International Pictures, which they owned jointly with Universal, into the dominant international film distributor; and worked out an elaborate system of legally and efficiently using foreign tax shelters and government subsides to finance their movies. As a result, they tripled the movie divisions' profits. Even so, the Paramount film business was nowhere as lucrative as the MTV and Nickelodeon cable business, both of which raked in money from advertisers and charged cable operators to carry them. Nor could an investment in a movie ever be as predictably profitable as one in MTV or Nickelodeon programming. So Freston replaced Dolgen, Lansing, and McGrath with the team of Brad Grey, a successful television producer, and Gail Berman, who had previously headed Fox television programming.

At News Corporation, Peter Chernin, who had headed Fox Broadcasting, is now chairman of the whole Fox Entertainment Group, which includes the movie studio as well as the Fox broadcast and cable networks. After the resignation in July 2005 of Murdoch's eldest son, Lachlan, from News Corporation, Chernin became Murdoch's undisputed heir apparent. Fox is not merely in the movie or television business, according to

Chernin, it is "in the business of creating and distributing original digital products . . . whether it's computer games on an Xbox or *X-Men* on DVD, whether on websites or in e-books, on iPods or ITV." The challenge for him is to find the most profitable way for the Murdoch empire to deliver these digital products. One way is by using the armada of satellites Murdoch now controls through DirecTV—America's largest satellite television company. Even before Murdoch had completed his acquisition of DirecTV, he announced, at Morgan Stanley's Global Media & Communications Conference, his plan to marry satellite signals above with TiVo-like personal video recorders below, so that digital content—including movies, TV series, and games—can be delivered into every subscriber's home. Chernin's mission will be to execute this grand strategy.

Finally, Universal is now a wholly owned subsidiary of NBC. As such, it is part of the domain of NBC CEO Robert C. Wright. In his nineteen-year tenure at NBC, Wright has brilliantly used the concept of programming, whereby programs are shifted from one time slot to another, or are even "repositioned" from a network to a cable channel, to maximize their ad revenues. The issue for Wright, as well as for his counterparts at the other studios, is whether such a programming strategy can be applied to the positioning of movies in the entertainment spectrum without damaging the creative process that has traditionally conferred value on them.

That all of Hollywood's new moguls—Stringer at Sony, Iger at Disney, Bewkes at Warner Bros, Freston at Paramount, Chernin at Fox, and Wright at NBC Universal—come from the realm of television reflects a singular, if dismal, reality: only 2 percent of Americans now go to movie theaters on a given day, while more than 95 percent watch something at home on TV. The same is true, with even greater force, in the key foreign markets of Europe and Asia. What used to be a business centered in movie houses has been transformed into a business centered around home television sets. Consequently, it is not surprising that the men now running it are more experienced with that mass audience than with the vanishing movie theater audience. For better or worse, this transformation is now part of the big picture.

Notes

Although there is no shortage of dazzling press releases about Hollywood's stars and performances, or, for that matter, data about its products' retail popularity at movie box offices,
on television channels, and at video stores, the numbers at the heart of Hollywood's
moneymaking are much harder to come by. The six world studios that shape today's film
business—Disney, Sony, Paramount, Twentieth Century Fox, Warner Bros., and NBC Universal—all make it a practice to keep secret from the public the data that accurately reflect
the real sources of their earnings. Each of these studios, however, furnishes precise data, including a detailed breakdown of their worldwide revenues from movie theaters, videocas-
sette, DVD, network television, local television, pay television, and pay-per-view—to the
Motion Picture Association (MPA), the international arm of its Motion Picture Association
of America (MPAA) trade organization, on condition that it will not be released to any
other parties. The MPA then consolidates these cash flows into a loose-leaf document called
the *MPA All Media Revenue Report*, which it then circulates back to the studios on a confidential basis. Each studio can then use this common pool of data—the 2003 report was
more than three hundred pages—to compare its own performance, and that of its subsidiaries, to that of the other major studios in sixty-four different markets. I had access to
the data between 1999 and 2004. Although MGM also reports its data to the MPA, it was
excluded because MGM no longer functions as a full-fledged studio. (In 2004, MGM announced it would sell its receiving assets to Sony and its corporate partners.) The data for
the six studios are referred to hereinafter as *MPA All Media Revenue Report.*

   In the case of the studios' earnings from individual movies, I relied on, when available,
participation statements. These are the semiannual reports of earnings that studios send to
stars, directors, writers, and other participants in the movies. (The "box-office gross" figures supplied to the media reveal the total take of theaters, not the portion of it that is ultimately remitted to studios.) The participation statements report the revenues (called

traditionally "rentals") the studio actually received from theaters and other sources, as well as the production, advertising, and distribution expenses charged against the films. Even after these statements are subjected to independent audits by participants, which is not uncommon in Hollywood, they generally prove accurate (at least on revenue flows). When participation statements were not available, I relied on estimates made for me by studio executives of films' performances. In comparing these executives' estimates to available participation statements, I did not find a significant difference.

A number of studio executives were extremely helpful in answering specific questions, both in person and in e-mail correspondence, between 1998 and 2004. At their request, they are not identified in the book by name.

Chapter 1: The Two Hollywoods

4   **a program that included:** Audience Research Inc., study quoted in *Variety,* February 23, 1949.

5   **studios produced nearly five hundred films in 1947:** Gene Brown, *Movie Time* (New York: Macmillan, 1995), p. 185.

7   **"about six producers today":** Quoted in Thomas Schatz, *The Genius of the System: Hollywood Filmmaking in the Studio Era* (New York: Metropolitan Books, 1988), p. 8.

9   **average cost of producing a film:** Brown, *Movie Time,* p. 185.

9   **Louis Mayer had proposed:** Mason Wiley and Damien Bona, *Inside Oscar: The Unofficial History of the Academy Awards* (New York: Ballantine Books, 1993), p. 2.

9   **censorship system:** Clayton R. Koppes and Gregory D. Black, *Hollywood Goes to War: How Politics, Profits, and Propaganda Shaped World War II Movies* (Berkeley and Los Angeles: University of California Press, 1990), pp. 113–14.

10 **Fox, the founder of Twentieth Century–Fox:** Neal Gabler, *An Empire of Their Own: How the Jews Invented Hollywood* (New York: Anchor Books, 1989), p. 419.

11 **the so-called Hollywood Ten:** Victor S. Navasky, *Naming Names: The Social Costs of McCarthyism* (New York: Viking Press, 1980), p. xii.

12 **television manufacturers were expecting:** *Film Daily Year Book of Motion Pictures* (New York: The Film Daily, 1949), p. 67.

12 **Disney had a different strategy:** Harvard Business School, Case Study 1-388-147, "The Walt Disney Company (A) (Boston: Harvard Business School Publishing Division 1996), p. 2; Richard Schickel, *The Disney Version: The Life, Times, Art and Commerce of Walt Disney* (Chicago: Elephant Paperbacks, 1997), pp. 126–36, 298, 310–14a.

13 **"business that no longer exists":** Schatz, *Genius,* p. 3.

15 **"a true full-service entertainment enterprise":** Michael Eisner, letter to shareholders, Walt Disney Pictures Annual Report, 2000, p. 4.

16 **film *Gone in 60 Seconds:*** The financial results come from Walt Disney Pictures Participation Statement, Statement #10, period ending December 31, 2003, author's files.

16 **one of the company's biggest "hits":** Walt Disney Pictures Annual Report, 2000, p. 37.

17 **accounted for less than half:** U.S. Economic Reviews, MPAA, 2003.

18　**Arnold Schwarzenegger received:** Letter Agreement, T-3 Productions, Intermedia Film Equities, and Oak Productions, regarding the acting services of Arnold Schwarzenegger, December 10, 2001.

19　**the studios recovered only $6.4 billion:** MPAA Economic Review.

19　**"Studios nowadays":** Frank Biondi, interview by author, 1999.

20　**Table 1:** Motion Picture Association, Worldwide Market Research, *2003 MPA All Media Revenue Report,* Encino, Calif., 2004 (hereinafter *All Media Revenue Report*). This privileged report, which is limited in its dissemination to major studios, contains the confidential cash-flow data furnished by the major studios and their subsidiaries from all their major sources, including movie theaters, video (both DVD and videotape), network television, local television, pay television, and pay-per-view. Although MGM—a studioless studio that in 2005 will become part of Sony—also provides data for this report, I have not included it. Consequently, the data here (and elsewhere in this book) are for the six major studios—Disney, Sony, Warner Bros., Paramount, NBC Universal, and Twentieth Century–Fox—and their subsidiaries (such as Miramax, New Line, and Sony Pictures Classics).

20　**By 2003, the home-entertainment share:** Document, MPA Worldwide Market Research, *All Media Revenue Report,* May 2004.

22　**F. Scott Fitzgerald noted:** Quoted in Schatz, *Genius,* p. 8

23　**"to avoid showing Wall Street":** Interview by author, 2004.

Chapter 2: The Creators

27　**the arcade business:** Neal Gabler, *An Empire of Their Own: How the Jews Invented Hollywood* (New York: Anchor Books, 1989), pp. 11–16.

28　**Zukor was one of the largest:** Gabler, *Empire,* p. 60.

31　**Within a year, Mickey Mouse:** Richard Schickel, *The Disney Version: The Life, Times, Art and Commerce of Walt Disney* (Chicago: Elephant Paperbacks, 1997), p. 122.

31　**"those Jews":** Leonard Mosley, *Disney's World: A Biography* (New York: Scarborough House, 2002), p. 207.

32　**local fan clubs were established:** Schickel, *Disney Version,* pp. 167–68.

34　**"world's biggest toy":** Ibid., p. 310.

34　**"Disneyland will never be completed":** Ibid., p. 315.

34　***Winnie the Pooh,* whose characters:** Bruce Orwall, "Disney Wins Bear-Knuckled 13-Year-Old Fight Over Royalties," *Wall Street Journal,* March 30, 2004, p. B1.

35　**"We don't do anything in one line":** Bruce Orwall and Emily Nelson, "Hidden Walls Shield Disney Culture," *Wall Street Journal,* March 30, 2004, p. 1.

35　**"powerful brand and character franchises":** Michael Eisner, letter to shareholders, Walt Disney Pictures Annual Report, 2000, p. 4.

36　**Wasserman aggressively expanded MCA:** Dennis McDougal, *The Last Mogul: Lew Wasserman, MCA, and the Hidden History of Hollywood* (New York: Crown, 1998), pp. 106–107.

37　**represented such top stars:** Thomas Schatz, *The Genius of the System: Hollywood Filmmaking in the Studio Era* (New York: Metropolitan Books, 1988), p. 470.

37　**MCA then took a 10 percent commission:** McDougal, *Last Mogul,* p. 228.

39 **Hitchcock became MCA's third-largest:** Schatz, *Genius*, pp. 488–89.

40 **Wasserman began Universal on:** Richard Evans, "And Now, for My Next Trick," *Barron's*, July 30, 2001, p. 1.

41 **"It always worked with cards":** Steve Ross, interview by author, 1988.

43 **"their share of his winnings":** Author's diary entry (Las Vegas trip), February 6, 1976.

44 **He bought the cable businesses:** Connie Bruck, *Master of the Game: Steve Ross and the Creation of Time Warner* (New York: Simon & Schuster, 1994), p. 68.

45 **"out of thin air":** Ross interview.

45 **"Can we really expect millions":** Ibid.

45 **"people could vote for":** Ibid.

46 **"a WASPy blue chip":** Richard M. Clurman, *To the End of Time: The Seduction and Conquest of a Media Empire* (New York: Simon & Schuster, 1992), p. 15.

46 **"beauty of the deal":** Ross interview.

46 **"a simple disc available":** "Reinventing a Giant," *Asia Week*, September 22, 1995 (Internet edition).

47 **At the age of ten:** John Nathan, *Sony: The Private Life* (Boston: Houghton Mifflin, 1999), p. 17.

47 **He received a draft notice:** James Lardner, *Fast Forward: Hollywood, the Japanese, and the Onslaught of the VCR* (New York: W. W. Norton, 1987), p. 39.

48 **Now he wanted to improve:** Akio Morita, *Made in Japan: Akio Morita and Sony* (New York: Dutton, 1986), pp. 1–44.

48 **Morita made his first trip:** Nathan, *Sony*, p. 4.

49 **"felt Jews were smart":** Quoted in ibid., p. 61.

49 **"the sense of being foreign":** Ibid., p. 62.

49 **the top executives of Sony:** Ibid.

49 **Morita meanwhile began:** Morita, *Made in Japan*, pp. 1–44.

50 **Morita had Sony's engineers:** Nathan, *Sony*, pp. 150–52.

51 **The resulting product, the Betamax:** Lardner, *Fast Forward*, pp. 94–96.

52 **"When we shake hands":** Ibid., p. 29.

52 **Eisner overrode this objection:** Eisner, letter to shareholders, p. 4.

53 **"software and hardware":** Norio Ohga, *The Melody of Sony* (Tokyo: Nihon Keizai Shimbun, 2003); also Norio Ohga and Gerald Cavanaugh, interview by author, 2004.

53 **"If I owned a movie studio:"** Quoted in Nancy Griffin and Kim Masters, *Hit and Run: How Jon Peters and Peter Guber Took Sony for a Ride in Hollywood* (New York: Simon & Schuster, 1996), p. 184.

54 **Plagued by financial scandals:** David McClintick, *Indecent Exposure: A True Story of Hollywood and Wall Street* (New York: William Morrow, 1982), pp. 1–18.

54 **Morita offered the starting price:** "Columbia 75th Anniversary," *Variety*, January 1999, pp. 62–78.

55 **"nothing to lose":** Ross interview.

56 **"Pearl Harbor Revenged":** Griffin and Masters, *Hit and Run*, p. 250.

57 **"These were not requirements":** Warren Lieberfarb, lecture at Wharton School of Business, "Knowledge at Wharton," March 13, 2002 (http://knowledge.wharton.upenn.edu/index.cfm?fa=viewArticle&id=530).

58 **When his father died, most:** William Shawcross, *Murdoch: The Making of a Media Empire* (New York: Simon & Schuster, 1993), pp. 54–68.

59 "His life had been an": Ibid., p. 15.

61 "a series of interlocking wars": Ibid., p. 15.

61 *Time* ran a cover: *Time*, January 17, 1977.

64 The ensuing panic: Shawcross, *Murdoch*, p. 14.

64 the financier Sir James Goldsmith: Author's notes, Cuixmala, Mexico, December 20–22, 1990.

65 an "opportunistic" decision: Rupert Murdoch, Morgan Stanley Global Media and Communications Conference, September 8, 2003.

65 He told financial analysts: Ibid.

66 "We didn't have a bathroom": Sumner Redstone, interview by author, 2000.

66 There he worked: Gretchen Voss, "The $80 Billion Love Affair," *Boston Magazine*, January 12, 2000 (www.bostonmagazine.com/highlights/sumner.shtml).

67 "Whatever cash flow": Sumner Redstone, *A Passion to Win* (New York: Simon & Schuster, 2001), p. 70.

68 David battling Goliaths: Redstone interview.

68 He also so impressed: Redstone, *Passion to Win*, p. 76.

68 He was at the Copley Plaza hotel: Voss, "The $80 Billion Love Affair."

68 "success isn't built on success": Internet interview, www.myprimetime.com/work/life/content/pm_redstone0606/.

70 "We were competing against": Redstone, *Passion to Win*, p. 156.

70 "a born litigator": Author's interview, 2003.

70 The settlement: Redstone, *Passion to Win*, p. 160.

70 "I learned that": Redstone interview.

70 "I had my eye on": Redstone, *Passion to Win*, p. 175.

71 "to succeed, you have": Internet interview.

72 "the price for gaining a studio": Redstone interview.

72 "What other business": Redstone, *Passion to Win*, p. 285.

73 "We are not going to pay": Ibid., p. 286.

73 "The paradigm was": Ibid., p. 301.

74 "We use our content": Redstone interview.

79 "Basically, we're the delivery": Marcy Carson and Tom Werner, "David Sarnoff," *Time*, June 14, 1999.

79 "The numbers made": Author's interview, 2002.

80 Table 2: *MPA All Media Revenue Report,* 2002–2003. Up until 2002, studios reported revenues from "contract sales," that is, the revenue that networks committed to pay the studios when programs aired. In 2003, however, they changed to reporting revenues actually received. For purposes of historic comparisons, the data for 2003 reflects contract sales (extrapolated from a 35 percent increase in the total 2003 studio revenues from networks).

82 "money machine": Ross interview.

Chapter 3: Americanizing the World

85 "The film has come": Quoted in David Puttnam, *Movies and Money* (New York: Alfred A. Knopf, 1998), p. 76.

86 By 1926, American films accounted: Ibid., p. 110.

86 These faithful copies: Ibid., p. 113.

87   **After war finally broke out:** Ibid., pp. 120–21.

87   **"a marginal activity":** Interview by author, 2002.

87   **"Decisions on what films":** Peter Bart and Peter Guber, *Shoot Out: Surviving Fame and (Mis)Fortune in Hollywood* (New York: G. P. Putnam's Sons, 2002), p. 25.

88   **Their share of the box office:** Puttnam, *Movies and Money,* p. 266.

88   **"transnational products":** Interview by author, 2003.

89   **"roots, heart and culture":** Quoted by Joseph Schuman, "Seeking Investor Respect, Murdoch Spurns Australia," *Wall Street Journal,* April 6, 2004 (Internet edition).

89   **"the reality that we are a U.S.–based":** Quoted in Geraldine Fabrikant, "News Corp. Plans to Follow Its Chief to the United States," *New York Times,* April 7, 2004, p. B1.

90   **"Murdoch is a shark":** Quoted in Mark Lewis, "Germany's Content King Is Dethroned," *Forbes,* March 26, 2002 (Internet edition).

91   **"out-Murdoch" Murdoch:** Interview by author, 2003.

91   **"The French cultural exception":** Quoted in Meara Cavanaugh, "Messier: Threat to French Culture?" CNN.com Europe, April 17, 2002.

91   **extend his American assets:** Richard Evans, "And Now, for My Next Trick," *Barron's,* July 30, 2001, p. 1.

Chapter 4: The Sexopoly

93   **"rabbit or duck" illusion:** E. H. Gombrich, *Art and Illusion* (Princeton, N.J.: Princeton University Press, 1960), p. 5.

94   **"race to the bottom":** Interview by author, 2002.

95   **"fair-competition" practices:** Tino Balio, *Grand Design: Hollywood as a Modern Business Enterprise, 1930–1939* (Berkeley: University of California Press, 1993), p. 20.

95   **Stars who refused to abide:** Ibid., p. 157.

95   **Department of Justice analysis:** Ibid., p. 158.

95   **"to respond to the barriers":** Motion Picture of America Association website, www.mpaa.org/about/.

96   **"State Department":** Ibid.

97   **"a legal way to avoid":** Steve Ross, interview by author, 1988.

98   **"I am a kind of Japanese Jew":** Quoted in John Nathan, *Sony: The Private Life* (Boston: Houghton Mifflin, 1999), p. 64.

99   **"the holy grail":** Interview by author, 2000.

100   **"to retain control over":** Ibid.

102   **"Bluhdorn loved Wasserman":** Quoted in Kim Masters, *Keys to the Kingdom: The Rise of Michael Eisner and the Fall of Everybody Else* (New York: HarperBusiness, 2000), p. 176.

104   **"combined libraries of Disney and Fox":** Bruce Orwall and Anna Wilde Mathews, "Disney, News Corp. Announce Deal to Offer Videos on Demand Online," *Wall Street Journal,* August 17, 2001 (Internet edition).

105   **Disney provided the Star:** News Corporation Limited, Form 20 F, SEC (December 18, 2000), p. 18.

Chapter 5: The Clearinghouse Concept

106 **"The studios are basically":** Quoted in David Puttnam, *Movies and Money* (New York: Alfred A. Knopf, 1998), p. 227.

106 **"mass production of prefabricated":** Hortense Powdermaker, *Hollywood: The Dream Factory, An Anthropologist Looks at the Movie Makers* (Boston: Little, Brown, 1950), p. 39.

108 **By adjusting the rates:** Christopher Oster, "Risky Game: Companies Scrimp on Insurance Costs," *Wall Street Journal*, August 1, 2002.

110 **Arnold Schwarzenegger lent his:** Oak Productions, Inc., Contract for the acting services of Arnold Schwarzenegger for *Terminator 3*, December 10, 2001, Exhibit D, Tax Reimbursement Agreement.

110 **"The [dinosaur] theme-park-ride":** Michael J. Wolf, *The Entertainment Economy* (New York: Times Books, 1999), p. 229.

111 **"money constantly gets paid":** Interview by author, 2002.

113 **"It's the ante":** Interview by author, 2002.

113 **One bank alone:** Martin Peers, "Financiers Flocked to Hoffman's Deals, Until the Claims Came In, Sparking Ire," *Wall Street Journal*, July 20, 2000, p. 1.

114 **ten separate lawsuits:** Peers, "Financiers Flocked."

114 **Entertainment-based characters accounted:** *The Licensing Letter*, "Licensing Business Survey, 2003" (Internet, www.epm.com).

114 **so-called product placement:** Bruce Orwall, "Miramax-Coors Deal Marries Advertising and Entertainment," *Wall Street Journal*, August 8, 2002 (Internet edition).

115 ***Gone in 60 Seconds,* for example:** Participation Statement, 2003.

115 **"to keep the lights on":** Interview by author, 2003.

116 **Sumner Redstone estimated:** Sumner Redstone, interview by author, 2000.

116 **By 2003, the six studios' annual take:** MPAA, All Source Numbers.

116 **7.2 billion worldwide:** MPAA data, May 2003.

116 **rebate from film labs:** Author's interview, 2004.

117 **only one out of ten:** Quoted in Charles Lyons, "Passion for Slashin'." *Variety*, June 26, 2000, p. 1.

118 **A knowledgeable Viacom executive:** E-mailed estimate, December 10, 2003.

120 **"Without the royalty system":** Interview by author, 2001.

121 **gross participations are considered:** John W. Cones, *The Feature Film Distribution Deal* (Carbondale: Southern Illinois University Press, 1997), p. 4.

122 **less than 5 percent of all studio films:** Ibid., p. 5.

122 **reported in deficit:** Ibid., pp. 7–8.

122 **the celebrated 1990 lawsuit *Buchwald*:** Pierce O'Donnell and Dennis McDougal, *Fatal Subtraction: The Inside Story of Buchwald v. Paramount* (New York: Doubleday, 1992), p. 408.

123 **any part of the video:** Oak Productions, Schwarzenegger contract: Contingent Compensation. Interview by author, 2002.

124 **the entire income of its film division":** Report, "Walt Disney," Morgan Stanley Equity Research, August 2002, p. 6.

124 **blame these contractual corridors:** Peers, "Financiers Flocked."

125 **"I'm not interested in box office"**: Quoted in Tom King, "Paramount Celebrates Birthday," *Wall Street Journal,* September 27, 2002 (Internet edition).

Chapter 6: Development Hell

129 **"Content is king"**: Quoted in "Still Rocking," *The Economist,* November 21, 2002 (Internet edition).
129 **"Without content, all the"**: Sumner Redstone, interview by author, 2000.
132 **"Spielberg's *Jurassic Park* had"**: Dean Devlin, interview by author, 1998.
132 **spent another $5.2 million:** Rachel Abramowitz, "Rage Against the Machines: T-3's Rocky Road," *Los Angeles Times,* March 11, 2002, Calender section (Internet edition).
133 **"Not only does the writer"**: Peter Bart and Peter Guber, *Shoot Out: Surviving Fame and (Mis)Fortune in Hollywood* (New York: G. P. Putnam's Sons, 2002), p. 31.
133 **"Without a script"**: Interview by author, 2003.
133 **In 2003, according to a Paramount estimate:** Interview by author, 2004.
136 **this story of "development hell"**: Bruce Feirstein, interview by author, 2003.
136 **"I did not expect that writing"**: Ben Stein, *Hollywood Days, Hollywood Nights: The Diary of a Mad Screenwriter* (New York: Bantam, 1988), p. 58.
136 **"be molded into star"**: Peter Guber in Bart and Guber, *Shoot Out,* p. 63.
136 **the studio commissioned six:** Laura M. Holson, "In This 'Superman' Story, the Executives Do the Fighting," *New York Times,* September 15, 2002 (Internet edition).
137 **"has a big hit"**: Lynda Obst, *Hello, He Lied: & Other Truths from the Hollywood Trenches* (New York: Broadway Books, 1996), p. 67.
138 **"materially alter Artist's role"**: Letter Agreement, T-3 Productions, Intermedia Film Equities, and Oak Productions, regarding the acting services of Arnold Schwarzenegger for *Terminator 3,* December 10, 2001.
138 **"Those at the top"**: Art Linson, *A Pound of Flesh: Perilous Tales of How to Produce Movies in Hollywood* (New York: Grove Press, 1993), p. 68.
138 **"clashing egos, screaming insults"**: Interview by author, 2003.
138 **"The conference calls"**: Interview by author, 2002.

Chapter 7: The Green Light

140 **"Most studios ask marketing"**: Peter Bart and Peter Guber, *Shoot Out: Surviving Fame and (Mis)Fortune in Hollywood* (New York: G. P. Putnam's Sons, 2002), p. 224.
140 **"The much tougher part"**: Interview by author, 2002.
140 **"Each day of shooting"**: Art Linson, *A Pound of Flesh: Perilous Tales of How to Produce Movies in Hollywood* (New York: Grove Press, 1993), p. 116.
141 **"financiers still want to"**: Quoted in 1978 interview by Mitch Tuchman, in *Steven Spielberg: Interviews,* eds. Lester D. Friedman and Brent Notbohm (Jackson: University Press of Mississippi, 2000), p. 52.
141 **the $187.3 million budget:** Budget, *Terminator 3,* March 11, 2002.
143 **"laser-beam their ads"**: Interview by author, 2001.
143 **"of only pennies"**: Ibid.

143   **invested $120 million in:** Marc Graser, "007's Big Ad-Venture," *Variety*, October 7–13, 2002, p. 1.

145   **"Stars can't pull in":** Interview by author, 2003.

145   **"there's no way to":** Jane Hamsher, *Killer Instinct: How Two Young Producers Took on Hollywood and Made the Most Controversial Film of the Decade* (New York: Broadway Books, 1997), p. 24.

145   **Lew Wasserman stressed:** Michael J. Wolf, *The Entertainment Economy* (New York: Times Books, 1999), pp. 156–57.

146   **"We live in the same small":** Steve Ross, interview by author, 1988.

146   **"We have the opportunity":** Linson, *Pound of Flesh*, pp. 137–38.

146   **"Whatever the":** Interview by author, 2000.

Chapter 8: Preparing the Illusion

149   **In the case of *Basic*:** Production Underwriting Summary, *Basic*, October 18, 2001.

149   **Arnold Schwarzenegger's contract:** Oak Productions, contract for the acting services of Arnold Schwarzenegger for *Terminator 3*, December 10, 2001.

150   **"a sort of stick-figured playback":** Art Linson, *A Pound of Flesh: Perilous Tales of How to Produce Movies in Hollywood* (New York: Grove Press, 1993), pp. 133–34.

150   **"visually click together":** Interview by author, 2001.

151   **Stone chose Cameron Diaz:** Interview by author, 2002.

153   **took a red pen to the script:** Bruce Orwall, "Why Michael Eisner Can Be Found Laboring in Walt Disney's Trenches," *Wall Street Journal*, November 7, 2001 (Internet edition).

Chapter 9: Lights, Cameras, Action

154   **"The director more often":** Peter Bart and Peter Guber, *Shoot Out: Surviving Fame and (Mis)Fortune in Hollywood* (New York: G. P. Putnam's Sons, 2002), p. 83.

156   **repeated the same two dozen:** *Wall Street* (1987), DVD, director's commentary.

156   **Brad Pitt not only proposed:** *Ocean's Eleven* (2001), DVD, director's commentary.

156   ***Sweet Smell of Success:*** John McDonough, "Movie Directors? Who Needs 'Em?," *Wall Street Journal*, March 25, 2002 (Internet edition).

157   **"It's a tough shot":** Jane Hamsher, *Killer Instinct: How Two Young Producers Took on Hollywood and Made the Most Controversial Film of the Decade* (New York: Broadway Books, 1997), p. 160.

157   **"to break down her door":** Ibid., pp. 165, 175.

159   **"B-12 shots and Vicodan":** Hamsher, *Killer Instinct*, p. 152.

162   **"Monster films do not":** Dean Devlin, interview by author, 1998.

Chapter 10: Bits and Pieces

165   **"CG cost more than":** Interview by author, 2002.

167   **$10,000 a day in 2003:** Nancy Griffin, "When A-List Actors Are Happy to Hide Their Faces," *New York Times*, July 6, 2003 (Internet edition).

168 **"the heart and soul"**: Quoted in John Nathan, *Sony: The Private Life* (Boston: Houghton Mifflin, 1999), p. 200.

169 **Paramount reportedly paid $1 million**: Tamara Connif and Carla Hay, "High Costs Have Biz Rethinking Soundtracks," *Hollywood Reporter*, October 7, 2002, p. 1.

169 **more than $2 million**: Jane Hamsher, *Killer Instinct: How Two Young Producers Took on Hollywood and Made the Most Controversial Film of the Decade* (New York: Broadway Books, 1997), pp. 184–85.

Chapter 11: Completing the Illusion

170 **"There are actually three"**: Roy Scheider, scene-specific commentary, *All That Jazz*, DVD (2003).

171 **"Shots go out of focus"**: Paul Seydor, "Notes from the Cutting Room," *The Perfect Vision*, no. 26 (September 1999), p. 25.

172 **"It requires sitting both"**: Interview by author, 2003.

172 **Kevin Costner did in**: Mielikki Org and Anna Wilde Mathews, "Engineering Blue Skies," *Wall Street Journal*, August 12, 2003 (Internet edition).

172 **"slight bump down in resolution"**: Interview by author, 2003.

Chapter 12: The Awareness Mission

177 **"These days we supply"**: Interview by author, 2001.

178 **"Movie marketing campaigns are"**: Interview by author, 1999.

178 **"If we release twenty-eight films"**: Interview by author, 2003.

179 **"First studios have to"**: Interview by author, 2003.

179 **"The easy part is generating"**: Interview by author, 2002.

180 **as "complicitous partners"**: Interview by author, 2003.

181 **"to alert millions of"**: Interview by author, 1999.

182 **"determine how well"**: Interview by author, 1999.

183 **"Getting multiplex chains to"**: Interview by author, 1998.

183 **theater owners often complain**: Nicole Sperling, "Trailer Wars," *Hollywood Reporter*, May 14–20, 2002, p. S30.

183 **"the key players were awash"**: Peter Bart, "Knowledge Is Power, Except in Hollywood," *Daily Variety*, May 6, 1999, p. A1.

Chapter 13: The Drive

184 **"the business was basically"**: Interview by author, 2003.

185 **"directed to desired audiences"**: Interview by author, 2002.

185 **"When you do research"**: Quoted in Stephen Galloway, "Alternate Angle," *Hollywood Reporter*, May 14–20, 2000, p. S14.

185 **the "key driver"**: Quoted in Stephen Galloway, "Where the Money Went," *Hollywood Reporter*, May 14–20, 2000, p. S8.

185 **studios spent $3.4 billion**: U.S. Entertainment Industry: MPA 2003 Market Statistics 2003, pp. 20–22.

185 **"laser-beamed"**: Interview by author, 2002.

185   studios spent $720 million on cable-television ads: MPAA Market Statistics 2003, pp. 20–22.

185   "The trick is to hit": Interview by author, 1999.

186   a "war council": Interview by author (PowerPoint presentation), 1999.

186   "Letterman and Leno act": Interview by author, 2001.

Chapter 14: D Day

187   "That is D day": Interview by author, 2000.

188   "Our job is to find": Interview by author, 2000.

188   "In a head-on collision": Interview by author, 2003.

188   "there is no longer a clear path": Interview by author, 2003.

189   "[Weinstein] and I": Laura M. Holson, "Miramax Blinks" *New York Times*, October 11, 2002, Business section, p. 1.

190   "The largest beneficiaries of": Randall Tierney, "Top Heavy," *Hollywood Reporter*, May 14–20, 2002, p. S28.

190   "not only establish movies": Interview by author, 2002.

191   "press junket": Interview by author, 2002.

Chapter 15: The Popcorn Economy

196   "We are really in": Interview by author, 1997.

196   "the most important technological": Interview by author, 1997.

198   "Efficiency requires trade-offs": Interview by author, 1997.

199   "free advertising": Interview by author, 1997.

200   As a result, studios: Kimberley A. Strassel, "Movie-Goers Toon Out Sex and Violence," *Wall Street Journal*, October 10, 2000, p. 28.

201   "In the end we": Jane Hamsher, *Killer Instinct: How Two Young Producers Took on Hollywood and Made the Most Controversial Film of the Decade* (New York: Broadway Books, 1997), p. 217.

201   "reportedly ran to more than $500,000": Interview by author, 1998.

201   "with movies, when school": Interview by author, 1997.

201   *Bourne Identity* to open: Doug Liman, *The Bourne Identity*, DVD, director's commentary (2002).

Chapter 16: Alien Territory

204   Table 4: MPAA All Media report, 2003.

205   For *Gone in 60 Seconds:* Participation Statement, Schedule 10, December 31, 2003.

205   seasonal "wastelands": Mark Zoradi, quoted in Michael Schneider, "Pic Launch Is World Shaking," *Variety*, July 17–23, 2000, p. 71.

206   "To get the same coverage": Interview by author, 1999.

206   example of *Gone in 60 Seconds:* Participation Statement.

206   *Midnight in the Garden of Good and Evil:* Warner Bros. Distribution Report #5, *Midnight in the Garden of Good and Evil*, June 30, 2000.

206 **Schwarzenegger's contract for** *Terminator 3,* **for example:** Oak Productions, contract for the acting services of Arnold Schwarzenegger for *Terminator 3,* December 10, 2001.

208 **"Even if it's not written":** Interview by author, 2000.

208 **"onerous," as one agency head put it:** Interview by author, 2000.

Chapter 17: The DVD Revolution

209 **In an average week in 2002:** Alexander & Associates video surveys.

209 **"the bonanza that saved Hollywood":** Sumner Redstone, interview by author, 2000.

209 **90 million a week:** Gene Brown, *Movie Time: A Chronology of Hollywood and the Movie Industry from the Beginning to the Present* (New York: Macmillan, 1995), pp. 193, 337.

212 **"limitless possibilities":** Norio Ohga and Gerald Cavanaugh, interview by author, 2004, and Norio Ohga, *The Melody of Sony* (Tokyo: Nihon Keizai Shimbun, 2003).

212 **"that digital satellite broadcasting":** Robert L. Cutts, *Toshiba* (London: Penguin Books, 2002), p. 143. Also, Koji Hase, interview by author, 2004.

212 **"135 digital minutes":** Warren Lieberfarb, lecture at Wharton School of Business, "Knowledge at Wharton," March 13, 2002 (http://knowledge.wharton.upenn.edu/index.cfm?fa=viewArticle&id=530).

213 **"it could be considered":** Viacom executive, interview by author, 2004.

213 **"the beginning of the end of the video rental system":** Interview by author, 2003.

214 **"It may seem perverse":** Interview by author, 2003.

214 **$27.6 million on . . .** *Midnight in the Garden***:** Warner Bros. Distribution Report #5, *Midnight in the Garden of Good and Evil,* June 30, 2000.

215 **Table 5:** *MPA All Media Revenue Report,* 1999, 2000, 2001, 2002, and 2003.

216 **Table 6:** MPA, Worldwide Market Research, "U.S. Entertainment Industry: 2003 MPA Market Statistics," pp. 29–31.

216 **For example, Wal-Mart:** Gary Younge, "When Wal-Mart Comes to Town," *The Guardian,* August 18, 2003 (Internet edition).

216 **"substituting bloodless kung fu":** Interview by author, 2003.

217 **"repackaging titles in new ways":** Merissa Marr and Martin Peers, "MGM's Library of Old Movies Puts It in Spotlight," *Wall Street Journal,* July 7, 2004, p. A1.

218 **"found money":** Author's correspondence with source, 2004.

218 **appreciated by an estimated $7 billion:** Interview by author, 2004.

Chapter 18: The Television Windfall

219 **"We are not just":** Steve Ross, interview by author, 1988.

220 **negotiated a seven-year contract:** Richard Schickel, *The Disney Version: The Life, Times, Art and Commerce of Walt Disney* (Chicago: Elephant Paperbacks, 1997), p. 313.

220 **having MCA churn out:** Dan E. Moldea, *Dark Victory: Ronald Reagan, MCA, and the Mob* (New York: Viking Press, 1986), pp. 176–77.

220 **studios closed their newsreel divisions:** Raymond Fielding, *The American Newsreel–1967* (Norman: University of Oklahoma Press, 1972), p. 308.

221 **broadcast-television revenues were fifteen times:** Cynthia Littleton, "Columbia TV Turns into Global Success," *Variety,* Columbia Pictures 75th Anniversary issue, January 1999, p. 18.

221 **Sumner Redstone reported that:** Judith Newman, "Fort Sumner," *Vanity Fair,* November 1999, p. 248.

221 **In 2003 the six studios earned:** "Hollywood's Haul," MIPCOM, *Variety,* October 7–13, 2002, p. A4b.

222 **In 2003 the studios earned:** *MPA All Media Revenue Report,* May 2004.

222 **That year, the six studios earned:** Ibid.

223 **the six studios earned $1.8 billion:** Ibid.

223 *Gone in 60 Seconds:* Participation Statement, December 31, 2003.

224 **As Table 7 indicates:** Ibid.

Chapter 19: License to Merchandise

226 **Another 250 million people:** Bruce Orwall, "Disney Aims for Bigger Share of Retailing with Revamp of Stores and New Products," *Wall Street Journal,* October 4, 2000, p. 8.

226 **estimated $500 million:** John Horn, "Can Anyone Dethrone Disney?" *Los Angeles Times,* June 1, 1997, p. 4.

226 **licensing rights made more money:** Ed Kirchdoerffer, "Licensing Diary: The Pink Panther," *Kidscreen,* June 1997, p. 18.

226 **"No one had any idea":** Interview by author, 2002.

227 **movie-based characters brought in $40 billion:** Jill Goldsmith and K. D. Shirkani, "Properties from Pics, TV Nearly Half of Toy Market," *Daily Variety,* February 11, 2000, p. 1.

228 **only ten to fifteen films:** Tamara Conniff and Carla Hay, "High Costs Have Biz Rethinking Soundtracks," *Hollywood Reporter,* October 7, 2002, p. 13.

Chapter 20: The Learning Imperative

230 **"high marketability":** Interview by author, 2002.

231 **"All it says is that":** Quoted in Rick Lyman, "Box-Office Letdown," *New York Times,* December 5, 2000, p. C2.

231 **"What is wrong with":** Interview by author, 2003.

233 **"action-based films":** Interview by author, 2003.

233 **"overly verbose":** Interview by author, 2003.

235 **Finally, Intermedia Entertainment:** Interparty Agreements, among IMF, *Terminator 3,* Union Bank of California, Warner Bros., Columbia TriStar, Intermedia, International Film Guarantors, et al., December 28, 2001, author's files.

Chapter 21: The Midas Formula

236 **"If it were not for":** Interview by author, 2003.

236 **"the billion-dollar club":** Interview by author, 2003.

237 **Table 8:** Studio estimates for rentals, Alexander & Associate estimates for video, studio estimates for TV.

238 **Among them was George Lucas:** Dale Pollock, *Skywalking: The Life and Films of George Lucas* (New York: Da Capo Press, 1999), p. 133.

239 **"a whisper of my":** Quoted in 1982 interview by Michael Sragow, in *Steven Spielberg: Interviews*, eds. Lester D. Friedman and Brent Notbohm (Jackson: University Press of Mississippi, 2000), p. 112.

240 **"The problem with American business":** Quoted in Sharon Waxman, "The Civil War Is a Risky Business: Miramax's Bet on 'Cold Mountain,' " *New York Times*, December 17, 2003 (Internet edition).

241 **"And these are the directors":** Interview by author, 2003.

Chapter 22: Homo Ludens

245 **"I don't make pictures just":** Charles Snow, *Walt: Backstage Adventures with Walt Disney* (Los Angeles: Communications Creativity, 1979).

245 **"The much talked about":** Ludwig von Mises, "Epistemological Problems of Economics," http://216.239.51.100/search?q=cache:erpZFOOV1C0C:www.mises.org/epofe/c5sec4.asp+Homo+economicus+theory&hl=en&ie=UTF-8.

246 **"the Jews that invented":** Neal Gabler, *An Empire of Their Own: How the Jews Invented Hollywood* (New York: Anchor Books, 1989), p. 5.

246 **Mayer was the highest-paid executive:** Ibid., p. 316.

247 **"the trivializing and demoralizing":** Quoted in ibid., p. 277.

247 **"the presence of outside bankers":** Tino Balio, *Grand Design: Hollywood as a Modern Business Enterprise, 1930–1939*, vol. 5 (Berkeley: University of California Press, 1995), p. 7.

247 **According to Balio:** Ibid., p. 7.

248 **By 1924, verging on:** Ibid., p. 10.

249 **"The deal on which we":** Preston Sturges, *Preston Sturges: His Life in His Words* (New York: Touchstone Books, 1991), pp. 304–305.

250 **"It doesn't cost forty":** Quoted in Kathryn Harris, "Edgar in Hollywood," *Fortune*, April 15, 1996 (Internet edition).

250 **"You just make the films":** Alan Ladd, Jr., and Giancarlo Parretti, interviews by author, 1989.

250 **"interested in making movies":** David McClintick, "Predator," *Fortune*, July 8, 1996 (Internet edition).

250 **Ben Stein called mere "voyeurs":** Ben Stein, *Hollywood Days, Hollywood Nights: The Diary of a Mad Screenwriter* (New York: Bantam, 1988), p. 154.

252 **"They lived in large palatial":** Gabler, *Empire of Their Own*, p. 6.

Chapter 23: The Communal Instinct

253 **"We see each other":** Quoted in 1978 interview by Mitch Tuchman, in *Steven Spielberg: Interviews*, eds. Lester D. Friedman and Brent Notbohm (Jackson: University Press of Mississippi, 2000), p. 39.

253 **a "feudal system":** Interview by author (e-mail communication), 2004.

254 **Office of War Information:** Clayton R. Koppes and Gregory D. Black, *Hollywood Goes to War: How Politics, Profits, and Propaganda Shaped World War II Movies* (Berkeley and Los Angeles: University of California Press, 1990), p. 61.

254 **"most of the producers"**: Otto Friedrich, *City of Nets: A Portrait of Hollywood in the 1940's* (Berkeley: University of California Press, 1986), p. 52.

254 **"a Jewish holiday"**: Quoted in Neal Gabler, *An Empire of Their Own: How the Jews Invented Hollywood* (New York: Anchor Books, 1989), p. 2.

255 **three stars under contract:** Tino Balio, *United Artists: The Company That Changed the Film Industry* (Madison: University of Wisconsin Press, 1987), p. 11.

255 **"I am a great believer in nepotism"**: Neil Chenoweth, *Rupert Murdoch: The Untold Story of the World's Greatest Media Wizard* (New York: Crown Business, 2001), p. 110.

256 **"establish the industry in"**: Mason Wiley and Damien Bona, *Inside Oscar: The Unofficial History of the Academy Awards* (New York: Ballantine Books, 1993), p. 3.

256 **"These ceremonies have taken"**: Interview by author, 2003.

256 **Unlike the industry's pioneers:** Friedrich, *City of Nets*, pp. 44–45.

256 **"a factory in the sun"**: Quoted in Natasha Fraser-Cavassoni, *Sam Spiegel: The Incredible Life and Times of Hollywood's Most Iconoclastic Producer* (New York: Simon & Schuster, 2003), p. 62.

256 **"marketplace of lies"**: Ibid., p. 61.

257 **decided against the film:** Sharon Waxman, "The Civil War Is a Risky Business: Miramax's Bet on 'Cold Mountain,' " *New York Times*, December 17, 2003 (Internet edition).

Chapter 24: The New Elites

259 **Mary Pickford, for example:** David Puttnam, *Movies and Money* (New York: Alfred A. Knopf, 1998), pp. 49–50.

260 **out of "almost obscurity"**: Otto Friedrich, *City of Nets: A Portrait of Hollywood in the 1940's* (Berkeley: University of California Press, 1986), p. 194.

261 **Oak Productions, owned by:** Letter of Agreement between T-3 Productions, Intermedia Films Equities, and Oak Productions, regarding the acting services of Arnold Schwarzenegger, December 10, 2001.

261 **In *Terminator 3*:** Ibid.

262 **"release, disseminate, divulge, publish"**: Ibid.

263 **"What it does mean"**: William Goldman, *Adventures in the Screen Trade: A Personal View of Hollywood and Screenwriting* (New York: Warner Books, 1984), p. 29.

264 **"Superstars do not get"**: Interview by author, 2003.

264 **Brad Pitt had to submit:** Memorandum, Fireman's Fund: Modified Cast Coverage, Brad Pitt, 2002.

265 **"Kidman is fully aware"**: Memorandum, Fireman's Fund, *Cold Mountain*.

265 **prided herself on arriving:** *Legally Blonde* (2001), DVD, director's commentary.

266 **"The consistency between"**: Interview by author, 2003.

267 **"twilight tandems"**: David Plotz, "Celebrity Dating," *Slate*, July 3, 2003 (Internet edition).

267 **"If stars aren't players"**: Interview by author, 2003.

267 **"pragmatists," as one studio:** Interview by author, 2003.

267 ***Terminator 3* got into difficulties:** *Terminator 3*, weekly budget reports.

268 **"one of the last big objects"**: Tom Wolfe, "The Ultimate Power: Seeing Them Jump," *The Power Game*, ed. Clay Felker (New York: Simon & Schuster, 1968), p. 238.

268 **"We always fly the"**: Quoted in Grant McLaren, "Star Turn for Executive Jets," *Rolls-Royce Magazine,* June 1998 (Internet edition).

268 **"be provided with exclusive"**: Oak Productions, contact for the acting services of Arnold Schwarzenegger for *Terminator 3,* December 10, 2001, Rider E.

268 **"It was just after"**: Quoted in Meredith Bodgas, "The Goods on Gwyneth," Univercity.com (www.univercity.com/sept02/gwynethpaltrow.html.).

268 **"an offer that even"**: Roberts Evans, *The Kid Stays in the Picture* (New York: Hyperion, 1994), p. 6.

269 **"Steve discovered the one perk"**: Quoted in Richard M. Clurman, *To the End of Time: The Seduction and Conquest of a Media Empire* (New York: Simon & Schuster, 1992), p. 331.

269 **For example, Barry Sonnenfeld:** *Late Show with David Letterman,* CBS, January 2, 2003.

269 **At MGM, Louis B. Mayer:** Friedrich, *City of Nets,* p. 13.

272 **John McTiernan was paid:** *Basic,* Preliminary budget, November 1, 2001.

272 **Donaldson received $4.4 million:** *The Farm* (original title), final budget, December 6, 2001.

272 **Mostow received almost $5 million:** Second Amendment Agreement, May 2, 2002.

273 **"each was the product of"**: John McDonough, "Movie Directors: Who Needs 'Em?" op. ed., *Wall Street Journal,* March 25, 2002 (Internet edition).

274 **films are a "collaborative effort"**: Quoted in 1978 interview by Steve Poster, in *Steven Spielberg: Interviews,* eds. Lester D. Friedman and Brent Notbohm (Jackson: University Press of Mississippi, 2000), pp. 62–63.

274 **"If actors believe we"**: Interview by author, 2001.

275 **"In terms of sheer numbers"**: Interview by author, 2000.

275 **CAA, which has the:** Author's e-mail correspondence, December 8, 2003.

276 **"mediated divorce settlements"**: Peter Bart and Peter Guber, *Shoot Out: Surviving Fame and (Mis)Fortune in Hollywood* (New York: G. P. Putnam's Sons, 2002), p. 137.

276 **"There are very few"**: Interview by author, 2002.

276 **"They are constantly whispering"**: Interview by author, 2002.

276 **"I'm not worried about"**: Quoted in Howard A. Rodman, "Talent Brokers," *Film Comment,* vol. 26, no. 1 (January–February, 1990).

277 **"Puck's unofficial reservations vetter"**: Quoted in Nikki Finke, "Wasted," *New York,* November 29, 1999 (Internet edition).

277 **"Since all agents charge"**: Interview by author, 2002.

277 **"What Does an Agent Really Do?"**: Rodman, "Talent Brokers."

278 **"Agents dwell in their own"**: Bart and Guber, *Shoot Out,* p. 136.

278 **One studio:** Friedrich, *City of Nets,* p. 73.

278 **"What's all this business"**: Bernard Weintraub, "Screenwriters May Walk Out Over Film Credit and Respect," *New York Times,* January 16, 2001, p. 1.

279 **John Howard Lawson:** Victor S. Navasky, *Naming Names: The Social Costs of McCarthyism* (New York: Viking Press, 1980), pp. 295–302.

279 **"All the writers sit"**: Quoted in Friedrich, *City of Nets,* p. 8.

281 **"The executive mantra goes"**: John Gregory Dunne, *Monster: Living Off the Big Screen* (New York: Random House, 1997), p. 8.

281 **"producers rushed to bring me"**: Dale Launer, interview by author, e-mail, February 4, 2003.

281 **"alienation problem"**: Interview by author, 2003.

281 **On *Chinatown*, for example**: Evans, *Kid Stays*, p. 264.

282 **Robert Evans has described**: Ibid.

282 **screenwriter Joe Ezterhas wrote**: *Premiere*, January 1989.

282 **"The writer is at once lionized"**: Bart and Guber, *Shoot Out*, p. 63.

283 **"It was inevitable"**: Eric Hamburg, *JFK, Nixon, Oliver Stone and Me* (New York: Public Affairs, 2001), p. 132.

284 **"too isolating"**: Interview by author, 2003.

285 **"getting our movies made"**: Interview by author, 2003.

285 **William Goldman spoke**: Goldman, *Adventures*, p. 39.

285 **"I was a big man"**: Evans, *Kid Stays*, p. 255.

285 **"You name 'em"**: Ibid., p. 410.

286 **"John is a brilliant executive"**: Quoted in Gregg Kilday, "Goldwyn Out at Par, In as Producer," *Hollywood Reporter*, November 24, 2003 (Internet edition).

286 **"Once your membership was"**: Peter Bart, quoted in Bart and Guber, *Shoot Out*, p. 7.

287 **"By the mid-thirties"**: Neal Gabler, *Empire of Their Own* (New York: Anchor Books, 1989), p. 291.

287 **"He was a lawyer living"**: Evans, *Kid Stays*, p. 68.

288 **"When that veil is pierced"**: Steven Seagal, interview, *Larry King Live*, August 31, 1997.

288 **"Michael was somebody"**: Ibid.

288 **"We'd like to make you"**: Seagal, *Los Angeles Times* interview.

288 **"What we're really doing here"**: Ibid.

289 **DiCaprio, for example, reportedly stayed**: Christine Dugas and Chris Woodyard, "How Broker to the Stars Came to Be Behind Bars," *USA Today*, April 17, 2000 (Internet edition).

289 **"You'd be standing there talking"**: Quoted in Anne-Marie O'Neill, Steve Erwin, Joseph Tirella, "Dana Giacchetto," *People*, November 20, 2000 (Internet edition).

289 **a U.S. district court sentenced**: SEC, *Administrative Proceedings*, Release no. 1957, July 31, 2001, File No. 3-10542.

Chapter 25: Hollywood at Work and Play

290 **"Buy more toys for myself"**: Dan Rather interview with George Clooney, *Sixty Minutes*, CBS, January 8, 2003.

291 **"fun whether you want to or not"**: *Full Frontal* (2002), DVD, rules (under "Special Features").

291 **"I'm into plastic bags"**: Quoted in *Full Frontal*, DVD, director's commentary.

292 **"There's no gamble"**: Quoted in Kim Masters, "Harvey, Marty and a Jar Full of Ears," *Esquire*, February 2002.

292 **"The most enriching thing"**: Ken Auletta, "Beauty and the Beast," *New Yorker*, December 16, 2002, p. 70.

292 **"They think I'm crazy"**: Quoted in Isabella Marchiolo, "Passion," *TuttoQui-Cinema*, September 21, 2002 (Internet edition).

292 **"I have a deep need"**: Richard Corliss and Jeff Israely, "The Passion of Mel Gibson," *Time*, January 27, 2003 (Internet Pacific edition).

292 **"could fuel hatred, bigotry":** "ADL Concerned Mel Gibson's 'Passion' Could Fuel Anti-Semitism if Released in Present Form," ADL press release, New York, August 11, 2003.

293 **"You can't make an immoral":** Quoted by Stephan Elliott, *Eye of the Beholder* (1999), DVD, director's commentary.

293 **"to take off their tops":** Eric Hamburg, *JFK, Nixon, Oliver Stone and Me* (New York: Public Affairs, 2001), p. 167.

293 **"the grooviest filmmaker":** "Spielberg Confirms Goldmember Cameo," Associated Press release, June 6, 2002.

294 **"It was so much fun":** Quoted in Meredith Bodgas, "The Goods on Gwyneth," Univercity.com (www.univercity.com/sept02/gwynethpaltrow.html.).

294 **"It was a blast":** Quoted in "Extra," New York *Daily News*, June 3, 2002 (Internet edition).

295 **"Unlike movies, TV episodes":** Interview by author, 2003.

Chapter 26: The Culture of Deception

296 **"What attracted you to the *Jaws*":** Quoted in 1974 interview by David Helpern, in *Steven Spielberg: Interviews*, eds. Lester D. Friedman and Brent Notbohm (Jackson: University Press of Mississippi, 2000), p. 8.

296 **the publicity business was:** Edward L. Bernays, *Public Relations* (Norman: University of Oklahoma Press, 1952), pp. 47–48.

297 **produced their own newsreels:** Raymond Fielding, *The American Newsreel, 1911–1967* (Norman: University of Oklahoma Press, 1972), p. 189ff.

298 **invented two dead wives:** David Plotz, "Celebrity Dating," *Slate*, July 3, 2003 (Internet edition).

298 **wedding for $1.55 million:** Jill Lawless, "Catherine Zeta-Jones, Michael Douglas Win Lawsuit over Wedding Pictures," Associated Press, April 11, 2003 (Internet edition).

298 **"to the apogee":** Leo Rosten, *Hollywood: The Movie Colony* (New York: Harcourt Brace & Company, 1941), p. 61.

299 **"Schwarzenegger is an instantly":** Laura Wides, "Settlement Allows for Governor Bobbleheads," New York *Daily News*, August 3, 2004, p. 5.

300 *O Brother, Where Art Thou?:* "George Clooney Confesses Dirty Makeup Secrets," *Celebrity News*, Internet Movie Database, December 11, 2000.

300 **"Eddie grew up with":** *I Spy*, DVD (2003), director's commentary.

301 **"confirmed" Pentagon reports:** Quoted by David Russell, *Three Kings* (1999), DVD, director's commentary.

301 **telling *Newsweek*, for example:** David Ansen, "Operation Desert Scam," *Newsweek*, October 18, 1999 (Internet edition), and *Three Kings*, director's commentary.

302 **"Oliver considered this to be acceptable":** Eric Hamburg, *JFK, Nixon, Oliver Stone and Me* (New York: Public Affairs, 2001), p. 121.

302 **revelations made to him by:** *The Bourne Identity*, DVD (2002), director's commentary.

303 **"the only real value is":** Ben Stein, *Hollywood Days, Hollywood Nights: The Diary of a Mad Screenwriter* (New York: Bantam Books, 1988), p. 49.

303 **a business with young faces:** Clayton R. Koppes and Gregory D. Black, *Hollywood Goes to War: How Politics, Profits, and Propaganda Shaped World War II Movies* (Berkeley and Los Angeles: University of California Press, 1990), p. 6.

304 **"bits and pieces":** François Truffaut, *Day for Night* (1973), DVD, director's interview.

305 **"There is usually a publicity person":** Interview by author, 2003.

305 **"The last thing publicists want":** Interview by author, 2003.

305 **"EPKs provide stars with":** Interview by author, 2003.

306 **"Nobody regulates":** Interview by author, 2004.

307 **"an unwanted invasion":** Bruce Feirstein, "Taking a Contract Out on Writers," *New York Observer,* March 20, 2003 (Internet edition).

307 **"I've been a real gentleman":** Telegram reprinted in Robert Evans, *The Kid Stays in the Picture* (New York: Hyperion, 1994), p. 343, but Evans deleted from it the last line "You did nothing on *The Godfather* other than annoy me and slow it down."

307 **As to his claim that:** Evans, *Kid Stays,* p. 218.

308 **"He had everybody believing":** Quoted in Peter Biskind, *Easy Riders, Raging Bulls: How the Sex-Drugs-and-Rock 'n' Roll Generation Saved Hollywood* (New York: Touchstone Books, 1998), p. 159.

308 **"The invariable rule":** Interview by author, 2003.

309 **"It is in everyone's interest":** Tad Friend, "This Is Going to Be Big," *New Yorker,* September 23, 2002 (Internet edition).

309 **"Richard Johnson, the editor":** Ken Auletta, "Beauty and the Beast," *New Yorker,* December 16, 2002, p. 76.

Chapter 27: The Pictures in Our Heads

313 **"The people here in the White House":** Ben Stein, *Her Only Sin: A Novel of Hollywood* (New York: St. Martin's Press, 1963), p. 66.

313 **"who gets what, when and how":** Harold Lasswell, *Politics: Who Gets What, When, and How* (Cleveland: Meridian Books, 1958), p. 1.

313 **"We define the world":** Walter Lippmann, *Public Opinion* (New York: Free Press, 1965), pp. 3–20.

314 **In 1894 a film producer:** Raymond Fielding, *The American Newsreel, 1911–1967* (Norman: University of Oklahoma Press, 1972), pp. 10–11.

314 **"It is like writing history":** Quoted in David Puttnam, *Movies and Money* (New York: Alfred A. Knopf, 1998), p. 78.

315 **Supreme Court ruled:** *Mutual Film Corporation* v. *Ohio,* 236 US 230 (1915).

315 **"What we wanted to":** Quoted in Puttnam, *Movies and Money,* p. 78.

315 **Tarzan film, for example:** Clayton R. Koppes and Gregory D. Black, *Hollywood Goes to War: How Politics, Profits, and Propaganda Shaped World War II Movies* (Berkeley and Los Angeles: University of California Press, 1990), p. 61.

316 **"While the Hollywood Jews":** Neal Gabler, *An Empire of Their Own: How the Jews Invented Hollywood* (New York: Anchor Books, 1989), p. 2.

317 **So the Hays Office began:** Tino Balio, *Grand Design: Hollywood as a Modern Business Enterprise, 1930–1939,* vol. 5 (Berkeley: University of California Press, 1995), p. 43.

Chapter 28: The Rules of the Game

321 **"the misuse and abuse":** Warren Lieberfarb, "Knowledge at Wharton," lecture at Wharton School of Business, March 13, 2002, http://knowledge.wharton.upenn. edu/index.cfm?fa=viewArticle&id=530; interview by author, 2000.

321 **"an integral part of the urban":** Egil Krogh, interview by author, 1977.

321 **"dog and pony" shows:** Edward Jay Epstein, *Agency of Fear: Opiates and Political Power in America* (New York: G. P. Putnam's Sons, 1977), pp. 165–69; also Krogh interview.

322 **"These White House people":** Interview by author, 1973.

322 **"The White House did view":** Quoted in Daniel Forbes, "Prime Time Propaganda," *Salon,* January 13, 2000 (Internet edition).

322 **In 1942 the NAACP:** *Papers of NAACP,* Part 18: Special Subjects, 1900–1955 (Ann Arbor, Mich.: University Publications of America, 1994).

322 **David Begelman, who had been:** Quoted in Ben Stein, *The View from Sunset Boulevard: America as Brought to You by the People Who Make Television* (New York: Basic Books, 1979), p. 38.

324 **"If you want to use the military's":** John Lovett, quoted in "Pentagon Provides for Hollywood," *USA Today,* May 29, 2001 (Internet edition).

324 **Pentagon's designated historical advisor:** Lawrence Suid, "Pearl Harbor Comes to the Big Screen," *Naval History Magazine,* June 2000 (Internet edition).

324 **depiction of American pilots:** Tony Perry, "The Pentagon's Little Pearler," *Los Angeles Times,* May 28, 2001 (Internet edition).

Chapter 29: The World According to Hollywood

327 **"Movies are powerful":** Quoted in David Puttnam, *Movies and Money* (New York: Alfred A. Knopf, 1998), p. 270.

328 **"essentially a Los Angeles export":** Quoted in Peter Biskind, *Easy Riders, Raging Bulls: How the Sex-Drugs-and-Rock 'n' Roll Generation Saved Hollywood* (New York: Touchstone Books, 1998), p. 348.

328 **"capitalism corrupting art":** Tim Robbins, interview by author, 2003.

329 **"wag-the-dog" manipulations:** Daniel Benjamin and Steven Simon, *The Age of Sacred Terrorism* (New York: Random House, 2002), pp. 358–62.

329 **"businessmen are bad, evil":** Ben Stein, *The View from Sunset Boulevard: America as Brought to You by the People Who Make Television* (New York: Basic Books, 1979), pp. 15, 18.

329 **"the murderous, duplicitous":** Ibid., p. 18.

329 **"the food chain of":** Interview by author, 2003.

331 *News from Nowhere:* Edward Jay Epstein, *News from Nowhere: Television and the News* (New York: Random House, 1973), p. 229.

331 **"Ever since Walt Disney":** Interview by author, 2001.

331 **"Everyone here at Disney":** Interview by author, 2001.

332 **"We don't make art films":** Quoted in Biskind, *Easy Riders,* p. 265.

332 featured **"action figures":** Dean Devlin, interview by author, 1998.

332 **"simple characters in exciting":** Sumner Redstone, interview by author, 2000.

337 **"confrontation" between good and evil:** Tracie Rozhon, "Toy Sellers Wish for Just a Bit of Evil," *New York Times*, December 24, 2003, Business section, p. 1.

337 **"totally about good and evil":** Jeff Sakson quoted in ibid.

Epilogue: The Once and Future Hollywood

338 **"Walking at dawn":** Quoted in Thomas Schatz, *The Genius of the System: Hollywood Filmmaking in the Studio Era* (New York: Henry Holt, 1988), p. 3.

338 **"making new combinations":** Frank E. Manuel, *The Prophets of Paris: Turgot, Condorcet, Saint-Simon, Fourier, and Comte* (New York: Harper Torchbooks, 1965), pp. 62–66.

339 **cultural anthropologists:** For example, Hortense Powdermaker, *Hollywood, the Dream Factory: An Anthropologist Looks at the Movie Makers* (Boston: Little, Brown, 1951).

339 **economists:** For example, Tino Balio, *Grand Design: Hollywood as a Modern Business Enterprise* (Berkeley and Los Angeles: University of California Press, 1995).

339 **political scientists:** For example, Otto Friedrich, *City of Nets: A Portrait of Hollywood in the 1940's* (Berkeley and Los Angeles: University of California Press, 1986).

339 **historians:** For example, Neal Gabler, *An Empire of Their Own: How the Jews Invented Hollywood* (New York: Anchor Books, 1989).

339 **industry insiders:** For example, Schatz, *Genius*.

340 **"ghost town making foolish efforts":** Quoted in ibid., p. 30.

341 **children influenced consumer sales:** David Barboza, "If You Pitch It, They Will Eat," *New York Times*, August 3, 2003, Business section, p. 1.

341 **"put merchandise on the studio store":** Terry Semel, quoted by Warner Bros. executive in interview by author, 1999.

341 **"The less dialogue the better":** Interview by author, 2003.

342 **"the world go round":** Quoted in Connie Bruck, *When Hollywood Had a King: The Reign of Lew Wasserman, Who Leveraged Talent into Power and Influence* (New York: Random House, 2003), p. 345.

342 **"a love affair":** Sumner Redstone, *A Passion to Win* (New York: Simon & Schuster, 2001), p. 23.

342 **$61.6 million in 2003:** U.S. Entertainment Industry: 2003 MPA Market Statistics, p. 18.

345 **a feat of identity theft:** Joe Fordham, "Mill Film's 'Gladiator' VFX," Creative Planet, *Post Industry Report*, May 19, 2000.

345 **Schwarzenegger had his facial:** Quoted in Paula Parisi, "The New Hollywood," *Wired*, December 1995, p. 3.

345 **"gone under the beam":** Quoted in ibid.

346 **"We can make an animal":** Quoted in ibid.

349 **"digital animation is the future":** *Terminator 3* (2003), DVD, director's commentary.

350 **"Certain actors can't do it":** Ibid.

350 **"For a filmmaker that":** Ibid.

351 **"It is like asking":** Quoted in Geraldine Fabrikant, "Troubles at Paramount: Is It Just Money?" *New York Times*, December 6, 2003 (Internet edition).

Acknowledgments

This book greatly benefited from a number of extraordinary books, including Neil Gabler's *An Empire of Their Own: How the Jews Invented Hollywood,* which brilliantly analyzes the rise and fall of the early moguls; Thomas Schatz's *The Genius of the System: Hollywood Filmmaking in the Studio Era,* which meticulously deconstructs the studio system; David Puttnam's *Money and Movies,* which puts Hollywood in a much needed international perspective; John Nathan's *Sony: The Private Life,* an extremely revealing corporate biography of Sony; James Lardner's *Fast Forward,* which lucidly tells the story of the video technology; and William Shawcross's elegant and resourceful *Murdoch: The Making of a Media Empire.* These pioneering works greatly aided my search for the logic that drives modern Hollywood.

The most daunting part of organizing my research was finding my way through the plethora of data about Hollywood, a forest overgrown with polemics, folklore, publicity releases, and celebrity trivia. For help in finding a conceptual path, I thank Andrew Hacker, James Q. Wilson, Claude Serra, and Sir James Goldsmith.

On this book, unlike my previous books, e-mail correspondence provided a new and invaluable research tool. It allowed me to query individuals with knowledge about particular aspects of filmmaking and for them to answer my questions in their own time frame or, if they did not know the precise answer, to forward them to others in their network. The answers I received, unlike conventional interviews, often contained Internet links that provided further details. I am especially grateful to Emma Wilcockson, Anthony Bregman, and Bruce Feirstein for their incredible patience and lucidity in answering my endless e mails between 1999 and 2004.

I am indebted to Joost Thesseling and Frederick Iseman at Caxton-Iseman Capital, Inc., for their unsparing assistance in analyzing and making sense of the corporate balance sheets of the studios, and, in Japan, to Ko Shioya and Yu Serizawa for their great help in researching the Japanese contribution to the entertainment economy.

I also thank June Eng and Dan Nessel for helping me deal with the resources of the Internet and establish my own website (www.edwardjayepstein.com) as a collection point.

The subject could not have been penetrated without the help (and documents) of a small number of studio and financial company executives who elected to remain anonymous. So while I cannot thank them by name, they have my utmost appreciation.

In shaping the material into a book, I am deeply thankful to Kent Carroll for the perceptive suggestions he made on reading early drafts; Kathryn Chetkovich, whose keen eye helped me further clarify the drafts; and Sarah-Marie Schmidt, who resourcefully fact-checked them.

I thank the William H. Donner Foundation, Lynde and Harry Bradley Foundation, and Randolph Foundation for providing funds for researching this project; the Social Philosophy and Policy Foundation for administrating the research grants; and Jeffrey Paul and Fred D. Miller, Jr., of the Social Philosphy and Policy Center for their intellectual as well as logistical support from the inception to the end of this book.

The list of individuals who provided invaluable insights, epiphanies, and inspirations during the writing of this book includes Renata Adler, Robert Alexander, Ken Auletta, Julie Baumgold, Tina Bennett, John Berendt, Richard Bernstein, Ed Bleier, Bob Bookman, Tina Brown, Adelaide de Clermonte-Tonnerre, Suzanna Duncan, Clay Felker, Michael Haussman, Hendrik Hertzberg, Felicitie Hertzog, Magui Iseman, Marty Kaplan, Dale Launer, Alexis Lloyd, Mike Milken, Sollace Mitchell, Victor Navasky, Linda Nessel, Camilla Roos, Charlie Rose, Randy Rothenberg, Rob Stone, Kim Taipale, and Victor Temken.

Finally, I am deeply indebted to my editor, Bob Loomis, for his indefatigable and heroic contribution. I thank him for transforming this work into a finished book.

Edward Jay Epstein
New York City
July 2004

INDEX

EDWARD JAY EPSTEIN studied government at Cornell and Harvard universities and received a Ph.D. from Harvard in 1973. His master's thesis on the search for political truth (*Inquest: The Warren Commission and the Establishment of Truth*) and his doctoral dissertation on television news (*News from Nowhere*) were both published. He taught political science at MIT and UCLA but decided that writing books was a more educational enterprise. *The Big Picture* is his thirteenth book. He lives in New York City. Visit the author's website at www.edwardjayepstein.com.

ABOUT THE TYPE

This book was set in Walbaum, a typeface designed in 1810 by German punch cutter J. E. Walbaum. Walbaum's type is more French than German in appearance. Like Bodoni, it is a classical typeface, yet its openness and slight irregularities give it a human, romantic quality.